PLAYFAIR CRICKET ANNUAL 1950

(*Third Innings*)

Edited by PETER WEST

Foreword . . . . by NEVILLE CARDUS
New Zealand Tour . . by REX ALSTON
Overseas Tours . . by CHARLES BRAY
The West Indies by LEARIE CONSTANTINE
Australia in South Africa by LOUIS DUFFUS
A Message . . . . from W. A. HADLEE
Statistics by ROY WEBBER

PUBLISHED BY

PLAYFAIR BOOKS LTD., 57 HAYMARKET, LONDON, S.W.1

PRINCIPAL FEATURES

A

ILLUSTRATIONS

Most of the photographs in this Annual were taken by : —

SPORT AND GENERAL LTD., Racquet Court, Fleet St., E.C.4;

A. E. WILKES AND SON, West Bromwich;

CENTRAL PRESS PHOTOS LTD., 119, Fleet St., E.C.4;

MRS. D. R. STUART, 57, Longridge Road, London, S.W.5.

Grateful acknowledgement is made to the *Nottingham Guardian* for photographs of Nottinghamshire, H. A. Brown and H. Winrow, and to the Lancashire Club for the group of their team taken by Photowork Ltd.; also to Eric Shore, Sports Editor of the *Durban Daily News*, for sending photographs from South Africa.

ASTERISKS AND AVERAGES

Throughout this Annual an asterisk where appropriate invariably denotes a not out innings or an unfinished partnership.

Averages in the county section are for all first-class county matches, championship or otherwise.

Foreword

by

NEVILLE CARDUS

WITH pleasure I respond to the invitation of the Editor of Playfair's Cricket Annual to contribute a foreword to the Edition for 1950, for when four years ago I returned to England from Australia and journeyed straight to Lord's from Tilbury, the first thing I saw on the bookstall by the Tavern was the attractive cover of this book, with the heraldic border of badges, including the Red Rose of Lancashire and the White Rose of Yorkshire, the White Horse of Kent and the Insignia of Middlesex—scimitars and all, as the immortal William Reeves once said, in a rather different context. *Playfair* is for me a sort of junior and less portly and more portable *Wisden*—(which God preserve and bless the shades of Sydney Pardon and Stewart Caine).

The season of 1950 is likely to command attention in three ways —as a time of preparation for another invasion of Australia; as a test of abilities of ourselves and the cricketers from the West Indies; and as a means of providing entertainment and recreation to the public in a period of austere challenge to the nation. And the greatest of these three will be entertainment.

The mass of English people nowadays are in no mood to pay at the gates, entertainment tax included, if no perceptible measure of entertainment is forthcoming. The first-class cricketer should realise once and for all that his first duty is not to play for his average, or even for a place in the next England XI, but for the health of the game, and the great cause of cheering us all up. I am not, of course, entering a plea for reckless hitting. The true cricketer will always suit the action to the state of the game, not to his own prominence on the score-sheet. Besides, the onus to play vitally and purposefully is not always on the batsman; the bowler can ruin many a sunny hour by " slow " cricket. I appeal to my colleagues in the Press-box to maintain a jealous watchfulness on the essentials, and to chastise even a Denis Compton if ever, in circumstances favourable to handsome batsmanship, he stays on view three hours and a half for his first or his fifteenth century of the season. But dull negative play doesn't emanate from the scorer's box; it comes from the minds of those who, " in the middle," are generally supposed, one and all, to be participating actively upon it.

The team from the West Indies will, I am confident, set the example in free action and conception. In a dry summer they might well beat our best. But I fervently hope, rain or fine, that the West Indians will not deny their own native genius for the game in any sort of emulation of what they imagine to be the Anglo-Australian Test Match *Realpolitik*. Like cricketers from " Ranji's " India, they have for long, winning or losing, added a rare attribute of their own to the game; they have mingled skill and science with a swiftness of movement and temperament flushed by warm impulsive blood coursing through daring and dusky nerve and muscle nurtured in a clime far different from ours. The genius of a Constantine adorns the game, exalts it beyond a game to an art expressive of race as well as of the individual. Brilliant batsmen such as Weekes and Worrell must never compromise, either to ideas or to physical atmosphere.

The West Indians will very likely provide a more searching test of our ability, with the Australian tour in view, than the New Zealanders were able to put before us last year. But we must pray for perpetual sunshine. Wet wickets are almost certain to put the West Indians out of countenance; and wet wickets are no help in the education of an English cricketer about to visit Australia for the first time.

There will be few " sinecures," we can already be sure, when the summer begins; few players at liberty to consider themselves elect by divine right. I doubt if there are three "indispensables" at the moment of writing, and wild horses wouldn't drag their names from me.

On the other hand, I am ready to risk some prophecy about young men who may presently be addressing themselves to the Selection Committee in no uncertain voice. And there's enough of them to make a quorum. Tompkin of Leicestershire, E. A. Bedser, S. M. Brown, T. W. Graveney—here are a " few to follow " as well as the more obvious candidates. It is the bowlers we lack—really fast, or really clever with spin and flight. But there's no occasion now for any of us to cultivate pessimism on the eve of an Australian tour. Bradman is "out of the way"; an enormous relief, from the point of view of an England cricket captain, who, naturally, always wishes to win. Bradman invariably played an innings which not only put his side quickly out of harm's way but in a position well placed for victory. The Australians have just demolished South Africa easily enough; yet the discerning eye of a critic can today see a fissure or two in the Australian rock not there in the Bradman—Ponsford—Woodfull—O'R.illy—Grimmett period.

Amongst the summer's delights anticipated with a smacking of lips none will be more richly savoured than the benefit match for Jim Sims—his second, because the first was not blessed by weather; and anyhow, the services of Sims to Middlesex and cricket at large are beyond mercenary computation. He has grown into the game's human and humourous texture of life and spirit. Few have excelled him as a leg-spin bowler, but with Sims, skill has been no more than contributory to the whole lovable man that is presented to us as he licks his fingers, curves his arm out sideways, then rolls to the wicket with a gait that invests it and all around with a starboard bow and scuppers, and a flowing sea. Then there is his batsmanship, sometimes diversified to originality; now insecure, with noises from the bat rather like the collapse of a deck-chair; but at other times majestic in poise, including a drive in front of the wicket which I can only describe as neo-Palladian. May the sun shine on his day from dawn to time of setting.

Also there will be a benefit for Hutton, our most classical batsman and the pride of Yorkshire. I have, by the way, received several letters from Leeds, Bradford, Sheffield, Hunslet, Laister-dyke and other wild places, informing me that during the cricket season of 1950 Yorkshire will knock Lancashire into the middle of next week at Whitsuntide; while as for Middlesex . . . ! It is possible that Middlesex will indeed dwindle a little in performance for want of variety of attack. But I am inclined to think a challenge to the county leadership might come from Lancashire.

We shall see; and praise the gods, at this time of the year we know that the time for seeing is really before us—days and days in the sun and air. Let us go forth to meet them, and see to it also that we get the best out of them. We'll none of us be so young again.

INTRODUCTION

THE PLAYFAIR Cricket Annuals of 1948 and 1949 proved so popular that the publishers have felt able to reinforce its third innings with an addition of 32 pages at no extra cost to the reader.

This has enabled the inclusion of several new features, the largest of which are the *Who's Who* and the Career Records. A great deal of work has gone into the compilation of both and it is thought that the *Who's Who* is as complete as anything of its kind ever published. The zealous Roy Webber has borne the greatest burden here, and it is worth noting that after many years of exacting research he has put together an exhaustive book of cricket records which will be published by Playfair Books in time for next Christmas. This, I firmly believe, will be an important addition to the cricket library.

Another new feature in this 1950 Annual is Playfair's "Eleven Cricketers of 1949." These are caricatured on page 80 and the reasons for their selection are given on the facing page. Much argument here, no doubt. There are also reviews of League cricket and of the Combined Services and on pages 16 and 17 there will be found the photographs of all the 26 professionals elected to be Honorary Members of M.C.C. On page 46 there is a message most kindly sent to us by W. A. Hadlee, the New Zealand captain of 1949—as modest and thoughtful a contribution as one would expect.

In the main, the Annual remains very much what it was. Those who may have acquired the Playfair habit will notice that this year's team of distinguished contributors is a new one. The 1949 team will, I hope, bat for us again on many future occasions and indeed E. W. Swanton has agreed to review the next M.C.C. tour in Australia for the 1951 Annual. Despite the problems of time and distance we shall hope to publish as usual in mid-April and to include his complete account.

Once again many people have given unstinted help in the compilation of this Annual. I record special gratitude to the County secretaries and to the 1950 University captains, Donald Carr and Hubert Doggart, all of whom have been pestered for sundry information throughout the winter. I think I must have made their lives a misery, but they must have felt it was in a worthy cause. I also thank Masters in charge of cricket at the schools and apologise for any drastic cutting which may have been necessary because of limited space. Mr. Frank Crompton, secretary of Bedfordshire and of the Minor Counties Cricket Association, has kindly provided a review of their cricket (there again one must regret the limited space devoted to the subject).

Once again my final thanks must be to Frank Lee, the Test match umpire, who for a second year has given up much of his time (very willingly, I think) to browsing through proofs with characteristic thoroughness and with a kindly index finger raised aloft.

THE EDITOR.

A memorable occasion last season was the match between the Duke of Edinburgh's XI and Hampshire at Dean Park, Bournemouth, in aid of the National Playing Fields Association. Hampshire, having been put in, made 254 for 8 wickets declared, Neville Rogers scoring 93. The Duke, bowling off-breaks round the wicket, as can be seen from the left-hand picture, took one wicket for 25 in nine overs. The late " Stan " Squires of Surrey made 80 and Denis Compton 52 for the Duke's team, who won a delightful match by one wicket. The Duke scored 12, including two handsome off-drives for four.

1949 ⤎ Looking Both Ways ⤏ 1950

THE stalemate in the Tests, the exciting county championship and some of the finest weather in living experience are outstanding memories of 1949; and so too is the New Zealand tour as a whole. What a grand side they were . . . every one of them, from the captain and manager down to Warwick Watts, scorer and king of commissariat. They came here as Saturday afternoon cricketers, modestly hoping to do well; they went away with the proud record of only one defeat, having given great delight on many fields.

It is now becoming reactionary to suggest that three days for Test matches in older days were quite long enough for positive results. This summer, the four Test matches with the West Indies are to run five days if necessary and, while they can be won in less, it is difficult to play in a five-day match without getting a five-day complex. What risks will be taken on the first day, on a good pitch? We are in danger of forgetting that cricket is a game to be played against the clock as well as against the other side; and that a draw can provide some very exciting cricket.

There are, of course, strong arguments in favour of the five-day match. Whether we like it or not, Test matches are more important to cricket's prosperity than ever and one must get results to maintain the public interest; and five-day games will bring more money into the till. Yet, for all this, many will regret that we cannot have a four-day compromise.

Our Test cricketers will have a bellyful indeed, what with a possible 20 days this summer, another 30 in prospect in Australia next winter and presumably another 25 against South Africa in 1951. Moreover there are to be two additional championship matches this summer—**28** instead of **26**. There is already too much first-class cricket (Devon's application for senior status has necessarily been refused on that account) but the counties must have good membership if they are to flourish and their players must be driven hard in the cause.

The resurgence of Yorkshire—delighting all those who aver that when their cricket is strong so also is England's—and the success of three of the midland counties were notable features of the championship. Worcester at one time looked as if they might achieve a big surprise but they were not a young side and they faltered at the end of a gruelling summer. Warwickshire's success was due reward for splendid leadership by their professional captain, Dollery, and the enterprise of a most progressive committee, and Northamptonshire's for the powerful captaincy of F. R. Brown. Surrey potentially were the best equipped side last year. In 1950 the prospects of Essex and Warwickshire surely cannot be ignored.

The outcome of one important event in 1949 cannot yet be measured. This was the formation of the *Cricket Enquiry Committee*, with Mr. H. S. Altham as Chairman. Its primary aim is to develop cricket for boys between the ages of 11 and 15 and then to provide facilities until they are called-up. The composition of artificial pitches and the technique of mass coaching (*vide* the Essex experiment at Westcliff) are only two subjects requiring much research. There is much hard work to be done and swift results could not be expected.

And now for 1950 and the West Indies; and for 1950-51 and Australia. At last there is no Don Bradman; our bowlers will not have the awful thought that to win a Rubber of five they have got to bowl him out ten times. Moreover, in South Africa, the Australian machine has been showing a chink or two in its armour. Our great need, as everyone knows, is some really quick bowling which will make them jump about a bit; but just as important is the right psychological approach. If England goes out there convinced she can win, then win she very well might.

Much can happen between May and August, and picking a team now is as foolish as it is intriguing. But unless something very startling occurs Messrs. Hutton, Washbrook, Denis Compton, Edrich, Simpson, Evans, Alec Bedser and Trevor Bailey should be assured of their passage. As captain, there is no one better qualified on every count than Norman Yardley; and Stephenson of Somerset may have strong claims as reserve wicketkeeper. Hollies and Jenkins for leg-spin, Doggart, Dewes, Tom Graveney, Lowson and Insole for batting, Eric Bedser as all-rounder (five of these are first-rate fielders) . . . all these may be strong candidates. It is still too early to talk about Preston going, but everyone naturally hopes he may make the grade; and perhaps about Berry of Lancashire also, the young left arm bowler for whom many fine judges have prophesied a brilliant future.

Quite recently, Mr. E. A. Dwyer, the Australian manager and selector in South Africa, proposed that there should be an exchange of umpires between countries so that, for instance, when M.C.C. go out to Australia they would take with them men like Frank Chester and Frank Lee to stand in State matches and thus give Australians the opportunity of studying their methods; and vice versa. The suggestion gains in force, perhaps, through coming from someone outside England.

Just as we went to press it was announced that Leslie Ames had been made a Test Match Selector in place of Group Captain A. J. Holmes, who had resigned because of ill health. The appointment was wholeheartedly welcomed everywhere. R. E. S. Wyatt is now Chairman of the Committee and the other members are A. B. Sellers and T. N. Pearce.

Australians in South Africa

The South Africans Are Overwhelmed

By LOUIS DUFFUS

THE first Australian side after the Bradman regime came to South Africa exuding friendliness and good humour, overflowing with cricket efficiency and loudly heralded for the power of its pace attack. Their arrival was contemplated with some trepidation for South African cricket was passing through a lean period when the test eleven badly needed rejuvenating. A signal batting weakness had persisted since the war and there were no signs of successors to Nourse and Mitchell who had been the backbone of the country's batting for the past twenty years.

It was no surprise therefore that the Australians were not beaten in any of their twenty-five matches. Because of the marked inability of their batsmen to adapt themselves to soft pitches they came close to defeat by the Transvaal and by South Africa in the third Test match, but in each instance recovered admirably and won the game. They took the rubber with four straight victories and in the majority of provincial games outclassed their opponents, frequently winning by an innings.

Financially, too, the tour was an outstanding success for the aggregate attendances reached the neighbourhood of 500,000 and a record of 83,000 was set up for the four days of the first Test match in Johannesburg.

Despite all these satisfactory accomplishments the Australians' general standard of play fell below expectations. There were two main reasons for this artificial decline. The opposition, particularly in the early part of the tour, was not strong enough to test their fullest capabilities and the comparatively slow pace of the South African pitches nullified the effectiveness of a predominately fast attack in which the leading figures were expected to be Ray Lindwall, Keith Miller and the left-hander, Alan Walker. Bill Johnston rarely used the new ball and for the most part bowled with spin and eminent success at medium pace.

Hidden resources in the team were plainly left unexposed for when in the third Test match at Durban they had been dismissed for 75—the lowest total made by any team against South Africa—and had to score 336 in the fourth innings on a responsive wicket, they rallied magnificently and won by five wickets.

No one distinguished himself more than Neil Harvey, the 21-years-old batsman and superb fielder who developed into the most aggressive and attractive left hander to visit the country since Frank Woolley. He not only exceeded the number of runs and centuries scored by J. H. Fingleton during the previous Australian tour and hit up the fastest hundred of the season, but on several occasions selflessly ended his innings when there seemed to him no special need to prolong it.

Like his colleagues he revealed imperfections of technique on a wet wicket but he played a masterful innings of 151 not out that lasted 5½ hours under the most adverse conditions in the third Test match which was, I think, the innings of the season. Harvey, indeed, usurped the position which everyone anticipated would be maintained by Arthur Morris, who did handsomely enough but fell below the high standard he had set himself in Australia and England. He became distinctly vulnerable when playing balls outside the off-stump, a weakness which reached a remarkable climax when he was dropped six times in the second Transvaal match, five of them off one bowler, the unfortunate Michael Melle.

The other successful members of the side, with play and personalities of sharp contrast, were colourful Keith Miller and phlegmatic Jack Moroney. Miller was summoned from Australia when Bill Johnston was involved in a motor accident and his combination of rich versatility, dramatics and

J. H. Fingleton scored 1,191 runs and six hundreds in South Africa in 1935-36—both records for an Australian batsman at the time. Harvey has now bettered both and, as will be seen on page 14, three other batsmen scored over 1,000 runs.

Thirty centuries were scored by the Australians in first-class matches. Harvey and Morris made 8—equalling Denis Compton's record in 1948-49; Moroney 6, including 3 in successive innings; Hassett 4; and Loxton, Miller, Archer and McCool one each.

South African batsmen scored four hundreds against the tourists—Nourse 2 and E. A. B. Rowan and O. Wynne one each.

Moroney, who scored a century in each innings of the fourth Test, is the eighth batsman to have achieved this feat since the war. Only six did so before 19439.

Never before in the history of Test cricket have averages shown such a complete superiority of one side over the other. Australia scored 2,710 runs for the loss of 51 wickets (avge. 53.13) and South Africa 1,991 for the loss of 90 wickets (avge. 22.12).

At the end of the series the Test scoreboard between South Africa and Australia reads as follows:— Played 29. Australia won 22, South Africa 1 (at Adelaide in 1910—11).

TEST AVERAGES

AUSTRALIA—BATTING

	Tests	Inns.	N.O.	Runs	Hghst.	Avge.
R. N. Harvey ..	5	8	3	660	178	132.00
A. L. Hassett ..	5	6	0	402	167	67.00
A. R. Morris ..	5	8	0	422	157	52.75
J. A. R. Moroney ..	5	8	1	352	118	50.28
S. J. E. Loxton ..	5	6	0	255	101	42.50
K. R. Miller ..	5	8	2	246	84	41.00
C. L. McCool ..	5	6	2	134	49*	33.50
I. W. Johnson ..	5	5	1	97	66	24.25
R. R. Lindwall ..	4	4	1	41	21	13.66
R. A. Saggers ..	5	4	2	25	14	12.50

PLAYED IN FIVE TESTS—W. A. Johnston, 1*, 2*.
G. Noblet played in one match but did not bat.

BOWLING

	Overs	Maidens	Runs	Wkts.	Avge.
G. Noblet ..	26.1	9	37	3	12.33
W. A. Johnston ..	160.5	31	392	23	17.04
R. R. Lindwall ..	94	13	248	12	20.66
C. L. McCool ..	83	14	272	13	20.92
K. R. Miller ..	135	17	390	17	22.94
I. W. Johnson ..	135.2	24	432	18	24.00

ALSO BOWLED—S. J. E. Loxton 34—6—104—2; R. N. Harvey 6—1—11—0; A. L. Hassett 1—0—5—0.

SOUTH AFRICA—BATTING

	Tests	Inns.	N.O.	Runs	Hghst.	Avge.
A. D. Nourse ..	5	9	0	405	114	45.00
E. A. B. Rowan ..	5	9	0	404	143	44.38
G. M. Fullerton ..	2	3	0	130	88	43.33
N. B. F. Mann ..	5	9	0	183	52	20.33
H. Tayfield ..	5	9	0	167	75	18.55
O. Wynne ..	3	6	0	106	33	17.66
J. Nel ..	5	9	0	139	38	15.44
J. Watkins ..	3	6	0	87	36	14.50
J. Cheetham ..	3	6	0	80	35	13.33
D. W. Begbie ..	2	3	0	30	24	10.00
P. L. Winslow ..	2	3	0	30	19	10.00
W. W. Wade ..	3	6	0	52	24	8.66
R. Draper ..	2	3	0	25	15	8.33
M. Melle ..	2	3	0	21	14	7.00
V. I. Smith ..	3	6	2	22	11*	5.50
C. McCarthy ..	5	9	7	10	4*	5.00

BOWLING

	Overs	Maidens	Runs	Wkts.	Avge.
M. Melle ..	68	5	303	8	37.87
N. B. F. Mann ..	194.2	29	623	16	38.93
H. Tayfield ..	198.4	21	726	17	42.70
J. Watkins ..	34	8	144	3	48.00
C. McCarthy ..	144	15	536	5	107.20

ALSO BOWLED—V. I. Smith 43—0—213—0; D. W. Begbie 14—0—92—1; E. A. B. Rowan 1—1—0—0; A. D. Nourse 1—1—0—0.

sense of fun made him a favourite with crowds wherever he played. Moroney came to the country labelled with a reputation for slow play which he immediately dispelled by establishing himself as one of the most improved batsmen in the side. On a few occasions—one during the fourth Test match when he became the only cricketer in matches between South Africa and Australia to score a century in each innings—he fell into moods of lethargy and became the butt of barrackers. He was one of the most prolific scorers in the team and if he hit boundaries unemotionally in the matter-of-fact manner of a butcher chopping cutlets, they were no less effective than the fours and sixes which Miller achieved so gracefully.

The Australians always hit the ball harder than the South Africans and their fielding, in which Ken Archer, who improved his free-footed batting considerably, seemed to me the most brilliant outfield seen in the Union, was always superior to their opponents'. Those who knew his previous form thought that Ron Saggers lost some of his earlier competence as a wicketkeeper. His understudy, Gil Langley, who was injured for a month, gave many impressive performances.

Amid much controversy the Australians introduced bumpers into South Africa but on account of the slow pitches they did not become a major factor in the attack. When there was a danger of their causing friction and retaliation on a lively wicket at Johannesburg during the fourth Test match, the Australians virtually banned them—a gesture which was widely appreciated. During the tour Lindsay Hassett, who captained the side

FIRST TEST — JOHANNESBURG
Played on Dec. 24, 26, 27, 28.
Australia won by an innings and 85 runs.

After a poor start—Morris and Moroney out with only two runs, both wides, in the book—the Australians regained their composure through the fine batting of Hassett. Loxton, Johnson, and reached a total considerably beyond the South Africans. Hassett, missed when 3, stayed 4¼ hours, but Loxton took only 2¼ hours over his first Test century, which included fourteen 4's.

In the first South African innings only Rowan and Watkins justified their selection. Miller, bowling at medium pace, dismissed half the side. Following on 276 runs behind, South Africa were 84-2 when rain intervened, and on an awkward pitch their resistance ended early next day.

South Africa could have saved the game had their fielding been sharper.

AUSTRALIA

A. R. Morris c Tayfield b McCarthy ..	0
J. A. R. Moroney run out ..	0
K. R. Miller b Mann ..	21
A. L. Hassett b Watkins ...	112
R. N. Harvey b Watkins ..	34
S. J. E. Loxton st Wade b Tayfield..	101
C. L. McCool b Tayfield ..	31
I. W. Johnson c Cheetham b Mann	66
R. A. Saggers lbw b McCarthy	14
R. R. Lindwall c Nel b Tayfield	21
W. A. Johnston not out..	1
B 5, lb 5, w 2..	12
Total	**413**

Bowling—McCarthy 25—0—90—2; Watkins 10—3—56—2; Smith 13—0—70—0; Tayfield 28—3—93—3; Mann 28.4—4—92—2.

SOUTH AFRICA

	First Innings		Second Innings
E. A. B. Rowan b Miller	60	— lbw b McCool	32
O. Wynne lbw b Johnston	3	— c Saggers b Johnston	33
J. Nel b Johnson	4	— c Saggers b Johnston	14
A. D. Nourse c Hassett b Johnson	0	— c Saggers b Johnson	36
W. W. Wade b Miller	2	— b Johnston	11
J. Cheetham lbw b Johnston	10	— c Hassett b Johnston	35
J. Watkins c Hassett b Miller	36	— c Miller b Johnson	0
H. Tayfield lbw b Miller	6	— c Miller b Johnson	0
N. B. F. Mann b Miller	0	— lbw b Johnson	13
V. I. Smith not out	1	— c McCool b Johnston	1
C. McCarthy b Johnson	0	— not out	1
lb 14, nb 1	15	Extras	15
Total	**137**	**Total**	**191**

Bowling—First Innings: Lindwall 10—1—22—0; Johnston 12—4—21—2; Miller 15—2—40—5; Johnson 18.2—6—37—3; Loxton 1—0—2—0. Second Innings: Lindwall 8—1—25—0; Johnston 20.1—5—44—6; Loxton 3—0—11—0; Johnson 13—0—50—3; McCool 10—3—19—1; Miller 11—1—27—0.

splendidly and whose success in batting was limited by ill health, made several similar concessions which did much to explode the view that Australians always play their cricket grimly. He was extensively criticised, however, when he batted throughout the last afternoon of the fourth Test match without making the customary token declaration.

The solid core of the Australian attack was supplied by Bill Johnston and Ian Johnson who were steady, accurate and tenacious. Except on rare fast wickets Lindwall was never a formidable force. In the early part of the season he put on weight and though his direction was always exemplary his pace was often moderate and he was played with increasing confidence. On the other hand Miller was consistently dangerous and often the fastest of all the bowlers. Alan Walker, who had done so well the previous season on the fast Sydney wicket, was also handicapped by the slow pitches and must have been the most disappointed member of the side.

It was however a tour with heavy emphasis on speed. The South Africans initiated the promising combination of Cuan McCarthy, who had taken

SECOND TEST — CAPE TOWN
Played on Dec. 31, Jan. 2, 3, 4. Australia won by 8 wkts.

Again Australia won the toss, and Harvey and Hassett built solidly upon the foundations laid by Morris, Moroney and Miller. Harvey's 178 came in four hours, his driving giving particular delight. South Africa replied in a manner much more businesslike than in the first Test. Rowan, Nel and Nourse all batting confidently, but gradually the Australians got on top. McCool, with leg-breaks, accounted for five men, and Nourse was obliged to follow-on. Against odds Nourse himself played a grand and courageous innings of 114 in 4½ hours; and Tayfield and Mann, taking heart from their captain's example, added 100 in an hour, during which the Australians were made to look moderate fieldsmen. Lindwall, bowling with rare fire, finished off the innings, and Australia, needing 86 runs, got home with only 25 minutes in hand.

AUSTRALIA

A. R. Morris c Watkins b Tayfield	42	— c and b Mann	24
J. A. R. Moroney c Cheetham b Mann	87	— lbw b Mann	19
K. R. Miller b Watkins	58	— not out	16
A. L. Hassett b Mann	57		
R. N. Harvey st Wade b Mann	178	— not out	23
S. J. E. Loxton b Tayfield	35		
C. L. McCool not out	49		
I. W. Johnson c Watkins b Mann	0		
R. R. Lindwall not out	8		
Extras	12	Extras	5
Total (7 wkts dec.)	526	Total (2 wkts)	87

R. A. Saggers and W. A. Johnston did not go in.

Bowling—First Innings: McCarthy 24—2—98—0; Watkins 12—2—59—1; Mann 28—3—105—4; Tayfield 37—4—141—2; Smith 25—0—111—0. Second Innings: McCarthy 4—1—18—0; Watkins 2—0—10—0; Mann 8—1—23—2; Tayfield 6—1—31—0.

SOUTH AFRICA

E. A. B. Rowan lbw b McCool	67	— c Harvey b Johnston	3
O. Wynne c Johnson b Miller	13	— c Saggers b Johnston	10
J. Nel lbw b Johnson	38	— c McCool b Johnson	19
A. D. Nourse c Johnston b Miller	65	— lbw b McCool	114
W. W. Wade c Saggers b Loxton	4	— b Johnston	11
J. Cheetham c McCool b Miller	5	— c Saggers b Lindwall	27
J. Watkins st Saggers b McCool	35	— c Saggers b Lindwall	9
H. Tayfield st Saggers b McCool	15	— b Lindwall	75
N. B. F. Mann b McCool	16	— b Lindwall	46
V. I. Smith not out	11	— lbw b Lindwall	4
C. McCarthy st Saggers b McCool	0	— not out	0
Extras	11	Extras	15
Total	278	Total	333

Bowling—First Innings: Lindwall 12—2—33—0; Johnston 17—3—53—0; Johnson 12—1—61—1; Miller 17—3—54—3; McCool 11 4—1—41—5; Loxton 6—0—25—1. Second Innings: Lindwall 15—2—32—5; Johnston 24—2—70—3; McCool 21—3—71—1; Loxton 4—1—6—0; Johnson 24—5—91—1; Harvey 3—1—5—0; Miller 11—0—43—0.

21 wickets against England, and 19 year-old Michael Melle, and neither of the leg-spin bowlers, Colin McCool and Ian Smith, was called on to make any major contribution to the attacks.

For South Africa it was a summer of upheaval and overhaul. Bold measures were adopted to groom young players and Bruce Mitchell, who was 40, was dropped after playing in 42 consecutive Test matches. An unfortunate injury kept Athol Rowan out of the Test series and the new eleven started badly by missing an excessive number of chances in the field. They were also set back through the inability of Billy Wade, Owen Wynne and Jack Cheetham to reproduce their batting form of the previous season.

Some compensation came from the striking improvement in the batting of three experienced players, Eric Rowan, Norman Mann and George Fullerton, the launching of Melle's career and the emergence of 22-year-old Hugh Tayfield, an off-spin bowler who took Athol Rowan's place, as a promising all-rounder. When the autumn came there was some cause to feel that the country's bowling was in good hands but the indifferent performances in the fifth Test match left South Africa woefully short of top-class batsmen.

THIRD TEST — DURBAN
Played on Jan. 20, 21, 23, 24. Australia won by 5 wkts.

SOUTH AFRICA

E. A. B. Rowan c Johnston b Miller	143	— c Saggers b Lindwall	4
O. Wynne b Johnston	18	— b Johnson	29
J. Nel c and b Johnson	14	— lbw b Johnston	20
A. D. Nourse c Saggers b Johnston	66	— b McCool b Johnson	27
W. W. Wade b Lindwall	24	— b Johnston	0
N. B. F. Mann b Johnston	9	— lbw b Johnson	0
J. Cheetham c Hassett b Johnston	4	— c Hassett b Johnson	1
J. Watkins b Lindwall	5	— st Saggers b Johnson	2
H. Tayfield run out	15	— b Johnston	3
V. I. Smith b Lindwall	1	— b Johnston	4
C. McCarthy not out	0	— not out	2
B 3, lb 7, nb 2	12	B 5, lb 1, nb 1	7
Total	**311**	**Total**	**99**

Bowling—First Innings: Lindwall 19—3—47—3; Miller 24—5—73—1; McCool 13—3—35—0; Johnston 31.2—5—75—4; Loxton 6—1—31—0; Johnson 16—5—38—1. Second Innings: Lindwall 4—1—7—1; Johnston 18.2—6—39—4; Miller 7—0—12—0; Johnson 17—2—34—5.

AUSTRALIA

A. R. Morris c Smith b Tayfield	25	— hit wkt b Tayfield	44
J. A. R. Moroney b Tayfield	10	— lbw b Tayfield	10
I. W. Johnson lbw b Tayfield	2		
K. R. Miller b Tayfield	2	— lbw b Mann	10
A. L. Hassett lbw b Tayfield	2	— lbw b Mann	11
R. A. Saggers c Cheetham b Mann	2		
C. L. McCool lbw b Mann	1	— not out	39
R. R. Lindwall b Mann	7		
R. N. Harvey c and b Tayfield	2	— not out	151
S. J. E. Loxton c Cheetham b Tayfield	16	— b Mann	54
W. A. Johnston not out	2		
B 3, lb 1	4	B 7, lb 9, nb 1	17
Total	**75**	**Total (5 wkts)**	**336**

Bowling—First Innings: McCarthy 6—2—8—0; Watkins 4—1—9—0; Mann 10—1—31—3; Tayfield 8.4—1—23—7. Second Innings: McCarthy 12—3—32—0; Watkins 6—2—10—0; Tayfield 49—5—144—2; Mann 50.6—13—101—3; Smith 5—0—32—0.

Brilliant Neil Harvey gave Australia the rubber after South Africa had seemed certain winners. The wisdom of Nourse's decision to bat again when the Australians had been shot out for their lowest total against South Africa and were 236 behind, will long be argued. Johnson and Johnston fully exploited the wearing pitch (at one period seven wickets fell for eight runs), and when Australia took fourth innings needing 336 the task looked much too big. Three wickets went for 59, but Harvey, using his feet superbly against the spin, held firm for 5¼ hours.

• • •

At the start, when the pitch was hard, Rowan and Nourse placed South Africa into a good position, which was made to look invincible when Tayfield's off-spinners on a soft pitch caused an Australian collapse.

AVERAGES IN ALL FIRST-CLASS MATCHES

BATTING——R. N. Harvey (V.), 1526 runs (H.S. 178) 76.30; A. L. Hassett (V.), 889 runs (H.S. 167) 68.39; A. R. Morris (N.S.W.), 1411 runs (H.S. 157) 58.79; J. A. R. Moroney (N.S.W.), 1331 runs (H.S. 160*) 55.45; K. Archer (Q.), 698 runs (H.S. 134) 43.62; S. J. E. Loxton (V.), 809 runs (H.S. 101) 40.45; K. R. Miller (N.S.W.), 557 runs (H.S. 131) 38.46; C. L. McCool (Q.), 438 runs (H.S. 100*) 29.20; W. A. Johnston (V.), 29 runs (H.S. 24*) 29.00; G. Noblet (S.A.), 138 runs (55*) 23.00; I. W. Johnson (V.), 350 runs (H.S. 70) 21.87; G. L. Langley (S.A.), 72 runs (H.S. 58) 18.00; R. A. Saggers (N.S.W.), 111 runs (H.S. 33) 13.87; R. R. Lindwall (N.S.W.) 150 runs (H.S. 28) 12.50; A. Walker (N.S.W.), 89 runs (H.S. 25*) 9.88.

BOWLING——W. A. Johnston, 56 wkts.——770 runs (av. 13.75); R. R. Lindwall, 50 wkts.——729 runs (av. 14.58); G. Noblet. 38 wkts.——557 runs (av. 16.65); I. W. Johnson, 78 wkts.——1276 runs (av. 16.35); K. R. Miller, 44 wkts.—— 728 runs (av. 16.54); S. J. E. Loxton, 12 wkts.——217 runs (av. 18.08); C. L. McCool, 51 wkts.——970 runs (av. 19.01); A. Walker, 25 wkts.—— 506 runs (av. 20.24); R. N. Harvey, 3 wkts.——71 runs (av. 23.66). Also bowled——A. L. Hassett, 1 wkt.——29 runs; K. Archer, 0 wkts.——30 runs; A. R. Morris, 0 wkts.——48 runs.

FOURTH TEST — JOHANNESBURG

Played on Feb. 10, 11, 13, 14. Match drawn.

Australia were checked in a high-scoring match in which Moroney established a record as the first Australian to complete two separate hundreds in a Test against them.

Morris and Moroney opened with 214 —Morris batted 4¼ hours, and his partner an hour longer —after which Miller, Hassett and Harvey hit out. Against all this Melle created a favourable impression as a pace bowler. South Africa struggled for runs. and lost six men for 148, but the enterprise of Fullerton, Tayfield and Mann enabled them to save the follow-on.

When Australia batted again there was little prospect of a decision, though Moroney's second century of the match, in 3¾ hours, another hundred from Harvey, and some brisk scoring by M⁽ller kept the game alive.

AUSTRALIA

A. R. Morris c Fullerton b McCarthy	111 — c Mann b McCarthy 19
J. A. R. Moroney c Fullerton b Melle	118 — not out 101
K. R. Miller c Fullerton b Melle	84 — not out 33
R. R. Lindwall b Melle	5
A. L. Hassett b McCarthy	53
R. N. Harvey not out	56 — b Melle 100
S. J. E. Loxton b Melle	6
C. L. McCool st Fullerton b Tayfield	8
I. W. Johnson c Tayfield b Melle	3
R. A. Saggers not out	5
B 8, lb 7, nb 1....	16 Extras 6
Total (for 8 wkts dec.)	465 (Total for 2 wkts) 259

W. A. Johnston did not go in.

BOWLING—First Innings: McCarthy 31—4—113—2; Melle 33— 3—113—5; Tayfield 31—4—103—1; Mann 25—2—85—0; Begbie 7—0—35—0. Second Innings: McCarthy 13—1—56—1; Melle 12—0—58—1; Tayfield 14—2—88—0; Mann 8—1—32—0; Begbie 3—0—19—0; Rowan 1—1—0—0; Nourse 1—1—0—0.

SOUTH AFRICA

E. A. B. Rowan b Lindwall	55
J. Nel run out	25
R. Draper c Saggers b Johnston	15
A. D. Nourse c Saggers b Lindwall	5
D. W. Begbie c McCool b Miller	24
P. L. Winslow c and b Miller	19
G. M. Fullerton c Hassett b McCool	88
H. Tayfield c Johnson b Miller	40
N. B. F. Mann b Lindwall	52
M. Melle lbw b McCool..	14
C. McCarthy not out	2
B7, lb 5, nb 1....	13
Total	352

BOWLING—Lindwall 26—3—82—3; Johnston 29—5—68—1; Miller 28—3—75—3; Loxton 10—2—22—0; Johnson 18—4—52—0; McCool 7—0—29—2; Hassett 1—0—5—0; Harvey 3—0—6—0.

···· FIRST-CLASS UMPIRES 1950 ····

FRANK CHESTER

The number of first-class umpires has been increased by two for 1950, the total now being 24. This is because of the increase in county championship matches from 26 to 28. C. N. Woolley (Northants.) and D. Hendren (Middx. & Durham) were not re-appointed and S. J. Staples (Notts.) has resigned because of ill health. The five newcomers are Parkin, Palmer, Welch (from the Minor Counties' list), Spencer and Mobey.

Frank Chester's Testimonial fund, spread over the seasons 1948 and 1949, was closed at just over £3,200.

W. H. Ashdown (Kent)
H. G. Baldwin (Surrey)
T. J. Bartley (Cheshire)
J. T. Bell (Glamorgan)
F. Chester (Worcs.)
A. R. Coleman (Leics.)
E. Cooke (Notts.)
D. Davies (Glamorgan)
Harold Elliott (Lancs.)
B. Flint (Notts.)

J. J. Hills
  (Kent and Glamorgan)
F. S. Lee
  (Middx. and Somerset)
A. Lockett (Staffs.)
K. McCanlis
  (Surrey and Beds.)
G. S. Mobey (Surrey)
H. Palmer (Cambs.)
H. L. Parkin (Staffs.)

H. W. Parks (Sussex)
A. E. Pothecary
  (Hants.)
W. F. Price (Middx.)
E. Robinson (Yorks.)
A. Skelding (Leics.)
T. Spencer (Kent)
C. H. Welch
  (Northants.)

FIFTH TEST — PORT ELIZABETH
March 3, 4, 6. Australia won by inns. and 259.

AUSTRALIA

A. R. Morris c Winslow b Melle	157
J. A. R. Moroney c Nourse b Melle	7
K. R. Miller c Nourse b Tayfield	22
R. N. Harvey b Begbie	116
A. L. Hassett c McCarthy b Mann	167
S. J. E. Loxton c Rowan b Mann	43
C. L. McCool c Fullerton b Tayfield	6
I. W. Johnson not out	26
R. A. Saggers not out	4
B 1	1
Total (for 7 wkts. dec.)	549

G. Noblet and W. A. Johnston did not go in.

BOWLING—McCarthy 29—2—121—0; Melle 23—2—132—2; Tayfield 25—1—103—2; Mann 36—4—154—2; Begbie 4—0—38—1.

SOUTH AFRICA

E. A. B. Rowan b Johnson	40	— c McCool b Miller	0
J. Nel b Miller	0	— lbw b Johnston	5
R. Draper c Johnston b Miller	7	— b Johnston	3
A. D. Nourse c McCool b Miller	37	— b Johnson	55
D. W. Begbie c Saggers b Noblet	1	— b Johnston	5
P. L. Winslow lbw b Noblet	0	— st Saggers b Johnson	11
G. M. Fullerton st Saggers b McCool	18	— c Saggers b Loxton	24
H. Tayfield st Saggers b McCool	6	— st Saggers b McCool	7
M. Melle b Miller	1	— c Harvey b McCool	6
N. B. F. Mann b Noblet	41	— lbw b Johnson	6
C. McCarthy not out	1	— not out	4
B 3, lb 3	6	B 5, nb 1	6
Total	158	Total	132

BOWLING—First Innings: Miller 14—3—42—4; Johnston 3—0—12—0; Noblet 17.1—7—21—3; Johnson 11—1—48—1; McCool 5—1—29—2. Second Innings: Miller 8—0—24—1; Johnston 6—1—10—3; Noblet 9—2—16—0; McCool 15.2—3—48—2; Loxton 4—2—7—1; Johnson 6—0—21—3.

After making the highest total by an Australian team in South Africa, the Australians out-played their opponents and gained their biggest win of the current series. The dismissal of Moroney and Miller for 49 raised South Africa's hopes, but Morris, Harvey and Hassett dashed them with merciless batting. Morris shared two three-figure partnerships —187 with Harvey and 114 with Hassett, who, like Morris, made his best score of the tour. Five catches were dropped.

* * *

Lindwall was omitted from the Australian side in favour of Noblet, who was given his first chance in Test cricket.

S. F. BARNES
(Staffordshire)

C. J. BARNETT
(Gloucestershire)

W. E. BOWES
(Yorkshire)

L. C. BRAUND
(Surrey & Somerset)

G. DUCKWORTH
(Lancashire)

THE 26 M.C.C.
A Personal Message

THESE are the photographs of all the twenty-six England professional cricketers who were made M.C.C. members in 1949—nearly all of them taken in the prime of their playing days. And this is a message from Patsy Hendren of Middlesex and England, who is now the Sussex coach:—

" It was a great gesture on the part of M.C.C. and I am very proud to be one of the selected. I have had such a great deal to do with Lord's, playing there for thirty years while I was a member of the M.C.C. staff, so I have such pleasant memories of the famous ground, which has been almost my

A. P. FREEMAN
(Kent)

G. GEARY
(Leicestershire)

G. GUNN snr.
(Nottinghamshire)

J. W. HEARNE
(Middlesex)

E. HENDREN
(Middlesex)

G. H. HIRST
(Yorkshire)

J. B. HOBBS
(Surrey)

H. LARWOOD
(Nottinghamshire)

M. LEYLAND
(Yorkshire)

C. P. MEAD
(Hampshire)

E. PAYNTER
(Lancashire)

W. RHODES
(Yorkshire)

PROFESSIONALS
From Patsy Hendren

A. C. RUSSELL
(Essex)

second home. It is a grand finale to many happy days spent there.

It will surprise many people that during all the time I was on the staff I never had any agreement or contract. Their word was always good enough! I began as a ground boy and was lucky enough to play for my county and country. What more could a boy wish than to become an honorary member of M.C.C.?

I appreciate the great compliment that has been paid me and in this I am quite sure I echo the feelings of all the other selected players."

Footnote: Harold Larwood is emigrating to Australia.

A. SANDHAM
(Surrey)

E. J. SMITH
(Warwickshire)

H. STRUDWICK
(Surrey)

H. SUTCLIFFE
(Yorkshire)

M. W. TATE
(Sussex)

E. TYLDESLEY
(Lancashire)

W. VOCE
(Nottinghamshire)

F. E. WOOLLEY
(Kent)

Fast Scoring, Fine Fielding

Played 28, Won 12, Lost 2, Drawn 14

THE popularity of this all-professional side was at all times proved by the record crowds at the matches in each of the three countries visited. The side was a formidable combination composed mainly of all-rounders. The batting was no doubt comparatively stronger than the bowling but any weakness in the attack was usually offset by what was often described as the finest fielding side seen in India.

Among the batsmen Worrell was outstanding and did nothing that did not enhance his already great reputation. Oldfield too showed again and again what a sound player he was—especially in the Test matches when he scored a century in each of the first three Tests. The main run-getters, in addition to these two, were Alley and Livingstone, both of whom topped the 1,000 mark.

As was expected Tribe was the mainspring of the attack. His well-flighted spinners earned him many wickets although it was unfortunate that he was often used as a stock bowler. Injuries and illness took toll from time to time and the greatest loss undoubtedly was Pepper's early return to England. This left Pettiford to bear the brunt of the leg-break bowling and a great gap was left when he could not play after the third Test at Calcutta.

All the players acquitted themselves well in the strange conditions —made even harder by the constant changing from turf to matting wickets and back again.

The Rubber, won by India by two matches to one with two drawn, proved very exciting and its issue was not finally decided until the final Test at Madras. There, in a game of changing fortunes, India won by 3 wickets with only six minutes to spare.

The Test match in Pakistan, due mainly to Tribe's devastating second innings spell of 5 for 8, was won very easily in three days.

LEADING TEST AVERAGES
COMMONWEALTH TEAM—BATTING

	Inns.	N.O.	Runs	H.S.	Avge.	100's
F. M. Worrell	9	2	684	223*	97.71	2
J. Pettiford	5	3	171	72	85.50	—
N. Oldfield	10	1	491	158	54.55	3
J. Livingstone	8	0	401	123	50.12	1
W. Alley	10	3	286	51*	40.85	—
F. Freer	8	0	288	132	36.00	1
J. K. Holt	6	1	149	84*	29.80	—
G. Tribe	7	2	119	61	23.80	—

BOWLING

	Overs	Mdns.	Runs	Wkts.	Avge.
D. Fitzmaurice	67	24	125	7	17.85
C. G. Pepper	75.4	22	191	7	27.28
F. Freer	197	48	470	14	33.57
G. Tribe	338	87	854	24	35.58
F. M. Worrell	158.1	52	262	7	37.42
H. Lambert	156	29	422	9	46.88
R. Smith	114.1	33	236	5	47.20

INDIA—BATTING

	Inns.	N.O.	Runs	H.S.	Avge.	100's
V. S. Hazare	10	3	677	175*	96.71	2
H. R. Adhikari	9	3	341	93	56.83	—
Mushtaq Ali	6	3	268	129	53.60	1
D. G. Phadkar	10	2	374	110	46.75	1
P. R. Umrigar	8	1	276	67	39.42	—
V. Mankad	8	0	163	91	20.37	—
R. S. Modi	10	0	196	58	19.60	—

BOWLING

	Overs	Mdns.	Runs	Wkts.	Avge.
D. G. Phadkar	195.5	30	593	21	28.23
N. Chowdhury	88.4	7	290	9	32.33
V. S. Hazare	144.3	22	356	10	35.60
C. S. Nayudu	137.3	12	520	10	52.00
V. Mankad	137	30	362	6	60.33

Livingstone was an adequate captain and in addition to his batting also kept wicket well. This was perhaps unfortunate for Dawkes who maintained the reputation he had gained in England but was kept out of the Test matches only because of Livingstone's greater run-getting ability.

The tour was a financial success and may well be the first of many similar enterprises. Already it has been suggested that another side should go to India next winter. This, no doubt, was influenced by the drawing power of a good side which included so many batsmen who maintained a rate of scoring seldom seen in first-class cricket.

COMMONWEALTH TEAM

J. Livingstone (N.S.W.) (Capt.)
W. Alley (N.S.W.)
C. G. Pepper (N.S.W.)
J. Pettiford (N.S.W.)
D. Fitzmaurice (Victoria)

F. Freer (Victoria)
H. Lambert (Victoria)
G. Tribe (Victoria)
W. Langdon (W. Australia)
G. Dawkes (Derbyshire)
N. Oldfield (Northants.)
W. Place (Lancashire)

G. H. Pope (Derbyshire)
Ray Smith (Essex)
J. K. Holt (Jamaica)
F. M. Worrell (Barbados)
Manager:—
G. Duckworth (Lancs.)

H. W. Parks (Sussex), now a first-class umpire, played in one match.

COMMONWEALTH TEAM IN INDIA, 1949-50
Standing: F. M. Worrell, D Fitzmaurice, J. Pettiford, W. Alley, H. Lambert, C. Pepper, R. Smith, G. Dawkes, W. Langdon, J. Holt.
Seated: N. Oldfield, G. Tribe, G. Duckworth (Manager), J. Livingstone (Capt.), F. Freer, G. H. Pope, W. Place.

INDIA—THIRD " TEST " (CALCUTTA), 1949-50
Standing: C. S. Nayudu, V. Mankad, M. K. Mantri, Mushtaq Ali, V. S. Hazare (Capt.), D. G. Phadkar, R. S. Modi, H. R Adhikari, P. Umrigar.
In front: N. Chowdhury, G. Kischenchand, Joshi (12th man).

FIRST TEST (New Delhi)—November 11 to 15.—COMMONWEALTH 608 for 8 dec. (Oldfield 151, Livingstone 123, Pettiford 65*) and 12 for 1; INDIA 291 (D. G. Phadkar 110, H. R. Adhikari 74, Pepper 4-57) and 327 (M. K. Mantri 54, P. R. Umrigar 55, V. S. Hazare 140, Tribe 4-65). Commonwealth won by 9 wickets.

SECOND TEST (Bombay)—December 16 to 20.—COMMONWEALTH 448 (Oldfield 110, Worrell 78, Pettiford 72, Freer 132, R. S. Modi 3-50) and 110-3 (Alley 51*); INDIA 289 (V. M. Merchant 78, Phadkar 78, Modi 58, Lambert 4-76, Freer 4-89) and 430 for 8 dec. (V. M. Merchant 94, Modi 51, Hazare 64, Adhikari 93, Umrigar 67, Tribe 4-156). Match drawn.

THIRD TEST (Calcutta)—December 30 to January 3.—INDIA 422 (V. Mankad 91, Hazare 175*, Tribe 5-144) and 117

for 3; COMMONWEALTH 190 (Livingstone 42; Phadkar 3-50, N. Chowdhury 4-52) and 348 (Oldfield 158, Livingstone 59, C. S. Nayudu 5-59). India won by 7 wickets.

FOURTH TEST (Cawnpore)—January 14 to 18.—COMMONWEALTH 446 (Livingstone 80, Worrel 223*, Tribe 61) and 237 for 3 dec. (Livingstone 81, Worrell 83*); INDIA 386 (Mushtaq Ali 129, Phadkar 64, Adhikari 61, Tribe 5-122, Worrel. 3-42) and 84 for 4 (Hazare 41*, Fitzmaurice 2-7). Match drawn.

FIFTH TEST (Madras)—February 17 to 21.—COMMONWEALTH 324 (Worrell 161, Phadkar 4-89) and 247 (Holt 84*, Phadkar 3-28); INDIA 313 (Hazare 77, G. Kishenchand 72, Tribe 4-90, Fitzmaurice 3-40) and 261 for 7 (Hazare 84, Umrigar 59). India won by 3 wickets.

New Zealand Report 1949-50　　　　*From Noel Macdonald*

More Records for B. Sutcliffe

THE Plunket Shield programme of six matches, all played during the Christmas-New Year period, proved rather disappointing despite the return of the touring team from England. Much of the play was of a poor standard—and uninteresting too because of slow scoring. Outstanding performances were few.

Wellington won the Shield because of the strength of their attack. They had six regular bowlers—Fenwick Cresswell, Rabone and Reid (all familiar names), and Arthur Cresswell, R. McK. Murray and C. W. L. Randall, who were quickish. In addition, E. W. Dempster, a slow medium left-hander, took four valuable wickets against Auckland. Of the batsmen only Reid and J. A. Ongley, the captain, showed any consistency.

Fenwick Cresswell was the linch-pin of their attack, bowling more than twice as many overs—half of them maidens—as any of his colleagues. Murray did the "hat-trick" against Otago and Wellington players occupied five of the top places in the Plunket bowling averages.

Auckland sent six players to England last year, but of these only Verdun Scott was available for the southern tour. Scott, the captain, was handicapped by a lack of bowlers, Cowie having transferred to Wellington in December

PLUNKET SHIELD
LEADING BATTING AVERAGES

	Inns.	N.O.	Runs	H.S.	Avge
B. Sutcliffe (Otago)	5	—	569	355	113.80
V. J. Scott (Auck.)	6	1	405	138	81.00
J. Hardstaff (Auck.)	4	—	269	135	67.25
J. R. Reid (Wgtn.)	6	1	291	112	58.20
W. M. Wallace (A.)	2	—	115	86	57.50
W. A. Hadlee (Cant.)	4	—	203	125	50.75
A. R. MacGibbon (C.)	5	1	194	94	48.50
J. G. Leggat (Cant.)	5	—	233	80	46.60
O. C. Cleal (Auck.)	6	—	254	81	42.33

AUSTRALIAN TOURING TEAM IN NEW ZEALAND

W. A. Brown (Queensland) (Captain), R. L. Ridings (S. Australia) (Vice-capt), R. Howard, J. Iverson, K. Meuleman and D. Ring (all Victoria), S. G. Sismey, J. Burke and A. Davidson (all N.S.W.), D. Duldig (S. Australia), L. Johnson and D. Tallon (Queensland), W. Driver and C. Puckett (W. Australia).

LEADING BOWLING AVERAGES

	Overs	Mdns.	Runs	Wkts.	Avge
A. M. Moir (Otago)	27	4	55	4	13.75
J. R. Reid (Wgtn.)	59.1	11	141	10	14.10
R. McK. Murray (W.)	82	29	190	13	14.61
G. F. Cresswell (W.)	186.3	93	204	12	17.00
E. W. Dempster (W.)	24	2	68	4	17.00
G. W. F. Overton(O.)	143	36	323	17	19.00
O. C. Cleal (A.) ...	69	23	154	8	19.25
C. L. W. Randall (W.)	80.3	24	186	9	20.66
S. M. Cameron (C.)	57.1	10	149	7	21.28
D. C Cleverley (A.)	66.2	22	132	6	22.00
T. B. Burtt (Cant.)	138	64	276	12	23.00

and Burke being unable to go. Hayes, who is only now recovered from a serious illness contracted on the voyage home, did not appear and Mervyn Wallace played only in the final game when he led the side to victory against Wellington. Sutcliffe, Auckland's star of previous seasons, represented Otago who have engaged him for a three-year term as coach. It was as well therefore that Scott himself had a great season, playing with more freedom than he had previously shown in the Dominion.

W. A. Hadlee was available only for the first two Canterbury matches. He scored a grand hundred in the victory against Auckland, but his 48 against Wellington was an even finer effort, entirely free from blemish and possibly the finest of all his innings for Canterbury. Leggat was consistently successful as an opening batsman and MacGibbon, who stands 6ft. 5ins., enhanced his reputation as a potential fast medium Test bowler, and batted very well too.

PHENOMENAL SUTCLIFFE

B. Sutcliffe's magnificent 355 for Otago v. Wellington is the highest score ever made by a New Zealand batsman; his aggregate of 569 runs is a record in Plunket Shield cricket; and his last nine innings have all exceeded 50.

Here are the details of his phenomenal successes in first-class cricket on the Carisbrook ground, Dunedin (Otago's home ground):

1946-47—197 & 128 v. M.C.C.
1947-48—99 & 103 Otago v. Auckland
118 & 125 Otago v. Canterbury
7 & 208* North Island v. S. Island
1949-50—355 Otago v. Auckland
117 & 51 Otago v. Canterbury
SUMMARY: 1,508 runs, average 150.80

As will be seen, five of the seven batsmen averaging more than 50 toured England in 1949, and a sixth was J. Hardstaff of Notts. who scored his 25,000th run in first-class cricket.

F. B. Smith scored 91 runs in five innings, Rabone 82 runs in six innings and three wickets for 192 besides. F. L. H. Mooney kept wicket as soundly as ever for Wellington but made only 66 runs in 5 innings. H. B. Cave was not selected for Wellington but played in minor association representative matches.

In the last four seasons his record against Canterbury has been :—
1946-47—111 & 62* for Auckland
1947-48—118 & 125 for Otago
1948-49—141 & 135 for Auckland
1949-50—117 & 51 for Otago
SUMMARY: 860 runs, average 122.85

L.S.D. IN THE COUNTIES 1949

Derby	£1.857†	Lancs.	£3.437	Surrey	£1.870
Essex	£1 942	Leics.	£1,664	Sussex	£526
Glamorgan	£1.336	Middlesex	—	Warwick	£1.138†
Glos.	£2.768	Northants.	£765	Worcs.	£765
Hants.	£1.951†	Notts.	£125†	Yorks.	£437
Kent	£3,171	Somerset	£2,341		† A loss.

SOME CRICKET BOOKS AND REPRINTS, 1950

FAREWELL TO CRICKET by Don Bradman. *Hodder & Stoughton.* 12/6 (May).

CRICKET IN THE BLOOD by Dudley Nourse. *Hodder & Stoughton.* 10/6. (May).

BATTING STROKES by Len Hutton & H. P. Crabtree. *Methuen.* 2/6. (May).

BOWLING by H. P. Crabtree. *Methuen.* 2/6. (May).

YORKSHIRE by J. M. Kilburn. *Falcon Press.* 7/6. (April).

ESSEX by Charles Bray. *Falcon Press.* 7/6. (April).

SUSSEX by Sir Home Gordon. *Falcon Press.* 7/6. (April).

MIDDLESEX by The Hon. Terence Prittie. *Falcon Press.* 7/6. (April).

SECOND INNINGS: More Autobiography by Neville Cardus. *Collins.* 12/6. (Feb.).

GOOD DAYS by Neville Cardus. *Rupert Hart-Davis.* 6/-. (Reprint, Available).

AUSTRALIAN SUMMER by Neville Cardus. *Rupert Hart-Davis.* 6/-. (Reprint, Available.)

DAYS IN THE SUN by Neville Cardus. *Rupert Hart-Davis.* 6/-. (Reprint, Available.)

SUMMER GAME by Neville Cardus. *Hart-Davis.* 6/- (Reprint, Available.)

WICKETS, TRIES AND GOALS by John Arlott. *Sampson Low.* 7/6. (Available).

PLAYING FOR ENGLAND by Denis Compton. *Sampson Low.* 7/6. (Reprint May).

BOYS' BOOK OF CRICKET, 1950. *Evans Brothers.* 10/6. (April 15).

THE RIGHT WAY TO BECOME A CRICKETER by John Board. *Right Way Books.* 5/-. (Just Published).

GONE TO THE CRICKETERS by John Arlott. *Longmans.* About 9/6. (May).

GENTLEMEN VERSUS PLAYERS by Sir Pelham Warner. *Harrap.* About 18/-. (July).

DENIS COMPTON by E. W. Swanton. *Playfair.* 5/- (Available).

Cricket books published by Stanley Paul and Werner Laurie are advertised on pages 24 and 42.

This list, kindly provided by W. H. Smith and Son, may prove a useful reference. Some books were published before this Annual went to press—one of them the latest autobiography by Neville Cardus; and no true cricketer should ho'd out against the lure and delight of any such offering. Learie Constantine with *Cricket Crackers* has also been setting off more gunpowder in his most irrepressible and provocative (Continued on page 29)

The West Indies Can Win

. . . By Being West Indian

By LEARIE CONSTANTINE

INDIA, South Africa, Australia and New Zealand have come to England since the war and all have emerged from their tours with enhanced prestige. Now it is the turn of the West Indies to stand their trial before the bar of English cricket opinion.

The West Indies players have been nurtured on true, hard and fast wickets in brilliant sunshine and now they face the inevitable rain and cold and varying wickets. It's too much to hope for a repetition of England's summer of 1949—though I hope I'm wrong! It is true to say that no Dominion or Colonial cricketer has deserved his spurs until he achieves success on an English tour. For only here, where the conditions vary from county to county, and where atmosphere plays so important a part, can technique and the capacity to adapt be really tested.

There are no bad wickets in England in the sense that a Barbados or a British Guiana wicket can be bad, or for that matter a Melbourne wicket in Australia. Many rude things have been said about the bad Melbourne wickets—or those of Brisbane—after rain, but I venture the opinion that their viciousness does not compare with wickets in the West Indies. I have seen a straight ball from a fast bowler pitch well over the batting crease and miss the wicket by at least half a foot. I am not exaggerating. Local players call a bad Barbados wicket " The Glue Pot "—and never were words truer spoken.

The 1950 tour should be a turning point in my country's cricket. It should put us up into the group that can challenge and threaten England in every Test match. But unless the peculiarly distinctive form of West Indian cricket is emphasised our team will fail in its objective. A weaker England side, backed by good and astute tactics and deeper experience, could finally stave off defeat.

Everton Weekes can play the sort of game I want to see. In the third Test match against India in 1948-9, his two gallant centuries were typical of the eager heart, the clear eye and daring wrists, and the flashing bat. These things to me specially mark out West Indian batting, or ought to do so. By such means we win matches.

Weekes made 162 not out in the first innings when he was carrying the side on his shoulders. He never allowed responsibility to tame him. 101 in his second knock was attained by blows that were a defiance to every batting prude. He made a new world record of five consecutive centuries in Tests, every one a sparkler. England will suit him; for he is a batsman who makes wickets and bowlers suit him. He broke all records in the Lancashire League last year—including the highest score and the greatest aggregate previously held by myself and George Headley respectively. I am not fond of making prophecies, but Everton Weekes, barring accidents and granted normal health, will combine orthodoxy and a rapid rate of scoring reminiscent of the great masters of yesteryear.

The West Indies produce batsmen equal to anyone in the world. Walcott, Worrell, Christiani, Stollmeyer and others can do the greatest things; but my country has nearly always suffered from bad technique or inexperience. The West Indies' tour of India was pathetic in its timidity and estimation of the relative strength and weakness of the contending forces. In the first two Tests our men made over 600 in one innings and then failed to win in five-day games ! In a shaking fever of desire not to lose, no effort was made to win. A team of eleven fine players all advanced at once in different directions. There was no well-laid plan, no ferocity†, no tactics. Imagine " W.G. " in such a position or even H. B. G. Austin†, then try to imagine them not winning the match ! You can't do it; the mind revolts. See what the Commonwealth side has done in a four-day match!

Tiger, Tiger

If the West Indies bank huge scores here this year—as well they may—and abandon attack in bowling, the team will go home with its tail between its legs. But if the team can put some " tiger " in its play we shall win the Rubber. But there must be a plan. Who will formulate it? That is the rub! We live in a period when the economy is planned, leisure planned and the peoples of the world yearn for security. But although some sort of planning is very necessary in a wise approach to the great game of cricket, must we over-emphasise the need of security and dispose once and for all of the element of chance which has helped to make the game what it is—the national game of the British Commonwealth?

Critics have said that the seeds of death of the true West Indian cricketing spirit were sown on the 1939 tour of England. I was the oldest player to take part in the tour, and I was roundly condemned for trying to put gunpowder into our batting and bowling, while younger players were obsessed by a pitiful anxiety not to take risks in either. Can you imagine a slow bowler being asked not to bowl his googly—for unless it is well-pitched he might give away runs? This is the kind of thing I mean, and this actually happened in 1939 on our tour.

Boldness must be our motto in 1950 if we are to beat England. How I would have loved to bowl some of my fastest overs against Compton and Edrich, Hutton and Washbrook, in the days when even Sir Donald Bradman sometimes moved his bat just after his wicket flew to bits!

† *Captain of West Indies teams in England, 1906 and 1923.*

Weekes, whom Pataudi has called " a more finished Archie Jackson," and his colleagues will get the big scores in England that are the essential foundation for a Test victory. And our fielding, which has, I hope, improved since the Indian tour (when it was alleged to be ragged and uncertain) could be top-class. But as to bowling, I am not sure. There must be a plan here too.

I have always held that a bowler of real pace is a pre-requisite for Test match success. But these bowlers are apt to set a defensive instead of an attacking field, and although this is quite in order when the conditions call for it, as a matter of policy I will not defend it. The matter of field placing is a question left entirely to the skipper's discretion. He ought to know when to let shots go to the boundary in return for a placing that increases the batsman's mental strain. No modern Test captain except Bradman has shown much conception of the part time plays in a cricket victory—and the joke of it is that Bradman has seldom needed to!

Of all Test-playing combinations the West Indies team alone is composed of men of different races. And there lies a difficulty which I believe few people realise—even the selectors. As I have often pointed out, Test match cricket is no sort of a game; it is a battle. And to win you do not only need the strenuous effort of individual players. The work of each player must be backed by a solidarity and a sense of loyalty and support—not only actually, but in the spirit, so to speak. The lack of this has been the chief weakness of the West Indies in big cricket.

It is a difficult obstacle, but not impossible to surmount. If the New Zealand team spirit of 1949 can be emulated (what a wonderful bunch of sportsmen they were) then no one need be afraid for the West Indies' showing this season. Our players, from captain down, must realise that every consideration should give way to the necessity of uniting in spirit and in truth to win through a series of Test matches; otherwise, the West Indies will never play, nor England see, the cricket which has fired the imagination of its great following in my country. In the West Indies almost everyone loves cricket.

Come on, West Indies! A great welcome awaits you. We have won Test matches before—against England, against Australia, against India. 1950 is the challenging year. We have the tools—can a good job be made with them?

In Retrospect . . .

by PAT LANDSBERG
(recently returned
from the West Indies)

A NGLO-WEST INDIES cricketing history is 55 years old this year. It was in 1895 that R. S. Lucas took a touring team to the hitherto unknown cricketing fields of Trinidad, Barbados and Jamaica. A year later, two teams went to the West Indies, one under Lord Hawke, the other under Arthur Priestley.

Four years later, in 1900, the West Indies made their first visit overseas and with R. S. A. Warner, brother of Sir Pelham, as captain, they brought a truly representative body of cricketers to this country. The side was gathered from Demerara, Granada and St. Vincent, in addition to the four chief cricketing centres of the West Indies—Jamaica, Trinidad, Barbados and British Guiana. Of the seventeen matches played, five were won. The tour did not rank as first-class.

In 1901-02 B. J. T. Bosanquet took a team to B.W.I. and they won thirteen of their nineteen games. Three years later Viscount Brackley toured with a side that included two professionals and they won eleven of the twenty games played. Then came 1906 and with it a name to be noted in West Indies cricket—Major H. B. G. Austin, later Sir Harold. His team in England included George Challenor, one of their greatest batsmen.

So far, all the tours to the West Indies had been, so to speak, under private enterprise, and were not officially recognised by the Marylebone Cricket Club. But in 1910-11 M.C.C. sponsored a tour and elected A. F. W. Somerset (of Sussex) to captain the side It won three, lost four, drew three and tied one of the eleven matches played. Another M.C.C. team—under Somerset again—toured in 1912-13, winning five and losing three of their nine matches.

The Tour of 1923

War intervened and it was not until 1923 that tours between the two countries were resumed. And then, as 17 years before, the captain of the touring side was Major H. B. G. Austin. With him, once again, was Challenor. Others were Karl Nunes (now President of the West Indies Board of Control), J. K. Holt, snr. (whose son has just returned from the Commonwealth tour of India), George Francis, a powerful and fearsome fast bowler (listed rather inappropriately as a " professional of unknown quantity ") and a man who was selected ninety per cent. for his acrobatica at cover point and the promise of his all-round ability—Learie Constantine. Of the twenty first-class games played, six were won, seven lost and seven drawn. But most encouraging for the tourists was their performance at Scarborough, when they emerged with flying colours from a match with a strong England XI. It was here that George N. Francis not only reached his 100 wickets in all matches on the tour, but with G. John had six of England's finest batsmen back in the pavilion in the second innings for 19 runs.

And so in 1925-26 the M.C.C. made their first post-war West Indies tour. Under the Hon. F. S. G. Calthorpe, the side lost only one game but drew ten of the thirteen matches played. One unofficial Test was won and two drawn. Then in 1928 the M.C.C. elevated the games between the countries to Test standard but the West Indies met with poor success in England that year. Coming as they do from a hemisphere where sticky wickets are very few and far between it was not perhaps surprising that they floundered against spin in a wet summer. All three of the Test matches were lost by an innings—and " Tich " Freeman did much of the damage, taking 22 wickets for 13.72 in the Tests.

The West Indies fared much better in 1929-30 when Calthorpe took out another M.C.C. side. England won one Test and West Indies one, the remaining two being drawn. The last Test, due to be played to a finish at Kingston, was cut short by the necessity to catch the homeward boat.

English cricketers were introduced during this tour to George Headley, the greatest West Indies bat of all time. Headley was a spare youth of 21, but his power was clearly shown with a century in the first Test, two centuries in the third and, for good measure, a double century in the last, in his native Jamaica.

The West Indies showed much improved form in England in 1933 and Ivan Barrow beat George Headley by a matter of minutes in becoming the first West Indies player to score a Test century on English pitches. This was at Manchester when he made 105 and Headley 169 not out. The series was lost, however, with one drawn and two lost.

1934-35 was jubilation year for the West Indies, who won a Test series for the first time. Two games were won, one drawn, one lost, and George Headley again proved an unpleasant thorn in the English side. His 270 not out at his favourite Sabina Park ground in Kingston is still the highest for

West Indies against England and the bowling of E. A. Martindale once again contributed considerably to the victory. Eric Hollies topped England's bowling. But in 1939, the year when the tour was cut short by seven games due to war, the West Indies lost the series by the only game in which there was a definite result; they were beaten by 8 wickets in the first Test at Lord's. Learie Constantine finished top of the bowling—and many will recollect his soaring six off the back foot on the second day of the last Test at the Oval. Hutton was in great form for England—480 runs in 6 innings for an average of 96.

The M.C.C. tour of 1947-8 completes the tale to date—and for the first time in M.C.C. history not a victory was achieved. But five of England's finest batsmen—Washbrook, Hutton, Edrich, Compton and Yardley—could not make the trip, and nor could A. V. Bedser and Wright; and no sooner had the team arrived than they were beset by injuries and illness. The captain, G. O. Allen, sent a desperate appeal to Lord's for reinforcement and Hutton flew out to score a century on his first appearance. But having drawn the first two Tests the West Indies deservedly won the third and fourth—and proved, if proof were needed, that in their own countries and in their own climate they are good enough for the toughest opposition in the world.

ENGLAND v. W. INDIES : TEST RECORDS 1928-1948

TEST SUMMARY	Matches Played	England won	W. Indies won	Matches drawn
1928 in England ...	3	3	0	0
1929-30 in West Indies ...	4	1	1	2
1933 in England ...	3	2	0	1
1934-35 in West Indies ...	4	1	2	1
1939 in England ...	3	1	0	2
1947-48 in West Indies ...	4	0	2	2
Total	21	8	5	8

HIGHEST INNINGS TOTALS

(ENGLAND)		(WEST INDIES)	
849	Kingston, 1929-30	535-7 dec.	Kingston, 1934-35
467	Barbados, 1929-30	498	Oval, 1939
438	Oval, 1928	497	Port of Spain, 1947-48
425-8 dec.	Port of Spain, 1929-30	490	Kingston, 1947-48

SMALLEST INNINGS TOTALS

103	Kingston, 1934-35	97	Lord's, 1933
107	Port of Spain, 1934-35	100	Oval, 1933
111	Georgetown, 1947-48	102	Barbados, 1934-35

HIGHEST MATCH AGGREGATE — 1815 for 34 wkts., at Kingston, 1929-30
LOWEST MATCH AGGREGATE — 309 for 29 wkts., at Barbados, 1934-35

RECORD WICKET PARTNERSHIPS
ENGLAND

1st	173	G. Gunn & A. Sandham	Kingston	1929-30
2nd	148	A. Sandham & R. E. S. Wyatt	Kingston	1929-30
3rd	264	L. Hutton & W. R. Hammond	Oval	1939
4th	259	A. Sandham & L. E. G. Ames	Kingston	1929-30
5th	86	E. Hendren & G. T. S. Stevens	Port of Spain ...	1929-30
6th	158	L. E. G. Ames & J. Iddon	Kingston	1934-35

7th	140	D. R. Jardine & R. W. V. Robins	Manchester	1933
8th	88	N. E. Haig & W. E. Astill	Barbados	1929-30
9th	62	E. R. T. Holmes & W. F. Farrimond	Port of Spain	1934-35
10th	31	L. E. G. Ames & G. G. Macaulay	Lord's	1933

WEST INDIES

1st	173	G. Carew & A. Ganteaume	Port of Spain	1947-48
2nd	228	R. K. Nunes & G. Headley	Kingston	1929-30
3rd	202	G. Headley & J. E. D. Sealey	Kingston	1934-35
4th	77	G. Headley & F. I. de Caires	Kingston	1929-30
5th	163	V. H. Stollmeyer & K. H. Weekes	Oval	1939
6th	118	J. E. D. Sealey & L. N. Constantine	Port of Spain	1934-35
7th	147	G. Headley & R. S. Grant	Kingston	1934-35
8th	93	K. Rickard & W. Ferguson	Kingston	1947-48
9th	33	C. R. Browne & E. St. Hill	Georgetown	1929-30
10th	26	G. N. Francis & H. C. Griffith	Lord's	1933

CENTURIES

ENGLAND

AMES. L. E. G. ....(3)
105 Port of S 1929-30
149 Kingston ..1929-30
126 Kingston ..1934-35
HENDREN. E. ......(2)
205* Port of S 1929-30
123 Georgetown 1929-30
HUTTON L ....(2)
196† Lord's 1939
165* Oval 1939
SANDHAM. A. ......(2)
152† Barbados ..1929-30
325¶ Kingston ..1929-30
BAKEWELL, A. H. ...(1)
107† Oval 1933
COMPTON. D. ......(1)
120† Lord's 1939
GRIFFITH. S. C. ....(1)

140‡ Trinidad ..1947-48
HAMMOND, W. R. ..(1)
138 Oval 1939
HOBBS, J. B. ......(1)
159 Oval 1928
JARDINE. D. R. ....(1)
127 Manchester 1933
PLACE, W. ....(1)
107 Kingston ..1947-48
ROBERTSON, J. D. ..(1)
133 Port of S 1947-48
TYLDESLEY. E. ....(1)
122† Lord's 1928

WEST INDIES

HEADLEY. G. ......(8)
176‡ Barbados ..1929-30
114 ⎫ Georgetown 1929-30
112 ⎭
223 Kingston ..1929-30

169 Manchester ..1933
270*¶ Kingston ..1934-35
106 ⎫ Lord's 1939
107 ⎭
ROACH. C. A. ......(2)
122 Barbados ..1929-30
209 Georgetown 1929-30
BARROW. I. ....(1)
105 Manchester 1933
CAREW. G. ....(1)
107 Port of S 1947-48
GANTEAUME. A. ....(1)
112‡ Port of S 1947-48
WEEKES. E. ....(1)
141 Kingston ..1947-48
WEEKES. K. H. ......(1)
137 Oval 1939
WORRELL, F. M. ....(1)
131* Georgetown 1947-48

* Not out. † Century on debut in series. ‡ On debut in Test cricket. ¶ Highest in series.

CRICKET BOOKS (Continued from page 22)

form. and that prolific author. John Arlott. this time in collaboration with Wilfred Wooller and Maurice Edelston. has produced a book with three-fold appeal. Bill Bowes' *Express Deliveries*, certainly one of the best and most engaging books ever written by a first-class cricketer is still available

One notes that when Stanley Paul are fielding an exceptionally strong team this year—Hammond. Yardley and Edrich. Yardley's book should be of particular interest as it is his first venture of the kind and one may expect it to be full of charm and sound sense and good humour.

Of the books not yet published the only one I have seen in proof form is *Cricket Companions* by Alan Mitchell of the New Zealand Press Association. He was the only New Zealand correspondent to cover the tour, of which he saw the whole; and a most entertaining review he has made of it. He cheerfully admits to being no great cricketer himself, yet his reflections on the game are sound and well-reasoned. and his descriptions of the touring players. are quite first-rate. I enjoyed reading this refreshing book immensely and many others will do so too.—P.W.

FUTURE TOURS

To U.K.		M.C.C. Tour to	1956-57	South Africa
1950-51		Australia & N.Z	1958	S. Africa
1951	S. Africa			It seems probable that New Zealand will tour England again in 1954 and West Indies in 1955.
1951-52		India		
1952	India			
1953	Australia			
1954-55		Australia & N.Z.	OTHER TOURS	
1956	Australia		1952-53 S. Africa to Australia	
			1954-55 N. Zealand to S. Africa	

THE TOURING TEAM

THERE is little doubt that the main power of the 1950 West Indies side will reside in its batting and pace bowling on firm pitches. Of their sixteen players, six are essentially batsmen—Weekes, Worrell, Stollmeyer, Rae, Trestrail and Marshall; three are all-rounders—Goddard (captain), Gomez and Williams; five are bowlers—Johnson, Jones, Pierre (all fast), Valentine and Ramadhin; and two are wicketkeepers—Walcott and Christiani (both class batsmen also). Worrell is a useful left-arm slow bowler and may perhaps be classified as an extra all-rounder.

Stollmeyer and Gomez are the only members of the team who toured England in 1939, and these two, with Goddard, Weekes, Rae, Walcott, Christiani and Jones, toured India in 1948-49. Only three—Rae, Valentine and Ramadhin—did not play against the M.C.C. in their own season of 1947-48. The manager of the team, as in 1933 and 1939, is Mr. J. M. Kidney.

The West Indies are undefeated in Test matches since the war. They won the Rubber of four against England in 1947-48 by two to nothing and that against India the following winter by one—nothing, the remaining four matches being drawn.

Full details of each player are included in the official Tour brochure, " Cricketers from the West Indies," published at 1s. 0d. by Playfair Books. Ages are correct at May 1st.

J. D. C. GODDARD (Barbados) (Capt.)

Age 31. John Douglas Claude. Solid left-hand batsman, useful bowler of medium right-arm off-breaks and grand fieldsman. Captained West Indies in last two Tests of 1947-48 and in five Tests in India in 1948-49 when he won the toss every time. In 1943-44 he made 218 not out v. Trinidad, and with Worrell shared in the then world record stand of 502 (unfinished) for 4th wicket. 411 runs in India (avge. 29.35) and 35 wickets (28.06)

J. B. STOLLMEYER (Trinidad)

Age 29. Jeffrey Baxter. Trinidad captain. Tall and elegant right-hand opening batsman, particularly strong on the on-side. In 1939, he scored 916 runs here (average 30.53), and in India his aggregate was 1,091 runs (60.61). Scored 244 not out v. S. Zone and with Rae made a record 239 for first wicket in Madras Test. Missed two Tests v. England (1947-48) because of injury. His 324 v. B. Guiana (1946-47) is highest innings in inter-colonial cricket.

G. E. GOMEZ (Trinidad)

Age 30. Gerald (" Gerry ") Gomez is a forcing right-hand batsman and accurate medium fast swing bowler. The Indian tour brought him into prominence as an all-rounder but earlier he had won fame for his tremendous batting form on matting wickets. He scored 719 runs (25.67) here in 1939, averaged 46.40 as batsman against England in all four Tests of 1947-48 and played in all five in India. There he made 658 runs (38.70) and took 71 wickets (18.70).

R. J. CHRISTIANI (British Guiana)

Age 29. Robert Christiani is a quick-footed, hard-hitting, right-hand batsman, a grand field, useful bowler of leg-breaks and reserve wicketkeeper. Just missed the 1939 tour, made 99 in his first Test v. England, 1947-48, and in India scored 785 runs at 41.31. The best batsman produced by British Guiana.

A. F. RAE (Jamaica)

Age 27. Allan Fitzroy Rae, opening left-hand batsman, has studied law in England for two years and with limited opportunities his first-class record is remarkable. Has played only three innings at home, scoring two hundreds in the same match (a feat never before achieved); and in India made 1,150 runs (6 centuries), average 46.00. In the Tests he made 374 runs at 53.42. Son of E. A. Rae who toured in 1928.

F. M. WORRELL (Barbados)

Age 25. Perhaps their finest batsman. He has every stroke in the trade—and the double-century habit. The only cricketer to have shared in two stands of over 500—502 (see Goddard), and 574 (unfinished) with Walcott for fourth wicket v. Trinidad in 1945-46. Both stands were world records at the time. Scored 294 runs in three Tests v. England in 1947-48 (147.00), averaged 118 in all matches against tourists. Did not tour India with West Indies but headed Test averages for Commonwealth team last winter. Was record scorer for Radcliffe in Central Lancs. League in 1949. Also a slow left-arm bowler.

E. WEEKES (Barbados)

Age 25. Everton de Courcy. One of the finest right-hand batsmen in the world today and a brilliant cover point: a cricketing musketeer with every stroke except the hook, which he half pulls because of lack of inches. Played in all four Tests against England, scoring 114 in the fourth; and followed this with four more consecutive Test hundreds against India—a world record. Was run out for 90 in his next Test. Scored 1,350 runs in India (90.00)—in Tests made 779 runs (111.28). Last summer he broke batting records for Bacup in Lancashire League.

C. L. WALCOTT (Barbados)

Age 24. 6ft. 1½ins. Clyde Walcott, No. 1 wicketkeeper, is a fast-scoring right-hand batsman, very strong off the back foot; a fine driver and puller. Shared in world record for 4th wicket (see Worrell) 1945-46 and played in all four Tests 1947-48, making seven dismissals at Kingston. In India his Test aggregate was 452 runs, average 64.57. Scored 1,366 runs all told (five hundreds)—highest aggregate on his side—at an average of 75.88.

P. E. JONES (Trinidad)

Age 32. Strong, persevering fast bowler who moves either way both in the air and off the seam. Headed averages in India with 51 wickets at 18.55 and bowled with splendid stamina and success in last two Tests. Stubborn tail-ender; fine slip field; has terrific throw-in. Played once against England, 1947-48.

H. H. JOHNSON (Jamaica)

Age 39. 6ft. 3ins. Hophnie Hines Johnson is a fast bowler with remarkable accuracy and control; swings very little at home but moves ball in off the pitch. Rarely bowls the bumper. Did not tour India but against England in 1947-48 had match figures of 10 for 96 in fourth Test. Because of his age will almost surely be nursed this summer. Good slip field; vigorous tail-ender.

L. R. PIERRE

L. R. PIERRE (Trinidad)

Age 28. 6ft. 2½in. Lance Pierre, surprise selection and fast bowler No. 3, moves either way, mostly out, rather quicker than Jones but less so than Johnson. Ability to swing the ball at home probably influenced his choice for this tour. Played against England at Georgetown 1947-48.

K. B. TRESTRAIL (Trinidad)

Ken Trestrail, attacking right-hand batsman with an upright style, was known as the "Boy Wonder" of the West Indies. His square cut and off-drive are joys to see; his fielding may remind us of Neil Harvey. Made his debut at 16, scored several centuries against Barbados but did not play against England in 1947-48 or tour India. Age 22.

C. B. WILLIAMS (Barbados)

Cecil Williams is called " Boogles," an appropriate name for a leg-break and googly bowler. He bowls at a quickish pace for his type and is also a good right-hand batsman.

R. MARSHALL (Barbados)

Roy Marshall is their third opening batsman. Scored readily at home when Indian tour was in progress and made 191 v. B. Guiana this year. Forceful and attractive to watch, he is also a good field and useful change bowler of off-breaks.

A. L. VALENTINE (Jamaica)

Age 20. Alfred Lewis Valentine, youngest of their players, is a slow left-arm bowler who flights well and has the right temperament for an important job in England.

K. T. RAMADHIN (Trinidad)

" Sonny " Ramadhin, off-break bowler, is the first East Indian to represent the West Indies. He was the most successful bowler in the recent Trials, taking 12 Jamaica wickets at 19.25. Can spin either way without change of action, according to reports.

Overseas Tours . . .

> *It is easy to magnify the pleasures of an overseas tour but it has its sterner aspects. This article is written by one well qualified to say so.*

. . . Are not all Beer and Skittles

By CHARLES BRAY
(Daily Herald Cricket Correspondent)

HOW frequently we hear it claimed that a first class cricketer's education is not complete until he has undertaken an overseas tour. Few will dispute it, for the experience gained from a visit to Australia, South Africa, the West Indies or any other country which from time to time receives a representative England team, is such that the player would indeed be lacking in intelligence if he did not benefit by it. But having now experienced three myself as a cricket writer, I would go further and say it is more than an addition to the first class cricketer's education—it is the acid test of an international.

Overseas tours are not all beer and skittles. If the young player can stand the strain and stress of playing cricket in exceptional heat without losing his form or his physical fitness; if he can travel thousands of tedious miles without being desperately tired; if he can "live in a suitcase" for six months on end and not allow the incessant packing and unpacking to become a nightmare and if he can accept the overwhelming hospitality without losing his head then indeed he is a worthy international and an ideal tourist.

But let me delve a little deeper into certain aspects on an overseas tour which are rarely publicised. This year another England team will set forth in quest of those mythical "Ashes" so it is appropriate if I refer specifically to Australia. Immediately the team arrives the players will quickly realise that the gay adventure of the boat trip from England changes into something far more serious. A battery of Australian pressmen will watch their first net practices with highly critical and perhaps somewhat biased

B

eyes. These critics include such great Test players as Bill O'Reilly, Bert Oldfield, Jack Fingleton, Clarry Grimmett, Arthur Mailey and Jack Whittington. It doesn't take them long (or their colleagues, who may not be so well known) to form an opinion of a player even at the nets and they do not mince words when it comes to voicing their views in their respective newspapers.

Therefore, within a week of their arrival, the visiting team will be reading frank and sometimes caustic comments which will continue throughout the tour. These can upset a team, give it an inferiority complex which can have a disastrous effect on its performances on the field, and even create such a sense of grievance with some players as to become almost an obsession. I should make it quite clear that this is not confined to teams visiting Australia or Australian cricket writers. Touring sides in England have frequently complained of similar treatment although I venture to add that rarely do English writers use such forthright language as some of our opposite numbers in Australia.

The player must expect criticism—he will certainly get it—and if he is to be a success he must not let it upset him. As an example I will mention Godfrey Evans. When the last English team arrived in Australia the critics took one look at Paul Gibb and Godfrey Evans, our two wicket-keepers, and then one of them wrote that neither Gibb nor Evans would get his place in a Grade A club side. At the end of the tour they hailed Evans as one of, if not the greatest, wicket-keepers in the world. Denis Compton was once described as " leaden-footed " and Bill Voce as not being good enough to be a " drink-waiter "—the man who takes the refreshments out to the fielding team.

Cricket Played " Hard "

It is hardly necessary for me to say that in Australia cricket is played " hard." They play to win. It is a contest, not a pastime. The letter of the law is meticulously respected but sometimes, we might think, the spirit is disregarded. I well remember Bill O'Reilly castigating the English team during a Test for failing to appeal against the light after every ball. The light was bad. Hutton made one appeal which was disallowed and then England went on batting to the close of play and lost several cheap wickets. The next morning O'Reilly in his report took England to task, reminding them that they were playing a Test match and that their duty was to win it. The batsmen, said O'Reilly, should have gone on appealing against the light. It was in their interests that play should stop.

During that tour I asked several Australian Test players why they appealed so frequently—sometimes for things they must have known were " not-out." Their reply was very frank: " The laws give us the right to appeal. The umpires can't give a decision unless we do—so why shouldn't we appeal?" I mention this not in any spirit of criticism of their methods but to illustrate my point that they play the game hard. To a youngster making his first tour it can be very disturbing, but he has got to school himself to expect it.

In addition to a " tough " press the tourist will experience a " tough " opposition on the field. Then there is the heat which can be most trying at times, not only in Australia but in the West Indies and South Africa. During the Test in Adelaide last time the temperature each day was over 100. And with the heat comes the stomach troubles as so many of us discovered who were in Africa or Burma during the war. Fair people seem to feel and be troubled by the heat more than dark ones and if I had to choose between two players of equal merit I would always go for the darker one to undertake an overseas tour in a hot country.

Then, too, there are the tedious and prolonged railway journeys. Anyone who thinks rail travel in England is bad should go to Australia or South Africa. Every effort is made to make the passengers as comfortable as possible but when it comes to spending days and nights in the confined space of a railway carriage, often on a single track line, with innumerable stops, great heat and the inevitable smuts, journeys become a trial and not a pleasure. I found South Africa far more trying than Australia in this respect simply because the rail journeys were more frequent and the stays in the various towns shorter. The hotels are good in both countries but even living in a most luxurious hotel becomes boring; and the constant packing and unpacking is the tourists' nightmare.

I would hate to give a wrong impression of these overseas tours. If I have emphasized the disadvantages it is because they are so rarely mentioned whereas the joys of a visit to any of the overseas cricketing countries are well-known. The good food, the friendliness of the people, the magnificent scenery of the Australian and South African coastal belts and the West Indian islands, the hospitality and pleasure of meeting new people and making new friendships, cannot be overlooked or even described. It is an education even to see, let alone to play, on the grounds at Melbourne or Sydney, or Ellis

Flash-back to 1946—W. R. Hammond, in cheerful mood, being presented with a lucky token before his M.C.C. team left Waterloo Station en route for Australia.

Park, Johannesburg, or the picturesque ones at Capetown, Adelaide, Barbados, Trinidad and Jamaica. And anyone who has experienced surf bathing at Sydney or the clear blue waters of the West Indies, the " breivlais " or barbecue at which you eat chunks of ox or succulent lamb chops roasted over an open fire, or the tropical splendour of the Jamaican and Trinidad mountains, must retain delicious memories.

Of course the pleasures far exceed the trials but it would be unwise, indeed foolish, not to warn our young Test players who will be making the trip to Australia in September that while there is plenty of honey on the bread it is not all honey.

The English selectors and the M.C.C.—for the latter have the final say—have no easy task picking a team to recapture the Ashes. Much must depend on current form but there are other important considerations.

Physical fitness and sound medical history are essential. It is a waste of time selecting a player whose form and health suffer in very hot weather. Loyalty to the captain and manager and an appreciation of the importance of team spirit are other vital qualities. Nothing disturbs the smooth running of a tour, and indeed the side's performance on the field, more than a player who resents or is irritated by the discipline—restricted as it may be—that has to be imposed on a Test team overseas. It is impossible for the captain or manager to explain in detail why he asks a player to do or not to do something. I can assure him he is given considerable licence but it should not be abused. Finally—and perhaps of greatest importance—is an ability to play the game hard; and by that I do not mean unfairly, but to be able to concentrate and equal their opponents in their determination to win.

To the M.C.C. I would make this appeal. Give the team, on its arrival in Australia, three full weeks, without any cricket, in which to settle down, find its landlegs and become acclimatised. Encourage air travel to reduce the tedious rail journeys and allow every member of the team a more generous out-of-pocket daily allowance. Hospitality to the individual is such that it becomes embarrassing if it cannot be returned in some small measure, and the out-of-pocket allowance given on previous tours has not been sufficient, particularly for the amateurs who get no cash payment for making the tour. Many have been seriously out of pocket . . .

The only other thing that remains is to find a team that can beat the Australians on their own ground—and thank heavens that's not my pigeon.

M.C.C. FIXTURES IN AUSTRALIA 1950-51

TWENTY-FIVE matches have been approved by M.C.C. for the tour of Australia next winter. Four of the five Test matches will last six days if necessary and the fifth will be played to a finish. The second Test will start on Friday, December 22, but there will be no play on Sunday (December 24) or Christmas Day. Fixtures:—

OCTOBER 13-17, one two-day match and a one-day match in Western Australia; 20-24, W. Australia (Perth); 27-31, S. Australia (Adelaide).

NOVEMBER 3-8, Victoria (Melbourne); 10-14, N.S.W. (Sydney); 17-18, N.S.W. country match (Newcastle); 21-22, N.S.W. country match (Lismore); 24-28, Queensland (Brisbane).

DECEMBER 1-7, FIRST TEST (Brisbane); 8-9, Queensland country match (Toowoomba); 12-13, Federal Capital Territory (Canberra); 15-19, Australian XI (Sydney); 22-29, SECOND TEST (Melbourne); 30-January 3, New South Wales (Sydney).

JANUARY 5-11, THIRD TEST (Sydney); 13-16, Tasmania (Hobart); 19-22 Combined Team (Launceston); 24-25, S. Australian country match (Denmark); 27-31, S. Australia (Adelaide).

FEBRUARY 2-8, FOURTH TEST (Adelaide); 10-14, Victoria (Melbourne); 16-17, Victorian country match (Geelong); 19-20, Victorian country match (Euroa); 23, FIFTH TEST (Melbourne) (played to a finish).

Bruce Miles's Australian Report

Without the Big Battalions

SYDNEY, March.

THIS country, with its big battalions in South Africa and New Zealand, would be an easy mark should a host of Anglo-Saxons invade us now. But there has been a close contest for the Sheffield Shield, New South Wales retaining the premiership by its outright, and unexpected, defeat of Victoria, and the season here has been full of interest.

With the possible exception of young Jim Burke there was no new batsman who looked like playing himself into the next Australian Test side. Burke himself started the season poorly and but for the clairvoyance of the State selectors would have played the year with Manly club side. About mid-way through the Shield series he found his form and displayed all his known defensive ability plus added power in his stroking. Another youngster from New South Wales, J. de Courcy, batted brilliantly at times, but lacked consistency. He was omitted from the New Zealand tour but may yet play his way into bigger cricket.

The discoveries of the season are bowlers—Jack Iverson of Victoria and Allan Davidson of N.S.W. Davidson, a youngster from Sydney's Northern Districts, was probably the best bowler of the year. Like Iverson, he tours New Zealand, and despite the presence of Allan Walker and Bill Johnston he may play for Australia in '50-51. He bowls fast left arm swingers.

THE ASTONISHING MR. IVERSON

Jack Iverson, of Victoria, 34 years old, 6ft. 3ins. tall, has achieved remarkable successes as an off-spin bowler, and the details of his most unusual grip— thumb and second finger only—already have spread round the cricket world. He bowls to a ring of three short legs.

Iverson taught himself this new method with a table tennis ball in New Guinea during the war. For twelve years, after being a fast bowler at school, he had played no cricket at all. His success, like that of Ian Johnson, marks a present trend in Australian cricket. Years ago, every player who attempted slow bowling spun from leg to off. Now the direction is changed.

The selectors have not been loudly applauded for their team in New Zealand. It is said that too many of the side have their best days behind them; that there is little team-building for the future. But the fact is that most of the young players available barely justified their selection for State sides.

Except for one div's play in a club game, nothing was seen of the dynamic Sydney Barnes. But he keeps himself in practice by coaching schoolboys and declares his intention to play again next season. W. A. Brown has announced this as his last year and Don Tallon's future is uncertain. Once this year, Tallon removed his pads and did some slow bowling. Toshack, for business reasons, has already retired.

In the absence of Saggers, Stan Sismey, the Australian Services wicket-keeper, made a welcome return to first-class cricket. He finished a brilliant season with six wickets in an innings in the Victorian match. It is a tragedy that both Saggers and Sismey are qualified for New South Wales, one of them is confined to keeping his club's wickets on Saturday afternoons.

D. R. Cristofani, hero of the Manchester Victory Test, has returned to England to continue his legal studies and perhaps to play a little cricket.

Attendances at first-class matches this season have been comparatively small, but boys in the street still play with their kerosene tin wickets and the playing memberships of all clubs are overflowing. No other Bradman, no other Neil Harvey seems in immediate prospect; but after all one can't expect new stars like that every day of the week.

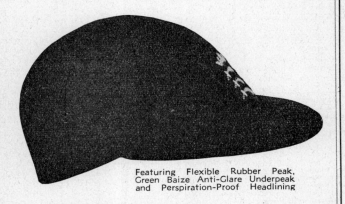

First-class matches
P. 32, W. 13, L. 1, D. 18
Other matches
P. 3, W. 2, L. 0, D. 1

A Grand Tour . . .

In Every Sense of the Word

By REX ALSTON

IF the be-all and end-all of a tour is the winning of Test Matches, then this one was not a success, but there was so much good cricket and good companionship in this most glorious of summers that mere winning or losing seemed almost of secondary consideration. Hadlee's team had greater success than any New Zealander could have anticipated, as only three of them in addition to the Captain— Wallace, Cowie and Donnelly—had had previous experience of first-class cricket in England. Yet by the end of the tour they had proved themselves the best side that had ever left New Zealand. Neither the full professional strength of England nor any one of the counties was able to beat them and they returned home with the proud record of only one defeat—and that by a good Oxford side who had them batting fourth on a horrible wicket.

The fact that the Test matches were drawn was scarcely New Zealand's fault. England, who won the toss on the first three occasions, had her chances to strike the right note, especially at Headingley on the first day, and at Old Trafford on the second day after New Zealand had been put in. But the leading England batsmen were unable to knock an extremely accurate attack off its length, concentrating too much on defence, which made a draw in the prevailing conditions almost inevitable. We saw the best cricket in the 4th Test, though New Zealand by then were feeling the effects of a long tour and did not show the resilience of earlier days. If Hadlee had won the toss at Headingley or Lord's, his side might have set an example which England must have followed, and so the Tests might have been saved from stagnation.

W. M. WALLACE   J. R. REID   F. B. SMITH

Although this New Zealand side contained several attacking batsmen of the highest quality, it was well suited to defensive play. Once the top five or six had been dismissed, the remainder rather lacked strokes. They were difficult to shift but they could not drive home an advantage, and a good hitter at No. 8 would have made a world of difference. But Sutcliffe, Scott, Hadlee, Wallace, Donnelly and Reid or Smith were a formidable proposition for any bowling, and almost always there was someone to come to the rescue and hold the side together after a collapse.

Quite the outstanding feature of the early part of the season was the brilliant form of Wallace, a grand little player on all types of wickets, with a very correct method, beautiful off-side strokes and a particularly punishing hook. Having made four centuries in the first five matches, he nearly scored 1,000 runs before the end of May, and his consistency in the first month virtually carried the batting. Thereafter he ran in o a bad patch and though still playing well, was right out of luck until early in August. Meanwhile his mantle had fallen on the two left-handers, Sutcliffe and Donnelly, who between them shared the batting honours of the Test matches. By their skill and stroke play they proved themselves two of the three best left-handers in the world. Sutcliffe arrived here with a tremendous reputation, but an inclination for hooking before he was set several times proved his undoing in the early matches. Yet his every stroke showed true class and the facility with which he made runs fast against all types of bowling marked him out as a great and attractive batsman. He was essentially a front of the wicket player and there is no more beautiful stroke in cricket than his extra cover drive.

Donnelly, who joined the team in England, from the very first match supplied the experienced stiffening which was to be expected from so talented and cultured a batsman, and for sheer consistency under all conditions throughout the season his performance was unrivalled. Whenever he batted in a Test match he faced a crisis, yet he always made over 50 until the 4th Test. Those who saw his masterly 206 at Lord's would probably vote it one of the finest innings ever played there in a Test match. His on-side

J. A. COWIE   G. O. RABONE   H. B. CAVE

play was magnificent. At his best no-one since Frank Woolley has " stroked " the ball so perfectly

Hadlee soon showed his sterling worth with a brave and very fine innings on a crumbling pitch against Surrey at the Oval, which won the match for his side. He didn't make as many runs as his undoubted ability indicated, partly due, doubtless, to the cares of captaincy, and partly to the unselfishness with which he sacrificed his wicket in forcing the pace. A fine upstanding driver, he was liable to hole out at extra cover and he had a weakness for flicking outside the off stump which more than once proved his undoing.

Scott, imperturbable opening partner and admirable foil for the brilliant Sutcliffe, had seemingly the broadest of bats with the shortest of back lifts, and he too was fallible outside the off stump. But he was always pushing the score along, almost imperceptibly keeping pace with more celebrated partners, and his good humour made him a great team man.

Smith and Reid played in two Test matches each and both more than justified their selection. If Smith was the hero at Headingley, then Reid undoubtedly saved the day at the Oval. They were totally contrasting in style; Smith, unorthodox and adventurous in the extreme, with a partiality for the square cut and for flashing at anything on the line of the off stump and beyond; Reid more solid and determined, with a watchful defence, a punishing on drive, and the most astonishingly powerful hook. He improved enormously during the season and should be a fine player on the next tour.

Rabone was one of the two genuine all-rounders of the team. He was not perhaps Test class either as batsman or bowler, but by sheer application he made himself indispensable whether as reserve opener or as a sticker in the middle of the order. He and Mooney, batting Nos. 7 and 8, exploded the fallacy that New Zealand had no body to support its elegant head by making 92 and 102 respectively against M.C.C. after six wickets had fallen for 94. Mooney was quick on his feet, but like Rabone was unable to force the pace. Apart from his century at Lord's he didn't play a big innings, but he always took a lot of shifting. These two had courage.

The bowling was not quite in the same class as the batting. Too much depended on the remarkable accuracy and big heart of slow left-hander Burtt. In match after match he took charge of one end and was rarely—if ever—collared, ending up with more than twice the number of wickets taken by any bowler on the side. A great performance. He really bowled

to his field and turned the ball just enough. Cowie, the one remaining bowler of the 1937 tour, was still a class performer, probably the best of his type in the country; though he rather wilted in the heat. He always attacked the stumps and was particularly dangerous in his opening overs. When Cowie and Burtt were bowling the New Zealand attack was Test class, but when either or both were resting it was no more than ordinary. Cave, who shared the new ball with Cowie, never quite fulfilled the promise of his beautiful high action. He obtained lift from the wicket and frequently bowled well, yet he didn't get many wickets. Cresswell, the other new ball bowler, was primarily an in-swinger, though he varied it with an occasional leg-cutter. He often had the best batsmen in trouble and was invaluable in keeping one end going in the county games. He had his reward when picked for the last Test and took six wickets.

Rabone, who could both spin and swing the ball, was steady in length without being particularly h o s t i l e, though he had several good performances against the Counties. Hayes, Cowie's understudy as a fast bowler, was unlucky with injury and never really justified himself. On the few occasions he let himself go he was pretty fast, but inaccurate. Burke, who with Hayes was the only man not to play in a Test match, was rather too slow through the air to trouble good players, neither did he spin the ball enough to beat them off the ground. But he bowled with accuracy and had one fine analysis against Derby. For one whose chances were necessarily rather limited, he definitely improved as the tour progressed.

TEST MATCH AVERAGES
ENGLAND—BATTING

	Tests	Inns.	N.O.	Runs	Hghst.	Avge.
†R. T. Simpson ..	2	2	0	171	103	85.50
C. Washbrook ..	2	3	1	157	103*	78.50
L. Hutton ..	4	6	0	469	206	78.16
†T. E. Bailey ..	4	5	2	219	93	73.00
†W. J. Edrich ..	4	6	0	324	100	54.00
D. Compton ..	4	6	0	300	116	50.00
†F. G. Mann ..	2	4	1	122	49*	40.66
†F. R. Brown ..	2	2	0	43	22	21.50
T. G. Evans ..	4	4	0	61	27	15.25
A. V. Bedser ..	2	2	0	20	20	10.00
W. E. Hollies ..	4	3	2	1	1*	1.00
J. A. Young ..	2	2	1	1	1*	1.00

PLAYED IN ONE MATCH.—D. B. Close. 0; C. Gladwin, 5; L. Jackson. 7*: J D. Robertson. 26. 121; A. J. Watkins. 6. 49*; A. Wharton, 7. 13; D. V. P. Wright, 0; J. C. Laker, 0.

ENGLAND—BOWLING

	Overs	Mdns.	Runs	Wkts.	Avge.
J. C. Laker ..	32	6	89	4	22.25
L. Jackson ..	39	14	72	3	24.00
D. Compton..	33	2	126	5	25.20
J. A. Young ..	62.4	13	158	6	26.33
A. V. Bedser ..	85	19	215	7	30.71
†T. E. Bailey ..	158	22	599	16	37.43
W. E. Hollies ..	175	54	385	10	38.50
†W. J. Edrich ..	27	3	97	2	48.50
†F. R. Brown ..	54	8	157	2	78.50
D. V. P. Wright ..	28	1	114	1	114.00

ALSO BOWLED. — D. B. Close. 42—14—85—1; C. Gladwin, 28—5—67—1; L. Hutton, 4—1—23—0; R. T. Simpson, 2—1—9—0; C. Washbrook, 2—0—8—0; A. J. Watkins, 3—1—11—0. † denotes amateur.

NEW ZEALAND—BATTING

	Tests	Inns.	N.O.	Runs	Hghst.	Avge.
F. B. Smith ..	2	3	1	173	96	86.50
M. P. Donnelly ..	4	6	0	462	206	77.60
B. Sutcliffe ..	4	7	0	423	101	60.42
J. R. Reid ..	2	4	0	173	93	43.25
W. A. Hadlee ..	4	7	1	193	43	32.16
G. O. Rabone ..	4	6	1	148	39*	29.60
T. B. Burtt ..	4	6	1	131	36	26.20
V. J. Scott ..	4	7	0	178	60	25.42
F. H. L. Mooney ..	3	4	0	99	46	24.75
W. M. Wallace ..	4	6	0	144	58	24.00
J. A. Cowie ..	4	5	3	35	26*	17.50
H. B. Cave ..	4	5	1	44	14*	11.00

PLAYED IN ONE MATCH.—G. F. Cresswell, 0*, 12*.

NEW ZEALAND—BOWLING

	Overs	Mdns.	Runs	Wkts.	Avge.
G. F. Cresswell ..	41.2	6	158	6	28.00
J. A. Cowie ..	147.1	23	451	14	32.21
T. B. Burtt ..	198.3	50	568	17	33.41
G. O. Rabone ..	87	22	327	4	81.75
H. B. Cave ..	141	19	465	4	116.25

ALSO BOWLED.—M. P. Donnelly, 5—0—20—0; J. R. Reid, 2—0—14—0; V. J. Scott, 1—0—9—0; B. Sutcliffe, 26—1—95—1; W. M. Wallace, 1—0—5—0.

The fielding, taking the season all through, was of very high class. There were at least four splendid cover points in Donnelly, Sutcliffe, Wallace and Smith, though the two left-handers usually lent distinction to other positions—Donnelly in the gully and Sutcliffe at backward short leg or in the deep. Hadlee, at mid-off, was an inspiration in the way he covered the ground with his enormous strides, and there was never a more whole-hearted chaser to the boundary. Rabone was an outstanding slip-field, Mooney a thoroughly good wicket-keeper, sound and unostentatious, whilst Reid, the deputy stumper, in addition to doing a bit of bowling was a fine field anywhere, particularly in the slips. A feature of the out-cricket was the quick and accurate throwing, which was well up to the best Australian standard.

Hadlee's part in making this tour a success was indeed a notable one. No touring side has had a more unselfish, conscientious, or thoughtful captain. He was an expert placer of his field, his judgement of a tactical situation was sound, and his wise handling of his team in the field, allied to his own splendid fielding, made him a captain to be remembered. His success on the field was equalled in the social and administrative sphere by Jack Phillipps, who proved the ideal manager.

The English successes of the summer were undoubtedly Bailey and Simpson. In Bailey England possesses her fastest bowler since the war—one who, if carefully nursed, might even trouble the Australians in Australia. But he cannot be expected to bear the brunt of the fast bowling and also be one of England's chief run-getters. Simpson's success, in a summer which particularly suited his style of play, was a real pleasure to watch, and he showed by his hurricane last 50 at Old Trafford that he can suit his game to the occasion. His opening partnership with Hutton at the Oval was the best of the summer. In addition he fielded gloriously.

Of the old hands, Hutton was the most prolific run-getter on either side, though only once in the 4th Test match did he show us the batting that the situation demanded of so great a player. In his second hundred he gave the most glorious display of forcing batting, every shot in the book being played immaculately, with the famous cover drive outstanding. One could not help wondering what a difference it might have made to the whole series if he had similarly let himself go in this way at Headingley and Old Trafford.

Compton, for him, had a comparatively unsuccessful summer. It is true he averaged 50 but we rarely saw the real Compton and undoubtedly he was stale. Edrich, too, was not the great player of 1947. He played like a man

F. L. H. MOONEY   V. J. SCOTT   G. F. CRESSWELL

N.Z. AVERAGES—ALL FIRST-CLASS MATCHES
BATTING

	Inns.	N.O.	Runs	H.S.	Avge.
M. P. Donnelly	45	8	2287	206	61.81
B. Sutcliffe	49	5	2627	243	59.70
W. M. Wallace	41	6	1722	197	49.20
J. R. Reid	40	4	1488	188*	41.35
V. J. Scott	40	1	1572	203	40.30
W. A. Hadlee	44	4	1439	119*	35.97
G. O. Rabone	39	8	1021	120*	32.93
F. B. Smith	40	4	1008	96	28.00
F. H. L. Mooney ..	39	5	774	102	22.76
T. B. Burtt	31	6	436	68*	17.44
H. B. Cave	23	9	228	36	16.28
J. A. Cowie	17	8	131	47	14.55
C. C. Burke	17	5	171	44*	14.25
G. F. Cresswell	15	11	50	12*	12.50
J. A. Hayes	6	2	20	9*	5.00

BOWLING

	Overs	Mdns.	Runs	Wkts.	Avge.
T. B. Burtt	1245	405	2929	128	22.88
G. F. Cresswell	695.1	184	1618	62	26.09
J. A. Cowie	616.5	129	1601	59	27.13
C. C. Burke	598.3	144	1611	54	29.83
J. R. Reid	127.4	20	390	13	30.00
J. A. Hayes	301.4	60	873	26	33.57
G. O. Rabone	558.4	118	1785	50	35.70
B. Sutcliffe	185.4	37	654	16	40.87
H. B. Cave	657	133	1809	42	43.07

ALSO BOWLED.—M. P. Donnelly, 21.3—0—130—3;
W. A. Hadlee, 5—1—30—0; F. H. L. Mooney, 1—1—0—0;
V. J. Scott, 4—0—23—0; F. B. Smith, 15—5—44—1;
W. M. Wallace, 5—1—30—0.

CENTURIES IN FIRST-CLASS MATCHES (29)

B. SUTCLIFFE (7).—187 v Surrey (Oval). 144 v Combined
Services (Gillingham). 183 v Scot'and (Glasgow). 101 v
England (Manchester) 243 & 100* v Essex (Southend).
110* v Middlesex (Lord's).

M. P. DONNELLY (5).—146 v Leics. (Leicester). 100* v
Hants. (Southampton). 206 v England (Lord's). 106 v
Warwicks. (Birmingham). 145* v H. D. G. Leveson
Gower's XI (Scarborough).

W. M. WALLACE (5).—126 v Yorks. (Bradford). 108 v
Worcs. (Worcester). 171 v. Leics. (Leicester). 197 v
Cambridge U. (Cambridge). 169* v Glamorgan
(Swansea).

V. J. SCOTT (4).—103 v Worcs. (Worcester). 109 v Hants.
(Southampton). 203 v Combined Services (Gillingham).
105 v Northants. (Northampton).

J. R. REID (4).—188* v Cambridge U. (Cambridge). 107*
v Northants. (Northampton). 151* v Warwicks. (Birmingham). 155 v Notts. (Nottingham).

W. A. HADLEE (2).—119* v Surrey (Oval). 114 v South of
England (Hastings).

F. H. L. MOONEY (1).—102 v M.C.C. (Lord's).

G. O RABONE (1).—120* v Notts. (Nottingham).

* Not Out

out of form, looking
worried and concentrating
too much on playing
himself in. In fact it may
well have been only his
brilliant slip - fielding
which kept him his place
in the Tests.

Washbrook pulled a
muscle in the first Test
and though he scored a
century in the second innings, he had to have a
runner and it probably
would have been better
both for himself and
England if he had re-
tired. He was not fit for
the second Test, and was
left out of the fourth in
favour of another bowler.

After Bailey, England's
best bowler was Hollies,
who kept a steady length
for long spells and was
always treated with res-
pect. He doesn't spin the
ball as much as some,
but he is far the most
accurate of his kind, and
was often relied on as a
stock bowler.

Alec Bedser was not
properly fit for much of
the summer, though he
made a splendid come-
back on his own home
ground at the Oval. For
the rest, the selectors
rung the changes on
Laker, Gladwin, Wright
and Young of the old
brigade, and tried out
two new men—Close and
Jackson. Close achieved
fame by being selected at the age of 18 and, whilst not a success if judged by
figures only, looked a real cricketer. Jackson bowled steadily, but without the
experience of Gladwin, whom he replaced.

The change in captaincy after the first two Tests gave England yet
another leg-spin bowler in F. R. Brown and probably sealed the fate of
Jenkins, who might otherwise have made the grade. Both Brown and
Mann in their respective ways set a fine example in the field and did their
utmost to force a decision. The England fielding always looked competent, but
lacked that concentrated hostility which characterises the best Australian sides.

A Message From W. A. Hadlee

I AM grateful to the Editor for an opportunity to express the gratitude of those seventeen New Zealanders lucky enough to tour Great Britain in 1949. To the administrators, players, cricket writers, and our many friends, both in Great Britain and in Germany, where B.A.O.R. were such grand hosts, we say " thank you " for the grand tour provided for us.

We came to England very well aware of our limitations—and we have returned to our small Dominion still knowing that the longer one plays cricket, the more there is to know about it. For example, we learnt that it pays to have infinite respect for a piece of turf known by some as the wicket, but better named the pitch, whose moods can vary, like those of a spoiled child.

*E*VEN under apparently unchanging conditions, pitches throughout our tour underwent sudden changes, perhaps encouraging the spin bowler for half an hour, and then spurning his most strenuous efforts to turn the ball. We were of the opinion that although wickets occasionally broke up on the third day, they generally lost their " bite " and played more slowly as the match progressed.

Much discussion takes place upon the relative merits of cricketers of this generation compared with some previous generation. One thing is certain—that in this generation Denis Compton and Len Hutton must be reckoned as great players by any standards. Those of us who had toured England in 1937 would, I think, agree that counties lack the all-rounders of the earlier period—and it is generally agreed that there is urgent need for fast bowlers. To bring on the latter, it is important that wickets should be made faster.

*B*UT there is nothing basically wrong with English cricket. As club cricketers, we did think we saw the need for two-day club matches played on a competitive basis, or the provision of some channel through which the Saturday afternoon player could appear in first-class matches. Perhaps a club conference side in the County Championship would be helpful. But these, no doubt, are matters which have been considered from time to time and are purely domestic problems.

As visitors, and guests, in our Motherland, we came to know that there is nothing amiss with this great Game which provided so much enjoyment for so many players and spectators alike. May it always be preserved as the traditional sport in Britain, for as such it will continue to strengthen the strong ties of fellowship within the Empire.

FIRST TEST—LEEDS

Played on June 11, 13, 14.   Match drawn

THERE was a time on the second day when New Zealand were in serious trouble; four men out for 80—three of them to Bailey—and only Donnelly, it seemed, to bolt the door. But Smith came in to join him and between them they made 120 together for the fifth wicket in less than an hour and a half. This was the turning point: Donnelly supreme master of a nasty situation, Smith chasing everything on the off - side with brave abandon. It was fine, challenging cricket—a bold answer to England's u n - imaginative batting on the first day.

Cowie could not bowl in the second innings and Mann set New Zealand to make 300 in two hours and a half—a very tall order indeed. Sutcliffe and Scott scored 82 in an hour before tea but afterwards no serious effort to get the runs was made. The pitch was still easy, the outfield q u i c k. New Z e a l a n d *might* have pulled it off.

Cowie and Burtt, ably supported by Cave and Rabone, bowled most accurately to splendid fielding on the first day. Hutton took four hours over a flawless hundred; Compton reached his century too but simply could not

ENGLAND

L. Hutton c Sutcliffe b Cowie	101	— c Mooney b Cave 0
C. Washbrook c Sutcliffe b Cowie	10	— not out 103
W. J. Edrich c Donnelly b Cowie	36	— b Cave 70
D. Compton st Mooney b Burtt	114	— c Mooney b Cave 26
A. Wharton lbw b Cowie	7	— b Sutcliffe 13
†F. G. Mann c Scott b Burtt	38	— not out 49
T. E. Bailey c Scott b Cowie	12	
T. G. Evans c Mooney b Burtt	27	
A. V. Bedser c Donnelly b Burtt	20	
J. A. Young st Mooney b Burtt	0	
W. E. Hollies not out	0	
B 3, lb 4..	7	B 4, lb 2 .. 6

Total 372   Total (for 4 wkts. dec.) 267

FALL OF WICKETS.—First Innings: 1-17, 2-92, 3-194, 4-214, 5-273, 6-322, 7-330, 8-353, 9-367. Second Innings: 1-0, 2-118, 3-162, 4-201.

	O.	M.	R.	W.	O.	M.	R.	W.
Cowie	43	6	127	5	..	—	—	—
Cave	27	5	85	0	.. 26	3	103	3
Rabone	18	7	56	0	.. 17	4	56	0
Burtt	39.3	16	97	5	.. 18	2	56	0
Donnelly	—	—	—	—	.. 5	0	20	0
Sutcliffe	—	—	—	—	.. 4	1	17	1
Scott	—	—	—	—	.. 1	0	9	0

NEW ZEALAND

B. Sutcliffe c Evans b Young	32	— c Bedser b Young .. 82
V. J. Scott c Washbrook b Bailey	1	— c Bedser b Young .. 43
†W. A. Hadlee c Edrich b Bailey	34	— not out 13
W. M. Wallace c Evans b Bailey	3	
M. P. Donnelly c Young b Bailey	64	
F. B. Smith c Compton b Edrich	96	— not out 54
G. O. Rabone c Evans b Edrich	13	
F. L. H. Mooney c Edrich b Bailey	46	
T. B. Burtt c Bedser b Compton	7	
H. B. Cave c Edrich b Bailey..	2	
J. Cowie not out	26	
B 2, lb 8, nb 7 ..	17	B 1, lb 2 .. 3

Total 341   Total (for 2 wkts.) 195

FALL OF WICKETS.—First Innings: 1-4, 2-64, 3-69, 4-80, 5-200, 6-251, 7-254, 8-273, 9-284. Second Innings: 1-112, 2-147.

	O.	M.	R.	W.	O.	M.	R.	W.
Bailey	32.3	6	118	6	.. 9	0	51	0
Bedser	22	8	56	0	.. 9	1	26	0
Edrich	9	2	18	2	.. 2	0	13	0
Young	22	6	52	1	.. 14	3	41	2
Hollies	25	6	57	0	.. 11	3	33	0
Compton	8	2	23	1	.. 1	0	5	0
Hutton	—	—	—	—	.. 3	0	23	0

UMPIRES—W. H. Ashdown and D Davies. † Captain.
TWELFTH MEN—A. J. Watkins (E.) and J. R. Reid (N.Z.).

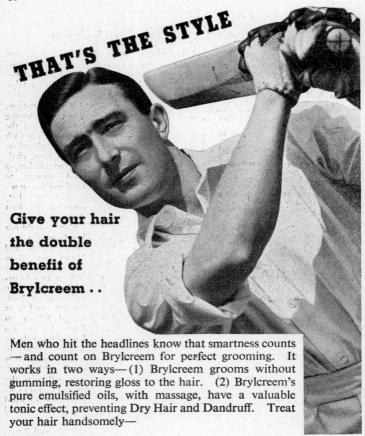

THAT'S THE STYLE

Give your hair the double benefit of Brylcreem ..

Men who hit the headlines know that smartness counts —and count on Brylcreem for perfect grooming. It works in two ways—(1) Brylcreem grooms without gumming, restoring gloss to the hair. (2) Brylcreem's pure emulsified oils, with massage, have a valuable tonic effect, preventing Dry Hair and Dandruff. Treat your hair handsomely—

BRYLCREEM

YOUR HAIR

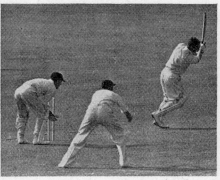

Two handsome strokes at Leeds . . . a pull (left) by B. Sutcliffe—note the perfect balance—and an off-drive (right) by England's captain, F. G. Mann.

find his rhythm; and a total of 307 for 5 was not enough. It needed a brisk and combative effort by the captain to cheer the heart.

Mann hit more fiercely still in the second innings, and one great hit, high over long-on, will surely be remembered. Washbrook's hundred was made under the handicap of lameness; he needed a runner.

Sutcliffe's batting in each innings was a sheer delight. Hadlee was going strong when Bailey had him at slip and Mooney presented stubborn opposition just when it was wanted. England's bowling on the whole was not so accurate as New Zealand's but Evans was in good form behind the wicket.

SECOND TEST—LORD'S

Played on June 25, 27, 28. Match drawn

A GREAT innings by Martin Donnelly, who held himself riigidly on leash so long as the situation demanded it but who cut loose in his most delightful fashion once the light was clear, enabled New Zealand to lead England for the first time in a Test match in England and to record their highest innings against us. On the second day Donnelly was restrained and exact but on the third morning his innings was a masterpiece of offensive play, worth coming a long, long way to see.

When England batted for a second time Hutton and Robertson began with a century stand, Robertson going on to complete a cultured hundred, and the closing stages were little more than a formality.

On the first morning Cowie's bowling was as good as any in the series. Hutton and Robertson, not without some luck—and they needed it against an attack of such quality—made 48 before Burtt had Hutton sparring down the wicket. Edrich got a brute of a ball which jumped and soon it was 112 for 5.

Now there was a stand of 189 for the sixth wicket between Compton and Bailey and, later, an illegal declaration which worried no one. If it was not

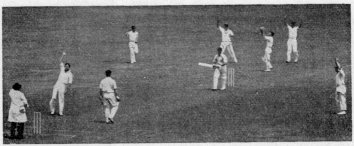

Robertson c. Mooney b. Cowie in the first innings at Lord's

a Compton innings of the best vintage it was no less welcome for that. As for Bailey, it was something of a triumph. The on-side was his strength, his sweeps outdoing even Compton's.

Sutcliffe began so briskly for New Zealand that one had visions of a hundred before lunch, but Gladwin teased him into flicking on the off. Scott did not much relish the leg-breaks of Hollies, the best English bowler, but Hadlee played with delightful assurance before he perpetrated rather a naughty shot in the last over before lunch. All the later batsmen gave Donnelly admirable support.

ENGLAND

L. Hutton b Burtt	23 — c Cave b Rabone	66
J. D. Robertson c Mooney b Cowie	26 — c Cave b Rabone	121
W. J. Edrich c Donnelly b Cowie	9 — c Hadlee b Burtt	31
D. Compton c Sutcliffe b Burtt	116 — b Burtt	6
A. J. Watkins c Wallace b Burtt	6 — not out	49
†F. G. Mann b Cave	18 — c Donnelly b Rabone	17
T. E. Bailey c Sutcliffe b Rabone	93 — not out	6
T. G. Evans b Burtt	5	
C. Gladwin run out	5	
J. A. Young not out	1	
B 9, lb 2	11	B 9, lb 1 .. 10
Total (for 9 wkts. dec.)	313	Total (for 5 wkts.) 306

W. E. Hollies did not go in.

FALL OF WICKETS—First Innings: 1-48, 2-59, 3-72, 4-83, 5-112, 6-301, 7-307, 8-307, 9-313. Second Innings: 1-143, 2-216, 3-226, 4-226, 5-252.

	O.	M.	R.	W.		O.	M.	R.	W.
Cowie	26.1	5	64	2	..	14	3	39	0
Cave	27	2	79	1	..	7	1	23	0
Rabone	14	5	56	1	..	28	6	116	3
Burtt	35	7	102	4	..	37	12	58	2
Sutcliffe	1	0	1	0	..	16	1	55	0
Wallace	—	—	—	—	..	1	0	5	0

NEW ZEALAND

B. Sutcliffe c Compton b Gladwin	57	FALL OF WICKETS — 1-89, 2-124, 3-137, 4-160, 5-197,
V. J. Scott c Edrich b Compton	42	6-273, 7-351, 8-436, 9-464.
†W. A. Hadlee c Robertson b Hollies	43	
W. M. Wallace c Evans b Hollies	2	
M. P. Donnelly c Hutton b Young	206	
F. B. Smith b Hollies	23	
G. O. Rabone b Hollies	25	
F. L. H. Mooney c Watkins b Young	33	
T. B. Burtt c Edrich b Hollies	23	
H. B. Cave c and b Young	6	
J. Cowie not out	1	
B 16, lb 3, w 3, nb 1	23	

		O.	M.	R.	W.
	Bailey	33	3	136	0
	Gladwin	28	5	67	1
	Edrich	4	0	16	0
Total	484	Hollies	58	18	133	5
		Compton	7	0	33	1
		Young	26.4	4	65	3
		Watkins	3	1	11	0

UMPIRES—F. Chester and W. H. Ashdown. † Captain.
TWELFTH MEN—L. Dolding (Lord's ground staff) (E.) and J. R. Reid (N.Z.).

THIRD TEST—MANCHESTER
Played on July 23, 25, 26. Match drawn

As the pitch seemed likely to give his pace bowlers some assistance in the first hour or so England's new captain, F. R. Brown, put New Zealand in. When four wickets were down for 83 his tactics were thoroughly justified but once again Donnelly came staunchly to the rescue and this time his chief henchman in crisis was Reid, whose first Test innings was the robust and courageous effort one would have expected of him. These two put on 116 for the fifth wicket and although both, with Mooney too, were dismissed in the middle of the afternoon Rabone and Burtt stood firm until stumps were drawn. It had been a stern day's play full of interest. The pitch gave no help to the spinners but the quicker bowling sometimes came through low. When New Zealand were all out next day Bailey's figures of 6 for 84 certainly did not flatter him.

Now it was the same old story — England struggling for the initiative against a precise attack admirably supported in the field, with Reid quite brilliant at mid-off to Burtt. But not for all the day. When Simpson had reached his first fifty in two hours he launched such a grand assault that in an exciting last hour 105 runs were added, and England still had a slight chance. Simpson made his second fifty in 30 minutes; he chanced his arm and exploited the lofted drive to

NEW ZEALAND

Batsman	1st Innings		2nd Innings	
B. Sutcliffe b Bailey	9	—	lbw b Compton	101
V. J. Scott b Bailey	13	—	b Jackson	13
†W. A. Hadlee b Bailey	34	—	c Brown b Hollies	22
W. M. Wallace c Washbrook b Close	12	—	lbw b Hollies	14
M. P. Donnelly lbw b Bailey	75	—	st Evans b Brown	80
J. R. Reid lbw b Jackson	50	—	b Bailey	25
G. O. Rabone c Brown b Bailey	33	—	not out	39
F. L. H. Mooney b Jackson	5	—	st Evans b Brown	15
T. B. Burtt st Evans b Compton	32	—	not out	27
H. B. Cave b Bailey	12			
J. Cowie not out	3			
B 3, lb 9, nb 3	15		B 2, lb 4, nb 6	12
Total	293		Total (for 7 wkts.)	348

FALL OF WICKETS—First Innings: 1-22, 2-23, 3-62, 4-82, 5-198, 6-205, 7-217, 8-269, 9-288. Second Innings: 1-24, 2-58, 3-109, 4-187, 5-235, 6-295, 7-313.

	O.	M.	R.	W.	O.	M.	R.	W.
Bailey	30.2	5	84	6	16	0	71	1
Jackson	27	11	47	2	12	3	25	1
Close	25	12	39	1	17	2	46	0
Hollies	18	8	29	0	26	6	52	2
Brown	18	4	43	0	21	3	71	2
Compton	6	0	28	1	8	0	28	1
Edrich	4	1	8	0	5	0	26	0
Simpson	—	—	—	—	2	1	9	0
Washbrook	—	—	—	—	2	0	8	0
Hutton	—	—	—	—	1	1	0	0

ENGLAND

L. Hutton st Mooney b Burtt	73	
C. Washbrook c Mooney b Cowie	44	
W. J. Edrich c Rabone b Burtt	78	
D. Compton b Cowie	25	
R. T. Simpson c Donnelly b Burtt	103	
T. E. Bailey not out	72	
†F. R. Brown c Wallace b Burtt	22	
T. G. Evans c Mooney b Burtt	12	
D. B. Close c Rabone b Burtt	0	
H. E. Hollies c Mooney b Cowie	0	
L. Jackson not out	7	
B 2, lb 2	4	
Total (for 9 wkts. dec.)	440	

FALL OF WICKETS — 1-103, 2-127, 3-172, 4-258, 5-363, 6-404, 7-419, 8-419, 9-419.

	O.	M.	R.	W.
Cowie	36	8	98	3
Cave	30	4	97	0
Burtt	45	11	162	6
Rabone	10	0	43	0
Sutcliffe	5	0	22	0
Reid	2	0	14	0

UMPIRES—F. Chester and F. S. Lee. † Captain.
TWELFTH MEN—S. Smith (Lancs.) (E) and F. B. Smith (N.Z.).

AT MANCHESTER
Above: the celebrated Hutton cover-drive. Mooney behind the wicket, Rabone at slip

Right: Reid pushes one away to leg. No wonder he generates such power from those shoulders and forearms!

very excellent purpose. Bailey too was no laggard.

At twenty to three on the final afternoon New Zealand were 109 for 3, and certainly not out of the wood, but Sutcliffe at last completed that first hundred in a Test match which so many were waiting to see and with Donnelly yet again, and with Reid and Rabone, he steered his side into safe waters.

FOURTH TEST—OVAL
Played on August 13, 15, 16. Match drawn

EVEN if the result was inconclusive again this match provided the brightest cricket of the series. As in the other three Tests there were moments when one side had a clear advantage but could not ram it home.

New Zealand at one time on the third afternoon had lost four wickets, including Donnelly's, and still were six runs behind. Now it was Wallace's turn—and most welcome too—to hold the fort; and Reid's again. These two stood firm for one vital hour but Wallace was out at 188 and England still had hopes. By now, however, Reid was seeing the ball exceptionally large and all further danger was averted. Shortly after bad light had caused a break in the play Hadlee made a formal declaration and the series was over.

The English selectors in their liberality had provided Brown with eight possible bowlers but Sutcliffe and Scott in their varying and effective ways had more than a hundred up for the first wicket in quick time and a big score seemed almost certain. Then England struck back and when Edrich had held two slip catches in the first two overs after tea it was New Zealand's turn to fight. Bedser bowled so well that his opponents must have been

How Wallace was out in the first innings at the Oval—two pictures from different angles at much the same moment

NEW ZEALAND

B. Sutcliffe c Bedser b Hollies 88	— c Brown b Bedser	..	54
V. J. Scott c Edrich b Bedser 60	— c Evans b Bedser	..	6
J. R. Reid lbw b Wright 5	— c Wright b Laker	..	93
W. M. Wallace c Edrich b Bedser 55	— st Evans b Hollies	..	58
M. P. Donnelly c Edrich b Bailey 27	— c Brown b Bedser	..	10
†W. A. Hadlee c Evans b Bedser 25	— c Edrich b Hollies	..	22
G. O. Rabone c Evans b Bailey 18	— lbw b Laker	......	20
T. B. Burtt c Evans b Bailey . 36	— c Compton b Laker	..	6
H. B. Cave b Compton 10	— not out	....	14
J. Cowie c Hutton b Bedser.. 1	— c Wright b Laker	..	4
G. F. Cresswell not out 12	— not out	....	0
Lb 1, w 1, nb 6 .. 8	B 10, lb 5, nb 6	..	21

Total 345   **Total (for 9 wkts. dec.) 308**

FALL OF WICKETS—First innings: 1-121, 2-134, 3-170, 4-239, 5-239, 6-272, 7-287, 8-311, 9-320. Second innings: 1-24, 2-68, 3-115, 4-131, 5-188, 6-276, 7-283, 8-299, 9-308.

	O.	M.	R.	W.		O.	M.	R.	W.
Bailey	26.1	7	72	3	..	11	1	67	0
Bedser	31	6	74	4	..	23	4	59	3
Edrich	3	0	16	0	..	—	—	—	—
Wright	22	1	93	1	..	6	0	21	0
Laker	3	0	11	0	..	29	6	78	4
Hollies	20	7	51	1	..	17	6	30	2
Brown	5	1	14	0	..	10	0	29	0
Compton	2	0	6	1	..	1	0	3	0

ENGLAND

L. Hutton c Rabone b Cresswell	206
R. T. Simpson c Donnelly b Cresswell	68
W. J. Edrich c Cave b Cresswell	100
D. Compton c Scott b Cresswell	13
T. E. Bailey c Reid b Cowie ..	36
†F. R. Brown c Hadlee b Cresswell	21
T. G. Evans c Donnelly b Cowie	17
J. C. Laker c Scott b Cowie ..	0
A. V. Bedser c Reid b Cowie ..	0
W. E. Hollies not out	1
D. V. P. Wright lbw b Cresswell	0
B 6, lb 11, nb 3 ..	20

Total 482

UMPIRES—D. Davies and F. S. Lee.
TWELFTH MEN—D. R. Cox (Surrey) (E.) and F. B. Smith

FALL OF WICKETS — 1-147, 2-365, 3-396, 4-401, 5-436, 6-469, 7-470, 8-472, 9-481.

	O.	M.	R.	W.
Cowie	28	1	123	4
Cresswell	41.2	6	168	6
Cave	24	4	78	0
Burtt	24	2	93	0

glad of his absence on other important occasions and Bailey and Hollies at times were dangerous also. England's fielding was very good, and Simpson's quite superb.

The second day, of course, was Hutton's. The England score was 147 for none and then, after Simpson was out, there was a stand of 218 between Hutton and Edrich, 100 of these runs coming in an hour after tea. Hutton took his time in the 'nineties but once he had reached his hundred he let himself go with glorious strokes all round the wicket.

FACTS AND FIGURES

RECORD WICKET PARTNERSHIPS

The following for New Zealand touring teams in England were recorded:

1st wkt. 243 B. Sutcliffe and V. J. Scott v. Combined Services (Gillingham).
3rd wkt. 246 G. O. Rabone and J. R. Reid v. Nottinghamshire (Nottingham).
4th wkt. 324 W. M. Wallace and J. R. Reid v. Cambridge U. (Cambridge).
7th wkt. 174 G. O. Rabone and F. H. L. Mooney v. M.C.C. (Lord's).
10th wkt. 57 F. H. L. Mooney and J. A. Cowie v. England (Leeds) (1st Test).

The following record wicket partnerships against New Zealand touring sides in England were recorded:

2nd wkt. 218 L. Hutton and W. J. Edrich for England (Oval) (4th Test).
4th wkt. 248 J. T. Ikin and K. Grieves for Lancs. (Manchester).
6th wkt. 189 D. Compton and T. E. Bailey for England (Lord's) (2nd Test).

Surrey's 645 for 9 (dec.) is the highest innings total ever made against New Zealand teams in England. J. F. Parker's 255 is also the highest individual innings recorded on any N.Z. tour.

B. Sutcliffe scored 243 and 100* v. Essex. Southend. His 243 is the highest individual innings by a New Zealand batsman in England and he was the first New Zealand batsman to make two hundreds in a match on a tour in England. This was the fourth time he had achieved this feat.

B. Sutcliffe and M. P. Donnelly became the first New Zealand batsmen to score over 2,000 runs on an English tour.

T. B. Burtt established a New Zealand record by taking 129 wickets (J. A. Cowie had 114 in 1937).

In August, B. Sutcliffe made six successive scores of over fifty: 243 & 100* v. Essex (Southend), 88 & 54 v. England (Oval) and 61 & 79* v. Lancs. (Liverpool).

TEST RECORDS

For the first time in history a series of more than three Test matches ended without a single Test reaching a definite conclusion.

The following wicket records were established by England: 147 for 1st wicket by L. Hutton and R. T. Simpson at the Oval, 218 for 2nd wicket by L. Hutton and W. J. Edrich at the Oval, 189 for 6th wicket by D. Compton and T. E. Bailey at Lord's, and 21 (unbroken) for 10th wicket by T. E. Bailey and L. Jackson at Manchester.

The following wicket records were established by New Zealand: 120 for 5th wicket by M. P. Donnelly and F. B. Smith at Leeds and 57 for 10th wicket by F. H. L. Mooney and J. A. Cowie at Leeds.

England's innings total of 482 at the Oval is their highest recorded against New Zealand in England. New Zealand's total of 484 at Lord's is their highest in any Test match.

M. P. Donnelly's 206 at Lord's is the highest individual innings for New Zealand in Test cricket. L. Hutton's innings of 206 at the Oval is the highest against New Zealand in England.

England declared their innings closed on the first day of the Lord's Test—a procedure found to be illegal. But New Zealand did not query it and the match proceeded quite happily.

In their Special Instructions to umpires in 1948, M.C.C. allowed a declaration after 300 runs had been scored on the first day of a three-day match, but this ruling did not apply to Test matches.

FINANCE

New Zealand's profit at the end of the tour was approximately £15.000—far in excess of any previous tour, most of which showed a financial loss.

Counties on whose grounds Tests were played received £3.173; other first-class counties had £1.058. Oxford and Cambridge each received £529. Minor Counties £181 and Combined Services £91.

NEW ZEALAND MATCH RESULTS 1949

(Played at County headquarters except where stated)

YORKSHIRE (Bradford)—April 30. May 2 & 3.—N.Z. 370 for 7 dec. (Sutcliffe 72, Wallace 82, Donnelly 69, Aspinall 5-80) and 244 for 6 dec. (Wallace 126, Donnelly 52); YORKS. 346 (Hutton 167, Lester 50) and 101 for 3. *Match drawn.*

WORCESTERSHIRE—May 7, 9 & 10.—N.Z. 425 (Scott 103, Hadlee 97, Wallace 108) and 220 for 5 dec. (Scott 75); WORCS. 279 (Yarnold 56, White 64) and 216 (Howorth 62*, Burke 7—102). *Won by 159 runs.*

SURREY—May 11, 12 & 13.—N.Z. 258 (Sutcliffe 83, McMahon 5—73) and 249 for 8 dec. (Hadlee 119*); SURREY 202 (Barton 85*, Cresswell 5—73) and 156 (Whittaker 50, Constable 55, Burtt 6 —47). *Won by 149 runs.*

LEICESTERSHIRE—May 14, 16 & 17.—N.Z. 430 (Wallace 171, Donnelly 146); LEICS. 119 (Cowie 6—54) and 207 for 1 (Lester 70*, Prentice 104*). *Match drawn.*

CAMBRIDGE UNIVERSITY—May 18, 19 & 20.—CAMB. U. 107 and 284 (Morris

56, Doggart 62. Insole 79*. Rabone 5—25); N.Z. 441 for 5 dec. (Reid 188*, Wallace 197). *Won by an innings and 50 runs.*

M.C.C.—May 21. 23 & 24.—M.C.C 379 (Edrich 57. Simpson 51, Compton 63, Watkins 69. Burtt 6—98) and 34 for 1. N.Z. 313 (Rabone 92. Mooney 102, Bailey 5—83). *Match drawn.*

OXFORD UNIVERSITY—May 25, 26 & 27. OXFORD U. 247 (Hofmeyr 95*. Winn 58. Rabone 5—60) and 72 (Burtt 6—18); N.Z. 110 (Wrigley 5—28) and 126. *Lost by 83 runs.*

SUSSEX—May 28. 30 & 31.—SUSSEX 276 for 7 dec. (John Langridge 154) and 130 (Cowie 5—22); N Z. 160 (Wallace 62 C. Oakes 5—19) and 247 for 5 (Sutcliffe 56. Reid 82, Donnelly 88*). *Won by 5 wickets.*

SOMERSET—June 1, 2 & 3.—SOMERSET 191 (Gimblett 53) and 43 for 1; N.Z. 297 for 9 dec. (Scott 81, Smith 93). *Match drawn.*

GLAMORGAN (Cardiff)—June 4, 6 & 7. N.Z. 312 for 8 dec. (Smith 72) and 111 for 3; GLAMORGAN 309 (Parkhouse 61, Wooller 80). *Match drawn.*

FIRST TEST MATCH AT LEEDS.

HAMPSHIRE—June 15. 16 & 17.—HANTS. 129 and 409 (McCorkell 67, Eagar 82. Arnold 110. Burtt 6—76); N.Z. 430 for 5 dec. (Sutcliffe 71. Scott 129, Reid 50. Donnelly 100*) and 109 for 3. *Won by 7 wickets.*

SURREY—June 18. 20 & 21.—N.Z. 465 (Sutcliffe 187. Scott 96. Rabone 51, Laker 6—112) and 127 for 3 (Rabone 52); SURREY 645 for 9 dec. (Whittaker 91. Parker 255, E. A. Bedser 65). *Match drawn.*

SECOND TEST MATCH AT LORD'S.

COMBINED SERVICES (Gillingham)—June 29 & 30.—C. SERVICES 72 and 347 (J. E. Manners 123. J. H. G. Deighton 59. R. G. Wilson 68); N Z. 469 for 7 dec. (Sutcliffe 144. Scott 203). *Won by an innings and 50 runs.*

GLOUCESTERSHIRE—July 2, 4 & 5—GLOS. 232 (Wilson 70. Burtt 6—73) and 155 (Rabone 5—66. Burtt 5—47); N.Z. 252 (Donnelly 89. Goddard 5—131, Cook 5—106) and 138 for 3 (Hadlee 56). *Won by 7 wickets.*

LANCASHIRE—July 6, 7 & 8.—LANCS. 467 for 5 dec. (Ikin 167. Grieves 128. N. D. Howard 50*); N.Z. 237 (Rabone 81. Grieves 5—64) and 204 for 7. *Match drawn.*

DERBYSHIRE—July 9. 11 & 12.—DERBY 121 (Burke 6—23) and 355 (Elliott 104, Revill 145*); N.Z. 371 for 8 dec. (Reid 66. Mooney 97. Burtt 68*) and 107 for 3. *Won by 7 wickets.*

NORTHAMPTONSHIRE—July 13, 14 & 15.—N.Z. 456 for 7 dec. (Sutcliffe 81, Scott 105, Hadlee 71, Reid 107*) and 194 for 4 dec. (Reid 72); NORTHANTS. 338 (Oldfield 76, Barrick 147*) and 182 for 8 (Brookes 97). *Match Drawn.*

SCOTLAND (Glasgow)—July 16, 18 & 19.

—N.Z. 423 (Sutcliffe 183. Smith 68) and 16 for 0; SCOTLAND 137 (Burtt 6—45) and 299 (Willatt 101. Crosskey 81, Cowie 6 —66). *Won by 10 wickets.*

THIRD TEST MATCH AT MANCHESTER

YORKSHIRE (Sheffield)—July 27, 28 & 29.—N.Z. 261 (Sutcliffe 91. Wardle 5—92) and 228 (Donnelly 95. Wardle 6—84); YORKS. 321 (Yardley 134. Close 51) and 108 for 8 (Cresswell 5-30). *Match drawn.*

GLAMORGAN (Swansea)—July 30. August 1 & 2.—N Z. 378 for 6 dec. (Wallace 169*. Smith 71); GLAMORGAN 73 (Cresswell 6-21). *Match drawn.*

WARWICKSHIRE—August 3. 4 & 5.—N.Z. 303 (Sutcliffe 58. Donnelly 106, Pritchard 6-96) and 280 for 2 (Rabone 58. Reid 151*); WARWICK 394 for 9 dec. (Gardner 70. Townsend 53, Ord 70, Dollery 84). *Match drawn.*

NOTTINGHAMSHIRE—August 6. 8 & 9. —NOTTS. 323 for 4 dec. (Keeton 64, Hardstaff 123*. Harris 83) and 229 for 4 dec. (Poole 67); N.Z. 329 for 4 dec. (Rabone 120. Reid 155) and 105 for 4 (Wallace 54*). *Match drawn.*

ESSEX (Southend)—August 10. 11 & 12. —N Z. 420 (Sutcliffe 243. Hadlee 55) and 218 for 8 dec. (Sutcliffe 100*, Hadlee 57); ESSEX 304 (Dodds 82, Vigar 89) and 216 for 4 (Cray 60, Eve 69). *Match drawn.*

FOURTH TEST MATCH AT THE OVAL

DURHAM (Sunderland)—August 18 & 19. —N.Z. 417 for 3 dec. (Scott 104. Rabone 56. Smith 106*, Mooney 104*); DURHAM 171 and 280 (Clarke 56, Burke 5-81). *Match drawn.*

LANCASHIRE (Liverpool)—August 20, 22 & 23.—LANCS. 318 (Washbrook 125, Greenwood 50) and 224 for 5 dec. (Washbrook 68. Ikin 57. Edrich 53); N.Z. 390 (Sutcliffe 61. Scott 87, Donnelly 80) and 153 for 1 (Sutcliffe 79*, Donnelly 56). *Won by 9 wickets.*

KENT—August 24. 25 & 26.—N.Z. 358 (Smith 58. Donnelly 68. Scott 74) and 204 for 6 dec. (Wallace 55); KENT 184 (Todd 54. Pawson 50. Burtt 6—56) and 250 for 5 (Ames 152*). *Match drawn.*

MIDDLESEX—August 27. 29 & 30.—MIDDX. 315 (Compton 148. Dewes 92. Cowie 5—87) and 169 (Dewes 60); N.Z. 328 (Sutcliffe 59. Wallace 58. Donnelly 72. Hadlee 50) and 157 for 1 (Sutcliffe 110*). *Won by 9 wickets.*

SOUTH OF ENGLAND XI (Hastings).—September 3. 5 & 6.—N.Z. 367 (Rabone 78. Hadlee 114. Reid 54); SOUTH OF ENGLAND XI 159 and 205. *Won by an innings and 3 runs.*

H. D. G. LEVESON GOWER'S XI (Scarborough)—September 7, 8 & 9.—L. GOWER'S XI 348 for 5 dec. (Hutton 54, Simpson 54. Hardstaff 123) and 202 for 3 dec. (Hutton 75. Simpson 58); N.Z. 388 (Reid 50. Donnelly 145. A. V. Bedser 5—101) and 217 for 4 (Sutcliffe 83, Donnelly 53*). *Won by 6 wickets.*

Championship Table 1949

	P.	W.	L.	D.	No. dec.	First Inns. lead L.	First Inns. lead D.	Pts.
POINTS AWARDED		12				4	4	
Middlesex ... ... (3)	26	14	3	9	0	1	5	192
Yorkshire ... ... (4)	26	14	2	10	0	0	6	192
Worcestershire ... ... (10)	26	12	7	7	0	2	5	172
Warwickshire ... ... (7)	26	12	5	8	1	0	6	168
Surrey ... ... (2)	26	11	8	6	1	2	4	156
Northants ... ... (17)	26	10	7	9	0	2	3	140
Gloucestershire ... ... (8)	26	10	7	7	2	0	3	132
Glamorgan ... ... (1)	26	7	6	12	1	2	7	120
Essex ... ... (13)	26	7	9	10	0	0	6	108
Somerset ... ... (12)	26	8	15	3	0	2	1	108
Lancashire ... ... (5)	26	6	7	13	0	0	7	100
Notts ... ... (14)	26	6	5	13	2	0	7	100
Kent ... ... (15)	26	7	15	4	0	1	2	96
Sussex ... ... (16)	26	7	10	7	2	1	2	96
Derbyshire ... ... (6)	26	6	13	6	1	2	2	88
Hampshire ... ... (9)	26	6	13	6	1	2	1	84
Leicestershire ... ... (11)	26	3	14	8	1	3	2	56

Figures in parentheses indicate positions in the 1948 table

COUNTY CHAMPIONS

1873 { Glos. Notts.	1889 { Surrey Lancs. Notts.	1906 Kent	1927 Lancs.
1874 Derby		1907 Notts.	1928 Lancs.
1875 Notts.	1890 Surrey	1908 Yorks.	1929 Notts.
1876 Glos.	1891 Surrey	1909 Kent	1930 Lancs.
1877 Glos.	1892 Surrey	1910 Kent	1931 Yorks.
1878 Middx.	1893 Yorks.	1911 Warwick	1932 Yorks.
1879 { Notts. Lancs.	1894 Surrey	1912 Yorks.	1933 Yorks.
	1895 Surrey	1913 Kent	1934 Lancs.
1880 Notts.	1896 Yorks.	1914 Surrey	1935 Yorks.
1881 Lancs.	1897 Lancs.	1915-18 No	1936 Derby
1882 { Notts. Lancs.	1898 Yorks.	competition	1937 Yorks.
	1899 Surrey	1919 Yorks.	1938 Yorks.
1883 Notts.	1900 Yorks.	1920 Middx.	1939 Yorks.
1884 Notts.	1901 Yorks.	1921 Middx.	1940-45 —
1885 Notts.	1902 Yorks.	1922 Yorks.	1946 Yorks.
1886 Notts.	1903 Middx.	1923 Yorks.	1947 Middx.
1887 Surrey	1904 Lancs.	1924 Yorks.	1948 Glamorgan
1888 Surrey	1905 Yorks.	1925 Yorks.	1949 { Middx. Yorks.
		1926 Lancs.	

BOOTH'S
DRY GIN

Definitely Superior!

BOOTH'S
FINEST DRY GIN

BOOTH'S
FINEST
DRY GIN
70° PROOF
LONDON

MAXIMUM PRICES : 32/4 PER BOTTLE ;
HALF BOTTLE 16/11 (U.K. ONLY)
THE ONLY GIN THAT HOLDS THE BLUE
SEAL OF THE INSTITUTE OF HYGIENE

| D. B. CLOSE | A. V. BEDSER | W. E. HOLLIES |

The County Championship

The First Tie for 60 Years

THERE being no really outstanding side in last year's Championship, possibly a tie was a suitable result. The success of Midland teams was a striking feature of the season.

Once again the finish was a most exciting affair. Middlesex lost to Surrey at Lord's but in their last home match defeated Derbyshire by three wickets to make sure at least of sharing the title; and Yorkshire, who finished with six victories off the reel, beat Glamorgan by 278 runs at Newport to become joint champions.

On August 10th Worcestershire shared the lead with Middlesex, with a game in hand, but they lost successive away matches to Somerset and Middlesex. At the same time Warwickshire dropped out of the hunt by losing to Glamorgan and Yorkshire, although they finished strongly, putting paid to Surrey's hopes by beating them at the Oval by 119 runs, Hollies taking 11 wickets for 76.

| J. HARDSTAFF | H. E. DOLLERY | L. E. G. AMES |

Derbyshire

Played 26, Won 6, Lost 13, Drawn 6, No decision 1

EVEN without George Pope, whose all-round talents were sorely missed, Derbyshire's attack was still quite formidable, its speed being well suited to home pitches. Tenuous batting accounted for a drop of nine places in the table to the position they held in 1946.

Having beaten Leicester on May 24, Derbyshire did not win again till June 28 (against Lancashire). Later, the "double" was completed against Somerset and the season ended brightly with an honourable defeat by Middlesex in their last and vital championship match at Lord's, and a second victory, this time by an innings, over Essex. Taking the season all through, an encouraging feature was the improved form of Revill, Rhodes and Gladwin as batsmen, and of Jackson as bowler. Carr, after the University match, and Eggar and Sale in August, brought welcome reinforcement to the batting, but of this amateur Repton contingent only Eggar really batted consistently well. Carr could not recapture his Oxford brilliance while Sale virtually limited himself to one lovely left-hander's innings at Old Trafford. Carr and Sale are Old Reptonians and Eggar, himself an Old Wykehamist, is in charge of Repton cricket.

BATTING

	Inns.	N.O.	Runs	H.S.	Avge.
†J. D. Eggar	14	2	501	219	41.75
A. Revill	41	5	1269	156*	35.25
C. S. Elliott	50	2	1477	104	30.77
D. Smith	37	2	1033	89	29.51
C. Gladwin	41	10	903	124*	29.12
A. E. G. Rhodes	46	1	1156	127	25.68
†L. Johnson	20	1	475	77	25.00
†R. Sale	12	0	273	146	22.75
†D. B. Carr	14	0	313	72	22.35
G. Dawkes	41	8	620	88	18.78
E. A. Marsh	26	1	437	71	17.48
†D. A. Skinner	35	1	474	63	13.94
A. F. Townsend	20	1	233	41	12.26
W. H. Copson	40	7	210	28	6.36
L. Jackson	39	12	126	24	4.66

ALSO BATTED.—†P. Vaulkhard, 4, 2, 13, 2; D. Snape, 0*, 0, 0; J. Rimmer, 1*, 0, 0*; †W. E. G. Payton, 24, 35*, 15, 19; †K. A. Shearwood, 4, 2; G. Lowe, 22, 0; T. R. Armstrong, 4*, 0; †T. A. Hall, 0; †M. Fredricks, 12, 2, 84; †D. C. Brooke-Taylor, 3, 4, 4.

BOWLING

	Overs	Mdns.	Runs	Wkts.	Avge.
C. Gladwin	917	267	2210	110	20.09
L. Jackson	885.5	210	2162	103	20.99
W. H. Copson	647.2	148	1823	67	27.20
†D. B. Carr	67.2	16	248	8	31.00
A. E. G. Rhodes	802	133	2549	66	38.62
J. Rimmer	63.3	3	264	5	52.80
†L. Johnson	83	12	297	4	74.25

ALSO BOWLED.—T. R. Armstrong, 18—6—34—3; †T. A. Hall, 15—4—55—0; E. A. Marsh, 123—38—320—3; A. Revill, 4—2—11—0; †D. A. Skinner, 39—2—182—2; D. Smith, 4.1—1—12—0; A. F. Townsend 4—1—9—0.

NEW CAP.—L. Jackson. † denotes Amateur.

Revill should make many runs in the future, besides saving many by his brilliant fielding close to the bat; he is a realistic, if not particularly elegant player. Rhodes believes in hitting the ball firmly, in a manner good to see (he made 100 before lunch against Notts.) but uncertain length made his bowling figures expensive. Elliott, consistent, if not brilliant, is rewarded with a testimonial this year, and Smith, now 43, remains to give delight with authentic left-hand strokes, having changed his mind about retirement. Johnson, an amateur from Barbados, showed promise, and Townsend, a rather uncertain starter, is capable of better things. Amateurs like Payton, a solid opener, and Vaulkhard, a forcing bat, played only rarely. Dawkes, one of our very best wicketkeepers, might usefully go in higher.

C. ELLIOTT   A. E. G. RHODES   R. SALE

Gladwin and Jackson both played for England and if neither perhaps is the sort to bowl out Australia next winter they would be excellent tour men. Gladwin's all-round play has made big strides since his South African tour. He has scored his first century and he will soon be achieving the " double." Jackson's arm is low but he is very industrious and if required would cheerfully bowl himself into the ground.

Copson has now retired after most honourable service; Marsh has not been re-engaged; and Skinner, a keen and pleasant leader, has resigned the captaincy for business reasons. A new batsman, A. Hamer, has been engaged (see Who's Who).

Essex

Played 26, Won 7, Lost 9, Drawn 10

HAD it not been for injuries Essex might well have achieved big things. Preston, the fast bowler, broke a leg in the soccer season and never once played for the 1st XI—being shrewdly restored to confidence and form in minor games—and Horsfall, a really fine batsman in the making, slipped a disc in his spine when trying to emulate Larwood at the nets in April, and missed all but the last six matches—when he showed renewed signs of quality. Then Avery, so often in the wars, missed two months through another hand injury, and Morris, a bat of distinct possibilities, was out for four weeks with similar trouble.

These things considered, Essex did very well to rise four places in the Table —and it might have been more had the weather not intervened in three matches when they had a grip on affairs. But when Essex lost they did not do it by halves: seven of the nine defeats were sustained in two days.

Progressive administration resulted in a new record membership total of 4,790 and gates were also up on 1948.

Avery had just scored two hundreds in a match when he was injured; may better luck be the lot of this correct and dependable batsman this year, for he takes a Benefit. Dodds once more surprised the unknowing by combining notable consistency with enterprising stroke play so refreshing to see and Cray improved in average and aggregate in Avery's absence. Vigar too had a better year with the bat and now that Price has returned north perhaps his leg-breaks will at last be given the chances they deserve.

Pearce scored only half as many runs as in 1948, yet he still presented the broadest of bats when set. At his own suggestion he now becomes joint-captain with Insole, who batted with wonderful success for the county after he had led Cambridge to victory at Lord's. He may be unorthodox, but he is extremely effective; and his fielding uplifts the heart.

BATTING

	Inns.	N.O.	Runs	H.S.	Avge.
†D. J. Insole	19	5	898	219*	64.14
A. V. Avery	25	2	906	143	39.39
F. H. Vigar	48	5	1449	136	33.69
T. C. Dodds	53	2	1696	123	33.25
†T. E. Bailey	38	7	1005	88*	32.41
S. J. Cray	35	1	1046	129	30.76
†T. N. Pearce	40	6	975	111*	28.67
‡S. C. Eve	28	2	717	120	27.57
R. Horsfall	10	1	235	95	26.11
W. B. Morris	20	1	443	68	23.31
R. Smith	44	4	771	78*	19.27
T. P. B. Smith	37	4	548	115	16.60
T. H. Wade	36	7	384	45	13.24
†G. R. Pullinger	19	10	51	14*	5.66
E. Price	32	9	118	19*	5.13

ALSO BATTED.—†G. H. West, 55, 8; W. J. Dines, 1*; J. Taylor, 2; †A. B. Lavers, 11, 10*, 21, 0, 6, 0; †F. St. G. Unwin, 15, 8, 6, 16; †D. Watkins, 2; †H. A. Faragher, 26.

BOWLING

	Overs	Mdns.	Runs	Wkts.	Avge.
†T. E. Bailey	710.1	139	2132	87	24.50
†A. B. Lavers	66	15	197	7	28.14
T. P. B. Smith	899.4	153	2472	82	30.14
R. Smith	1175.5	251	3248	104	31.23
F. H. Vigar	234.2	31	909	28	32.46
E. Price	613.5	133	1765	54	32.68
†G. R. Pullinger	459.3	101	1333	38	35.07

ALSO BOWLED.—†D. J. Insole, 3—1—5—0; W. J. Dines, 11—0—42—0; T. C. Dodds, 1—0—3—0; †D. Watkins, 22.3—4—86—3; †T. N. Pearce, 4—0—20—0; T. H. Wade, 0.3—0—3—0; W. B. Morris, 70—20—233—2.

NEW CAPS.—†D. J. Insole, †G. R. Pullinger. † denotes Amateur.

It was better fielding, plus the all-round prowess of T. E. Bailey, that had most to do with the county's improved fortunes. Bailey took all ten wickets in an innings against Lancashire and became the first amateur to achieve the "double" since V. W. C. Jupp (for Northants.) in 1933. If Preston comes on as hoped then the Essex opening attack will sharpen up the laggards.

Ray Smith was the only bowler to take 100 wickets for the county, bowling far more overs than anyone else. His batting remains unpredictably exhilarating. Peter Smith still batted skilfully when required, though his bowling, perhaps with less spin, was not so consistently successful. Eve, a forceful bat, played several good innings; another amateur, Pullinger, bowled with spirit and accuracy; and Wade, no mean left-hand bat, kept a good wicket in his usual quiet way.

D. J. INSOLE   F. H. VIGAR   S. J. CRAY

Glamorgan

Played 26, Won 7, Lost 6, Drawn 12, No decision 1

IT was simply not Glamorgan's year. Possibly any luck that was going had been theirs in 1948; last season it was not. When the weather in most places was beneficent rain withheld from them almost sure victory in two, and maybe three, of the early games, and later the side was ill-equipped for a succession of firm wickets. The loss of W. E. Jones with a cracked knee-cap early in July was severe: it robbed them at once of a dangerous and attractive left-hand bat, a brilliant outfield and a more than useful slow left-armer.

So virtually there were just four bowlers left—Wooller and Hever, Muncer and Watkins—and with conditions favouring the batsmen they had considerable trouble in bowling out their opponents twice. Too often a " tight " attack had to be the order of the day.

Wooller never spared himself and would have achieved the " double " if his innings against the R.A.F. had been allowable, but Hever was best used in short spells and Muncer seemed rarely free from a nagging groin injury. Yet Muncer still obtained 105 wickets for the county at very reasonable cost in a summer certainly not made

BATTING

	Inns.	N.O.	Runs	H.S.	Avge.
W. E. Jones	22	4	680	128	37.77
W. G. A. Parkhouse ..	49	4	1491	145	33.13
S. Montgomery ..	6	0	183	117	30.50
A. J. Watkins ..	39	2	1087	129	29.37
E. Davies ..	50	1	1287	158	26.26
P. Clift	50	3	1226	125*	26.08
†M. Robinson ..	40	1	899	190	23.05
†W. Wooller ..	46	5	943	80	23.00
B. L. Muncer ..	42	5	746	81	20.16
J. Pleass ..	25	2	330	49	14.34
H. G. Davies ..	42	6	457	45	12.69
J. Eaglestone ..	35	3	395	62	12.34
N. G. Hever ..	34	22	148	23*	12.33
†S. Trick	6	4	23	15	11.50

ALSO BATTED.—G. Lavis, 4, 3; †A. Porter, 10, 1*; J. Pressdee, 0; †J. C. Clay, 0, 2.

BOWLING

	Overs	Mdns.	Runs	Wkts.	Avge.
B. L. Muncer ..	1024.2	303	2378	105	22.64
A. J. Watkins ..	659.2	169	1609	66	24.37
†W. Wooller ..	1127.2	290	2947	120	24.55
N. G. Hever ..	801	217	1851	70	26.44
†M. Robinson ..	81	14	242	9	26.88
W. E. Jones ..	307	72	834	31	26.90
†S. Trick ..	129.2	42	291	10	29.10

ALSO BOWLED.—W. G. A. Parkhouse, 17—1—75—0; E. Davies. 55—8—143—2; †J. C. Clay, 26—2—63—0; P. Clift, 36—2—123—0; G. Lavis, 9—5—10—0; J. Pressdee, 19—5—35—0.

NEW CAPS.—Nil. † denotes Amateur.

to order for off-spinners, and, fortunately, Watkins showed great improvement as a seam bowler in the latter part of the season.

The batting on the whole showed a steady improvement but it lacked stability. Emrys Davies, who has now scored 20,000 runs, Clift and Watkins all had a lean time in August, a dismal month in which only one match was won and which culminated in that depressing defeat at the hands of Yorkshire (whom Glamorgan have still to beat for the first time). Watkins could not find consistent form throughout the season but Clift was settling in well at No. 1 and the batting of Parkhouse was another encouragement for the future. His career should be assured, for he has the skill and the right temperament for big cricket.

The amateur, Robinson, who could not turn out in 1948, played the highest Glamorgan innings of the summer but lacked consistency; Montgomery,

W. G. A. PARKHOUSE   H. G. DAVIES   P. B. CLIFT

formerly of Essex, hit his maiden hundred against Hampshire and shared in a record 5th wicket 264; and Muncer's batting was very useful once again.

The ground fielding was still supremely good, but fewer miraculous catches were held and Haydn Davies's wicketkeeping, though often brilliant, was not quite so reliable as usual. Gates were down on 1948, but membership rose to a new record of 6,000

Gloucestershire

Played 26; Won 10; Lost 7; Drawn 7; No decision 2.

Gloucestershire made a slight advance on 1948, rising from eighth to seventh place; and nothing was more remarkable in their season than the performances of Tom Goddard at the ripe age of 49. Having experienced rather leaner fortunes in 1948, he arrived at the end of May, 1949, with 16 wickets to his name at a horrid cost of 41 apiece; but reinvigorated by continuous sunshine, he found his most deadly form and finished up at the top of the first-class averages. A magnificent feat.

The batting, deprived in two short years of the genius of Hammond and Barnett, was less resilient and too much depended on Nos. 1 to 6. Early in the summer Crapp was unduly defensive but in the last six weeks he batted better and more successfully than ever before, and became the first left-hander to score 2,000 runs in a season for the county. Emmett, a model opening batsman—consistent, elegant and aggressive without a suggestion of crude violence—also surpassed previous achievements with a similar aggregate.

Tom Graveney had a wonderfully successful second season but he tired and could not keep up his brilliant early form. His forward play is beautifully straight yet his back strokes are sometimes a little across the line. With improved technique on turning wickets he should reach the highest grade. Milton is also a player of the richest promise; he plays the ball remarkably late and is very strong off the back foot for one so young. His cover drive is a beauty; he fields gloriously; and he is a steady out-swinger. Moreover, he does well at times of stress.

Allen could not quite maintain his tremendous form at the start of the season but still scored over 1,500 runs. There being no successor with all the right qualifications available, the county are pleased that he continues as captain.

The problem of an opening partner for Emmett was a constant one. Allen himself went in first for a time, and so did Wilson, Tom Graveney and Young. Wilson, a fine batsman-wicketkeeper, scored consistently yet again, playing one big innings against Sussex, but he is probably a better bat in the middle. With more

BATTING

	Inns.	N.O.	Runs	H.S.	Avge.
J. F. Crapp	48	4	2014	140	45.77
G. M. Emmett	51	2	2095	116	40.91
T. W. Graveney ..	49	1	1656	159	34.50
†B. O. Allen	48	3	1489	134	33.08
A. E. Wilson	49	1	1287	188	26.81
C. A. Milton	45	3	960	92*	22.85
D. M. Young	20	2	349	63*	19.38
C. J. Scott	11	3	151	40*	18.87
†C. Monks	17	2	248	51	16.53
J. K. Graveney ..	33	4	462	62	15.93
G. Lambert ..	43	7	568	61	15.77
L. M. Cranfield ..	12	2	157	41	15.70
†Sir D. Bailey ..	10	2	70	29	8.75
A. G. S. Wilcox ..	7	1	52	13	8.66
T. W. Goddard ..	40	13	227	20	8.40
C. Cook	38	14	133	18	5.54

ALSO BATTED.—L. Harbin, 13. 2.

BOWLING

	Overs	Mdns.	Runs	Wkts.	Avge.
T. W. Goddard ..	1187.2	326	3069	160	19.18
C. Cook ..	1052.2	343	2397	101	23.73
J. K. Graveney ..	504.4	100	1547	57	27.14
G. Lambert ..	771.5	146	2401	73	32.89
L. M. Cranfield ..	102.4	30	275	7	39.28
C. J. Scott ..	203.5	41	552	13	42.46
C. A. Milton ..	265	71	640	11	58.18

ALSO BOWLED.—†Sir D. Bailey, 13—3—49—2; †B. O. Allen, 6.4—1—54—0; †C. Monks, 18—4—42—1; G. M. Emmett, 35—8—109—1; L. Harbin, 45—8—133—9; J. F. Crapp, 5—2—14—0.

NEW CAPS.—†Sir D. Bailey, C. A. Milton, J. K. Graveney. † denotes Amateur.

chances and the confidence they bring, Young should solve the problem.

If Cook's flight and spin were on a par with his phenomenal accuracy he would be the leading slow left-hander of the day. Lambert's best ball is devastating but interludes of inaccuracy make his wickets expensive. Scott has been learning the art of off-break bowling so that he may succeed Goddard, and Kenneth Graveney, the elder, showed great promise as a fast medium bowler with the out-swinger at his command. He is not yet consistent but he achieved several excellent feats, notably that of taking all ten wickets in an innings at Chesterfield. Cranfield must curse the fates for making him an off-spin bowler in the same side as Goddard. For details of those not regularly re-engaged please turn to *Valete*.

J. K. GRAVENEY

G. LAMBERT

C. A. MILTON

NEW ZEALANDERS IN ENGLAND, 1949

Standing: J. H. Phillipps (Manager), F. B. Smith, T. B. Burtt, C. C. Burke, G. F. Cresswell, G. O. Rabone, H. B. Cave, J. A. Hayes, J. R. Reid, F. L. H. Mooney, W. Watts (Scorer). Seated: B. Sutcliffe, V. J. Scott, W. M. Wallace (Vice-Capt.), W. A. Hadlee (Capt.), J. A. Cowie, M. P. Donnelly. Inset: Alan Mitchell (N.Z. Press Association).

C

ENGLAND—FOURTH TEST (THE OVAL), 1949

Standing: T. G. Evans, D. Compton, A. V. Bedser, J. C. Laker, D. V. P. Wright, W. E. Hollies.
Seated: R. T. Simpson, W. J. Edrich, F. R. Brown (Captain), T. E. Bailey, L. Hutton.

AUSTRALIANS IN SOUTH AFRICA, 1949-50
Back row: R. N. Harvey, G. L. Langley, J. A. R. Moroney, C. L. McCool.
Middle row: S. J. E. Loxton, R. A. Saggers, G. Noblet, W. A. Johnston,
K. Archer, R. R. Lindwall.
Seated: W. Ferguson (scorer), I. W. Johnson, A. L. Hassett (Capt.)
E. A. Dwyer (Manager), A. R. Morris (Vice-capt.), A. K. Walker,
C. Cartledge (S.A. Manager).

SOUTH AFRICA—THIRD TEST, DURBAN, 1950
Standing: H. Stacey (Manager), V. I. Smith, J. Watkins, C. McCarthy,
H. Tayfield, J. Nel, M. North (scorer).
Seated: O. Wynne, J. Cheetham, E. A. B. Rowan, A. D. Nourse (Capt.),
W. W. Wade, N. B. F. Mann, O. C. Dawson (twelfth man).

MIDDLESEX—JOINT CHAMPIONS, 1949

Standing: J. A. Young, S. M. Brown, L. H. Gray, J. J. Warr, L. H. Compton, H. Sharp, D. Richards (Masseur). Seated: J. D. Robertson, J. Sims, R. W. V. Robins, F. G. Mann (Captain), W. J. Edrich, D. Compton. On ground: A. Thompson, J. G. Dewes.

YORKSHIRE—JOINT CHAMPIONS, 1949

Standing: H. Halliday, B. Heyhurst (Masseur), D. B. Close, W. H. H. Sutcliffe, J. V. Wilson, A. Mason, H. Walker (Scorer), E. Lester. Seated: E. P. Robinson, L. Hutton, N. W. D. Yardley (Captain), D. V. Brennan, W. Watson. On ground: F. A. Lowson, E. S. Barraclough.

WORCESTERSHIRE, 1949
Standing: H. Yarnold, L. Outschoorn, E. Cooper, R. Howorth, D. Kenyon,
G. Darks, R. O. Jenkins.
Seated: R. E. Bird, A. F. T. White (Joint Captain) and R. E. S Wyatt
(Joint Captain), R. T. D. Perks, P. F. Jackson.

WARWICKSHIRE, 1949
(Tom Dollery's Benefit team)
Standing: R. E. Hitchcock, G. Austin (Scorer), C. W. Grove, A. Townsend,
T. L. Pritchard, F. C. Gardner, A. V. Wolton, F. Reed (Masseur),
R. T. Spooner.
Seated: W. E. Hollies, P. Cranmer, H. E. Dollery (Captain), A. H. Kardar,
J. S. Ord.

SURREY, 1949

Standing: G. J. Whittaker, H. Strudwick (Scorer), E. A. Bedser, H. S. Squires,
J. W. McMahon, G. A. R. Lock, S. Tait (Masseur), T. H. Clark.
Seated: L. B. Fishlock, E. A. Watts, M. R. Barton (Captain), J. F. Parker,
A. V. Bedser.
On ground: A. J. McIntyre, B. Constable.

NORTHAMPTONSHIRE, 1949

Standing: F. Jakeman, D. Barrick, P. Davis, W. Barron, V. H. Broderick,
R. G. Garlick, R. W. Clarke, E. Davis.
Seated: N. Oldfield, J. Webster, F. R. Brown (Captain), D. Brookes,
A. E. Nutter.

England v. New Zealand

Five pictures from the Fourth and final Test match at The Oval which illustrate the pyrotechnics, the triumphs and the strident voice of Godfrey Evans.

Wicket-keepers are sometimes airborne . . . here Sutcliffe puts Bedser away past cover's right hand.

●

And sometimes they are quite the reverse . . . The batsmen are Tom Burtt and Cave. Fielders (left to right): Brown, Hollies, Edrich and Wright (bowling).

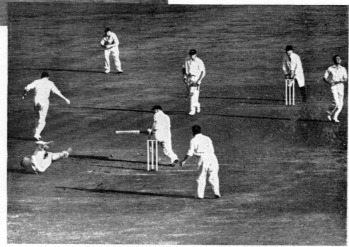

At other times they have an apprehensive look. Wallace slips when playing Laker but safely regains his ground.

●

But there are moments of loud and confident appeal . . . such as when Reid goes lbw to Wright.

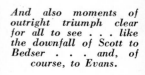

And also moments of outright triumph clear for all to see . . . like the downfall of Scott to Bedser . . . and, of course, to Evans.

GLOUCESTERSHIRE, 1949
Standing: **C. Monks, G. Lambert, C. J. Scott, B. S. Bloodworth (Scorer), L. M. Cranfield, T. W. Graveney, C. A. Milton, C. Cook.**
Seated: **G. M. Emmett, T. W. Goddard. B. O. Allen (Captain), J. F. Crapp, A. E. Wilson.**

GLAMORGAN, 1949
Standing: **P. B. Clift, J. Eaglestone, W. G. A. Parkhouse, N. G. Hever, A. J. Watkins, J. Pleass.**
Seated: **W. E. Jones, H. G. Davies, W. Wooller (Capt.), E. Davies, B. L. Muncer.**

ESSEX, 1949

Standing: Ray Smith, W. B. Morris, E. Price, T. C. Dodds, S. J. Cray,
S. C. Eve.
Seated: G. R. Pullinger, Peter Smith, T. N. Pearce (Captain), T. E. Bailey,
T. H. Wade.

SOMERSET, 1949

Standing: M. Coope, E. Hill, M. F. Tremlett, F. L. Angell, H. W. Stephenson,
J. Lawrence.
Seated: H. Gimblett, A. W. Wellard, G. E. S. Woodhouse (Captain),
S. S. Rogers, H. T. F. Buse.

LANCASHIRE, 1949
Standing: A. Wilson, G. A. Edrich, K. Grieves, P. Greenwood, A. Wharton,
J. T. Ikin.
Seated: W. B. Roberts, C. Washbrook, N. D. Howard (Captain), R. Pollard,
W. Place.

NOTTINGHAMSHIRE, 1949
Standing: H. Winrow, F. W. Stocks, P. F. Harvey, B. H. Farr, F. G. Woodhead,
E. A. Meads, C. J. Poole.
Seated: C. B. Harris, W. W. Keeton, W. A. Sime (Captain), R. T. Simpson,
J. Hardstaff.

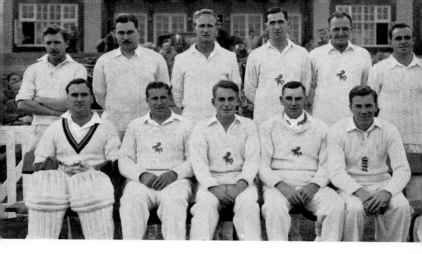

KENT, 1949

Standing: B. Edrich, H. J. Pocock, A. H. Phebey, E. Crush, R. R. Dovey,
F. Ridgway.
Seated: T. G. Evans, A. E. Fagg, D. G. Clark (Captain), L. J. Todd,
D. V. P. Wright.

SUSSEX, 1949

Standing: A. E. James, J. Oakes, J. Wood, J. Cornford, D. V. Smith, C. Oakes.
Seated: John Langridge, S. C. Griffith, H. T. Bartlett (Captain),
James Langridge, G. Cox.

DERBYSHIRE, 1949

Standing: A. Revill, M. D. Snape, E. A. Marsh, C. Gladwin, L. Allen (Scorer), L. Jackson, W. H. Copson, G. Dawkes.
Seated: A. E. G. Rhodes, D. Smith, D. A. Skinner (Captain), P. Vaulkhard, C. S. Elliott.

HAMPSHIRE, 1949

Standing: C. Walker, D. Shackleton, N. H. Rogers, G. Dawson, J. R. Gray, N. McCorkell.
Seated: J. Bailey, C. J. Knott, E. D. R. Eagar (Captain), D. E. Blake, J. Arnold.

LEICESTERSHIRE, 1949
Standing: **V. Munden, J. E. Walsh, M. Tompkin, J. Sperry, G. Watson, G. Lester, T. A. Chapman.**
Seated: **F. T. Prentice, L. G. Berry, S. J. Symington (Captain), P. Corrall, V. E. Jackson.**

CAMBRIDGE—WINNERS OF UNIVERSITY MATCH, 1949
Standing: **A. G. J. Rimell (Charterhouse), A. C. Burnett (Lancing), M. H. Stevenson (Rydal), J. J. Warr (Ealing G.S.), O. J. Wait (Dulwich), P. J. Hall (Geelong G.S., Victoria), O. B. Popplewell (Charterhouse),**
Seated: **R. J. Morris (Blundell's), G. H. G. Doggart (Winchester), D. J. Insole (Monoux, Walthamstow) (Captain), J. G. Dewes (Aldenham).**

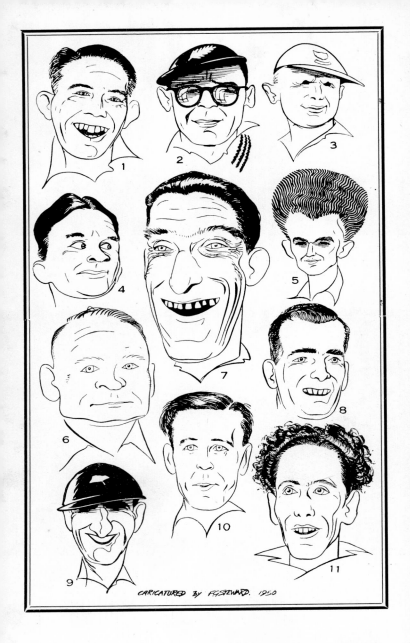

CARICATURED by F.G.STEWARD. 1950

PLAYFAIR'S
ELEVEN CRICKETERS OF 1949

Being the outstanding cricketers of the past summer, not on figures alone, but for their play or for what they did for the game.

THIS is a new Playfair feature. It is not seriously intended as a rival to that of Wisden, which selects its " Five Cricketers of the Year." To be selected for that is to achieve one of cricket's highest honours, but once included, a player cannot achieve the same distinction again. In the Playfair list we might include the same player ten times running.

Our choices won't please everybody: that is sure. But at least they may lead to lively argument. All true Yorkshiremen—and others—may be exasperated by the omission of D. B. Close, They may ask: " What more can a lad of 18 achieve in his first season? " Although the views of many were canvassed on this feature it was the majority opinion of our final panel—composed of an England captain, a first-class umpire and myself—that Close should be our 12th man.

Other notable omissions will spring to mind—Denis Compton or Joe Hardstaff (top of the batting list) to name but two. But we could not quite find room for them. We left out Compton with a fairly clear conscience. He did not have the best of summers but he is quite likely to appear in all future issues.

We made eleven selections because that is a very good cricket number, and we gave our artist free rein to display his victims in any order. Goddard catches the eye first not because we think him No. 1 but because . . . well, he makes a very good centre-piece.

Wally Hadlee (2) is in the list because he was a grand captain on a memorable tour and because he did *so much good* for cricket; Martin Donnelly (10) and Bert Sutcliffe (8) for the delight of brilliant batting and fielding; Tom Burtt (6) because without him New Zealand might have found things very difficult. Leonard Hutton (9) is there for superb technique and 3,000 runs; Tom Goddard (7) because at the age of 49 he virtually headed the bowling list—in a dry summer—after being prematurely " written off " at the end of May.

John Langridge (3) is there for his wonderful batting run, and Freddie Brown (4) for what he did for Northants. Reggie Simpson (5) we chose for gay and delightful batting, and for superb fielding; Trevor Bailey (11) for cheering us with something pretty quick and with all-round skill. And Roley Jenkins (1) we chose because we thought him the unluckiest cricketer in England.—PETER WEST.

Hampshire

Played 26; Won 6, Lost 13; Drawn 6; No decision 1

HAMPSHIRE do best in damp summers (*vide* 1946, when they finished tenth, and 1948, when they were ninth). In 1947 they were sixteenth, and last summer, when the three close finishes all went the wrong way, they finished one from the bottom again. The policy of giving youth every chance, with which Eagar, their dynamic captain, has much to do, must surely bear dividends soon.

One Hampshire problem—the lack of a good leg-break bowler—remains, but another, the lack of a penetrating opening attack, should have been solved by the advent of Shackleton and Carty. Shackleton came on so fast that he almost achieved the " double." He is a lively bowler who moves the ball either way and makes the batsman play him; and he will make many more runs yet. Carty does not yet move the ball a lot but he did very well when he was fit and he should improve with more experience. This pair provided Hampshire with their most hostile attack in years, although one must not forget Ransom, an amateur who has always done stout work despite the lack of regular first-class practice.

In the absence of a leg-spinner Knott and Bailey once again had to shoulder heavy burdens. Each, perhaps, have had better seasons, but it was not their sort of summer. Knott is one of the cleverest off-spinners and Bailey, who is a batsman of rare value when the ball is turning, has that cheerful philosophy born of years on the job.

None of the batsmen could find their form at the start of the season—a fact which accounted for the slow tempo of run - making at that stage, but by September seven of them had made more than 1,000 runs; and three of the last six matches were won.

McCorkell, relieved of regular wicketkeeping cares, had his most prosperous summer and played mostly with delightful freedom, while

BATTING

	Inns.	N.O.	Runs	H.S.	Avge.
N. McCorkell	52	3	1871	143*	38.18
G. Dawson	34	3	1032	158*	33.27
N. H. Rogers	56	1	1691	107	30.74
J. Arnold	44	5	1151	110	29.51
J. Bailey	50	3	1254	89	26.68
C. Walker	50	9	1087	112	26.51
†E. D. R. Eagar	47	3	1132	118	25.72
D. Shackleton	48	9	914	87*	23.43
L. Harrison	11	4	137	24*	19.57
†D. R. Guard	17	0	319	89	18.76
G. Hill	36	5	561	53	18.09
†D. E. Blake	18	0	311	60	17.27
†V. J. Ransom	11	1	143	58	14.30
R. Carty	15	3	154	53	12.83
A. W. H. Rayment	14	2	154	35	12.83
†C. J. Knott	35	13	188	21	8.54

ALSO BATTED.—J. R. Gray, 4, 30, 0, 22*; J. Taylor, 6. 8*, 8, 2; R. Dare, 4*, 2, 7; R. Prouton, 0; †J. R. Bridger, 0, 1, 46, 1, 52; T. A. Dean, 17*, 25*, 4, 6, 0, 5*; G. E. M. Heath, 9*, 0*,5, 3, 2, 12.

BOWLING

	Overs	Mdns.	Runs	Wkts.	Avge.
R. Carty	276.4	42	878	34	25.82
D. Shackleton	941.2	206	2616	100	26.16
†C. J. Knott	897.4	175	2717	101	26.90
J. Bailey	1026.4	267	2662	86	30.95
T. A. Dean	100.1	25	316	10	31.60
G. E. M. Heath	153.3	22	512	16	32.00
G. Hill	432.4	110	1237	27	45.81
C. Walker	366.4	94	1063	22	48.31
†V. J. Ransom	238.2	53	691	13	53.15

ALSO BOWLED.—†E. D. R. Eagar, 5.2—0—42—1; A. W. H. Rayment, 8—2—42—0; J. Arnold, 7—0—40—2; R. Dare, 49—10—143—3; J. R. Gray, 4—0—13—0; G. Dawson, 1—0—2—0; N. McCorkell, 1—0—6—0; N. H. Rogers, 0.5—0—8—0.

NEW CAPS.—V. J. Ransom, D. Shackleton, C. Walker.
† denotes Amateur.

Arnold, despite injury, recovered well from a most unpropitious beginning. Arnold is still a very nimble cover point and Rogers, who scored attractively, is also a grand field. Walker established himself as a sound all-rounder, being a teasing bowler of medium pace and, sometimes, a batsman with the minimum of back-lift; yet he can score quite freely too. Hill is a much more capable all-rounder than his figures suggest and one would like to see him getting more chances. Of the younger batsmen Guard, Rayment and Gray showed considerable promise, and Blake has possibilities as a wicketkeeper-batsman. Harrison—batsman, wicketkeeper and splendid field—still could not find a regular place. Cannings has been registered from Warwickshire, and Debnam from Kent. Players not re-engaged are listed in *Valete*.

D. SHACKLETON   G. HILL   C. WALKER

Kent

Played 26, Won 7, Lost 15, Drawn 4

KENT won nearly twice as many matches as in 1948—7 against 4; but as they lost 15 (as against 11 in 1948) their final position was little better—13th instead of 15th.

Nevertheless, Kent contrived to play the cricket that earned them this tribute from Billy Griffith : "Playing against Kent is always something to be enjoyed." The Kent XI does play as if it understands that cricket should be played against the clock as well as against the other side.

There were two main reasons for Kent's comparatively poor showing— injuries, and, most important, the lack of reserves. In addition, neither Todd nor Fagg did so well—Todd, indeed, in the early months was sadly out of form and luck; he came back, however, with a splendid 174 at Maidstone and thereafter batted with his old skill and steadiness. Fagg was disappointing; that he can be one of the most precise and powerful batsmen in England anyone must acknowledge; but for one reason or another he wasn't the big run-getter his technique and ability make us expect.

Thus Ames, in his 44th year, had to carry a bigger burden than ever. He batted magnificently, and scored over 2,000 runs with seven centuries— including a masterly 152 not out, out of 250 for 5, to save the game against the New Zealanders. He has now scored 95 centuries and every man of Kent and Kentish man looks forward to his 100th in 1950.

BATTING

			Inns.	N.O.	Runs	H.S.	Avge.
L. E. G. Ames	..		47	2	2125	160	47.22
†H. A. Pawson			12	1	420	54*	38.18
A. E. Fagg	..		42	2	1508	129	37.70
†J. G. W. Davies			14	0	462	99	33.00
L. J. Todd	..		49	1	1460	174	30.41
P. Hearn			33	2	729	74	23.51
B. Edrich	..		42	3	893	193*	22.99
T. G. Evans	..		42	1	870	76	21.21
A. H. Phebey	..		28	0	554	68	19.78
D. V. P. Wright			29	18	184	50*	16.72
†E. Crush			36	3	486	51	14.72
†D. G. Clark	..		44	6	537	58*	14.13
F. Ridgway			35	5	415	89	13.83
R. R. Dovey	..		46	8	482	52*	12.68
R. Mayes		..	8	0	90	37	11.25

ALSO BATTED.—J. Aitchison, 0, 2; J. Walker, 0, 19*; †J. W. Martin, 3, 10, 0, 14; †H. J. Pocock, 0, 20, 11, 8, 10, 4; A. Debnam, 2, 10, 4, 0, 2, 4; G. Ward, 6*, 4, 4*, 5; C. Lewis, 0, 20, 0, 2*, 0, 0*; †D. G. Ufton, 27*, 0, 14, 11; †B. J. K. Pryer, 0, 7; †A. W. H. Mallett, 14, 3, 34*, 1, 3.

BOWLING

			Overs	Mdns.	Runs	Wkts.	Avge.
D. V. P. Wright	..		727.1	124	2715	128	21.21
F. Ridgway	..		825.1	177	2201	97	22.69
C. Lewis	..		46.1	19	194	8	24.25
†J. W. Martin	..		104.1	17	286	11	26.00
R. R. Dovey	..		954.1	289	2234	73	30.60
B. Edrich	..		432.2	112	1228	37	33.18
†J. G. W. Davies	..		199.4	53	522	15	34.80
A. Debnam	..		67	11	219	6	36.50
†E. Crush	..		536	106	1563	36	43.41
†A. W. H. Mallett	..		150	33	373	8	46.62
L. J. Todd	..		79	25	192	3	64.00

ALSO BOWLED.—L. E. G. Ames, 18—0—86—2; T. G. Evans, 3—0—12—0; J. Aitchison; 7.3—0—33—3; †H. J. Pocock, 11—0—53—1; R. Mayes, 2—0—18—0; P. Hearn, 7—3—13—1; †D. G. Clark, 1—0—5—0; †H. A. Pawson, 2—0—22—0; †B. J. K. Pryer, 22—0—96—4.

NEW CAPS.—†D. G. Clark, B. Edrich, †A. W. H. Mallett. † denotes Amateur.

Pawson and Davies strengthened the side when they could play, but Evans was a great disappointment as a batsman; with so much ability and with Kent's urgent need for a run-getter at 7 or 8 he earned justifiable criticism by his lack of restraint. Phebey, Hearn and Brian Edrich all showed again that they could bat—indeed Edrich's 193 at Tunbridge Wells involved a control and judgement beyond his years. But too often the Kent batting reports could read: "The last 7 wickets fell for 60 runs."

The bowling on paper looked well balanced though in practice upset by injuries and absences. Ridgway was faster than in '48, and can genuinely bowl the out swinger; he bowled over 800 overs, always tried hard and deserved his best season.

Dovey bowled thoughtfully and steadily again; he is a better bowler than figures show. Edrich had two excellent performances, but otherwise his right-hand off-breaks were expensive. Finally Wright: out of the game for part of the season and in and out of form, he won several matches by unplayable bowling. At his best he is still the finest of his kind.—J.H.C.

F. RIDGWAY

B. EDRICH

P. HEARN

Lancashire

Played 26, Won 6, Lost 7, Drawn 13

ONLY three times since 1919 have Lancashire finished lower than sixth; last season was one of them. Yet they finished well with a successful August.

Everyone was delighted to see Pollard rewarded with a fine Benefit after years of valiant service, but on the firm wickets he was not the force of old and, however well Greenwood did as an opening bowler, the lack of really effective pace was the county's biggest handicap. Then, too, Nigel Howard's captaincy was criticised and the members' enclosure seemed divided into opposing factions on the matter. Certainly, once made captain, he should have been better supported. Inevitably he made mistakes, but he brought to the job a refreshing zest and enthusiasm and his declaration when the second New Zealand match at Liverpool might easily have fizzled out did a fine service to cricket. No wonder his stylish batting suffered with the controversy buzzing around his ears.

Washbrook's sound judgement and advice were too often lacking as he was twice seriously injured and out of the side for many matches. When he played his batting was in a class of its

BATTING

		Inns.	N.O.	Runs	H.S.	Avge.
C. Washbrook	.. ..	24	0	1262	141	52.58
A. Wharton	.. ..	38	4	1480	139	43.52
K. Grieves	.. ..	42	5	1407	128	38.02
G. A. Edrich	.. ..	42	4	1436	136*	37.78
W. Place	.. ..	37	2	1287	226*	36.77
J. T. Ikin	.. ..	49	5	1588	167	36.09
†J. H. G. Deighton	..	6	1	151	79	30.20
R. Tattersall	.. ..	21	13	235	39	29.37
J. Kelly	.. ..	6	1	124	58	24.80
†B. J. Howard	.. ..	9	1	187	56	23.37
P. Greenwood	.. ..	32	6	572	52	22.00
†N. D. Howard	.. ..	49	4	847	95	18.82
W. B. Roberts	.. ..	24	5	267	41*	14.05
R. Pollard	.. ..	34	4	365	52	12.16
A. Barlow	.. ..	18	3	160	44	10.66
M. Hilton	.. ..	6	1	49	15	9.80
J. G. Lomax	.. * ..	6	0	51	14	8.50
R. Berry	.. ..	16	1	86	22	5.73
A. Wilson	.. ..	19	8	25	8*	2.27

ALSO BATTED.—R. Alderson, 55; D. Stone, 1*, 0, 46.

BOWLING

		Overs	Mdns.	Runs	Wkts.	Avge.
W. B. Roberts	..	813.4	339	1365	66	20.68
†J. H. G. Deighton	..	114	16	305	12	25.41
P. Greenwood	..	858.4	259	1927	75	25.69
K. Grieves	..	699.4	189	1705	63	27.06
R. Tattersall	..	430.3	137	976	36	27.11
R. Berry	..	372.4	127	823	30	27.43
J. T. Ikin	..	460.2	117	1212	44	27.54
R. Pollard	..	884.4	241	2062	73	28.24
J. G. Lomax	..	143	33	322	11	29.27
A. Wharton	..	58	12	150	5	30.00
M. Hilton	..	129.3	35	328	10	32.80

ALSO BOWLED.—G. A. Edrich, 4—2—2—0; J. Kelly, 2—0—14—0; D. Stone, 60—8—253—3.

NEW CAPS.—P. Greenwood, K. Grieves. † denotes Amateur.

own. Place, cheerful and philosophical even in adversity, could not find consistent form as an opener though playing several innings of true quality, and after injury he went in lower down, thus allowing Ikin, who had prospered at No. 1 in Washbrook's absence, to go in first. This seemed to suit Ikin, who played a really fine innings against the tourists at Manchester.

In the early part of the season much depended on Wharton as batsman and Grieves as all-rounder. Wharton played so well that he won an England cap, although technique against spin remains his Achilles heel, and Grieves, who comes from a country where the bad ball is sure to be hit

K. GRIEVES   R. BERRY   P. GREENWOOD

hard, did really good work. He might easily have achieved the "double" if he had been bowled more in the latter part of the season. The greatly improved all-round form of Greenwood was also most encouraging. He may very well revert to off-breaks when pace bowlers are found—perhaps Lomax or Stone, who has the right build for the job. Geoffrey Edrich lost his place at one time but came back again to show the fine form of which he is capable.

Lancashire will need to sort out their spin department as they have three slow left-handers, Roberts, Berry and M. Hilton, none of whom played regularly and all of whom are worth a regular place in any side. Each has his virtues, Roberts being the most experienced, Berry the most promising. Tattersall achieved good performances with his well-spun off-breaks pushed through quicker than most, his height producing lift off the pitch. Wicket-keeping remained a problem and the genial Barlow might prove the man if he could feel assured of a regular place. The fielding was variable; it could be very good. Kelly, an opening bat of promise, has been released to Derbyshire. Stanley Worthington, the former Derbyshire and England player, succeeds George Duckworth as assistant coach to Harry Makepeace.

Leicestershire

Played 26, Won 3, Lost 14, Drawn 8, No decision 1

LEICESTERSHIRE had their poorest season since the war; it was in 1939 that they last finished at the bottom with the wooden spoon. They beat Notts., Surrey and Glamorgan and won first innings points against Somerset, Middlesex, Kent, Northants. and Worcestershire.

The batting generally was an improvement on that of 1948, with Berry playing almost as well as he has ever done in his twenty-fifth season with the county, and Prentice, Tompkin, Lester and Jackson all scoring well over 1,000 runs; but the bowling figures were considerably poorer than those of the previous summer. Walsh sometimes bowled superbly well—and when he does there is no one more dangerous—but his 132 wickets for the county cost 28 runs apiece as against 170 for an average of 18 the year before.

Jackson and Sperry were more expensive than usual, too, and there is a most crying need for another pace bowler of merit. Sperry must have support because he can bowl quite brilliantly at times.

BATTING

		Inns.	N.O.	Runs	H.S.	Avge.
L. G. Berry	.. ..	46	3	1853	162	43.09
F. T. Prentice	..	46	1	1742	191	38.71
M. Tompkin	..	51	2	1735	126	35.40
G. Lester	..	53	5	1599	131	33.31
V. E. Jackson	..	50	3	1335	143	28.40
A. Riddington	..	23	3	502	72	25.10
†S. G. Symington		36	5	659	65	21.25
J. E. Walsh	..	46	3	785	97	18.25
G. Watson	..	22	2	337	63	16.85
V. Munden	..	31	5	426	67	16.38
T. A. Chapman	..	27	1	414	38	15.92
†G. Evans	..	15	2	192	65*	14.76
P. Corrall	..	42	10	370	38	11.56
J. Sperry	..	39	15	201	30	8.37

ALSO BATTED.—†P. Jaques, 55, 14; †G. S. Smith, 22, 7; C. Wooler, 6*; P. Konig, 3; †N. Dunham, 3, 12*; †E. L. Williams, 14, 3.

BOWLING

		Overs	Mdns.	Runs	Wkts.	Avge.
J. E. Walsh	..	1061.1	135	3800	132	28.78
V. E. Jackson	..	959.1	302	2275	75	30.33
J. Sperry	..	920	190	2397	72	33.29
G. Lester	..	449	92	1323	38	34.81
†G. Evans	..	197.5	42	664	16	41.50
†S. J. Symington	..	411.5	83	1312	30	43.73
A. Riddington	..	128	23	349	7	49.85
V. Munden	..	175.5	26	667	8	83.37

ALSO BOWLED.—F. T. Prentice, 21.4—4—56—1; C. Wooler, 44—6—132—3; M. Tompkin, 1—1—0—0; †N Dunham, 18—4—60—0; †E. L. Williams, 13—4—33—2.

NEW CAPS.—†G. Evans, †S. J. Symington. † denotes Amateur.

Symington led the side keenly and bowled with plenty of guts and go before Evans, the old Oxford and Glamorgan player, succeeded him, but he could not fully solve the county's biggest problem. Then, too, Munden, who should become a very useful left-hand bat if he can curb his impulses, did not come on as a bowler, and the fielding was very uneven. If all of the catches had been held the bowling figures would have looked a deal more handsome. Perhaps Wooler, who is now qualified, may be the seam bowler required.

Berry plays more off the back foot than he used to but so remarkably consistent a bat is perfectly entitled to adjust his method. He has now scored more runs and more centuries than any other Leicestershire player. Prentice and Lester each made more runs than before; Prentice, forceful and enterprising with a fine shot past mid-on, Lester, a sound and solid opener and useful googly bowler too. It was good to see Tompkin in better fettle again; he takes time to warm up and sometimes plays across the line but his powerful cover strokes are a joy.

G. LESTER

A. RIDDINGTON

V. E. MUNDEN

The middle batting lacked stability although Riddington played some good innings when fit from an injury sustained at practice. He seems to show more concentration at No. 1 and his steady left-arm slows might well be used more.

To everyone's pleasure Corrall had a record county Benefit and he kept wicket as well as ever. Prentice and Watson have a joint Testimonial this summer and the county are playing a match at Coalville for the first time in many years. Mr. G. O. J. Elliott resigned soon after the season finished. He had been secretary since November, 1945. C. H. Palmer (Worcs.) has been appointed in his stead and will captain the side when registered by M.C.C.

Middlesex

Played 26, Won 14, Lost 3, Drawn 9

MIDDLESEX finished up joint leaders in the Championship in spite of the cavalier and unreliable nature of their play and limited bowling strength. The batting did not acquit itself as well as expected, and often during the later games major burdens fell on Sims, Young and Leslie Compton. In addition, matches were jeopardised by strange fielding errors which extra fielding practice failed to correct. Denis Compton had a satisfactory batting season, but was not often seen at his scintillating best; his bowling was often more than useful, while his fielding and elan often infused new life into the side. Edrich displayed little of his inherent greatness, his batting acquiring an awkward and studious quality. Brown had a patchy season, scoring a double century against Kent, and, though full of shots on occasion, is still allergic to the ball that moves in to him. Robertson, graceful and correct as ever, was often out as a result of some wayward shots.

Sharp established himself as a solid batsman whose best place is probably No. 1; Thompson, forceful as ever, was unlucky to lose his place at the end of the season. Dewes, a hard

BATTING

	Inns.	N.O.	Runs	H.S.	Avge.
D. Compton	41	4	1931	182	52.18
J. D. Robertson ..	45	1	1710	331*	38.86
†W. J. Edrich ..	40	3	1422	182	38.43
S. M. Brown	45	1	1568	200	35.63
H. Sharp	36	5	1020	102	32.90
†J. G. Dewes ..	16	1	491	92	32.73
A. Thompson ..	24	3	682	89	32.47
†R. W. V. Robins ..	21	2	521	68	27.42
L. H. Compton ..	41	7	884	88	26.00
†F. G. Mann ..	38	1	791	86	21.37
J. A. Young ..	28	6	423	62	19.22
J. Sims	38	6	523	61	16.34
†J. J. Warr ..	14	7	98	47	14.00
L. H. Gray ..	23	14	52	7	5.77

ALSO BATTED.—†G. O. Allen, 10, 91, 0, 98; †R. S. Cooper, 36, 4, 8; L. Devereux, 32, 11; R. Routledge, 1*, 12; †L. B. Thompson, 0, 13; †H. Brearley, 18, 2, 24, 11; †E. A. Ingram 0*; †J. L. Swann, 19, 13; F. Titmus, 13, 4*; †M. L. Laws, 0*.

BOWLING

	Overs	Mdns.	Runs	Wkts.	Avge.
†G. O. Allen	67.2	9	179	13	13.76
J. A. Young	1249.1	489	2423	131	18.49
†J. J. Warr	273.4	60	743	31	23.96
L. H. Gray	692.4	167	1566	63	24.85
J. Sims	1159	188	3284	126	26.06
H. Sharp	136.5	27	373	12	31.08
†R. W. V. Robins ..	90.2	12	314	10	31.40
D. Compton	659.4	119	2069	63	32.84
†W. J. Edrich ..	412.2	73	1157	30	38.56

ALSO BOWLED.—A. Thompson, 4—0—30—0; †L. B. Thompson, 14—8—18—0; R. Routledge, 40—7—141—2; S. M. Brown, 3—1—6—0; †F. G. Mann, 3.5—0—22—0; †E. A. Ingram, 48—21—80—2; L. H. Compton, 10—2—27—1; F. Titmus, 2—0—9—0; †J. L. Swann, 14.1—1—53—2.

NEW CAPS.—†J. G. Dewes, †J. J. Warr. † denotes Amateur.

hitting and aggressive Cambridge bat, took his appearances with Middlesex rather seriously and his batting for them was cramped and less attractive. Leslie Compton improved both in wicketkeeping and batting, and with Young and Sims became one of the team's mainstays. Young fielded well, bowled his left-arm slows for long periods, and his batting improved out of all knowledge, especially against slow and medium bowling.

Sims became almost first favourite at Lord's, the crowd always appreciative of his keenness and long service; a tower of strength in several crises, he hit boundaries when the better known batsmen had been struggling. Gray had his usual measure of hard work and bad luck, but was eventually displaced by Warr of Cambridge, a promising medium fast bowler.

Mann hit attractively but was unreliable, and is still inclined to hit across the line of the ball against spin bowling, while his captaincy lost something of its virile quality. G. O. Allen and Robins played well on their infrequent appearances, but the reserves did not display any outstanding talent except for young Titmus, a sound batsman of even temperament who drives well.

With their several failings, Middlesex yet remained one of the most attractive sides in the country and drew large, enthusiastic crowds wherever they went. Although they might feel more certain of honours if some of Yorkshire's determination was infused into them, those honours might be won at the expense of sparkle, and that of course would be a great loss to the county game.—WALTER FLACK.

| H. SHARP | A. THOMPSON | J. G. DEWES |

Northamptonshire

Played 26, Won 10, Lost 7, Drawn 9

THE renaissance of Northamptonshire cricket, so long awaited and so welcome to all without exception, was due in very large part to the powerful and able leadership of F. R. Brown (and he completed the " double " in all first-class matches for good measure). But it was also a fine reward for all the hard work put in since the war to build up a successful team.

BATTING

		Inns.	N.O.	Runs	H.S.	Avge.
N. Oldfield	.. ..	47	3	2192	168	49.81
D. Brookes	.. ..	50	5	2022	257	44.93
D. Barrick	.. ..	18	4	595	147*	42.50
E. Davis	.. ..	26	1	851	171	34.04
W. Barron	.. ..	30	1	908	109	31.31
F. Jakeman	.. ..	33	2	963	169	31.06
†F. R. Brown	.. ..	40	3	1001	94	27.05
P. Davis	.. ..	17	1	427	104	26.68
J. E. Timms	.. ..	23	0	531	113	23.08
R. W. Clarke	.. ..	40	12	627	51*	22.39
†A. C. L. Bennett	.. ..	5	0	104	45	20.80
V. H. Broderick	.. ..	39	2	757	100	20.45
R. G. Garlick	.. ..	31	9	358	51	16.27
A. E. Nutter	.. ..	33	5	314	44	11.21
K. Fiddling	.. ..	25	12	116	23	8.92
†J. Webster	.. ..	7	2	27	13	5.40

ALSO BATTED.—†C. B. Clarke, 5, 0*, 4, 2*; †K. Ablack, 4*; †W. M. E. White, 2, 4, 13*, 17*; G. Brice, 3, 4*, 20; D. Constable, 8, 12; †A. F. Skinner, 10, 2.

BOWLING

		Overs	Mdns.	Runs	Wkts.	Avge.
†F. R. Brown	..	839.2	222	2226	94	23.68
A. E. Nutter	..	634.4	159	1544	62	24.90
R. G. Garlick	..	787	193	2052	81	25.33
†J. Webster	..	98.4	17	286	11	26.00
V. H. Broderick	..	711.5	213	1759	63	27.92
R. W. Clarke	..	842.5	156	2467	88	28.03
G. Brice	..	62	11	200	5	40.00
D. Barrick	..	60.4	3	285	5	57.00

ALSO BOWLED.—†K. Ablack, 31—6—111—1; †W. M. E. White, 45—10—122—2; D. Brookes, 3—0—24—0; W. Barron, 3.5—0—15—2; J. E. Timms, 23—8—42—0; †C. B. Clarke, 55—6—185—3.

NEW CAPS.—R. G. Garlick, R. W. Clarke. † denotes Amateur.

Kent were beaten twice (Northampton's first " double " in 20 years), and so, too, were Sussex; and during August successive innings victories were gained over Derby, Notts and Gloucestershire. This makes happy reading compared with only seven wins and thirty-nine losses in the three previous seasons! Their best position between the wars was 12th in 1919. Only twice in their history have they finished higher than in 1949—in 1912, when they were runners-up to Yorkshire, and in 1913, when they were fourth.

In Brookes and Oldfield, Northampton had one of the best pair of openers in the country. Oldfield, showing extraordinary consistency, scored two thousand runs for the first time at the age of thirty-nine, and set up a new county aggregate record. Brookes did not strike his best form until late in the season but he also topped 2,000 and his 257 against Gloucestershire equalled Bakewell's record for the highest individual score for the county. All the other batsmen had to fight for their places— a healthy sign. Barron (No. 3) and Jakeman, two robust left-handers, would easily have scored their 1,000 if they had played regularly. Barron was apt to nibble outside the off-stump, but he certainly played some good innings. Jakeman should be very useful indeed with more concentration.

D. BARRICK   F. JAKEMAN   R. W. CLARKE

Davis lost his place as opener to Oldfield and E. Davis could not establish himself but Barrick, who made a notable debut by scoring 147 not out against the New Zealanders, will be a most useful addition to the side, especially as he shows promise as a googly bowler.

R. W. Clarke made good progress, taking 88 wickets with his left-arm fast medium " swingers," and Garlick was much more successful with his off-spinners. Broderick's length was not so accurate as usual and Nutter took fewer wickets, perhaps because he was conscious of a weakness behind his knee.

Fiddling, who was kept out of the team for some time owing to injuries, was usually dependable behind the wicket and occasionally brilliant. The fielding, inspired by F. R. Brown, was of a consistently high standard, with Nutter outstanding in the slips and Barron very good in that position also.

Timms, who joined the County as far back as 1925, completed his last season and now pursues a more leisurely sport as assistant professional to the Buckingham Golf Club.—BRIAN KEMP.

Nottinghamshire

Played 26, Won 6, Lost 5, Drawn 13, No decision 2

NOTTS. improved by three places on 1948 and finished eleventh; and if their bowling had been stronger they might have been well up amongst the leaders. In only two of their victories—both against Sussex in the course of one August week—did they bowl the other side out twice. In the other four, against Northants, Surrey, Leicester and Hampshire—all at Trent Bridge—their opponents declared and the Notts. batting achieved astounding things against the clock. Wilfred Wooller, by the way, was not to be caught in the same manner: he put the home county in after winning the toss, but rain interfered with his scheming.

At the end of the season, if one takes 15 innings as a minimum qualification, Notts. had Hardstaff (top), Simpson and Keeton in the first five of the first-class averages—a remarkable achievement even if about half their innings were played at Trent Bridge, which should add more than a decimal to an average. These three between them scored over 6,000 runs for the county, some 2,000 more than the rest of the team put together. It was a fine performance on the part of Keeton to score so freely at the age of 44. Hardstaff can hardly have had a better season and Simpson was one of the players of the year. His tour to South Africa must have done him a power of good, and he played spin with an improved technique born of extra experience.

No batsman in the team made g r e a t e r strides than Poole, an attacking left-hander who played a notable part in

BATTING

	Inns.	N.O.	Runs	H.S.	Avge.
J. Hardstaff	36	8	2005	162*	71.60
†R. T. Simpson	34	4	1977	238	65.90
W. W. Keeton	38	1	2049	210	55.37
C. J. Poole	34	4	1293	154*	43.10
C. B. Harris	29	6	844	100*	36.69
R. Giles	11	1	269	59	26.90
H. Winrow	32	3	746	105*	25.72
J. D. Clay	9	4	124	57*	24.80
P. W. Stocks	22	2	466	61	23.30
A. Jepson	29	7	487	45*	22.13
†W. A. Sime	29	3	432	63	16.61
P. F. Harvey	20	4	233	50*	14.56
E. Martin	7	2	41	18*	8.20
H. J. Butler	15	4	87	26*	7.90
E. A. Meads	25	7	133	25	7.38
F. G. Woodhead	24	3	145	40*	6.90

ALSO BATTED.—†B. H. Farr, 2, 3, 0; †A. J. Underwood, 0*; †B. Notley, 0; †E. Rowe 1*, 0; A. Richardson, 0, 4*, 0*, 0, 5.

the races against the clock. Against Leicester he scored his hundred in an hour—the quickest of the season. That ripe character, Harris, who was troubled by injury in his Benefit year, still did well—this time in the middle of the order, where perhaps he can suit his tempo to the needs of the situation. Winrow had a fair

BOWLING		Overs	Mdns.	Runs	Wkts.	Avge.
H. J. Butler	..	487.4	112	1227	44	27.88
P. F. Harvey	..	567.1	120	1698	58	29.27
C. B. Harris	..	430.4	135	834	26	32.07
†R. T. Simpson	..	203.4	71	491	14	35.07
F. G. Woodhead	..	829.4	249	1916	53	36.15
A. Jepson ..	..	799.3	155	2213	61	36.27
†W. A. Sime ..	..	379.5	95	990	25	39.60
F. W. Stocks	..	124	29	402	10	40.20
A. Richardson	..	99	25	280	5	54.00
H. Winrow ..	..	265.2	75	769	10	76.90

ALSO BOWLED.—J. D. Clay, 6—1—25—0; J. Hardstaff, 63—12—202—4; †A. J. Underwood, 62—19—175—1; †B. H. Farr, 36—6—130—1; †B. Notley, 28—3—90—1.

NEW CAPS.—P. F. Harvey, C. J. Poole. † denotes Amateur.

summer but little would go right for Stocks, who looked so promising in 1946.

The decline in bowling was largely due to an injury to the luckless Butler in the first match; he was lost to the side for a long period. The accurate Woodhead had more success than in 1948 but Jepson, a great trier, was taxed severely by the demands which had to be made on him and he became rather stale. Richardson looked as if he might make a pace bowler.

The fielding was much improved. Rarely was it not good; at times it was very fine. Simpson, Hardstaff and Poole were all outstanding, but the most improved was Harvey, whose bowling may not have come on as much as hoped, but who held some thrilling catches in the slips and off his own attack. Sime had safe hands in the silly positions and Jepson, mostly at short leg, seldom missed a chance.

C. J. POOLE   F. G. WOODHEAD   H. WINROW

Somerset

Played 26, Won 8, Lost 15, Drawn 3

ALTHOUGH Somerset lost as many matches as anyone they drew the least, two facts which may not reflect much credit on their batting. They enjoyed a prosperous August and were concerned in several tight finishes. At Taunton, Northants. found the strain of making only 64 to win, so early in the season, almost too much for their nerve, and Buse, affirming that straight bowling would do the trick, was proved all but right: he had 7 for 26.

Somerset had a most varied attack and it was good to see Hazell doing so splendidly in his Benefit year—and a dry one at that—and Lawrence taking over 100 wickets for the first time, his twiddlers bemusing Hampshire in particular. His batting but he fielded with great agility and held 37 catches. Hazell headed the averages for the third successive year, bowling always with accuracy. Against Gloucester he set up a world record by bowling 17 successive maidens.

Wellard's pace at so advanced an age remained one of the wonders of cricket; it is good that the county had second thoughts and re-engaged him for mid-week matches in 1950,

BATTING

	Inns.	N.O.	Runs	H.S.	Avge.
†M. M. Walford	16	2	763	120	54.50
H. Gimblett	50	3	2063	156	43.89
†H. E. Watts	13	0	483	110	37.15
M. F. Tremlett	43	1	1012	104	24.09
H. T. F. Buse	48	3	1020	117	22.66
†S. S. Rogers	20	2	400	61	22.22
M. Coope	42	1	826	102*	20.14
†G. E. S. Woodhouse	49	7	841	59	20.02
H. W. Stephenson	43	4	735	88	18.84
E. Hill	40	1	718	60	18.41
†F. Castle	6	0	102	52	17.00
W. T. Luckes	8	4	66	30*	16.50
†G. R. Langdale	10	1	138	63*	15.33
A. W. Wellard	46	3	603	54	14.02
J. Lawrence	49	7	583	45	13.88
H. L. Hazell	39	23	185	29	11.56
†N. S. Mitchell-Innes	14	0	157	42	11.21
L. Angell	18	2	160	45	10.00
J. Redman	10	3	45	12	6.42

ALSO BATTED.—†R. Genders, 3, 22, 0, 4; †R. J. O. Meyer, 14, 11; Roy Smith, 0, 40.

BOWLING

	Overs	Mdns.	Runs	Wkts.	Avge.
H. L. Hazell	923.1	303	2065	106	19.48
M. F. Tremlett	492	116	1324	61	21.70
J. Lawrence	771.3	123	2433	107	22.73
H. T. F. Buse	729.2	163	2017	79	25.53
A. W. Wellard	1019.1	221	2725	87	31.32
J. Redman	153.1	19	498	11	45.27

ALSO BOWLED.—Roy Smith, 7—1—29—0; †W. R. Genders. 4—2—6—0; H. Gimblett, 20—4—60—1; M. Coope, 17—1—93—1; †R. J. O. Meyer, 47—10—150—3; E. Hill, 3—0—25—1; †G. R. Langdale, 81—9—307—3.

NEW CAPS.—E. Hill, H. W. Stephenson, †S. S. Rogers. † denotes Amateur.

because they still need him. Tremlett's length and direction were still uncertain but he could not bowl in ten matches and so probably missed the "double," a distinction which might fall to Buse one of these days (Buse was the most successful all-rounder, moving the ball a lot whenever conditions suited and remaining happy under any stress). Tremlett's batting already is a force and his fielding close in on the off is top-rate.

In batting, until August arrived, the county once more leaned very heavily on Gimblett, who enjoyed perhaps his best season with five hundreds, including two in the Hampshire match at Taunton, in his first 2,000 run aggregate. At Taunton also he hit Thomas Goddard very firmly into the river—an achievement which always gives him (Gimblett) much pleasure. Hill was out of form and luck, but will surely come again, and Coope, who can be so good, was so unpredictable that he was not re-engaged. A decision which the county may have regretted. Soon there came welcome news that he was to remain.

Walford, more restrained than usual, and Watts, more successful for the county than before, brought welcome reinforcement in August. Earlier, Rogers had enjoyed a hard-hitting purple patch which along with his zestful fielding endeared him to home crowds, but then was injured and met with less success; Mitchell-Innes could not find his touch in May and

Woodhouse, a keen and unselfish leader, may have found his batting affected by the burden of captaincy. Angell showed promise as a sound player.

Stephenson succeeded Luckes as wicketkeeper and at once won the highest praise. He missed several matches, yet still had 83 victims, a county record. But it was his method which impressed more than figures; and he is a very useful bat.

As Woodhouse cannot play regularly in 1950, Somerset announced during the winter that their new captain was to be Rogers. He will bring great enthusiasm to the task. Brigadier E. H. Lancaster has now resigned after being honorary secretary since 1937.

H. W. STEPHENSON   H. L. HAZELL   G. E. S. WOODHOUSE

Surrey

Played 26, Won 11, Lost 8, Drawn 6, No Decision 1

SURREY'S final position, fifth, did not do full justice to their powers; but they were not one of the best fielding sides and their batting had weaknesses against googly bowling.

Certainly their attack was the most varied they have had for years. Alec Bedser, however jaded after his South African trip, still had one of his fine records, and Laker and Surridge have never bowled better—Laker after being troubled by early injury. But quite the most improved cricketer in the side —and in England too—was Eric Bedser, who developed into one of the very best off-spin bowlers in the country. His all-round prowess might very well take him to Australia without the bother of paying his own fare. Lock, too, came on very well as a slow left-arm bowler. An attack like this, ably reinforced by Parker's medium pace, was always good enough to dismiss opponents for moderate scores.

The batting figures look impressive enough. Fishlock once more was at the top; what wonderful consistency he shows. He is moreover a very young forty in the field. Parker, too, essentially a forward player, liked the firm wickets and had a very good season, playing the highest innings of his career against the New Zealanders.

BATTING

	Inns.	N.O.	Runs	H.S.	Avge.
L. B. Fishlock	53	2	2219	210	43.50
J. F. Parker	46	4	1740	255	41.42
H. S. Squires	49	3	1720	210	37.39
G. J. Whittaker ..	29	4	924	148	36.96
E. A. Bedser	54	5	1654	163	33.75
D. G. W. Fletcher ..	23	1	633	111	28.77
B. Constable	31	0	863	100	27.83
A. J. McIntyre ..	51	3	1188	143*	24.75
†M. R. Barton ..	48	4	931	101*	21.15
A. V. Bedser	31	8	444	53*	19.30
J. C. Laker	37	6	538	100	17.35
E. A. Watts	10	1	119	44	13.22
G. A. R. Lock ..	32	14	211	29	11.72
†W. S. Surridge ..	28	2	300	41*	11.53
J. W. McMahon ..	15	7	21	6*	2.62

ALSO BATTED.—D. R. Cox, 9, 2*, 7, 0*; P. Westerman, 5, 1*, 10*, 0, 6, 2; T. H. Clark, 59; A. F. Brazier, 20, 11, 0, 0, 7; G. N. G. Kirby, 14*, 0; †E. R. T. Holmes, 50*, 23.

BOWLING

	Overs	Mdns.	Runs	Wkts.	Avge.
A. V. Bedser	848.2	226	1820	96	18.95
J. C. Laker	1121.1	399	2276	117	19.45
E. A. Bedser	823	251	2009	84	23.91
G. A. R. Lock	713.1	279	1529	61	25.06
J. F. Parker	529.5	124	1299	49	26.51
†W. S. Surridge ..	548.5	98	1813	68	26.66
E. A. Watts	111	21	331	11	30.09
P. Westerman	95	23	258	7	36.85
H. S. Squires	168.1	33	452	11	41.09
J. W. McMahon ..	238	46	807	19	42.47
D. R. Cox	66	11	238	5	47.60

ALSO BOWLED.—B. Constable, 82—13—283—4; L. B. Fishlock, 3—1—8—0; T. H. Clark, 4—0—10—0.

NEW CAP.—G. J. Whittaker. † denotes Amateur.

Whittaker has always been in the wars and last season a strained knee put him out just when he was batting with fine power and promise. Constable could not find a regular place but he got runs at critical times and fielded with immense zest. Probably he would do even better if he could feel his place was secure. Fletcher did not really fulfil his great promise of 1947 and one noticed that his on-side play had developed at the expense of his handsome strokes to the off—a reflection perhaps of a modern bowling trend.

As he made as many " ducks " last season as he is likely to notch in the next three summers, McIntyre did very well to reach 1,000 runs again. He kept wicket splendidly, his method with spin bowling being much improved. Barton, whose technique is best suited to hard wickets, might have been expected to score more runs; yet he is the best captain Surrey have had since the war, and he often batted well in a crisis.

Watts's Benefit—a county record—delighted all without exception; may Fishlock have equal fortune this summer. These are happy thoughts, but during the winter there came the saddest news—the death of Squires, who had enjoyed so splendid a season. An obituary notice appears on page 129.

E. A. BEDSER   A. J. McINTYRE   G. J. WHITTAKER

Sussex

Played 26, Won 7, Lost 10, Drawn 7, No Decision 2

EARLY in the season Sussex promised to make a big improvement on their position in 1948. John Langridge was in wonderful form from the start and the fielding, with Jack Oakes holding some remarkable catches, made the most of hostile bowling by Cornford and Wood.

The bowling rather lost its sting and later on there were some alarming lapses in the field. A first-class slow bowler, or any real spinner, would have lifted Sussex much higher. Mainly because of John Langridge the batting, usually so inconsistent, was better than in previous years.

Cox had his ups and downs but on the whole batted very well, if not perhaps with all his old freedom. The Oakes brothers were disappointing with the bat, although Jack, one of the finest hitters in county cricket, began in great style. He is inclined to pick the wrong ball too early in an innings.

James Langridge once again provided stability in the middle and sometimes held the side together on his own.

In the latter half of the season Sussex were lucky to have Doggart and Sheppard. Doggart showed signs of staleness towards the end but played some fine innings, notably a match-winning effort against Middlesex which disproved any theory that he cannot play spin. Sheppard, a beautiful back player, has a remarkable temperament for his years and should clearly go far. Smith has possibilities as a left-hand opener and among the youngest players Suttle—also left-hand—and Parks, a son of Jim, showed promise.

Generally speaking, the bowling once again lacked length and accuracy. Cornford began well enough but he lost his fire as the long, hard season progressed.

BATTING

	Inns.	N.O.	Runs	H.S.	Avge.
John Langridge	49	5	2850	234*	64.77
†D. S. Sheppard	21	0	913	204	43.47
G. Cox	54	6	1938	212*	40.37
James Langridge	51	9	1640	133*	39.04
†G. H. G. Doggart	23	1	715	155	32.50
C. Oakes	52	1	1459	112	28.60
J. Oakes	43	7	990	99	27.50
D. V. Smith	25	0	673	85	26.92
†H. T. Bartlett	42	6	920	111	25.55
†C. E. Winn	8	0	203	71	25.37
†S. C. Griffith	38	4	776	111	22.82
K. Suttle	9	3	127	43*	21.16
A. James	29	11	331	37*	18.38
J. Cornford	36	12	252	34	10.50
R. T. Webb	9	0	75	16	8.33
D. J. Wood	30	7	94	12*	4.08

ALSO BATTED.—†P. L. Winslow, 8, 16; G. Potter, 5; G. T. Hurst, 9, 2, 0; †R. J. Tillard, 3, 0; †J. N. Bartlett, 4*, 0; J. M. Parks, 12, 1*, 6, 7; †W. W. Davidson, 0, 1, 6; †D. M. W. Gay, 0, 5; †P. G. Laker, 8*, 6.

BOWLING

	Overs	Mdns.	Runs	Wkts.	Avge.
J. Cornford	880.5	200	2476	97	25.52
James Langridge	765.1	183	2076	69	30.08
G. T. Hurst	54	10	157	5	31.40
C. Oakes	582.3	123	1766	53	33.32
D. J. Wood	973.2	199	2905	84	34.58
A. James	611.2	166	1523	44	34.61
J. Oakes	377.2	80	1168	28	41.71
G. Cox	314.2	73	843	20	42.15

ALSO BOWLED.—D. V. Smith, 1—0—2—0; †P. L. Winslow, 7—1—23—0; K. Suttle, 4—0—6—0; John Langridge, 11.4—3—28—2; †J. N. Bartlett, 10—2—20—0; J. M. Parks, 4—1—9—1; †D. M. W. Gay, 23—6—76—3; †G. H. G. Doggart, 80.1—20—218—4; †C. E. Winn, 1—0—9—0; †H. T. Bartlett, 6—1—25—2; G. Potter, 14—2—63—0; P. G. Laker, 5—0—40—0.

NEW CAPS.—J. Oakes, †G. H. G. Doggart, †D. S. Sheppard. † denotes Amateur.

Wood also bowled with plenty of life early on, but he had to assume the role of stock bowler and his record suffered. James, a clever and extremely promising bowler in 1948, did not always do himself justice, and a lack of success worried him into changing his method. Charles Oakes took his fifty wickets as usual; one would like to see him bowling more.

Considering the bowling at his disposal Bartlett captained the side shrewdly again and Griffith, who kept wicket as well as ever, made his maiden first-class hundred in England. It must be comforting to have so genial and imperturbable a player on the side. As deputy stumper Webb showed glimpses of real ability. Bartlett has now resigned and Griffith, having taken a news-paper appointment, will be available mid-week only. R. G. Hunt and G. H. G. Doggart are now joint captains.

D. J. WOOD   G. COX   J. OAKES

Warwickshire

Played 26, Won 12, Lost 5, Drawn 8, No decision 1

IN the controversy of Amateur v. Professional captains, the traditionalists have been given considerable food for thought by Warwick-shire's success in their first full season under a professional skipper: they finished fourth, equalling their best season (1934) since the Great War.

Whatever one's views, Tom Dollery must be given full credit; he carried out his duties with vast and unassuming competence and well earned his record benefit. Nor did his batting suffer as he topped 2,000 runs and scored his maiden double-century. He was merciless against loose bowling and took 50 off a tired Hampshire attack in eleven minutes.

The most consistent of the other regular batsmen was Gardner. Although his style is somewhat cramped he watches the ball and has the gift of concen-tration. Another newcomer, Wolton, who is a brilliant outfielder, has the strokes and drives beautifully, but is inclined to get himself out thoughtlessly.

The batting averages, as in 1947, were headed by the Marlborough school-master, Thompson, who is a most talented attacking batsman. Ord had rather a disappointing season, although improving towards the end.

In Kardar, Townsend and Derief Taylor, Warwickshire had three good all-rounders. The unflurried Kardar, as good as any of his kind, bowled his left-arm spinners intelligently, varying length and flight, but did not do himself full justice with the bat. Townsend, scoring his 1,000 runs, showed much promise. He drove well, fielded superbly at slip, where he held more catches in a season than any Warwickshire fielder, and with more confidence should take many wickets with his inswingers. T a y l o r, chosen originally for his spin bowling, developed into a useful batsman. T h e w i c k e t keeper, Spooner, was neat and most competent, but his batting did not improve as much as was hoped.

Both opening bowlers, Pritchard and Grove, had a good season. Pritchard moved the ball either way, was quick off the pitch and attacked the s t u m p s. Grove kept an immaculate length with his inswingers and earned his success. The patient and tireless Hollies took 144 wickets with consistently accurate leg-breaks and googlies, but his batting somewhat disappointed his large number of light-hearted admirers; he was unable to emulate his 1948 feat of reaching double figures.—BRIAN KEMP.

BATTING

	Inns.	N.O.	Runs	H.S.	Avge.
†J. R. Thompson	12	2	609	103	60.90
H. E. Dollery ..	48	4	2084	200	47.36
Derief Taylor ..	14	4	438	121	43.80
F. C. Gardner ..	53	5	1657	140*	34.52
A. V. Wolton ..	43	9	978	111*	28.76
J. S. Ord ..	50	3	1308	156*	27.82
†A. H. Kardar ..	21	3	471	57	26.16
†R. H. Maudsley ..	11	0	269	107	24.45
†P. Cranmer ..	7	1	144	57	24.00
A. Townsend ..	48	4	1056	76	24.00
R. T. Spooner ..	34	9	587	70	23.48
V. H. D. Cannings ..	9	5	77	26*	19.25
K. A. Taylor ..	15	0	247	89	16.46
C. W. Grove ..	43	3	511	81	12.77
T. L. Pritchard ..	35	4	332	44	10.70
L. Croom ..	8	0	73	26	9.12
W. E. Hollies ..	24	13	47	8*	4.27

ALSO BATTED.—R. G. Thompson, 17, 0*; H. E. Roberts, 1, 30, 2, 0; J. T. Kendall, 4, 18*, 0; †N. A. Shortland, 4, 13, 21, 6*; †J. M. A. Marshall, 8*, 5, 18, 28, 0; D. D. Taylor, 54, 26, 5, 38, 8; †E. B. Lewis, 6, 7, 51; R. Brindle, 42, 32; P. H. Bromley, 4, 1*; D. Heath, 6, 9, 0, 9; R. E. Hitchcock, 15, 0; †D. G. Shaw, 17; L. Flint, 2, 1*, 7*, 1, 0*.

BOWLING

	Overs	Mdns.	Runs	Wkts.	Avge.
D. D. Taylor ..	42	16	129	7	18.42
W. E. Hollies ..	1369.1	497	2858	144	19.84
C. W. Grove ..	949.1	244	2243	95	23.61
A. Townsend ..	435	100	1052	44	23.90
†A. H. Kardar ..	573.2	216	1148	48	23.91
T. L. Pritchard ..	1043	189	2794	113	24.72
Derief Taylor ..	205	79	402	12	33.50
V. H. D. Cannings ..	163.4	55	311	9	34.55
L. Flint ..	92	24	210	4	52.50

ALSO BOWLED.—J. S. Ord, 3—1—6—0; †P. Cranmer, 6—0—29—0; †J. M. A. Marshall, 35—10—57—1; †R. H. Maudsley, 41—15—98—2; †N. A. Shortland, 3—1—2—0; R. G. Thompson, 24—9—66—1; P. H. Bromley, 6—2—15—0; A. V Wolton, 5—0—21—0; †D. G. Shaw 34—8—106—2.

NEW CAPS.—F. C. Gardner, A. V. Wolton, †A. H. Kardar. † denotes Amateur.

F. C. GARDNER

A. H. KARDAR

A. TOWNSEND

Worcestershire

Played 26, Won 12, Lost 7, Drawn 7

AT the start of the season most people could have got very long odds on Worcestershire being champions; yet they very nearly pulled it off and enjoyed their best summer since 1907, when they were second. Once again their strength was bowling—even if Jackson had a lean season—but the batting was much improved. The fielding was only moderate, although Yarnold * had 110 victims behind the stumps—more in a year than any other

BATTING

	Inns.	N.O.	Runs	H.S.	Avge.
E. Cooper	50	6	1916	193	43.54
†C. H. Palmer ..	19	1	722	136	40.11
†M. L. Y. Ainsworth ..	13	1	397	96	33.08
D. Kenyon ..	54	1	1691	182	31.90
R. E. S. Wyatt ..	23	2	654	112	31.14
L. Outschoorn ..	52	4	1289	215*	26.85
†R. E. Bird ..	42	4	1016	116	26.73
R. O. Jenkins ..	46	7	982	91*	25.17
†A. F. T. White ..	30	2	643	64	22.96
G. Dews	15	2	255	45	19.61
R. Howorth ..	49	4	860	72	19.11
†P. E. Richardson ..	7	0	108	39	15.42
H. Yarnold ..	44	11	485	61	14.69
F. Cooper ..	12	2	131	52	13.10
R. T. D. Perks ..	47	4	503	51	11.69
P. F. Jackson ..	27	12	115	29	7.66

ALSO BATTED.—N. K. Whiting, 18, 5, 56, 1; H. Horton, 12, 11; †P. J. Whitcombe 4, 8*; G. Darks, 8*, 4, 20; †R. C. M. Kimpton, 93*, 0; †C. R. Maxwell, 31; J. Flavell, 6.

BOWLING

	Overs	Mdns.	Runs	Wkts.	Avge.
R. Howorth ..	1113.4	386	2278	117	19.47
R. Jenkins ..	982.5	159	3314	159	20.84
R. T. D. Perks ..	1051.2	281	2829	116	24.38
†R. E. Bird ..	77.3	9	303	9	33.66
P. F. Jackson ..	617.1	129	1704	48	35.50
†C. H. Palmer ..	265	77	698	18	38.77
†R. E. S. Wyatt ..	124	44	278	5	55.60

ALSO BOWLED.—F. Cooper, 4—0—23—0; G. Darks, 43—4—182—2; L. Outschoorn, 57.4—11—201—2; J. Flavell, 7—1—39—0; †M. L. Y. Ainsworth, 1—0—6—0.
NEW CAP.—†M. L. Y. Ainsworth. † denotes Amateur.

'keeper except Ames— and at the end of a hard day, especially late in the season, the age of the side began to tell. The running between wickets was sometimes not too sprightly, nor the chasing to the boundary; yet age and experience counted for much in other ways.

All this erroneously suggests the team were a lot of greybeards with several feet in the grave. But, certainly, if the county are to maintain their position, they will have to find quite a few new players.

Eddie Cooper, who had easily his best season, developed into a really good opener, precise and consistent, and Kenyon too came on fast, looking a class player whenever he made runs, although commendable enterprise was sometimes his undoing. There was no telling what Outschoorn might do; he had a fair summer and needed some luck before he made a big score. Still, he is just about the best slipper or gully in the country.

Palmer was perhaps a little stale after his South African winter and needed longer to play himself in but he did well in August and once more was a useful change bowler, spin or seam. Ainsworth, strong on the off but not too reliable against spin, was again a force when available, and Wyatt, after a poor beginning, was still rewarded by sound technique. That he is a very good captain goes almost without saying. Bird, perhaps with more concentration, began in fine fettle but fell away in mid-season. White, joint captain and a hard hitter when under way, had a moderate summer. Because there

* *A feat for which his county made him a gift of £100.*

H. YARNOLD   E. COOPER   D. KENYON

were few injuries Dews, F. Cooper and Whiting had limited chances—Dews especially is a much improved batsman. Richardson, a young left-hander, showed good promise.

Perks was still one of the very best bowlers in the country in his opening spell, but he tired quickly. He is a great trier and not unwilling to experiment. Howorth's batting was inconsistent but his bowling was just about as effective as ever. He is very dangerous when the pitch helps him and accurate and experienced enough when it is not to let batsmen dismiss themselves. Jenkins, after his South African tour, made great strides but could not win another England cap. Sometimes he bowled badly but then came back with matchwinning spells. He bowled more quickly when the pitch helped, batted in a solid dependable way, fielded admirably and achieved a very good " double."

Yorkshire

Played 26, Won 14, Lost 2, Drawn 10

HUTTON'S golden summer, Lowson and Close achieving wonders in their first seasons, Wardle finding his best form at a vital time— these are some reasons why Yorkshire climbed back to the top. But there were others, less obvious but no less important, such as Yardley's grand captaincy, the improved fielding (due to the youth of the team) and a return of the old combative spirit, especially towards the end. Their only defeats were by Worcestershire at Sheffield and by Surrey at The Oval.

Hutton scored more runs in June (1,294) than had ever been scored in a single month, another 1,000 in August and 3,429 all told—more than any Yorkshire cricketer. Technically he remains supreme but in Test matches one could sometimes wish for an increased freedom of stroke. Perhaps he will be more carefree on big occasions in this his Benefit year.

Lowson scored more runs in his first season than any cricketer before him— and he really looked the part. Always willingly learning, he could in a year or two be Hutton all over again. His style quite naturally " tightened " a little against the accuracy of first-class bowling. The only query against his name is that of stamina. Close, too, is a " natural," but possibly he did not

BATTING

	Inns.	N.O.	Runs	H.S.	Avge.
L. Hutton	44	6	2640	269*	69.47
J. V. Wilson	41	5	1460	157*	40.55
E. Lester	49	3	1774	186	38.56
†N. W. D. Yardley	49	10	1413	134*	36.23
F. A. Lowson	51	4	1678	104	35.70
H. Halliday	23	0	773	113	33.60
†W. G. Keighley ..	9	2	211	40	30.14
D. B. Close	42	8	958	88*	28.17
W. Watson	35	2	853	119	25.84
A. Coxon	32	9	487	65*	21.17
G. A. Smithson ..	15	2	256	46*	19.69
†W. H. H. Sutcliffe ..	12	0	218	38	18.16
J. H. Wardle ..	28	4	412	70	17.16
J. P. Whitehead ..	7	3	59	23*	14.75
J. Leadbeater	6	1	68	29*	13.60
E. P. Robinson ..	22	8	151	40	10.78
†D. V. Brennan ..	32	11	123	17*	5.85
A. Mason	9	1	42	22	5.25

ALSO BATTED.—F. P. McHugh, 0; J. Firth, 18, 2, 22*; E. Barraclough, 3, 24*; R. Aspinall, 9, 5, 0, 3, 17*; C. W. Foord, 2*, 0*, 1*, 4, 6*; F. Trueman, 10, 1*, 0, 1, 0*, 0.

BOWLING

	Overs	Mdns.	Runs	Wkts.	Avge.
R. Aspinall	133.1	32	289	30	9.63
A. Coxon	920.2	238	2100	101	20.79
J. H. Wardle ..	1060.1	404	2213	100	22.13
F. Trueman ..	243.3	49	719	31	23.19
J. P. Whitehead ..	137	31	325	14	23.21
D. B. Close	1089	291	2703	105	25.74
A. Mason	464.3	164	1038	37	28.05
E. P. Robinson ..	737.3	239	1458	46	31.69
C. W. Foord ..	185.5	31	520	16	32.50
†N. W. D. Yardley ..	350	106	689	21	32.80
H. Halliday ..	106	31	242	7	34.57
L. Hutton	98	28	263	7	37.57
J. Leadbeater ..	136.1	28	427	8	53.37

ALSO BOWLED.—†W. G. Keighley, 4—0—9—0; F. P. McHugh, 59—13—147—4; E. Barraclough, 24—10—34—1; E. Lester, 13—5—26—0; J. V. Wilson, 7—0—25—0; G. A. Smithson, 3—0—27—0; †W. H. H. Sutcliffe, 20.2—1—68—2; F. A. Lowson, 3—0—15—0; W. Watson, 2—0—7—0.

NEW CAPS.— F. A. Lowson, D. B. Close. † denotes Amateur.

learn quite so much as Lowson. Instinctively he wants to get a move on. His versatility was quite astonishing but it was a pity that because of Aspinall's injury he had to bowl seamers before off-spin. Before the end of the season he was very very tired; and no wonder.

That ebullient and realistic cricketer Lester had a fine summer on the dry pitches. Wilson, a forthright left-hander with a splendid temperament, had a fine season too and of course Yardley's batting was a power, especially at times of stress. Halliday did well amidst sciatic infliction but Watson, although he had a good August, had an in and out summer and needs more assurance; and Smithson, who is not technically sound, quite lost his confidence.

If Aspinall had not strained an Achilles tendon after four matches—he missed the rest of the season—Yorkshire almost certainly would have won outright. He was a vastly improved bowler and his figures speak for themselves. Coxon once again did nobly with all his heart and soul; Whitehead, pretty quick, looked a very useful reserve; and Trueman, built for the job of a fast 'un, and with the spirit too, showed fine possibilities for a few seasons hence. Yorkshire will not hasten his development or that of any other promising player.

Wardle lost his place for six weeks possibly because he was persuaded into altering his action, but in his absence the county were admirably served by Mason, who bowled very steadily on unhelpful pitches. Leadbeater looked an accurate bowler of leg-breaks and an agile field, and McHugh showed promise of effective pace. Brennan, whose rather frail physique must be a handicap in a hard summer, once again was one of the three or four best 'keepers in England.

Close, at the age of 18 was the youngest player ever to achieve the " double " or to play for England. There had been no previous instance of a " double " in a first season.

N. W. D. YARDLEY   F. A. LOWSON   J. V. WILSON

County Captains and Secretaries

	Captains	*Secretaries*
DERBY	—	W. T. Taylor, 18, St. James's Chambers, Derby
ESSEX	{ T. N. Pearce { D. J. Insole	R. F. T. Paterson, 3, Crane Court, Chelmsford
GLAMORGAN	W. Wooller	W. Wooller & L. M. Spence, 6, High St., Cardiff
GLO'SHIRE	B. O. Allen	Lt.-Col. H. A. Henson, County Ground, Bristol
HAMPSHIRE	E. D. R. Eagar	E. D. R. Eagar & R. C. Court, County Ground, Southampton
KENT	D. G. Clark	N. Christopherson, St. Lawrence Ground, Canterbury
LANCS.	N. D. Howard	C. G. Howard, County Ground, Old Trafford
LEICESTER	—	C. H. Palmer, Market Place, Leicester
MIDDX.	R. W. V. Robins	R. W. V. Robins, Lord's Cricket Ground, St. John's Wood, London, N.W.8
NORTHANTS	F. R. Brown	Lt.-Col. A. St. G. Coldwell, County Ground, Northampton
NOTTS.	W. A. Sime	H. A. Brown, County Ground, Nottingham
SOMERSET	S. S. Rogers	N. Daniell, County Cricket Ground, Taunton
SURREY	M. R. Barton	B. K. Castor, Kennington Oval, London, S.E.11
SUSSEX	{ R. G. Hunt { G. H. G. Doggart	Secretary, County Ground, Hove, 3
WARWICK	H. E. Dollery	L. T. Deakins, County Ground, Edgbaston
WORCS.	—	Brig. M. A. Green, County Ground, Worcester
YORKS.	N. W. D. Yardley	J. H. Nash, Old Bank Chambers, Leeds, 1

A blank indicates that no appointment had been made at time of going to press.

Highest Innings for each County

Derbyshire	..	..	274 G. Davidson, v. Lancashire, at Manchester	.. 1896
Essex	..	..	343* P. A. Perrin, v. Derbyshire, at Chesterfield	.. 1904
Glamorgan	..		287* E. Davies, v. Gloucestershire, at Newport	.. 1939
Gloucestershire		..	318* W. G. Grace, v. Yorkshire, at Cheltenham	.. 1876
Hampshire	..		316 R. H. Moore, v. Warwickshire, at Bournemouth	.. 1937
Kent	..	..	332 W. H. Ashdown, v. Essex, at Brentwood	.. 1934
Lancashire	..		424 A. C. MacLaren, v. Somerset, at Taunton	.. 1895
Leicestershire		..	252* S. Coe, v. Northamptonshire, at Northampton	.. 1914
Middlesex	..		331 J. D. Robertson, v. Worcestershire, at Worcester	.. 1949
Northamptonshire		257	{ A. H. Bakewell, v. Glamorgan, at Swansea	.. 1933
			{ D. Brookes, v. Gloucestershire, at Bristol	.. 1949
Nottinghamshire		..	312* W. W. Keeton, v. Middlesex, at the Oval	.. 1939
Somerset	..		310 H. Gimblett, v. Sussex, at Eastbourne	.. 1948
Surrey	..	..	357* R. Abel, v. Somerset, at the Oval	.. 1899
Sussex	..		333 K. S. Duleepsinhji, v. Northants, at Hove	.. 1930
Warwickshire	..		305* F. R. Foster, v. Worcestershire, at Dudley	.. 1914
Worcestershire		..	276 F. L. Bowley, v. Hampshire, at Dudley	.. 1914
Yorkshire	..	..	341 G. H. Hirst, v. Leicestershire, at Leicester	.. 1905

* Not Out

GENTLEMEN v PLAYERS

Played at Lord's on July 13, 14, 15. Players won by 4 wkts.

NEEDING 139 for victory, the Players found themselves in serious trouble when Compton, their captain, was sixth out at 69, but Evans and Jenkins came to the rescue with brave and cheerful batting and were still together when the winning hit was made directly after lunch. Evans was never more audacious; and with his equally courageous partner he enjoyed some hairbreadth escapes as they hit at and ran for everything.

On the first day, in poor light, Hollies made things very unpleasant for the batsmen with clever leg-breaks, and the Gentlemen, after much indecisive batting, were dismissed in two and a half hours. A fifty stand between Hutton and John Langridge then gave the Players an immediate " edge," but a minor breakdown developed and the score became 63 for four. Yet Compton and Evans, splendidly supported by Close, averted rout, and the Players obtained a lead of 129. Close showed a maturity beyond his years, playing the highest individual innings of the match.

After Dewes and Simpson had knocked off 54 of the arrears, Jenkins busied himself with leg-spin and so upset the amateurs that half the side were gone and a deficit of 44 remained; but Bailey and van Ryneveld rose to the occasion with a brave stand of 115, Bailey scoring freely to leg and van Ryneveld excelling with forward strokes. Mann also used his feet well to improve the position of his side.—A.S.

GENTLEMEN

R. T. Simpson lbw b Jackson	6	— c Langridge b Close .. 28
J. G. Dewes b Jackson	16	— b Jenkins 33
W. J. Edrich c Evans b Perks	7	— st Evans b Jenkins .. 4
G. H. G. Doggart c Evans b Hollies	3	— c Evans b Jenkins .. 4
N. W. D. Yardley lbw b Hollies	7	— lbw b Jenkins 9
C. B. Van Ryneveld c Evans b Hollies	18	— lbw b Hollies 64
†F. G. Mann c Evans b Hollies	17	— c Compton b Jackson 43
T. E. Bailey not out	15	— lbw b Hollies 53
F. R. Brown c Langridge b Close	7	— st Evans b Hollies .. 2
A. H. Kardar hit wkt. b Close	2	— not out 16
S. C. Griffith lbw b Hollies ..	0	— c Jenkins b Jackson .. 1
B 4, lb 3 ..	7	B 4, lb 6 .. 10
Total	105	Total 267

	O.	M.	R.	W.		O.	M.	R.	W.
Perks	13	3	22	1	..	17	1	60	0
Jackson	13	3	30	2	..	20.2	7	33	2
Hollies	17.3	7	32	5	..	26	10	51	3
Close	7	2	14	2	..	22	3	52	1
Compton	—	—	—	—	..	6	1	13	0
Jenkins	—	—	—	—	..	21	8	48	4

PLAYERS

L. Hutton c Edrich b Brown ..	25	— c Kardar b Bailey .. 11
John Langridge lbw b Bailey..	31	— c Kardar b Bailey .. 10
J. D. Robertson b Bailey	1	— c Kardar b Brown .. 5
†D. Compton lbw b Yardley ..	33	— c Doggart b Brown .. 17
T. W. Graveney c Kardar b Brown	2	— b Bailey 5
D. B. Close c Simpson b Brown	65	— c Edrich b Brown .. 2
R. O. Jenkins b Bailey	5	— not out 41
T. G. Evans c Griffith b Brown	41	— not out 40
R. T. D. Perks c Dewes b Brown	13	
W. E. Hollies c Bailey b Kardar	5	
L. Jackson not out	8	
Lb 2, nb 3 ..	5	B 5, lb 3 .. 8
Total	234	Total (for 6 wkts.) 139

	O.	M.	R.	W.		O.	M.	R.	W.
Bailey	22	4	59	3	..	12	1	35	3
Edrich	9	1	30	0	..	3	0	13	0
Brown	24.4	1	80	5	..	15	2	71	3
Yardley	10	3	18	1	..	—	—	—	—
Van Ryneveld	3	0	17	0	..	—	—	—	—
Kardar	5	1	25	1	..	7	1	12	0

UMPIRES—T. J. Bartley and H. Elliott. † denotes captain.

The Universities

Oxford

(P. 15; W. 7†; L. 5; D. 3)

(† *Includes 2-day match v. M.C.C.*)

OXFORD reached peak form in the Parks. On tour the batting became uncertain and the bowling less accurate and at Lord's the side did itself no sort of justice. This was a disheartening end to what in many ways had been an outstandingly good season, including as it did the solitary defeat of the New Zealanders, victories against Yorkshire, Middlesex, Sussex, Hampshire, the Free Foresters and M.C.C., and honourable defeats by Worcestershire, Warwickshire and Surrey.

Van Ryneveld had very little experienced batting to build on so it was as well that Carr held the fort with two brilliant centuries in May. Such impressive form won an invitation

BATTING

	Inns.	N.O.	Runs	H.S.	Avge.
M. B. Hofmeyr	23	3	879	154	43.95
D. B. Carr	22	0	821	170	37.31
C. E. Winn	22	0	705	95	32.04
C. B. Van Ryneveld	24	0	767	102	31.95
P. A. Whitcombe	13	1	353	68	29.41
H. J. Potts	6	0	142	49	23.66
J. N. Bartlett	7	2	104	28	20.80
R. V. Divecha	14	6	145	68*	18.12
A. H. Kardar	12	0	211	60	17.59
I. P. Campbell	12	0	202	43	16.83
C. R. P. Rudd	20	4	260	54	16.25
G. H. Chesterton	17	6	160	43	14.54
J. W. E. Wiley	8	0	103	30	12.87
B. Boobbyer	12	0	143	28	11.91
M. H. Wrigley	14	4	69	17	6.90

ALSO BATTED.—P. Gardiner-Hill, 28, 50; P. V. Harvey, 9; D. Henderson, 9, 1; M. Ivey, 1; M. E. A. Keeling, 16; J. A. C. C. Law, 10, 12, 0, 0; D. Lewis, 7; R. C. Lewis, 34; K. A. Shearwood, 28, 0, 6*; J. P. D. Tanner, 18, 0, 0*, 1*, 17, 13.

BOWLING

	Overs	Mdns.	Runs	Wkts.	Avge.
A. H. Kardar	337.3	148	592	43	13.76
M. H. Wrigley	314.4	75	792	38	20.84
G. H. Chesterton	423.2	129	1010	46	21.95
J. N. Bartlett	145	31	448	17	26.35
P. A. Whitcombe	212.1	53	536	20	26.80
R. V. Divecha	194.1	52	471	17	27.70
C. B. Van Ryneveld	352.3	60	1064	31	34.32

ALSO BOWLED.—D. B. Carr, 23—3—83—3; D. Henderson, 16—2—55—0; R. C. Lewis, 19—6—44—1.

to Lord's after one appearance. Winn, an enterprising player who opened in 1948, became the No. 3 and though he made only one big score (95 v. Worcs.) his figures justly reflected consistency; while Hofmeyr, sound and watchful, at once secured one of the vacant opening positions. He carried his bat through an innings (95 not) against the New Zealanders—a sort of dress rehearsal for Lord's. The other place went finally to Boobbyer who came back to the side on tour after being dropped. Van Ryneveld, a fine all-round cricketer who hits the ball very firmly in front of the wicket and a leg-break bowler who can disturb the best, was No. 5.

Kardar, like Whitcombe, joined the side late because of Schools. Whitcombe could not find his bowling form of 1948 but Kardar more than maintained his, yet lost touch and timing with his batting. The No. 7 position fell to Rudd, an elegant stroke maker. Whitcombe was no mean bat at No. 8.

Campbell, an unorthodox quick-footed batsman with a remarkably good eye, was selected as wicket-keeper in preference to J. D. P. Tanner. R. V. Divecha, J. N. Bartlett (a Blue in 1946) and Tanner went on tour but were not selected for Lord's.

There being no off-spinner worthy of a place, Chesterton, an accurate medium-paced in-swinger, quickly established himself as a stock bowler and in fact took more wickets than anyone else. Whitcombe bowled splendidly against the New Zealanders but Wrigley was the more successful opening bowler throughout the season, using his height to get considerable pace and lift off the pitch. Many good judges thought Kardar the most dangerous slow left-arm bowler in England, so that with van Ryneveld (whose figures did him scant justice) Oxford had an attack well above average.

The fielding, if not brilliant, was on the whole well up to standard. Winn, at cover or in the deep, Carr and van Ryneveld close to the bat, and Boobbyer anywhere were outstanding. Old Blues who played at Lord's were van Ryneveld, Winn (the secretary), Kardar and Whitcombe.

Cambridge

(P. 15; W. 2; L. 3; D. 10†)
(† *Includes 2-day match v. Army*)

A COMPARISON of performances on the covered wickets at Fenner's with those in the Parks—which are often affected by rain—can be misleading. It may have led to an under-estimation of Cambridge strength; but certainly at Fenner's they took a long time to settle down (the scoring leaning overmuch on the Old Blues) and it was only on tour that the batting became consistently effective. They came to Lord's with an attack quite obviously weaker than Oxford's; it lacked spin and penetration, although Warr was a potential matchwinner. In the event, steadiness served them well, supported moreover by aggressive fielding, able captaincy and a fine team spirit.

Insole, Doggart and Dewes occupied high places in the first-class batting averages at the end of the summer. Insole really came into his own when playing for Essex but the other two each scored over 1,000 runs for Cambridge. To a remarkable consistency Dewes added increased freedom and power of stroke; and Doggart more than maintained his brilliant progress. Doggart began at No. 3, and then moved to 4, which let in Stevenson, whose left-arm bowling originally won him a place.

An opening partner for Dewes was immediately forthcoming in Morris, who gained in confidence and batted well at Lord's. No. 5 position went to Rimell, a left-hander who found his form with a vengeance (230 runs in two innings v. Worcester and 50 against Oxford) after a scrappy start, and

BATTING

		Inns.	N.O.	Runs	H.S.	Avge.
G. H. G. Doggart	..	24	5	1280	219*	67.36
J. G. Dewes	..	22	2	1175	204*	58.75
D. J. Insole	..	18	3	636	128*	42.40
A. C. Burnett	..	20	5	565	79*	37.66
A. G. J. Rimell	..	16	1	467	160	31.13
R. J. Morris	..	19	0	550	96	28.94
M. H. Stevenson	..	19	0	483	82	25.42
O. B. Popplewell	..	16	4	267	37	22.25
P. J. Hall	..	11	3	165	49	20.62
J. H. H. Anton	..	15	1	264	45	18.85
J. J. Warr	..	10	5	84	32*	16.80
O. J. Wait	..	8	2	19	7	3.16
B. J. K. Pryer	..	13	3	31	12	3.10

ALSO BATTED.—W. N. Coles, 14, 0, 12; G. H. C. Griffiths, 8, 3; R. B. Hawkey, 2, 13, 2, 8; Sir J. C. Hoskyns, 1, 11, 9, 42*; P. A. Kelland, 0, 1*; I. N. Mitchell, 10, 1, 25, 27; S. N. Roberts, 3, 1; I. Sutherland, 9.

BOWLING

		Overs	Mdns.	Runs	Wkts.	Avge.
O. J. Wait	..	284.5	58	842	33	25.51
J. J. Warr	..	330.2	68	842	33	25.51
D. J. Insole	..	89	17	233	9	25.88
P. A. Kelland	..	60.5	15	172	6	28.66
A. G. J. Rimell	..	201.2	75	473	16	29.56
G. H. G. Doggart	..	163.4	49	408	13	31.38
P. J. Hall	..	289.4	52	826	24	34.41
B. J. K. Pryer	..	332	63	953	23	41.43
M. H. Stevenson	..	276	88	728	14	52.00

ALSO BOWLED.—J. G. Dewes, 2—0—22—0; G. H. C. Griffiths, 14—1—53—1, R. B. Hawkey, 48—11—139—1; R. J. Morris, 67—19—192—2; S. N. Roberts, 2—0—21—0; I. Sutherland, 5—1—23—0.

Cambridge picture (with schools) in art inset

the No. 7 was Burnett, a firm forward player who averaged little under 40 although out of luck at Lord's. Popplewell, a neat, unobtrusive wicket-keeper, Hall and Warr all played useful innings and Cambridge batted pretty solidly down to No. 9.

Pryer, the only bowler remaining from 1948, lost his place on tour (along with J. H. H. Anton, a batsman) and there being no spinner of class available Insole relied on the seam attack of Warr, Wait and Hall, with Rimell and Doggart to bowl off-breaks to a length. Warr has a fine temperament and unbounded energy; he moves the ball either way and took close on 70 wickets throughout the summer; clearly a bowler of great possibilities. Wait, in-swing with a rather stiff action, may well have been impeded by an injury in the Trials, and Hall, though sometimes inaccurate, was certainly lively and he took two vital first innings wickets at Lord's.

The fielding generally was very good indeed with Insole setting an inspiring example in the covers and Doggart outstanding also. Burnett held several fine catches in the slips and Dewes was a notable outfield. Old Blues at Lord's were Insole, Doggart and Dewes, the side including an unprecedented number of seven Freshmen.

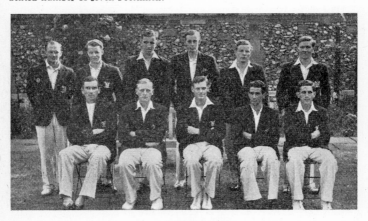

OXFORD, 1949
Standing: M. B. Hofmeyr (Pretoria H.S., S.A.), C. R. D. Rudd (Eton), G. H. Chesterton (Malvern), M. H. Wrigley (Harrow), I. P. Campbell (Canford), B. Boobbyer (Uppingham).
Seated: P. A. Whitcombe (Winchester), C. E. Winn (K.C.S., Wimbledon), C. B. van Ryneveld (Diocesan Coll., S.A.), A. H. Kardar (India), D. B. Carr (Repton).

OXFORD v. CAMBRIDGE
At Lord's: July 2, 4, 5. Cambridge won by 7 wkts.

THE favourites' path is often no easy one in University sport. Taking the match all through there was no doubt the better side won and once Cambridge had taken a grip on the game they never relaxed it. They fielded supremely well and made the utmost of their bowling, its consistent accuracy pinning Oxford in their first innings to unnatural defence.

Oxford missed a chance or two early on the Saturday. It was one of those days, perhaps, when luck was with the batsmen. Cambridge were 99 for one at lunch and 226 for three at tea, but Oxford redeemed themselves by taking five more wickets for 113 before the close. Mostly it was a day of good batting—particularly by Doggart, whose innings proclaimed true class —against splendid slow bowling by Kardar and van Ryneveld. Of five fine catches close to the bat the best were held by Carr, Boobbyer and the captain. Some admirable running between wickets was marred by two crises occasioned by Stevenson in the afternoon, both of which should have led to the end of Doggart.

Oxford at once hit trouble on the Monday; 20 for 2 and 50 for 3 when van Ryneveld was run out through a change of mind on Hofmeyr's part. Cambridge dictated their own terms and Hofmeyr carried his bat, the innings lasting 4¼ hours.

Oxford's performance on the Tuesday was much more in character. At lunch they were 155 for 3, with Carr and van Ryneveld still in skilful possession, but the fourth and vital wicket ended for 70 when Carr was run out at 179, and soon the score was 202 for seven. Sturdy resistance from the tail gave the bowlers something to shoot at but Dewes batted quite admirably in his second innings and Cambridge, aided by some rather ragged fielding, cruised home to their first victory against Oxford since 1936 after 12 minutes of the extra half-hour.

CAMBRIDGE

J. G. Dewes c Carr b Kardar	48	— c Campbell b Carr ..	45
R. J. Morris b Wrigley	46	— st Campbell b Van Ryneveld	25
M. H. Stevenson c Boobbyer b Wrigley	70	— c Hofmeyr b Van Ryneveld	37
G. H. G. Doggart b Whitcombe	60	— not out	6
A. G. J. Rimell c Kardar b Chesterton	57	— not out	8
†D. J. Insole c Van Ryneveld b Kardar	5		
A. C. Burnett b Kardar	0		
P. J. Hall c and b Van Ryneveld	12		
O. B. Popplewell st Campbell b Van Ryneveld	17		
J. J. Warr not out	15		
O. J. Wait c and b Van Ryneveld	2		
B 10, lb 17 ..	27	B 5, lb 5, w 2 ..	12
Total	359	Total (for 3 wkts.)	133

	O.	M.	R.	W.		O.	M.	R.	W.
Whitcombe	21	4	48	1	..	1	0	5	0
Wrigley	18	3	67	2	..	5	0	22	0
Chesterton	16	4	40	1	..	4	0	20	0
Kardar	49	21	79	3	..	7.5	0	41	0
Van Ryneveld ..	38.1	8	98	3	..	8	1	28	2
Carr	—	—	—	—	..	1	0	5	1

OXFORD

M. B. Hofmeyr not out	64	— c Doggart b Rimell ..	54
B. Boobbyer b Wait	10	— c Burnett b Doggart	17
C. E. Winn c Doggart b Wait	2	— b Warr	30
†C. B. Van Ryneveld run out ..	12	— c Popplewell b Warr..	47
D. B. Carr c Burnett b Hall..	13	— run out	35
A. H. Kardar lbw b Doggart..	25	— c Doggart b Wait ..	11
I. P. Campbell c Popplewell b Doggart	0	— b Doggart	16
C. R. D. Rudd b Hall	5	— b Warr	0
P. A. Whitcombe c Popplewell b Warr	14	— lbw b Doggart	47
G. H. Chesterton b Warr	9	— not out	39
M. H. Wrigley b Warr	0	— c Burnett b Warr	11
B 10, lb 3, w 1, nb 1 ..	15	— B 3, lb 7, w 2, nb 3 ..	15
Total	169	Total	322

	O.	M.	R.	W.		O.	M.	R.	W.
Warr	21.3	7	43	3	..	33.2	6	91	4
Wait	18	6	31	2	..	20	5	66	1
Hall	17	3	46	2	..	19	4	64	0
Rimell	12	9	7	0	..	10	3	29	1
Doggart	8	3	10	2	..	21	7	57	3
Stevenson	4	0	17	0	..	—	—	—	—

UMPIRES—F. Chester and E. Cooke. † denotes captain.

Good Cricket in Good Company

P. 6, W. 1, L. 3, D. 2

IF the results were not impressive it should be remembered that success in county cricket depends not only on a high standard of skill but regular practice in the first-class atmosphere. Service players taking part in occasional three-day games are certainly at some disadvantage; and, what is more, Service commitments prevent their regular appearance.

Results apart, there is no doubt that the Combined Services play an important role in the country's cricket. Young players from the county ground staffs can get good cricket during their period of National Service, and assimilate useful experience of first-class play without the fierce competition of championship matches. The regular serving man also has chances to develop his game in good company.

Peter May, at the age of 19, was the outstanding performer in 1949. Both in concentration and stroke-range he is uncommonly well equipped for his years, and his technique against spin, as the New Zealanders were quick to spot, is remarkably mature. His on-side play is particularly strong although he is inclined at the moment to over-do the cross-bat push off his legs. A lot more

P. B. H. MAY

COMBINED SERVICES—BATTING

	Inns.	N.O.	Runs	Hghst.	Avge.
P. B. H. May (R.N.) ..	12	1	695	175	63.18
R. G. Wilson (R.A.F.)..	10	2	298	100	37.25
J. E. Manners (R.N.) ..	8	0	281	123	35.12
A. Oakman (Army) ..	6	2	98	79*	24.50
J. H. G. Deighton (Army)	10	0	238	59	23.80
A. H. Parnaby (Army)	12	0	268	87	22.25
W. E. G. Payton (R.A.F.)	6	0	133	45	22.16
A. C. Shirreff (R.A.F.)	12	2	173	54	17.30
J. M. Vernon (R.N.) ..	4	0	67	25	16.75
M. L. Y. Ainsworth (R.N.)	10	0	159	46	15.90
A. G. Coomb (R.N.) ..	4	2	30	16	15.00
†W. R. Ford (R.A.F.) ..	6	0	65	36	10.83
P. I. Bedford (R.A.F.)	8	2	47	15	7.83
W. T. Greensmith (R.A.F.)	6	0	26	10	4.33
D. W. M. Gay (Army)	4	1	11	11	3.66

ALSO BATTED.—B. R. M. Hayles (Army), 4, 6; I. J. M. Lumsden (R.A.F.), 13, 47; H. Crick (R.A.F.), 1*; †J. F. Roberts (R.A.F.), 36, 16; M. P. Murray (R.A.F.), 17, 6*; †M. D. Fenner (R.A.F), 2, 0*; A. L. Thackara (R.N.), 7, 42.   † denotes left-hand batsman.

BOWLING

	Overs	Mdns.	Runs	Wkts.	Avge.
R. G. Wilson ..	152	18	421	16	26.31
J. H. G. Deighton ..	211.1	45	564	21	26.85
A. C. Shirreff ..	257.2	63	728	23	31.65
D. W. M. Gay ..	69	11	212	6	35.33
A. G. Coomb ..	47.4	6	165	4	41.25
P. I. Bedford ..	71.4	3	351	5	70.20

ALSO BOWLED.—A. Oakman, 44—12—137—2; W. T. Greensmith, 49—10—152—2; J. M. Vernon, 14—3—44—2; M. L. Y. Ainsworth, 2—0—6—0.

will be heard of him—both at Cambridge, where he is now in residence, and with Surrey, for whom he is qualified.

Deighton and Wilson bowled and batted with great heart, both being all-rounders of real merit. Manners (123 v. New Zealanders), Ainsworth and

(*Continued on page 113*)

Lancashire II Champions Again

By FRANK CROMPTON

*(Hon. Secretary of the Minor Counties C.A.
and Bedfordshire C.C.C.)*

TWO outstanding achievements of 1949 were those of M. Hilton of Lancashire II, who took 103 wickets for 10.89 runs each in a batsman's summer, and of A. F. Brazier of Surrey II, who scored 1,212 runs for an average of 80.80. Brazier's aggregrate was a Minor Counties record.

Lancashire II defeated Oxfordshire in the Challenge Match by an innings and 150 runs, and so won the championship for the second year in succession, and the fifth in all. Thirty-one counties took part in the competition as compared with twenty-eight in 1948, the new counties being Hampshire II, Middlesex II, and Warwickshire II. Northamptonshire II will compete in 1950, but Gloucestershire II and Glamorgan II will withdraw from the competition in 1951 for domestic reasons.

Lancashire once again had a well-balanced side. Their bowling was particularly strong, for apart from M. Hilton they had another clever slow left-arm bowler in R. Berry, who took 7 wickets for 40 in the Minor Counties match against Yorkshire at Lord's.

Oxford experienced their most successful season since 1939, when they won the championship. R. V. Divecha, their best bowler, took 74 wickets, and finished second to Hilton in the complete averages.

Bedfordshire, who were runners-up to Lancashire II in 1948, finished tenth. Two of their matches were lost by small margins, repre-

LEADING BATTING AVERAGES
(Qualification: 8 innings)

	Inns.	N.O.	Runs	H.S.	Avge.
A. F. Brazier (Surrey II)	18	3	1212	216*	80.80
N. H. Humphries (Devon)	11	2	627	216*	69.66
D. R. Guard (Hants. II)	8	2	372	77	62.00
E. Martin (Notts. II)	10	2	493	123	61.62
B. Constable (Surrey II)	10	1	552	249*	61.33
N. F. Borrett (Devon) ..	14	3	661	134*	60.90
B. J. Howard (Lancs. II)	17	4	755	114	58.09
J. F. Mendl (Oxfordshire)	18	2	923	195	57.68
G. L. B. August (Bedfordshire)	12	3	509	126*	56.55
G. J. Whittaker (Surrey II)	8	0	447	117	55.87
C. Monks (Gloucester II)	14	3	586	135	53.27
T. H. Clark (Surrey II) ..	15	2	688	209*	52.92
J. A. R. Oliver (Bedfordshire)	11	1	521	128	52.10
D. V. Smith (Sussex II) ..	11	1	512	111	51.20
A. Woollett (Kent II) ..	19	3	808	212*	50.50
D. G. W. Fletcher (Surrey II)	11	3	402	77	50.25
T. S. Worthington (Northumberland)	13	1	593	94	49.40

LEADING BOWLING AVERAGES
(Qualification: 20 wickets)

	Overs	Mds.	Runs	Wks.	Ave.
M. Hilton (Lancs. II) ..	602.2	256	1122	103	10.89
R. V. Divecha (Oxfordshire)	377.1	120	826	74	11.16
L. Hemming (Oxfordshire)	178.4	58	402	35	11.48
R. Tattersall (Lancs. II)	213.4	76	406	35	11.60
V. H. D. Cannings (Warwicks. II)	368.1	123	682	58	11.80
S. Crump (Staffs.) ..	162.3	66	293	23	12.73
G. Heath (Hampshire II)	239	68	486	38	12.78
L. M. Cranfield (Gloucester II)	155.4	48	388	30	12.93
J. H. Wardle (Yorkshire II)	168.1	73	313	24	13.04
T. Greenhough (Lancs. II)	294	84	727	24	13.21
D. Stone (Lancs. II) ..	131.5	37	317	24	13.21
R. Halton (Staffs.) ..	178.4	53	427	32	13.34
B. Notley (Notts. II) ..	109	23	249	24	13.70
B. Shardlow (Staffs. ..	338	102	737	53	13.90
F. Berry (Berkshire) ..	238	84	467	33	14.15
W. K. Laidlaw (Durham)	260.4	51	830	57	14.56
A. J. Hughes (Bucks.) ..	251.5	49	585	40	14.62
S. Norcup (Staffs.) ..	192.2	49	491	33	14.87

CHAMPIONSHIP TABLE 1949

	P.	W.	L.	1st inns. W.	1st inns. L.	No Result	Pts.	Avge. pts. per match
Lancashire II	20	13	2	1	2	2	141	7.83
Oxfordshire	10	7	2	1	-	-	75	7.50
Hampshire II	10	6	1	2	1	-	73	7.30
Staffordshire	10	6	1	2	1	-	73	7.30
Gloucestershire II	14	6	1	4	2	1	86	6.61
Buckinghamshire	10	6	2	-	2	-	66	6.60
Hertfordshire	10	5	2	1	2	-	61	6.10
Surrey II	16	5	1	7	2	1	91	6.06
Yorkshire II	14	5	2	3	3	1	74	5.69
Bedfordshire	8	3	2	3	-	-	45	5.62
Warwickshire II	10	3	2	4	1	-	53	5.30
Middlesex II	8	1	-	5	2	-	41	5.12
Berkshire	10	2	2	5	1	-	48	4.80
Dorset	10	3	3	1	3	-	44	4.40
Essex II	10	2	2	2	4	-	42	4.20
Durham	8	2	3	2	1	-	33	4.12
Worcestershire II	14	3	4	2	4	1	52	4.00
Sussex II	12	2	2	1	6	1	43	3.90
Suffolk	8	2	3	1	2	-	31	3.87
Northumberland ...	10	1	3	4	1	1	33	3.66
Nottinghamshire II ...	10	1	3	3	3	-	34	3.40
Kent II ...	12	1	4	4	2	1	36	3.27
Cambridgeshire	8	-	2	2	4	-	22	2.75
Devon	12	-	3	3	6	-	33	2.75
Derbyshire II	10	-	3	2	5	-	25	2.50
Lincolnshire	10	-	4	3	3	-	24	2.40
Norfolk	10	1	6	2	1	-	23	2.30
Glamorgan II	10	-	5	3	1	1	18	2.00
Cornwall	8	-	4	1	3	-	14	1.75
Wiltshire	10	-	5	1	4	-	17	1.70
Cheshire	10	-	7	-	3	-	9	.90

SCORING

Ten points for a win in a Completed Two Day Match, and for a lead on the first innings in a One Day Match, provided the match cannot be played out.

Five points to the winner and three to the loser in a Two Day Match decided on the first innings.

Matches in which there is No Result on the first innings are ignored.

When the match is a tie the points are equally divided.

For tie on first innings in an unfinished match, four points to each side.

senting their second and third defeats since 1939. Hampshire did well to reach third place on their first appearance in the competition.

All the sides, in fact, enjoyed a good season and there is a wealth of cricket talent in the Minor Counties which might easily be developed for Test match purposes if the selectors are minded to organise a scheme for spotting it.

As proof of the quality of players who have appeared in Minor Counties cricket, one is reminded of that great bowler S. F. Barnes, who played for Staffordshire and England, M. Falcon (Norfolk), Frank Edwards of Buckinghamshire, the famous slow bowler, and W. B. Franklin, wicketkeeper and captain of Buckinghamshire for thirty-five years, and now Chairman of the Minor Counties. Franklin kept wicket for the Gentlemen and in his prime was probably the finest wicketkeeper of his day. S. F. Barnes last appeared for the Minor Counties in 1929 when he took 8 for 41 against the South Africans at Stoke-on-Trent.

The Minor Counties Cricket Association was formed in 1895 on the suggestion of P. Foley of Stourbridge, Worcestershire, and the inaugural meeting took place at Birmingham. The intention was to harness up in competitive cricket those counties not then recognised as " first-class," which accounts for the title " Minor Counties." It has often been suggested that a title more appropriate to the excellent class of cricket played might be adopted, but so far no one has yet suggested a suitable alternative. The Minor Counties act as " feeders " to the first-class counties; and second elevens of all the first-class counties (except Leicestershire and Somerset) are now in the competition.

The Association received official recognition by M.C.C. in 1901. Worcestershire won the Championship in the years 1895 to 1898 inclusive—once jointly with another county—before their entry into first-class cricket. Northamptonshire also won the championship four times (once jointly) before being elevated. Staffordshire have won the championship six times outright and Buckinghamshire a similar number (once jointly). Lancashire II have won it five times, including the seasons 1948 and 1949, and Durham also, but twice jointly.

The Minor Counties XI will play M.C.C. at Lord's on July 22, 24 and 25, and the West Indies at Norwich on September 6, 7 and 8.

THE CHALLENGE MATCH

At Old Trafford, Sept. 7 & 8 : *Lancashire II won by an innings and* 150 *runs.*

Oxfordshire, without four of their regular players, were no match for their opponents. Quickish swing bowling dismissed them in two hours before lunch on the opening day and by the close Lancashire had made 314 for 5 wickets against a weak attack. Oxfordshire made a good start to their second innings but Hilton, who reached his 100 wickets for the season, was too clever for them: Scores:—

Oxfordshire 78 (R. V. Divecha 31 not, J. G. Lomax 5-16, E. W. F. Highton 5-31) and 138 (M. Hilton 7-21); Lancashire II 356 (R. Alderson 63, B. J. Howard 112, J. G. Lomax 75, Divecha 5-61).

THE COUNTIES IN BRIEF

BEDFORDSHIRE, though dropping eight places, were keenly led by A. B. Poole, in his 22nd year with the County. The side was strengthened by the return of R. J. O. Meyer from Somerset. **BERKSHIRE** undoubtedly missed D. W. Stokes, their captain, who fell ill and was unable to play in any of their games. **BUCKINGHAMSHIRE** improved greatly, the batting being more consistent than for many years. O. G. Battcock and A. J. Hughes bowled splendidly, and P. Isherwood headed both sets of averages.

CAMBRIDGESHIRE did better than in 1948, but their bowling remained weak. C. E. Coote and M. A. Crouch were mainstays of the batting. **CHESHIRE**, a young side, lost their first three matches and finished bottom. Bowling caused most concern. **CORNWALL**, too, did not win a match. It was one of their poorest seasons, with bad catching (particularly in the slips) mainly responsible. R. Whitehouse, a newcomer, headed the batting.

N. F. Borrett, the squash champion, and N. H. Humphries batted grandly for **DEVON**, but too often the bowling lacked penetration, and no game was won. **DORSET** were early beset by injuries and had to call upon many inexperienced players. W. L. Creese, ex-Hampshire, took 52 wickets. **DURHAM**, who finished half-way, twice took first-innings points from the ultimate Champions. The Scot, W. K. Laidlaw, secured 58 wickets in an outstanding season.

ESSEX II began well enough with two wins, but afterwards were disappointing. H. A. Faragher hit 501 runs (including two centuries) in his first season. **GLAMORGAN II**, included some talented young players who should prove of worth in the future. J. Pressdee (slow left) and D. Shepherd (medium right) were promising bowlers. **GLOUCESTERSHIRE II** lost only their first match, and with stronger bowling they would have run Lancashire a close race. In his seven innings G. W. Parker scored 519 runs, including three centuries, average 103.80. Consistent batting and the experience of G. Heath and O. W. Herman in attack enabled **HAMPSHIRE II** to finish joint third. D. R. Guard of Winchester scored 372 runs for an average of 62. *(continued on page* 134)

A. V. AVERY (Essex)	**J. SIMS** (Middlesex)	**J. S. ORD** (Warwickshire)
v. Worcs. (Romford) *(May 27, 29, 30)*	*v. Yorks. (Lord's)* *(June 17, 19, 20)*	*v. Middx. (Birmingham)* *(July 8, 10, 11)*

This is Their Benefit Year

May the Sun Shine for Them All

In 1949 Denis Compton of Middlesex received a Benefit of £12,200. Other approximate amounts were:—R. Pollard (£8,500), H. E. Dollery (£6,362), E. A. Watts (£5,000), C. B. Harris (£3,500), R. Howorth (£3,000), H. L. Hazell (£2,300) and P. Corrall (£2,300). W. H. Copson's Testimonial amounted to about £2,500 and J. E. Timm's to £1,650. E. P. Robinson was granted £1,500. This season Jim Sims has his second Benefit in four years; his Sussex match in 1946 was marred by rain.

J. ARNOLD	**J. BAILEY**	**N. McCORKELL**

These three Hampshire professionals, along with **G. HILL** and **O. W. HERMAN**, have a joint benefit spread over the seasons **1948-49-50**.

H. J. BUTLER
(Notts.)

v. Yorks. (Trent Bridge)
(July 8, 10, 11)

L. HUTTON
(Yorkshire)

v. Middx. (Leeds)
(July 15, 17, 18)

L. B. FISHLOCK
(Surrey)

v. Middx. (Oval)
(July 29, 31, August 1)

1950 TESTIMONIALS

S. BULLER (Worcs.)

L. M. CRANFIELD
(Glos.)

P. DAVIS (Northants.)

C. S. ELLIOTT (Derby)

G. LAVIS (Glamorgan)

W. T. LUCKES
(Somerset)

G. WATSON,
F. T. PRENTICE
(Leics.)

D. V. P. WRIGHT
(Kent)

v. Hants. (Canterbury)
(August 5, 7, 8)

J. CORNFORD
(Sussex)

v. Kent (Hastings)
(August 12, 14, 15)

* * *

COMBINED SERVICES (continued from page 108)

Payton are all good county bats, and Shirreff, another capable all-rounder, captained the side with zest and skill.

Bedford's leg-breaks and googlies were disappointingly expensive, due perhaps to lack of regular practice. Oakman played infrequently but showed considerable promise; he should attack the bowling more. Greensmith improved from match to match and should develop into a useful county all-rounder; he is a good on-side batsman. He must learn to flight the ball more and to push it through quicker when conditions demand.

E

W. T. TAYLOR
(Derby). Appointed
1908: senior county
secretary.

W. WOOLLER
(Glamorgan). Joint
secretary with L. M.
Spence. Appt. 1948.

E. D. R. EAGAR
(Hants.). Joint
secretary with R. C.
Court. Appt. 1946.

N. CHRISTOPHERSON
(Kent). Appointed
1950.

C. G. HOWARD
(Lancs.). Appointed
1949.

G. de L. HOUGH
(Kent). Appt. 1933;
resigned 1950.

R. W. V. ROBINS
(Middx.). Appointed
1935.

R. F. T. PATERSON (Essex). Appointed
1947. Photograph taken in the caravan
which takes him the round of the Essex
festivals.

**Lt.-Col. A. St. G.
COLDWELL**
(Northants.). Appointed
1946.

Lt.-Col. H. A. Henson (Glos.). Appointed 1936. The inkstand on his desk is a souvenir of W. G. Grace's hundredth 100. This is the ball off which he made his 100th run and the cork comes from the bottle drunk to toast the feat.

Col. Coldwell's photograph by Eric Ager; Mr. Deakin's by Birmingham Post and Mail; Col. Henson's by Picture Post Library.

H. A. BROWN (Notts.). Appointed 1920.

✦ COUNTY SECRETARIES ✦

Brig. E. H. LANCASTER (Hon. Somerset secretary). Appointed 1937; resigned 1949.

B. K. CASTOR (Surrey). Appointed 1947. Essex secretary 1930-47.

S. C. GRIFFITH (Sussex). Appointed 1946; resigned February, 1950.

L. T. DEAKINS (Warwick). Appointed 1944.

Brig. M. A. GREEN (Worcs.). Appointed 1946.

J. H. NASH (Yorkshire). Appointed 1930.

Their True Intent was all for Our Delight

WILLIAM HENRY COPSON (Derbyshire) was one of the few fast bowlers able to bridge the years of the war. After touring Australia and New Zealand in 1936-7 and heading the averages, he played twice for England against the West Indies in 1939, taking 12 wickets at 15.41; and in 1947 he was still good enough to play for England against S. Africa at the Oval. He was a very fine bowler in his prime, moving the ball in or out, and although his arm was not high he generated great haste off the pitch.

Sandy-haired and stiffly built, Bill Copson had a quiet and happy temperament. 1937 was his great season. Against Warwickshire at Derby he had 8 for 11, including 4 in 4 balls, and he achieved hat-tricks against Lancashire at Burton and Oxford at Oxford. Born at Stonebroom, near Alfreton, on 27th April, 1909, he made his debut in 1932 and had Andy Sandham of Surrey caught at slip off his very first delivery. In 1936 when Derbyshire were champions, he played a great part with 140 wickets in Championship matches. Now he will play for Lidget Green in the Bradford League.

JOHN E. TIMMS (Northants.) gave consistently good service to his county over a period of 20 years. Never a very good starter, he was a stylish right-hand bat when under way. He moved his feet well, was a good cutter and driver, and was pretty severe on anything short. He was a brilliant cover point and a useful change bowler of medium pace; and he was always immaculate in appearance.

He made his debut in 1925 as an amateur, turning professional in 1927. During his career he played in 471 matches for his county—his only other appearance being in the Test Trial of 1932. He scored more than a thousand runs eleven times between 1928 and 1947. Highest innings: 213 v. Worcs. (Stourbridge) 1934. Best bowling: 6-18 v. Worcs. (Worcester) 1938. In 1939 he scored two hundreds v. Sussex at Kettering and in 1940 a Testimonial brought him £1,650. He was born at Silverstone on 3rd November, 1907, and is now Assistant at Buckingham Golf Club.

EDWARD A. WATTS (Surrey) enjoyed a record county Benefit last season (£5,000)—very proper reward for a most popular cricketer. A right-arm medium fast bowler who kept the ball well up to the batsman, so giving it some room to move—chiefly away—he was troubled by knee injury when cricket was resumed after the war. His batting would have prospered more in a weaker batting side.

Born at Peckham on 1st August, 1911, he made his debut as an amateur in 1933 and turned professional in 1934 when he scored 928 runs and took 91 wickets. Against Yorks. at Bradford he hit his first hundred (123) in under two hours. He toured the Argentine in 1937-8 and New Zealand in 1938-9 (both privately organised) and in 1939 took all 10 Warwickshire wickets for 67 in an innings at Birmingham. This season he is playing in the Birmingham League and coaching at Whitgift School.

T. L. BRIERLEY (Lancs.) a useful right hand batsman and wicketkeeper, joined Glamorgan in 1931 and played as a batsman once Haydn Davies had taken over the gloves in 1938. In 1946 he joined Lancashire as regular wicketkeeper but lost his form and was appointed assistant county coach. He was born at Southampton on 15th June 1910; and now lives in Canada.

GILBERT DAWSON (Hants.), a right hand bat from the Bradford League, joined the county in 1947, won his cap in 1948, and scored more than 1,000 runs in each of the past two seasons.

ELLIS P. ROBINSON (Yorks.) was a right arm off-break bowler who really spun the ball and kept a fine length. He was, moreover, a splendid field near the wicket, where his ability was not so very far short of the very best.

Having made his debut in 1934 he toured Jamaica with his county in 1935-6 and played a notable part in three of Yorkshire's Championships by taking over 100 wickets in 1938, 1939 and 1946. He played in the Lord's Test Trial in 1946 and took over 100 wickets again in 1947. Best bowling: 8-34 (13-115 match) v. Lancs. (Leeds) 1939. He held 7 catches (6 in one innings) v. Leics. at Bradford, 1937.

In 1946 he finished fourth in the first-class bowling averages with 167 wickets. At the end of 1949 the county made him a testimonial award of £1,500.

WALTER T. LUCKES (Somerset) who has handed over the gloves now that Stephenson has proved so able a successor, was a most competent wicketkeeper of the unobtrusive kind, and a much better bat than was indicated by his position in the order.

He made his debut in 1924, played regularly from 1927, missed most of the 1929-30-31 seasons through ill health and became a fixture in the side from 1932. Against Kent at Taunton in 1934 he conceded only one bye in an innings of 577 and put on 112 with J. W. Lee for the 10th wicket; in 1939 he let no byes in a Glamorgan total of 574-7 at Newport. In 1946 he topped the wicketkeepers' list with 75 victims and he made eight dismissals v. Worcs. at Worcester in 1948. During his career he played in 365 matches—all for Somerset—and made one century (121* v. Kent at Bath, 1937). He takes a well-deserved Testimonial this season.

OSWALD W HERMAN (Hants.) for many years was a bowling mainstay of his side. Right-arm, of medium pace, he chiefly moved the ball in but varied his attack with one that straightened out. He was a great trier and always good-natured—and he could be quite a useful hitter.

He joined Hampshire in 1929 and except for 1939, when professional at Rochdale, he played regularly, taking over 100 wickets in a season 5 times. He represented the Players in 1932, and in 1937 took 142 wickets and scored 801 runs. In that year too he did the "hat-trick" v. Glamorgan (Portsmouth). In 1947 he took 3 S. African wickets in 4 balls at Southampton. He shares a joint Benefit (1948-50) with Arnold, Bailey, Hill and McCorkell. He was born at Oxford on 18th September, 1907.

THOMAS A. DEAN (Hants.) spent his early years in South Africa but returned to join the county in 1939, his leg-breaks taking 4 wickets in 5 balls—including the "hat-trick"—v. Worcs. at Bournemouth in his second match. But after the war he could not re-find his form.

GEORGE E. M. HEATH (Hants.) a right arm medium paced bowler, moved the ball either way—chiefly off the seam He made his debut in 1937 but played irregularly in the past two seasons. He was born in Hong Kong on 20th February, 1913. Best bowling: 7-49 v. Derby (Portsmouth).

ERIC A. MARSH (Derby), a genial left hand bat and slow left arm bowler, made his debut in 1946 and won his county cap in 1947. He was born at

Bolsover on 17th July, 1920, and played originally in the Bradford League. He is now to play for Westhoughton in the Bolton League.

C. MONKS (Glos.), a right hand bat and change bowler, made his debut in 1935 as an amateur and turned professional in 1936. He left the county in 1939 but played again as an amateur in 1946 and fared quite well in 1947 and 1948, scoring 120 at Cambridge. In 1949 he turned professional once again.

ERIC PRICE (Essex) made his debut for Lancashire as a slow left arm bowler in 1946 and showed such promise that he was picked for the Canterbury Test Trial, won his county cap and headed the county averages. In 1948 he joined Essex under special registration. He was born at Middleton on 27th October 1918; and has now returned there as League professional.

K. A. TAYLOR (Warwicks.) a right hand bat, made his debut and won his county cap in 1946. He scored 1,259 runs in 1947, including his only century —102 v. Glos. at Birmingham. He is now with the Electricity Board.

A. G. S. WILCOX (Glos.), a left hand bat, made his debut as amateur in 1939 and turned professional in 1946. Highest score: 73 v. Hants. (Bournemouth) 1948.

WILLIAM J. DINES (Essex), a right-hand batsman and medium pace bowler, took two wickets in his second over in county cricket in 1947 and shortly afterwards scored two fifties in the Brentwood

festival, but could not maintain his early form. Born Colchester, Sept. 14, 1916.

JIM EAGLESTONE (Glamorgan), an attacking left-hand batsman, joined the Welsh county from Middlesex for the 1948 season. He had begun propitiously at Lord's, and won a Glamorgan county cap in 1948. He played regularly in 1948 and 1949 but failed to make the advance expected. He was offered another contract for 1950 but declined it. Born London, July 24, 1923.

Others released from regular engagements at the end of 1949 were: A. H. Mills (Glos.), J. Taylor and R. O. Prouton (Hants.), J. Bowes (Lancs.), P. Konig (Leics.) and R. Brindle, L. C. Croom, D. Flint and J. T. Kendall (Warwicks.) and H. Horton (Worcs.).

CAREER RECORDS FOR VALETE

	Runs	HS	Avge	100's	Runs	Wkts	Avge
Bowes, J.	106	39	8.83	—	602	21	28.66
Brierley, T. L.	6046	116*	18.83	4	45	0	—
Brindle, R.	74	42	37.00	—	—	—	—
‡Coope, M.	2789	113	21.12	2	479	8	59.87
Copson, W. H.	1710	43	6.84	—	20655	1092	18.91
Croom, L.	73	26	9.12	—	—	—	—
Dawson, G.	2643	158*	26.43	4	7	0	—
Dean, T. A.	283	26	9.75	—	1587	51	31.11
Dines, W. J.	431	69*	18.73	—	980	15	65.33
Eaglestone, J.	1420	77	15.77	—	—	—	—
Flint, L.	33	11	4.71	—	465	12	38.75
Heath, G. E. M.	586	34*	5.58	—	11359	404	28.11
Herman, O. W.	4336	92	11.38	—	28222	1045	27.00
Horton, H.	129	21	8.06	—	32	0	—
Kendall, J. T.	26	18*	8.66	—	—	—	—
Konig, P.	3	3	3.00	—	—	—	—
Luckes, W. T.	5705	121*	16.20	1	—	—	—
Marsh, E. A.	1627	86	18.28	—	1698	44	38.59
Mills, A. H.	81	39	16.20	—	62	3	20.66
Monks, C.	1510	120	20.68	1	1619	36	44.97
Price, E.	558	54	8.71	—	5722	215	26.61
Prouton, R. O.	0	0	0.00	—	—	—	—
Robinson, E. P.	2625	75*	12.44	—	15575	753	20.68
Taylor, J.	76	27*	15.20	—	24	0	—
Taylor, K. A.	3145	102	21.68	1	33	1	33.00
Timms, J. E.	20457	213	25.03	31	6619	149	44.42
Vickery, A.	89	21	8.09	—	—	—	—
Watts, E. A.	6158	123	21.41	2	19004	729	26.06
Wilcox, A. G. S.	835	73	15.75	—	—	—	—
Winslow, P. L.	24	16	12.00	—	23	0	—

‡Coope's record should appear in Career Records for those still playing—a section which went to press before his re-engagement by Somerset was announced.

THE SERVICES

THE ARMY v. R.A.F.
R.A.F. 184 for 9 wkts. dec. (M Murray 74), and 107 for 6 wkts. dec.; THE ARMY 187 for 7 wkts. dec. (B. A. Gomm 84, W. Greensmith 4-34) and 72 for 5 wickets. Match drawn.

ROYAL NAVY v. THE ARMY
THE ARMY 177 (A. H. Parnaby 68) and 128 for 7 wkts. dec. (J. D. Sayer 5-41); ROYAL NAVY 211 (J. M. Vernon 58, A. J. H. Cassels

4-38) and 96 for 1 wkt. (J. M. Vernon 51 not). Royal Navy won by 9 wickets.

ROYAL NAVY v. R.A.F.
ROYAL NAVY 283 for 7 wkts. dec. (P. B H. May 162 not, J. Hodges 58 not, W. Greensmith 5-73) and 154 for 5 wkts dec. (P. B. H. May 58 not) R.A.F 191 for 1 wkt. dec (W E. G. Payton 107 not, M. Murray 76 not) and 122 for 4 wkts. Match drawn.

The Leagues   *By Kenneth Wolstenholme*

Fine Cricket in a Golden Summer

AT the start of yet another cricket season, secretaries of the northern League clubs have one prayer—let us have another summer like 1949. For 1949 was a record in numerous ways. Never has the weather been better, the gate receipts higher, the cricket so sparkling or the interest in League cricket so much increased.

CENTRAL LANCASHIRE LEAGUE

First Division

	P.	W.	L.	D.	Pts.	Agg.
MILNROW	26	14	6	6	48	87½
STOCKPORT	26	13	4	9	48	91½
RADCLIFFE	26	9	3	14	41	63
HEYWOOD	26	9	5	12	39	56½
ROCHDALE	26	9	6	11	38	71
WERNETH	26	9	6	11	38	68
CASTLETON MOOR ..	26	9	9	8	35	53½
ROYTON	26	7	5	14	35	73
MIDDLETON	26	7	6	13	34	53
ASHTON	26	7	9	10	31	51
WALSDEN	26	7	11	8	29	65
LITTLEBOROUGH ..	26	3	10	13	22	40
OLDHAM	26	3	15	8	17	47
CROMPTON	26	3	18	5	14	39

Second Division

	P.	W.	L.	D.	Pts.
STOCKPORT	20	13	3	4†	43½
MILNROW	20	11	3	6†	39½
ROYTON	20	12	6	2	38½
WALSDEN	20	10	4	6	36
ROCHDALE	20	11	9	0	33
OLDHAM	20	8	6	6	30
WERNETH	20	8	6	6	30
CROMPTON	20	6	7	7	25
RADCLIFFE	20	6	10	4	22
ASHTON	20	6	12	2	20
MIDDLETON	20	4	9	7	19
CASTLETON MOOR ..	20	5	12	3†	18½
LITTLEBOROUGH ..	20	4	10	6	18
HEYWOOD	20	4	11	5†	17½

† *Tied Match*

WHITTAKER CUP " A "

	P.	W.	L.	D.	Pts.
WERNETH	8	6	1	1	19
CROMPTON	8	3	2	3†	12½
ROYTON	8	3	3	2†	11½
OLDHAM	8	3	3	2	11
MILNROW	8	0	6	2	2

† *Tied Match*

WHITTAKER CUP " B "

	P.	W.	L.	D.	Pts.
ROCHDALE	10	7	0	3	24
HEYWOOD	10	6	2	2	20
RADCLIFFE	10	5	3	2	17
LITTLEBOROUGH ..	10	3	5	2	11
CASTLETON MOOR ..	10	2	7	1	7
WALSDEN	10	1	7	2	5

Werneth won the Cup by beating Rochdale in the Final

Last season, too, led to the tour of India by the Commonwealth team, captained by Jock Livingston and managed by George Duckworth, the ex - Lancashire and England wicket-keeper. Nearly all the players in the party were highly-paid professionals with Lancashire and Central Lancashire League clubs. In addition, two of the leading players on the Indian side, Hazare and Mankad, are professionals in the Central Lancashire League, while P. R. Umrigar, India's opening bat, signed forms to play in the same League for Werneth in 1950.

Probably the Lancashire League has the greatest talent among the professionals, but they start the new season mourning the loss of their secretary, Mr. Gideon Holgate, who died in November. Mr. Holgate was a great worker for cricket in all its spheres and he is the type of man we cannot afford to lose.

Last season, East Lancashire, the enterprising Blackburn club, carried all before them in this League. With Bruce Dooland, the Australian Test Match leg - break bowler, in brilliant form as their professional, they won the Worsley Cup, the League championship and the 2nd XI championship. Dooland took 117 wickets in 331 overs at a cost of 10.47 each and scored 857 runs. But East Lancashire, whose ground is so pretty that you would never think you were within a mile of an industrial town, were no one-man team. They have in Cyril Looms, the son of Blackburn's Chief Constable, a most promising amateur batsman who scored 359 runs during 1949 and is still improving, and Tom Dickenson, a young bowler, is regarded as one of the best young pace men in the county. He is still at Blackburn Grammar School, who have first claim on his services. Nevertheless, his 25 wickets in the League only cost him 13 runs each, a brilliant performance considering the strong opposition.

LANCASHIRE LEAGUE

			P.	W.	D.	L.	Pts.
EAST LANCS.	..	..	26	17	3	6	57
RAWTENSTALL		..	26	13	2	11	50
TODMORDEN	..	..	26	13	6	7	46
BACUP	..	..	26	10	4	12	42
BURNLEY		..	26	10	7	9	39
CHURCH	..	..	26	10	8	8	38
COLNE	..	..	26	9	8	9	36
NELSON		..	26	8	9	9	33
LOWERHOUSE	..		26	7	13	6	27
RISHTON	..	..	26	6	12	8	26
ENFIELD	..		26	6	13	7	25
RAMSBOTTOM		..	26	5	11	10	25
ACCRINGTON	..		26	4	13	9	21
HASLINGDEN	..	..	26	3	12	11	20

BRADFORD LEAGUE
First Division

			P.	W.	L.	D.	Pts.
SALTS	..	..	22	13	6	3	42
BOWLING OLD LANE	..		22	13	7	2	41
PUDSEY ST. L'CE		..	22	12	6	4	40
WINDHILL		..	22	11	7	4	37
ECCLESHILL	..		22	10	8	4	34
IDLE	..	..	22	9	8	5	32
GREAT HORTON		..	22	10	11	1	31
UNDERCLIFFE		..	22	9	10	3	30
BINGLEY	..		22	8	11	3	27
YEADON	..	..	22	7	15	0	21
SPEN VICTORIA		..	22	4	14	4	16

Second Division

			P.	W.	L.	D.	Pts.
BAILDON GREEN		..	22	14	4	4	46
QUEENSBURY	..		22	12	6	4	40
BRADFORD	..		22	11	7	4	37
LIGHTCLIFFE	..		22	11	8	3	36
BANKFOOT	..		22	10	9	3	33
BRIGHOUSE	..		22	10	9	3	33
FARSLEY	..		22	9	10	3	30
SALTAIRE	..		22	8	13	1	25
EAST BIERLEY	..		22	7	12	3	24
KEIGHLEY	..		22	6	14	2	20
LIDGET GREEN		..	22	5	14	3	18

Cecil Pepper had a great season. He became the first man ever to complete the " double," completing the feat on the last Saturday but one in the season. Then, on the last Saturday, Vijay Hazare equalled the feat. Hazare was the outstanding professional, topping both batting and bowling averages. Altogether, five professionals topped the 1,000 runs and four captured 100 or more wickets.

It is grand that we shall be able to see Eddie Paynter in action in the League as an amateur. He played a few games in 1949 and scored 388 runs for an average of 43.11.

George Tribe will be in the League this season as he replaces Hazare at Rawtenstall. A magnificent left-arm spin bowler, he established a Central Lancashire League record in 1948 by taking 148 wickets. He equalled it last year, but, with another two wickets in the championship play-off, his final total was 150. Certainly he will be a great drawing power in the Lancashire League. Hazare, who goes to Royton (their professional, Livingston, has joined Northants), will be an equal attraction in the Central Lancashire League.

One of the most successful professionals was Everton Weekes, who came to Bacup and struck brilliant form. Two league records fell to him. He beat the previous aggregate record by scoring 1,470 runs, and by hitting 195 in an innings he beat the previous highest score of 188. Both these records were previously held by West Indians—the aggregate record by George Headley and the highest innings by Learie Constantine.

Another West Indian—Frank Worrell—also held the batting limelight in the Central Lancashire League, which produced the best finish in its history.

Stockport and Milnrow shared all the honours. Milnrow won the Wood Cup (the knock-out competition), Stockport the 2nd team championship and the two clubs shared the first team title. Even a play-off failed to bring a definite result.

Worrell, playing for Radcliffe, beat the previous aggregate record by scoring 1,501 runs for an average of 88.29. His last five innings produced 500 runs and he was only out once! It will be a long time before this League sees magnificent batting like this.

Worrell's opening partner, Bill Greenhalgh—a newcomer to the side—was the League's outstanding amateur. He scored 813 runs and twice in successive weeks helped Worrell to put on over 100 for the first wicket. Certainly Radcliffe would have won the league title if their bowling had been as strong as their batting.

Central Lancashire

Like all other types of cricket, the Central Lancashire League proved a heartbreaking outing for bowlers during the perfect summer. In fact the aggregate of runs scored—53,479—was a new record for the League, and in addition to Worrell's record-breaking feats with the bat, Vinoo Mankad, the Indian, also broke the previous aggregate record by scoring 1,466 runs for Castleton Moor, three other batsmen topped 1,000 runs and 21 amateurs completed 500 or more runs. Mankad, in addition to scoring almost 1,500 runs, took 124 wickets for 11.79 to become the leading all-rounder. George Pope (ex-Derbyshire) did well with the ball. He took 148 wickets at a cost of 10.12, but only the veteran Ellis Achong and Des Fitzmaurice among the others took more than 100 wickets.

As evidence of the tremendous enthusiasm for this sort of cricket, I can only record that many League games drew £200 gates (one shilling admission, the gate receipts not including member's subscriptions), and the total cup gate receipts were more than £2,000.

The cup tie between Rochdale (with Charlie Barnett, of Gloucestershire and England fame) and Castleton Moor (with Mankad) attracted receipts of more than £600 and produced 700 runs.

The Bradford League cannot match such figures; here the accent is not on high-salaried professionals but on producing young cricketers for the county. Each side is allowed four professionals, but they are not the crowd-drawing players we see in Lancashire. Nevertheless, the cricket is first-class and every club has a fair sprinkling of Yorkshire Colts.

Nearly all the honours were in doubt until the last day of the season, and there was an unfortunate scene after Salts had beaten Pudsey in the last game to make certain of the 1st Division title. Although Pudsey failed to lift the championship, they had the distinction of providing the outstanding batsman in Hamer, whose 1,106 runs was a League record. Never before has a batsman scored 1,000 runs in a Bradford League season. Powell of Queensbury, one of the promoted sides, was the leading bowler with 94 wickets, but we must not forget Matthews, the ex-Glamorgan star, who played in the last few matches for Undercliffe and took 34 wickets in 87 overs for 6.88 runs each.

For the second year in succession, the Priestley Cup winners were relegated. This time it was Yeadon; in 1948 it was Keighley, who finished next to the bottom of Division 2 last season. Yeadon's fate was very hard on Falkingham, who scored 255 runs in Cup games and was only out once. Sad to say he never reproduced that form in League games.

Birmingham League

By *Frank Pemberton*
("*Birmingham Mail*")

Cricket with Pre-War Flavour

THE most consistently fine weather ever known in the sixty-one years' history of the Birmingham & District Cricket League enabled its ten clubs to experience a flourishing season. Attendances were large throughout, records being reached at some grounds, and there was a pre-war flavour about the cricket which was brighter than for many years, with sporting declarations that led to exciting finishes and often decisive results.

Aston Unity, one of the original members of the League, won the First Division title for the eleventh time, thus equalling the record set up in 1948 by West Bromwich Dartmouth. In 1948, when the Unity did not have professional assistance, the first team won only one match and finished last, but last year Nichols, the old Essex fast bowler, took 69 wickets for them at an average of 12.23.

The former Yorkshire all-rounder, Frank Smailes, helped Walsall to second place with a batting average of 25.94 and a bowling record of 55 wickets at 17.47. For West Bromwich Dartmouth "Alf" Gover (ex-Surrey and England) captured 70 wickets (more than any other in the League) for 13.84 each, though his club colleague, Fred Allen, had the season's best analysis — 43 wickets, 9.37 average.

Smethwick's "pro.", Frank Woodhouse, was more effective with the bat and Bill Merritt, the old New Zealand Test player, once more proved the mainstay of the Dudley side. He and Bill Andrews (ex-Somerset) of Stourbridge are still grand all-rounders. With the ball, however, Jack Holroyd (Kidderminster) probably did better than anyone (252 overs, 46 maidens, 664 runs, 58 wickets, 11.4 average). His services will be missed at the Chester Road ground next season.

George Paine (Moseley), "Alf" Pope (Mitchells and Butlers) and Albert Thomas (Old Hill) bore the brunt of the attack for their respective clubs. It was Thomas's last season, for the former Northamptonshire player has retired at the age of 58, leaving pleasant memories of sportsmanship, club loyalty, and many fine performances.

Division I

	P.	W.	L.	D.	Pts.
Aston Unity	18	9	3	6	33
Walsall	18	9	4	5	32
W. Bromwich Dartmouth	18	8	5	5	29
Smethwick	18	6	5	7	25
Moseley	18	5	5	8	23
Dudley	18	5	6	7	22
Kidderminster	18	4	6	8	20
Old Hill	18	3	6	9	18
Stourbridge	18	5	10	3	18
Mitchells & Butlers	18	2	6	10	16

Division II

	P.	W.	L.	D.	Pts.
Mitchells & Butlers	18	10	1	7	37
Walsall	18	9	4	5	32
Moseley	18	8	6	4	28
Smethwick	18	7	6	5	26
Kidderminster	18	6	5	7	25
Aston Unity	18	6	7	5	23
Dudley	18	5	6	7	22
W. Bromwich Dartmouth	18	5	7	6	21
Old Hill	18	5	8	5	20
Stourbridge	18	2	13	3	9

Cricket at the Schools 　　　　*Edited by Albert Sewell*

LONDON

Ten victories in sixteen matches gave **ALLEYN'S** a good record, much of their success being due to J. F. Pretlove's fine bowling. M. J. Stewart again batted soundly.

HARROW won only three of fourteen games, the batting being rather unstable. In a season of exciting finishes M.C.C. and Harlequins were beaten and defeats suffered at the hands of Winchester and Eton. Harrow decisively beat Malvern and had the better of a draw with Charterhouse. The most successful bowlers were R. G. Marlar (50 wickets at 13 runs apiece with off-breaks), R. A. Jacques and M. Kok.

HIGHGATE defeated Mill Hill, St. Paul's and Merchant Taylors'. Their most prominent cricketer was W. Knightley-Smith, who scored 501 runs, average 41.75. R. D. Owen, the captain, hit 436, including one innings of 100 not out.

MERCHANT TAYLORS' had a well-balanced eleven, and with a little luck would have won more often. They beat Whitgift, Beaumont, U.C.S. and Buccaneers, lost to Highgate and M.C.C., and drew on five occasions. Banwell, Ross, Ingram, Sims (a fine all-rounder) and Prodger (slow left-arm—27 wickets at 7.93) were outstanding. **MILL HILL** failed to reach expectations, poor batting being responsible; the only win was against Old Millhillians.

ST. PAUL'S, captained by C. J. Godfrey, beat Brighton and Mill Hill in school matches, and gained an exciting win by three runs against Free Foresters, N. B. W. Widlake (fast-medium) taking 6-19. They drew with M.C.C. and Merchant Taylors' and lost to The Leys, Highgate and Dulwich.

KENT

In 1947 **CRANBROOK** won six school matches, drew one; in 1948 they won five, drew one; and in 1949, despite losing the toss each time, they beat King's Rochester, Dover, Ardingly and Sutton Valence. The Whitgift, M.C.C. and Band of Brothers matches were lost. J. M. Cochrane, captain, once more bowled off-breaks effectively, well supported by A. R. C. Galpin (medium) and B. H. Wardle (quite fast). B. B. Moore, R. T. Nye and Cochrane were the best batsmen, and the fielding was always good.

A young **DOVER** side was capable of good scores, but it lacked experience and failed to win a school game. **ELTHAM**, the first school to defeat Bancroft's for four years, had their best season since 1935.

Because of indifferent batting, **ST. DUNSTAN'S** lost six games, compared with five won. Their outstanding member was D. P. Thomas (captain), an excellent all-rounder. J. A. Pierce, slow left-arm, took 52 wickets.

Strong and varied bowling and inconsistent batting—particularly in the middle of the order—sums up the season at **SUTTON VALENCE**, who won as many games as they lost. A. F. Tipples, a punishing batsman and good leg-break bowler, captained the side keenly. M. A. Whittaker (medium), M. C. Parnell (inswing), A. J. Knight (stock) and J. A. Roper (slow left) all took wickets, and most of the runs came from Tipples, J. B. Sanders and K. C. Goodwin.

At **TONBRIDGE**, M. C. Cowdrey, the captain, was in a class by himself. He hit four hundreds and narrowly missed 1,000 runs for the season. He made 119 v. Lancing, 181 not out v. Buccaneers, 140 v. Old Tonbridgians (all those games being won) and fought magnificently for 123 out of 196 v. Haileybury in a match lost through erratic bowling. Cowdrey, with leg-breaks, was also bowler-in-chief. Tonbridge should prosper again in 1950, since Cowdrey is available (for his sixth season) with six old colours.

SURREY

CHARTERHOUSE, undefeated by schools, beat Eton and Westminster, and drew with Harrow and Winchester. A. Kamm showed tremendous enthusiasm as captain, and J. W. H. May, his 1950 successor, played several fine innings. D. H. G. Goodliffe and M. S. Scholfield batted attractively, and C. E. Holt enjoyed much success as a bowler.

CRANLEIGH had a poor season, best results being a win against a strong Cryptics team and a creditable loss to M.C.C. D. J. Lister scored 508 runs (average 39.07) and N. A. Paul promised well as an all-rounder. A disappointment was the failure of M. A. Fairbairns, the captain, to reproduce his bowling form of the previous three seasons.

EPSOM, well-equipped in all departments, won every school match. Christ's Hospital, Dulwich, Cranleigh and St. John's, Leatherhead, being defeated. J. S. Hall was a capable all-rounder, and P. Adlington hit the only century.

WHITGIFT won five school matches, lost four and drew one. Subba Row hit two not-out centuries, and R. N. Lewis took 53 wickets for 9.8 runs each. An outstanding performance was the dismissal of M.C.C. before lunch for 110.

R. H. Etheridge headed the **WHITGIFT MIDDLE** batting averages, scoring 330 runs. J. D. Fowler took over 50 wickets at cheap cost (including all ten for 23 against Purley C.S.). Most of last year's side are available again.

SUSSEX

BRIGHTON had their strongest team for several years, and finished the season with wins against Lancing, Cranleigh, Christ's Hospital and Old Brightonians, and a draw with M.C.C. Their best batsman was A. B. D. Parsons, a Colt who scored 570 runs, average 51.8. P. Kemp and J. A. Gibson formed a capable opening attack, and J. A. Ince was a good captain.

HURSTPIERPOINT, a fine fielding side, did extremely well, winning all their inter-school matches. (Illness prevented fixtures against Lancing and Cranbrook.) K. R. Jenkin, captain, achieved outstanding success; his 419 runs included a century against XL Club and three fifties off school bowlers. In addition he took 34 wickets, average 10.06. P. R. Boan and R. G. Bartlett (batsmen) and C. L. Carter and G. L. Hill (bowlers) were useful players.

LANCING'S results were poor, yet they had some exciting cricket. A strong Old Boys XI won on time, and Sussex Martlets just drew with nine wickets down. Lancing drew with Eastbourne and lost to Tonbridge, Bradfield, Brighton and Westminster. The batting was quite strong, but the bowling weak.

EASTERN COUNTIES

FELSTED, who beat M.C.C. for the first time since 1935, were undefeated in school matches. K. F. G. Thomas and I. M. Peek were reliable opening batsmen and A. A. Mitchell and A. H. Knight useful all-rounders.

FRAMLINGHAM returned to form, winning five school matches and losing one. D. A. Walton, I. B. Stiles and C. M. M. Ford were dependable batsmen, and G. A. Warner and Ford the mainstays of a very strong attack.

GRESHAM'S had a fine season, defeating Norwich, Ipswich and Framlingham, and drawing with Felsted. Only one match was lost. C. W. R. Chapman (400 runs, average 40) and R. W. Gillett (34 wickets at 9.24 runs each) were outstanding.

	Won	Drawn	Lost		Won	Drawn	Lost
Alleyn's‡	10	2	3	King William's, I.O.M.	5	6	2
Allhallows	9	4	3	Lancing*		1	4
Beaumont*	3	–	5	Leeds G.S.	5	6	5
Bedford	6	5	3	The Leys	1	3	1
Bedford Modern	4	2	3	Loretto	2	1	2
Bloxham	6	1	3	Marlborough	7	4	3
Bradfield	5	3	5	Merchant Taylors'	4	5	2
Brighton	5	5	4	Mill Hill	1	3	7
Bromsgrove	5	4	3	Newcastle R.G.S.	7	4	5
Charterhouse	3	5	5	Oakham	6	6	3
Cheltenham	3	5	4	Reading	6	5	5
Clifton*	2	2	1	Repton	4	3	8
Cranbrook	5	4	4	Rossall	7	3	3
Cranleigh	2	6	5	St. Albans	6	1	4
Dean Close	–	1	9	St. Bees	4	1	7
Denstone	5	3	2	St. Dunstan's*	5	1	6
Downside	6	1	3	St. Edward's	4	8	3
Dover*	–	3	5	St. Paul's	4	4	7
Durham	1	4	9	St. Peter's, York*	2	–	4
Edinburgh Academy*	7	–	1	Stamford	8	4	0
Eltham	6	2	3	Stonyhurst	3	3	8
Epsom‡	7	2	2	Stowe	5	2	7
Eton	4	4	4	Solihull	2	5	2
Felsted	6	4	4	Sutton Valence	6	3	6
Fettes	2	2	4	Taunton	6	4	4
Framlingham	11	1	3	Tonbridge	5	–	10
George Watson's, Edinburgh	7	2	6	Trent	3	4	6
Gresham's	6	6	1	Trinity College, Glenalmond	6	6	6
Haileybury & I.S.C.	1	2	2	Uppingham*	2	1	2
Harrow	3	7	4	Wellingborough	1	2	7
Highgate	5	6	3	Wellington College*.	1	1	3
Hurstpierpoint	6	2	4	Whitgift*	5	1	4
Ipswich	3	4	6	Whitgift Middle*	5	6	2
Kelly	8	1	6	Winchester*	2	2	–
K.C.S., Wimbledon	3	2	5	Worcester R.G.S.	7	6	3
King Edward's, B'ham	8	7	1	Worksop	3	4	5
King's College, Taunton	1	4	7	Wrekin	2	7	7
Kingswood*	5	–	2	* School Matches only. ‡ Also one tie.			

STAMFORD remained unbeaten all season during the course of 12 games. **IPSWICH** had a moderate summer, R. G. Cadman and I. A. Young being their most successful batsman and bowler respectively.

THE LEYS did not enjoy the best of luck. I. T. Craig, with 49 wickets at 9.88 runs each, was the backbone of the bowling, and D. J. W. Thomas also did well with spin. N. R. Nesbitt was easily the most consistent bat. Nine old colours are available this year.

HERTS. AND BEDFORDSHIRE

It was a flourishing season at **BEDFORD**, where the cricket this summer should be of a similar high standard as six of the side remain. Undefeated by schools, Bedford had two good all-rounders in J. W. Fry (captain) and J. A. Spooner, and two promising newcomers, M. S. Meeson (aged 15), who made 540 runs, average 41.54, and M. H. J. Allen, a slow left-arm bowler.

Once more **BEDFORD MODERN** depended largely on R. E. G. Jeeps and P. G. Miller, their captain, for runs. The most successful bowlers were K. Tait and P. F. W. Wright.

HAILEYBURY and I.S.C. whose best win was that by six wickets against Tonbridge, were inconsistent. They lost to Uppingham and Cheltenham, and games with Harrow and Wellington were drawn. J. H. V. Dicks, who made a hundred against Wellington, hit 632 runs, average 52.67, and J. G. H. Jeffers, A. D. Watts and A. Fox were the best of the bowlers.

ST. ALBANS did well despite uncertain batting, to which M. G. Smith, a lefthander, proved the exception. Bowling honours were shared by D. J. George (captain) and H. A. F. Malden, both medium-fast.

BUCKS., BERKS. AND OXON.

With M B. Sheridan, their captain and wicketkeeper, below his 1948 form, **BEAUMONT** achieved only moderate results. One of their three victories was an exciting one-run affair against Oratory at Lord's. A. B. Wallerstein, who headed the averages with 58 wickets in his first season, bowled encouragingly well. Sheridan dropped to eighth place in the batting averages, which were headed by P. A. Dingli (421 runs)

BLOXHAM won all their school games, but fell away in club matches. J. W. Barton, the captain, developed as an attacking bat, and also took 27 wickets.

BRADFIELD, despite a loss of form in mid-season, improved on recent years, the Butterflies, Incogniti, Lancing, Wellington and Free Foresters being defeated. H. W. Joynt headed the batting with 511 runs; he was also the most economical bowler.

For **ETON**, of course, a satisfactory event was the seven-wickets win over Harrow at Lord's. They beat Wellington also but lost to Charterhouse and Marlborough and drew with Winchester. Batsmen to attract attention were I. R. Lomax and A. C. Ingleby-Mackenzie (aged 15) who made the only century of the season. J. S. Guthrie (47 wickets with off-breaks) and M. G. C. Jeffreys (quick) excelled in attack. J. A. Bailey was an able captain of a good fielding side.

READING had to build almost a new team, but they won six and drew five out of sixteen games. J. C. Rudd and K. Cotterell batted very well, and D. Wilson was the spearhead of the attack.

STOWE beat Bradfield and St. Edward's. but lost to Oundle, Bedford and Radley, and drew with Malvern. The Coningtons, J. F. (379 runs) and D. E. (352) led the batting. Of the bowlers, M. D. Cobham (57 wickets—including 9-20 v. Bradfield—average 11.93) took more wickets than the rest of his colleagues combined.

ST. EDWARD'S improved greatly, beating Bradfield, Bromsgrove, Eastbourne and Radley. They lost to Stowe and Wellington. D. Lattey, with 425 runs in 16 innings, was the most productive batsman. R. Lock and H. E. Lucas did best as bowlers, and D. S. Gilbert-Smith kept wicket very well in a good fielding side.

The reasons for **WELLINGTON'S** poor season were inconsistent batting and lack of penetration in attack. They beat St. Edward's, lost to Marlborough, Eton and Bradfield and had the better of a drawn game with Haileybury. The fielding improved, and eight colours remain for 1950.

MIDLANDS

DENSTONE, unbeaten by a school, scored 347 for six wickets against Stonyhurst— the biggest total in their history. J. Oliver contributed 170 not out, and W. G. Tobias (slow left-arm) hastened victory with match figures of ten for 50. Wrekin, Trent and Worksop were other schools defeated.

REPTON lost twice as many games as they won. In R. D. Bailey, who took 63 wickets at 9.2 runs each, they had a bowler who was at times as fast as anyone in England. A. C. W. Lewis, captain in 1950, made progress as an all-rounder and was the best batsman in the side.

UPPINGHAM, beginning with only two colours, became a useful side. They beat Haileybury and Oundle, drew with Repton, and were defeated by Shrewsbury and Rugby. C. K. R. Vartan (captain this year) was a good all-rounder, and P. B. Scotcher brought vigour to the batting. The fielding was steady.

·········MATCHES AT LORD'S·········

HARROW (128 and 151); ETON (176 and 107 for 3 wkts.). ETON won by seven wickets.

CLIFTON (248) beat TONBRIDGE (112 and 119) by an innings and 17 runs.

MARLBOROUGH (337 for 6 wkts. dec.) beat RUGBY (156 and 177) by an innings and 4 runs.

CHELTENHAM (240) beat HAILEYBURY & I.S.C. (140 and 99) by an innings and 1 run.

SOUTHERN SCHOOLS v. THE REST

THE REST 180 (Griffiths 86, Jeffreys 3-13) and 149 (Dicks 78 not, Marlar 4-28, Cowdray 4-44); SOUTHERN SCHOOLS 192 for 7 wkts. dec. (Cowdrey 85, Stewart 63, Bailey 3-55) and 139 for 3 wickets. (Worlidge 54 not). Southern Schools won by 7 wickets. Teams:—

SOUTHERN SCHOOLS—M. H. Bushby (Dulwich), D. R. W. Silk (Christ's Hospital), M. C. Cowdrey (Tonbridge), M. J. Stewart (Alleyn's), P. F. Worlidge (Marlborough), H. W. Joynt (Bradfield), A. Kamm (Charterhouse), D. C. P. Jowett (Sherborne), R. G. Marlar (Harrow), M. G. C. Jeffreys (Eton), I. St. G. Lindsay (Pangbourne).

THE REST—D. R. Wright (Rugby), J. H. V. Dicks (Haileybury & I.S.C.), P. M. Davies (Llandovery), C. J. Griffiths (Brentwood), J. F. Tucker (Cheltenham), J. M. Phillips (Rossall), A. G. Phillips (Shrewsbury), J. M. Fry (Bedford), T. R. Summers (Shrewsbury), R. D. Bailey (Repton), M. D. Cobham (Stowe).

COMBINED SERVICES v. PUBLIC SCHOOLS

COMBINED SERVICES 194 (Griffiths 3-40) and 222 for 8 wkts. dec. (Cowdrey 5-62); PUBLIC SCHOOLS 258 (Dicks 104, Kamm 56) and 140 for 8 wickets. (Stewart 63). Match drawn.

PUBLIC SCHOOLS XI—M. H. Bushby, D. R. W. Silk, M. C. Cowdrey, M. J. Stewart, C. J Griffiths, J. H. V. Dicks, P. F. Worlidge, H. W. Joynt, A. Kamm. R. G. Marlar, M. G. C. Jeffreys.

Three of **WORKSOP'S** five defeats came in the final week—a sign of strain on a young and inexperienced team. School victories were gained over Trent and St. Peter's, York. Prospects this year are favourable, although bowlers are scarce.

In a moderate summer at **WREKIN**, J. B. Nichols, the captain, achieved success as batsman and bowler, but the side was young and lacked experience.

An inability to bowl out their opponents' tail sometimes proved costly to **TRENT**, whose captain, F. Smit, again scored attractively and hit two centuries (against Craven Gentlemen and Mount St. Mary's). B. Nicholson, a bowler much above average, took 28 wickets at 9.39 runs each.

KING EDWARD'S, BIRMINGHAM, had a very fine season, losing only one of their sixteen matches. The team batted down to No. 11 (though this was seldom necessary). P. Hutchings and B. Lobb were good opening bowlers, and F. B. Revill and D. H. Benson clever with slows. A. J. Homer, P. A. Gough, I. R. McClelland and J. R. Charlesworth (wicket-keeper) batted consistently.

Three players, R. W. Evans (236 runs), T. N. Mitchell (234) and J. Faull (232) proved the best batsmen for **BROMSGROVE**, who won five games and lost three. Of the bowlers, J. D. Link was outstanding with 45 wickets, average 8.57.

WELLINGBOROUGH had a disappointing season. Their batting was unreliable, and only F. J. Cook was consistent. R. N. Bates and M. W. White bowled with most success.

OAKHAM gained splendid victories over Lincolnshire Gentlemen, Northants. Amateurs and Old Oakhamians. They also beat Wellingborough and Trent, drew with Stamford and Ratcliffe, and lost to Bedford Modern.

The Thompson twins dominated events in a successful season at **WORCESTER R.G.S.**, where J. W. (captain) dismissed 31 men from behind the stumps, and A. S., bowling leg-breaks, took 66 wickets—a record for the school. R. G. Woodcock, in his first year, obtained 29 wickets and looked a most promising bat.

SOLIHULL had a moderate year, A. E. Bannister, a fine opening bat, being unable to find his true form.

WEST COUNTRY

WINCHESTER'S best performance was a comfortable win over Marlborough, P. M. Welsh and R. J. Armitage bowling spinners skilfully. Harrow were beaten by 12 runs with five minutes to spare, due largely to a brave innings of 57 by the captain, J. P. Raison, and steady bowling by J. G. A. Varley. Against Charterhouse, Winchester had the better of a drawn game, but Eton made them follow on and it needed a fine not-out century by M. R. Coulman, potentially a very good player, to save them.

CHELTENHAM were undefeated in all six school games. Having drawn against St. Edward's, Marlborough and Malvern, they beat Repton, Clifton and Haileybury and I.S.C. R. T. Procter handled the team astutely; D. M. Richards was a successful medium-pace bowler, and J. F. Tucker hit nearly 500 runs, including a century against Marlborough.

MARLBOROUGH beat Wellington, Eton and Rugby, lost to Winchester and Sherborne, and drew with Cheltenham and Clifton. Their outstanding batsman was P. F. Worlidge, the captain, well supported by J. A. Tyzack, M. F. Pope, A. M. B. Salmon, K. A. C. Patteson and M. G. Case. C. J. Denham Davis, Tyzack and Pope made up an adequate pace attack, variety being provided by J. A. Burnett's leg-breaks and J. A. Kidd's off-spinners. The fielding reached a high standard, with J. M. Coates an excellent wicketkeeper.

CLIFTON, who beat Tonbridge and Sherborne, lost to Cheltenham and drew with Rugby and Marlborough. The batting largely depended on D. B. Bird (captain) and R. V. Turner, and their strength lay in bowling. J. D. C. Rees (off-breaks) took 58 wickets for 9.1 runs, including 12 for 90 v. Cheltenham and 8 for 45 v. Tonbridge.

DOWNSIDE had a keen XI which improved greatly. E. A. McGuire scored freely, and M. F. Daly (captain) took 32 wickets, average 9.72, with medium-pace out-swingers. K. Wylie was a fine hitter, and R. J. Adamson and J. M. A. Nicholson were promising batsmen. M.C.C., Beaumont, Canford, Blundell's and King's School, Bruton, were beaten.

CANFORD began with good prospects, but their season was moderate. P. W. Littman was the most successful batsman, and G. A. Milnes (leg-breaks) the best bowler. M. Hayes was above average as wicketkeeper, and the fielding was always good.

KINGSWOOD won five school matches and lost two—a good record. J. G. Smith excelled as batsman and bowler.

ALLHALLOWS enjoyed their best summer for a long time, their team-work being notably good. There were six reliable batsmen and four bowlers, whose value was increased by crisp fielding. M. Ray Hills, the captain, hit two centuries at the end of term, and S. J. Harvey, K. F. Keightley and R. Taylor all took over 30 wickets.

KELLY COLLEGE, with eight wins, had a good side, although strength in bowling was at times off-set by uncertain batting on easy-paced pitches. They had good wins against Exeter, Wellington, West Buckland, Plymouth College and Devon Dumplings. The 1950 side should be above average.

NORTH

ROSSALL were one of the outstanding sides of the year. Against schools they scored 1,256 runs, and lost only 27 wickets in doing so. There were decisive victories against St. Bees, Sedbergh and Stonyhurst, and five centuries were hit. J. M. Phillips (564 runs, average 51.27), K. V. Holmes, W. Nabb and G. P. Marsland all batted finely. J. A. Carter, in his fourth year and second as captain, headed the bowling averages, followed by S. L. Watson, a Colt, and Marsland.

STONYHURST had a disappointing season, but P. J. Leyden (average 70.33) batted splendidly and P. S. Delisle showed exceptional batting promise at the age of 14.

ST. BEES won four matches and lost seven. D. Whitehead headed the batting averages and D. Holliday the bowling.

KING WILLIAM'S COLLEGE, Isle of Man, beat Liverpool College (by 7 runs) and Merchant Taylors', Crosby, but lost to Birkenhead. R. N. Waters topped the batting averages with 22.3, and B. D. Galbraith took 37 wickets at 10.5 runs each.

For ST. PETER'S, York, P. T. Baker, the captain, hit the highest individual score (63 not out v. M.C.C.) and D. Walter bowled well.

DURHAM had a lean year. Their batting relied overmuch on T. Bourn, D. I. Mort and T. G. Smailes, the captain. Despite many lifeless pitches the bowling was good, without being brilliant.

NEWCASTLE R.G.S. proved a strong combination, and were beaten only by Manchester G.S. in ten inter-school matches. Their captain, D. R. Lowther, scored 479 runs.

At LEEDS G.S. the season was the best since the war, and with tighter fielding they would have done even better. Metcalfe, Booth and Balmforth were batsmen of quality, and Hufton, Howard and Duncan bowled effectively.

SCOTLAND

EDINBURGH ACADEMY had the best record in Scotland—seven wins, one defeat. In a season of many fine performances, all were overshadowed by the all-round brilliance of J. M. Allan, who took 85 wickets (6.05 runs each) and scored 573 runs, average 35.8. A. S. Hay, captain of FETTES, made 668 runs, his average, 51.38, being the highest among Scottish schools in 1949.

TRINITY COLLEGE, Glenalmond, were handicapped by injuries, and their captain, I. C. Burnett, did not regain true all-round form after damaging his hand. A. C. Denholm (543 runs, average 31.94), scored consistently and kept wicket admirably, and H. J. J. Denholm took 45 wickets. They beat George Watson's College and Edinburgh Academy, lost to Loretto and Fettes, and drew with Merchiston.

OBITUARY 1949

SIR SAMUEL HILL-WOOD died on January 4th. He was captain of Derbyshire from 1899 to 1901, his four sons (W. W., B. S., C. K. and D. J.) also playing for the county. He was also well known as the Chairman of Arsenal F.C.

F. H. GRESSON died on February 1st aged 81. An Oxford Blue, he played in three University matches and later appeared for Sussex.

GEORGE COX (sen.) died on March 25th while his son, George Cox jun., was on his way home from coaching in South Africa. A Sussex stalwart for over 30 years, he took seventeen wickets in a match in 1926 and assisted in a last wicket partnership of 156 with H. Butt.

C. A. OLLIVIERRE died on March 26th aged 72. One of the best West Indies bats of the early days, he toured England with the 1900 team and stayed behind to qualify for Derbyshire, for whom he played with success until 1907.

S. CHRISTOPHERSON died on April 4th aged 87. He was educated at Uppingham and played for England v Australia at Lord's in 1884. He was President of the M.C.C. from 1939 to 1946.

J. CANNON died on April 21st aged 82. He was on the Lord's staff for 65 years, starting as a ball boy. in the tennis courts in 1879 and ending as chief clerk to the M.C.C. for more than 40 years. On his retirement in 1944 he was elected an honorary member of M.C.C.

G. WATTS died on April 22nd aged 82. He was born in the Cambridge cricket pavilion and played as wicketkeeper for Surrey and Cambridgeshire. Later he assisted the club as umpire.

F. WALDEN died on May 3rd aged 61. For several years he was a valuable member of the Northants team. but he was even better known on the football field, playing for England, Northampton Town and Tottenham Hotspur. On retiring from cricket he became an umpire and " stood " in the Oval Test match of 1938.

M. WRIGHT died on May 16th. He was the professional coach to Eton College for 52 years and played a few matches for Notts. in his youth before playing for 26 seasons with Bucks.

LORD HAZLERIGG died on May 26th. He was the Leics. captain from 1907 to 1910. His son, A. G. Hazlerigg, also captained the county.

T. OATES died on June 20th aged 73. He played for Notts. as wicketkeeper for 28 years and dismissed nearly 1.000 batsmen during the seasons 1897-1925.

W. F. GIFFEN, who died on June 29th, was the younger brother of G. Giffen. He toured England in 1893. without appearing in a Test match, but played in three Test matches in Australia.

T. A. HIGSON died on August 3rd aged 75. During his cricket career he played for three counties— Lancs., Derby and Cheshire. In 1932 he was appointed Chairman of the Lancashire C.C.C. From 1931 to 1938 he was a member of the England Test Selection Committee. He was one of the most famous legislators in the game.

W. E. ROLLER died on August 27th aged 91. Educated at Westminster and Cambridge University, he played for Surrey as an all-rounder from 1881 to 1890. During that time Surrey won the championship in six successive years.

R. V. RYDER died on September 2nd. A famous figure on the legislative side of cricket, he was secretary of Warwickshire from 1895 to 1944.

F. WORSLEY died on September 15th. Famous as the producer of the B.B.C. show " I.T.M.A.," he played two matches for Glamorgan, one in 1922 and one in 1923.

C. L. A. SMITH died on November 25th aged 70. He played for Sussex from 1898 to 1911, being joint-captain with C. B. Fry in 1906 and captain in 1909.

D. D. HINDLEKAR died on March 3rd. A fine wicketkeeper and useful bat, he toured England with the 1936 and 1946 India teams, but was unfortunate to receive an injury on each tour.

T. W. REESE died on April 13th. Although a very useful cricketer he will always be better known for two notable works on New Zealand cricket.

A. L. OCHSE died in May. A good pace bowler, he toured England with the 1929 South African team, taking 52 wickets at 35 runs each.

K. R. B. FRY died in June. A cousin of C. B. Fry, he gained a Cambridge Blue in 1904. He later appeared in two matches for Sussex.

F. HEARNE died in South Africa in July. He was one of the few players to appear in Test cricket for two countries—England and South Africa. He toured South Africa with C. A. Smith's team in 1888-89 and stayed there on a coaching engagement. Before settling in South Africa he played with success for Kent. His son, G. A. L., toured England with the 1924 South African team.

A. FIELDER died on August 30th aged 71. Making his debut as a fast bowler for Kent in 1903, he quickly gained a place in first-class cricket and toured Australia in 1903-04 and 1907-08, appearing in six Test matches for England. His best season was 1906 when Kent won their first championship and he set the seal on his fame by taking all ten Gentlemen wickets in an innings at Lord's; he totalled 172 wickets during the summer. Another record that stands to his credit was his share in the last wicket stand of 235 for Kent v Worcs. (Stourbridge) in 1909, his partner being Frank Woolley. This is still an English record.

L. H. GAY died on November 1st aged 78. Educated at Brighton, he won Cambridge Blues as wicket-keeper in 1892 and 1893. He played for Somerset in 1894, but then transferred to Hampshire. A good goalkeeper, he gained his soccer Blue at Cambridge and later played for England in internationals.

E. HUMPHRIES died on November 1st. He was a fine slow left-arm bowler but the presence of Colin Blythe in the great Kent team of the early 1900s restricted his bowling opportunities. He was also a very good batsman and a fine specialist fielder at mid-on. He made one overseas tour, to the West Indies with the M.C.C. in 1912-13. After retiring from cricket he was coach at Uppingham before becoming chief coach at Canterbury. During the first World War he took part in the raid on Zeebrugge.

H. S. SQUIRES

The untimely death of H. S. Squires of Surrey was reported on January 24th, 1950. He died in Richmond Royal Hospital as the result of leuchaemia, an unusual disease of the blood.

Those who know county cricketers intimately may say that there was no one more popular than " Stan " Squires. He was universally respected and admired, his demeanour and attitude to the game being an ideal model for young professional cricketers to follow. No one ever saw Squires try anything but his very hardest in the field.

Although he was a more than useful bowler of off-breaks (306 wickets at 35.35) it is as a batsman, precise and cultured, that he will, of course, be remembered. Between 1928 and 1949 he scored 19,186 runs (average 31.24) and made 37 hundreds. Eleven times he passed the 1,000 mark. His style was so essentially sound that he might well have played for England had it not been for the handicap of poor sight.

He first played for Surrey as an amateur in 1928 and 1929 but joined their staff in 1930. In the 'twenties he had been coached by that master of the craft, G. A. Faulkner, the South African cricketer, and later he joined his staff. He hoped to become a coach himself when he retired—quite probably at the end of this season and very possibly at Oxford. He had a Benefit in 1948 which realised £2,900. His best score was 236 against Lancashire at the Oval, 1933, and his best bowling figures were 5 for 34 against Leicester at the Oval in 1947. He was born at Kingston on February 22nd, 1909.

645—9 dec. Surrey v N. Zealanders
(Oval)
623—5 dec. Middx. v Worcs.
(Worcester)

LOWEST INNINGS TOTALS
49 Kent v Glamorgan (Swansea)
52 Derbyshire v Surrey (Oval)
54 F. Foresters v Oxford U. (Oxford)
58 Essex v Derbyshire (Buxton)
59 Hampshire v Surrey (Oval)

Matters of Fact

SOME 1949 STATISTICS
Compiled by
ROY WEBBER

BATTING

DOUBLE CENTURIES

331*	J. D. Robertson	.. .. ..	Middlesex v Worcs. (Worcester)
269*	L. Hutton	.. .. ..	Yorks. v Northants. (Wellingborough)
257	D. Brookes	.. .. ..	Northants v Glos. (Bristol)
255	J. F. Parker	.. .. ..	Surrey v New Zealanders (Oval)
243	B. Sutcliffe	.. .. ..	New Zealanders v Essex (Southend)
238	R. T. Simpson	.. .. ..	Notts. v Lancs. (Manchester)
234*	John Langridge	.. .. ..	Sussex v Derby (Ilkeston)
226*	W. Place	.. .. ..	Lancs. v Notts. (Nottingham)
219*	G. H. G. Doggart	.. .. ..	Cambridge U. v Essex (Cambridge)
219*	D. J. Insole	.. .. ..	Essex v Yorks. (Colchester)
219	J. D. Eggar	.. .. ..	Derby v Yorks. (Bradford)
215*	L. Outschoorn	.. .. ..	Worcs. v Northants. (Worcester)
212*	G. Cox	.. .. ..	Sussex v Yorks. (Leeds)
210	H. S. Squires	.. .. ..	Surrey v Derby (Oval)
210	W. W. Keeton	.. .. ..	Notts. v Yorks. (Sheffield)
210	L. B. Fishlock	.. .. ..	Surrey v Somerset (Oval)
208	W. W. Keeton	.. .. ..	Notts. v Glamorgan (Nottingham)
206	M. P. Donnelly	.. .. ..	New Zealand v England (Lord's)
206	L. Hutton	.. .. ..	England v New Zealand (Oval)
204*	J. G. Dewes	.. .. ..	Cambridge U. v Essex (Cambridge)
204	D. S. Sheppard	.. .. ..	Sussex v Glamorgan (Eastbourne)
203	V. J. Scott	.. .. ..	N. Zealanders v Combined S. (Gillingham)
201	L. Hutton	.. .. ..	Yorks. v Lancs. (Manchester)
200*	R. T. Simpson	.. .. ..	Notts. v Surrey (Nottingham)
200	S. M. Brown	.. .. ..	Middlesex v Kent (Canterbury)
200	H. E. Dollery	.. .. ..	Warwick. v Glos. (Gloucester)

A CENTURY IN EACH INNINGS OF A MATCH

117	100	A. V. Avery	..	Essex v Glamorgan (Ebbw Vale)
111	118	L. B. Fishlock	..	Surrey v Notts. (Nottingham)
115	127*	H. Gimblett	..	Somerset v Hants. (Taunton)
100*	114*	J. Hardstaff	..	Notts. v Northants (Nottingham)
165	100	L. Hutton	..	Yorks. v Sussex (Hove)
115	129	John Langridge	..	Sussex v Lancs. (Manchester)
143	102*	R. T. Simpson	..	Notts. v Leics. (Nottingham)
243	100*	B. Sutcliffe	..	New Zealanders v Essex (Southend)

CENTURIES IN SUCCESSIVE INNINGS

Four — John Langridge (Sussex): 115* v Camb. U. (Cambridge), 115 and 129 v Lancs. (Manchester), 120 v Glos. (Chichester).

Three—W. W. Keeton (Notts.): 109* v Hants. (Nottingham), 208 v Glamorgan (Nottingham), 134 v Lancs. (Manchester).

BEST WICKET PARTNERSHIPS
† unfinished.

1st	318	W. W. Keeton & R. T. Simpson	Notts. v Lancs. (Manchester)
	260	L. B. Fishlock & E. A. Bedser	Surrey v Somerset (Oval)
	251	L. J. Todd & A. E. Fagg	Kent v Leics. (Maidstone)
	247	B. Sutcliffe & V. J. Scott	N.Z. v Combined S. (Gillingham)
	238	John Langridge & D. S. Sheppard	Sussex v Leics. (Hove)
	229	B. Sutcliffe & V. J. Scott	N.Z. v Surrey (Oval)
	208†	D. Brookes & N. Oldfield	Northants. v Yorks. (Wellingborough)
	207	J. D. Robertson & S. M. Brown	Middlesex v Lancs. (Manchester)
2nd	429†	J. G. Dewes & G. H. G. Doggart	Camb. U. v Essex (Cambridge)
	261†	L. Hutton & J. V. Wilson	Yorks. v Scotland (Hull)
	251†	R. T. Simpson & C. J. Poole	Notts. v Leics. (Nottingham)
	227	S. M. Brown & W. J. Edrich	Middlesex v Northants. (Lord's)
	219	R. T. Simpson & C. J. Poole	Northants. v Sussex (Hastings)

	218	L. Hutton & W. J. Edrich	England v New Zealand (Oval)
	220	L. B. Fishlock & E. A. Bedser	Surrey v Hants. (Oval)
	204	J. D. Robertson & W. J. Edrich	Middlesex v Hants. (Bournemouth)
3rd	246	G. O. Rabone & J. R. Reid	N.Z. v Notts. (Nottingham)
	241	C. H. Palmer & L. Outschoorn	Worcs. v Northants. (Worcester)
	204	H. S. Squires & B. Constable	Surrey v Essex (Southend)
	201	G. Lester & M. Tompkin	Leics. v Oxford U. (Oxford)
4th	326†	James Langridge & G. Cox	Sussex v Yorks. (Leeds)
	324	W. M. Wallace & J. R. Reid	N.Z. v Cambridge U. (Cambridge)
	299	W. M. Wallace & M. P. Donnelly	N.Z. v Leics. (Leicester)
	248	J. T. Ikin & K. Grieves	Lancs. v N.Z. (Manchester)
	210	D. Compton & J. G. Dewes	Middlesex v N.Z. (Lord's)
5th	264	M. Robinson & S. Montgomery	Glamorgan v Hants. (Bournemouth)
	230	J. D. Robertson & G. O. Allen	Middlesex v Worcs. (Worcester)
7th	176	G. O. Rabone & F. H. L. Mooney	N.Z. v M.C.C. (Lord's)
9th	161	B. Edrich & F. Ridgway	Kent v Sussex (Tunbridge Wells)

CARRYING BAT THROUGH COMPLETED INNINGS
(Innings total in brackets)

109*	(236)	L. G. Berry	Leics. v Somerset (Leicester)
140*	(283)	F. C. Gardner	Warwick v Worcs. (Birmingham)
95*	(247)	M. B. Hofmeyr	Oxford U. v New Zealanders (Oxford)
64*	(169)	M. B. Hofmeyr	Oxford U. v Cambridge U. (Lord's)
78*	(153)	L. Hutton	Yorks. v Worcs. (Sheffield)
119*	(261)	J. T. Ikin	Lancs. v Middlesex (Manchester)

BOWLING
"HAT-TRICKS"

R. Jenkins	Worcs. v Surrey (Worcester—1st inns.)
R. Jenkins	Worcs. v Surrey (Worcester—2nd inns.)
J. T. Ikin	Lancs. v Somerset (Taunton)
T. L. Pritchard	Warwick v Kent (Maidstone)
J. E. Walsh	Leics. v Notts. (Loughborough)
D. V. P. Wright	Kent v Hants. (Canterbury)

3 WICKETS IN 4 CONSECUTIVE BALLS

H. L. Hazell	Somerset v Worcs. (W-super-M)
R. Jenkins	Worcs. v Combined S. (Worcester)
R. Tattersall	Lancs. v Surrey (Manchester)

ROY WEBBER

9 OR 10 WICKETS IN AN INNINGS & 15 IN A MATCH

10—90		T. E. Bailey	Essex v Lancs. (Clacton)
9—53		J. Cornford	Sussex v Northants. (Peterborough)
9—61	15—107	T. W. Goddard	Glos. v Derby (Bristol)
	15—164	J. E. Walsh	Leics. v Notts. (Loughborough)
10—66		J. K. Graveney	Glos. v Derby (Chesterfield)
9—51	15—163	D. V. P. Wright	Kent v Leics. (Maidstone)

TEN OR MORE SUCCESSIVE MAIDEN OVERS

17	H. L. Hazell	Somerset v Glos. (Taunton)
14	J. A. Young	Middlesex v Glos. (Bristol)
10	C. Gladwin	Derby v Glos. (Chesterfield)

FIELDING AND WICKET-KEEPING
FIELDERS—FIVE CATCHES IN AN INNINGS

5	G. O. Rabone	New Zealanders v Oxford U. (Oxford)

FIELDERS—SIX CATCHES IN A MATCH

6	W. J. Edrich	Middlesex v Surrey (Lord's)
6	J. T. Ikin	Lancs. v Oxford U. (Oxford)

WICKET-KEEPERS—SIX DISMISSALS IN AN INNINGS

6	(3ct—3st)	P. Corrall	Leics. v Hants. (Leicester)
6	(6ct)	G. N. G. Kirby	Surrey v Cambridge U. (Guildford)
6	(5ct—1st)	E. A. Meads	Notts. v Kent (Nottingham)
6	(4ct—2st)	F. H. L. Mooney	New Zealanders v Worcs. (Worcester)
6	(3ct—3st)	H. Yarnold	Worcs. v Hants. (Worcester)

WICKET-KEEPERS—EIGHT OR MORE DISMISSALS IN A MATCH

9	(8ct—1st)	T. G. Evans	Kent v New Zealanders (Canterbury)
9	(8ct—1st)	E. B. Lewis	Warwick v Oxford U. (Birmingham)
9	(5ct—4st)	H. Yarnold	Worcs. v Hants. (Worcester)
8	(6ct—2st)	H. W. Stephenson	Somerset v Sussex (Eastbourne)
8	(4ct—4st)	H. Yarnold	Worcs. v Kent (Dover)

THE CRICKETER'S "DOUBLE"

Four cricketers achieved the "double" of 1,000 runs and 100 wickets in a season —T. E. Bailey (Aug. 1st), R. Jenkins (Aug. 20th), F. R. Brown (Aug 25th) and D. B. Close (Sept. 2nd).

WICKETKEEPERS' LAURELS

	Ct.	St.	Total			Ct.	St.	Total
H. Yarnold	63	47	110	T. H. Wade	47	18	65
A. J. McIntyre	72	23	95	R. T. Spooner	46	14	60
H. W. Stephenson	42	43	85	E. A. Meads	39	18	57
G. Dawkes	69	11	80	P. Corrall	38	18	56
T. G. Evans	58	22	80	S. C. Griffith	45	8	53
L. H. Compton	57	15	72	K. Fiddling	39	13	52
A. E. Wilson	50	19	69	H. G. Davies	41	9	50
D. V. Brennan	47	19	66	J. R. Reid	26	6	32
F. H. L. Mooney	46	20	66	A. Wilson	22	10	32
				N. McCorkell	25	6	31
				A. Barlow	23	7	30

FIELDSMEN'S LAURELS

Catches

L. Outschoorn	54		M. R. Barton	
W. J. Edrich	52		F. R. Brown	
J. T. Ikin	45		R. O. Jenkins	
L. Hutton	43		G. A. R. Lock	
B. O. Allen	} 38		C. Oakes	} 27
J. Lawrence	}		N. H. Rogers	
E. A. Bedser	} 35		W. S. Surridge	
P. Clift	}		J. H. Wardle	
A. Townsend	33	A. V. Bedser } 29	W. Wooller	
K. Grieves	}	D. Compton }	E. D. R. Eagar	} 26
Jn. Langridge	} 32	A. Coxon	J. C. Laker	}
B. Sutcliffe	}	G. H. G. Doggart	M. F. Tremlett	}
V. E. Jackson	} 31	A. E. Fagg } 28	J. F. Crapp	}
A. Revill	}	C. A. Milton }	T. W. Graveney	} 25
J. D. Robertson	30	A. J. Watkins	J. F. Parker	}
		A. W. Wellard	D. Smith	}
			C. Walker	}

HOW THE RUNS WERE SCORED IN 1949

	Matches played	FOR			AGAINST		
		Runs	Wkts.	Avge.	Runs	Wkts.	Avge.
England	4	2180	47	46.38	2314	58	39.89
New Zealanders	32	15659	400	39.14	14108	467	30.20
Derbyshire	27	10233	445	22.99	10640	385	27.63
Essex	29	12042	432	27.87	13051	416	31.37
Glamorgan	29	10523	430	24.47	11152	428	26.05
Gloucestershire	29	12454	459	27.13	11838	448	26.42
Hampshire	29	13034	495	26.33	13501	425	31.76
Kent	28	12013	489	24.56	12619	444	28.42
Lancashire	30	12167	413	29.46	12033	438	27.47
Leicestershire	29	12897	475	27.15	13756	399	34.47
Middlesex	29	13099	408	32.10	13049	508	25.68
Northamptonshire	28	12535	412	30.42	11934	430	27.75
Nottinghamshire	27	11767	340	34.60	11973	323	37.06
Somerset	29	11524	505	22.81	12309	465	26.47
Surrey	32	14253	487	29.26	13822	554	24.94
Sussex	30	14834	465	31.90	13951	423	32.98
Warwickshire	30	12003	440	27.27	12213	499	24.47
Worcestershire	30	12716	479	26.54	12359	488	25.32
Yorkshire	33	14242	440	32.36	14073	549	25.63
Oxford U.	13	5633	219	25.72	5352	222	24.10
Cambridge U.	14	6525	197	33.12	6215	183	33.96
M.C.C.	5	2566	71	36.14	2482	74	33.54
Combined Services	6	2915	116	25.12	2984	84	35.52
Miscellaneous	—	8429	330	—	8551	284	—
Total		256,243	8994	28.49	256,243	8994	28.49

HERE AND THERE

J. D. ROBERTSON scored 331 not out in the course of a day's play (6¼ hours) for Middlesex v. Worcs. (Worcester). The Middlesex total at the close was 623 for five wickets.

E. B. LEWIS dismissed nine batsmen (8 ct., 1 st.) in his first match in first-class cricket—Warwick. v. Oxford U. (Birmingham). This is a record debut for a wicketkeeper.

D. V. P. WRIGHT established a new world record by recording the seventh "hat-trick" of his career v. Hants. (Canterbury). T. W. Goddard and C. W. L. Parker hold second place with six each.

H. L. HAZELL (Somerset) bowled 105 consecutive balls without conceding a run v. Glos. (Taunton)——a world record.

G. J. WHITTAKER hit nine sixes in his innings of 148 v. Northants. (Northampton) but the on-side boundary was rather short. The record number of sixes for one innings is eleven.

Notts. scored 279 for the loss of one wicket in 107 minutes to defeat Leics. by nine wickets. R. T. SIMPSON and C. J. POOLE added 251 in an unbroken second wicket partnership in 97 minutes, Poole reaching his century in an hour.

M. B. HOFMEYR carried his bat through a completed innings in the University match——only the second time the feat has been achieved in the series—— and also for Oxford against the New Zealanders.

T. G. EVANS straight drove a ball from T. E. Bailey for a six all-run in the Gentlemen v. Players match at Lord's.

J. CORNFORD took the first nine wickets in the Northants. first innings at Rushden, but the tenth batsman was dismissed by G. Cox.

T. E. BAILEY completed the "double" on 1st August—the first amateur to achieve the feat since V. W. C. Jupp, of Northants, in 1933.

J. HARDSTAFF has now scored a century against each of the other 16 first-class counties. At the beginning of 1949 he needed hundreds against Lancs. and Yorks. and scored them in successive matches at the end of June.

In the first three Derbyshire matches of the season DAWKES conceded only one bye while opposing batsmen scored 989 runs.

Only two cricketers, V. E. JACKSON and M. TOMPKIN (Leics.), have appeared in every match for their county since the resumption of cricket in 1946.

* * *

The Minor Counties in Brief (*continued from page* 111)

HERTFORDSHIRE began with four victories and with a little luck would have finished higher than seventh. T. W. Tyrwhitt-Drake was an inspiring captain. **KENT II** had a moderate summer, but were heartened by the form of several young players, among them A. Woollett, B. H. Lock, R. Mayes, A. Marshall and the Cambridge Blue, R. J. Morris. Bad fielding marred **LINCOLNSHIRE'S** efforts, and the batting was inconsistent, although five players made centuries—a county record. **MIDDLESEX II** discovered little fresh talent, the burden being shared mostly by already seasoned players. The Indian, R. S. Cooper, headed the bowling. **NORFOLK** were still weak in batting and had another poor year. An exception was B. A. Clements (501 runs)——their best all-rounder. E. H. Edrich returned from Lancashire to keep a fine wicket and C. S. R. Boswell again had much success with spin.

For **NORTHUMBERLAND** L. Liddell the captain, made a hurricane 221 against Lancashire II at Newcastle——the highlight of their season. T. S. Worthington (ex-Derbyshire) added strength to the batting, and the side showed all-round improvement. **NOTTINGHAMSHIRE II**, admirably led by E. A. Marshall, enjoyed better fortune, though the bowling was still below par. E. Martin, C. J. Poole and R. Giles were the best batsmen.

In their first season for twenty years **OXFORDSHIRE** led the field until the concluding stages, when Lancashire II overtook them. J. F. Mendl batted extremely well, and R. V. Divecha excelled as an all-rounder.

STAFFORDSHIRE'S advance was a most satisfactory performance under their new captain, D. M. Haynes. R. Smith (588 runs) and F. R. Bailey (512) scored consistently; S. Crump and B. Shardlow, both slow, were as good as ever. **SURREY II**, who won five games and lost only one, had a wealth of batting talent but the side was strong in all departments. Brazier's 1,212 runs included 249 not out against Norfolk at Guildford. B. Constable, G. J. Whittaker and D. G. W. Fletcher all scored many runs and G. Smith again headed the bowling.

SUSSEX II, in their second season, did reasonably well, though the attack was at times weak. D. S. Sheppard, K. P. A. Matthews and D. V. Smith were the most successful batsmen; K. G. Suttle, P. J. Wales and J. M. Parks showed much promise.. **WARWICKSHIRE II** under W. E. Houghton gave youth every opportunity. 17-years-old D. Heath was top batsman and H. E. Roberts, a left-handed opener, scored 570 runs. V. H. D. Cannings (58 wickets) bowled excellently.

Injuries deprived **WILTSHIRE** of a regular pace bowler, and this handicap proved too much. In a fairly strong batting side A. E. H. Rutter, aged 20, hit 539 runs, and J. A. Wheeler (511) also gave some delightful displays. **WORCESTERSHIRE II** did not attach overmuch importance to their moderate final placing. They preferred to introduce young cricketers rather than keep a regular eleven. N. Whiting scored 842 runs and P. E. Richardson (only 18) 577.

YORKSHIRE II had a satisfactory summer, though falling five places. W. G. Keighley, the new captain, K. Swales and E. S. Barraclough batted well, and C. W. Foord, F. S. Trueman, E. Leadbeater and B. Brooke were promising bowlers.

First-class Averages 1949

BATTING and FIELDING

(Qualification: 10 innings. † denotes left-hand batsman)

	I.	N.O.	R.	H.S.	Avge.	100	50	Ct/St
J. Hardstaff	40	9	2251	162*	72.61	8	12	5
L. Hutton	56	6	3429	269*	68.58	12	17	43
P. B. H. May	12	1	695	175	63.18	1	5	2
R. T. Simpson	46	6	2525	238	63.12	6	18	11
†M. P. Donnelly (N.Z.)	45	8	2287	206	61.81	5	13	24
J. R. Thompson	12	2	609	103	60.90	2	4	4
John Langridge	53	5	2914	234*	60.70	12	8	32
†B. Sutcliffe (N.Z.)	49	5	2627	243	59.70	7	15	32
W. W. Keeton	38	1	2049	210	55.37	6	8	4
D. J. Insole	39	9	1640	219*	54.66	4	14	14
C. Washbrook	27	1	1419	141	54.57	6	6	9
M. M. Walford	16	2	763	120	54.50	2	4	3
W. Oldfield	47	3	2192	168	49.81	4	16	14
†M. Wallace (N.Z.)	41	4	1722	197	49.20	5	11	2
D. Compton	56	4	2530	182	48.65	9	11	29
E. Dollery	48	4	2084	200	47.36	7	9	12
†E. G. Ames	47	2	2125	160	47.22	6	9	21
†G. H. G. Doggart	51	4	2063	219*	45.84	5	11	28
†J. F. Crapp	48	4	2014	140	45.77	7	7	25
†L. B. Fishlock	56	3	2426	210	45.77	7	13	11
†J. G. Dewes	42	3	1752	204*	44.92	7	5	5
D. Brookes	54	5	2163	257	44.14	7	11	19
M. B. Hofmeyr	23	3	879	154	43.95	1	2	10
†Denis Taylor	14	1	438	121	43.80	1	2	24
E. Gimblett	52	4	2093	156	43.60	4	12	14
E. Cooper	50	6	1916	193	43.54	3	14	3
D. S. Sheppard	21	0	913	204	43.47	3	1	7
†C. J. Poole	34	4	1293	154*	43.10	3	6	11
L. G. Berry	46	3	1853	162	43.09	4	10	8
G. J. Whittaker	31	5	1117	148	42.96	2	6	6
D. Barrick	18	4	595	147*	42.50	1	2	6
†A. Wharton	41	4	1567	139	42.35	4	9	5
†J. D. Eggar	14	2	501	113	41.75	1	2	8
J. R. Reid (N.Z.)	40	4	1488	188*	41.33	4	4	26/6

Batting (Cont.)

	I.	N.O.	R.	H.S.	Avge.	100	50	Ct/St
G. M. Emmett	51	2	2005	116	40.91	3	12	18
†J. F. Parker	48	4	1789	255	40.65	5	7	25
†J. V. Wilson	41	5	1460	157*	40.55	2	9	8
G. Cox	54	6	1938	212*	40.37	6	8	11
A. E. Fagg	46	2	1774	129	40.31	3	11	28
V. J. Scott (N.Z.)	19	1	1572	203	40.30	4	6	15
C. H. Palmer	40	1	722	136	40.11	1	3	9
J. D. Robertson	57	5	2244	331*	40.07	7	6	30
A. V. Edrich	62	9	2253	182	39.52	5	14	52
A. V. Avery	25	2	906	143	39.39	3	2	6
†James Langridge	51	9	1640	133*	39.04	2	7	18
F. T. Prentice	46	1	1742	191	38.71	2	8	4
N. McCorkell	52	3	1871	143*	38.18	5	14	25/6
H. A. Pawson	12	1	420	54*	38.18	–	3	3
K. Grieves	42	5	1407	128	38.02	2	9	32
A. C. Burnett	20	5	565	79*	37.66	–	2	18
E. Lester	51	3	1801	186	37.52	4	8	8
N. W. D. Yardley	54	11	1612	159	37.48	2	10	23
R. G. Wilson	10	2	298	107	37.25	1	1	4
H. S. Squires	51	3	1785	210	37.18	4	9	15
G. A. Edrich	46	4	1561	136*	37.16	2	14	17
†H. E. Watts	13	6	483	100*	37.15	1	–	2
C. B. Harris	29	6	844	100*	36.69	1	6	10
M. Tompkin	53	2	1860	128	36.47	4	10	10
W. Place	38	2	1305	226*	36.25	3	4	13
F. A. Lowson	55	5	1799	104	35.98	2	13	9
W. A. Hadlee (N.Z.)	44	4	1439	119*	35.97	1	6	24
T. E. Bailey	50	11	1380	93	35.38	–	10	14
†W. E. Jones	24	4	706	128	35.30	1	3	4
A. Revill	41	5	1269	156*	35.25	2	4	3
†F. Ikin	53	5	1685	167	35.10	4	9	31
†C. Gardner	53	5	1657	140*	34.52	2	6	45
E. A. Bedser	56	5	1740	163	34.11	2	10	18
S. M. Brown	49	1	1636	200	34.08	3	6	35
E. Davis	26	1	851	171	34.04	2	6	15
†P. H. Vigar	48	5	1449	136	33.69	1	7	22
F. Halliday	23	0	773	113	33.60	1	2	17
G. Lester	53	5	1599	131	33.31	1	2	7

Batting (Cont.)

	I.	N.O.	R.	H.S.	Avge.	100	50	Ct/St
G. Dawson	34	3	1032	158*	33.27	3	4	10
T. C. Dodds	53	2	1696	123	33.25	3	10	6
W. G. A. Parkhouse	49	4	1491	145	33.13	2	10	16
T. W. Graveney	55	1	1784	159	33.03	4	8	25
J. G. W. Davies	14	0	462	99	33.00	—	3	9
J. O. Rabone (N.Z.)	39	8	1021	120*	32.93	1	6	24
H. Sharp	36	5	1020	102	32.90	1	5	9
R. E. S. Wyatt	27	2	812	125	32.48	2	3	13
A. Thompson	24	3	682	89	32.47	—	5	7
D. Kenyon	54	1	1691	182	31.90	3	7	23
B. J. Howard	13	1	382	114	31.83	1	1	7
†W. Barron	30	1	908	109	31.31	2	5	21/1
†A. G. J. Rimell	16	1	467	160	31.18	1	1	7
†F. Jakeman	33	2	963	169	31.06	2	3	7
†B. O. Allen	52	3	1520	134	31.02	2	9	38
†D. B. Carr	39	0	1210	170	31.02	3	8	21
C. S. Elliott	50	2	1477	104	30.77	1	8	15
S. H. Cray	35	1	1046	129	30.76	2	4	5
N. H. Rogers	58	1	1747	107	30.64	4	8	27
L. J. Todd	49	1	1460	174	30.41	2	6	9
†C. E. Winn	30	0	908	95	30.26	—	6	8
†A. J. Watkins	48	4	1331	129	30.25	4	5	28
C. B. Van Ryneveld	30	0	905	102	30.16	1	6	13
J. Arnold	44	5	1151	110	29.51	—	9	4
†D. Smith	37	2	1033	89	29.51	—	5	25
P. A. Whitcombe	13	1	353	68	29.41	—	2	10
†R. Tattersall	21	13	235	39	29.37	—	—	7
C. Oakes	56	1	1607	112	29.21	2	11	27
T. N. Pearce	43	7	1043	111*	28.98	1	6	18
R. J. Morris	19	0	550	96	28.94	—	3	4
A. V. Wolton	43	9	978	111*	28.76	—	4	8
B. Constable	33	0	939	100	28.45	1	7	7
V. E. Jackson	50	3	1335	143	28.40	1	7	31
E. O. Jenkins	53	11	1183	100	28.16	1	5	27
F. B. Smith (N.Z.)	40	4	1008	96	28.00	1	7	10
J. S. Ord	50	3	1308	156*	27.82	1	8	5
†D. G. W. Fletcher	25	1	667	111	27.79	1	3	8
S. C. Eve	28	2	717	120	27.57	1	4	6
J. Oakes	43	7	990	99	27.50	—	6	21
†D. V. Smith	50	10	1098	88*	27.45	1	4	19
	25	0	673	85	26.92	—	4	3
R. Giles	11	1	269	59	26.90	—	2	—
L. Outschoorn	52	4	1289	215*	26.85	1	6	54

Batting (Cont.)

	I.	N.O.	R.	H.S.	Avge.	100	50	Ct/St
†A. E. Wilson	49	1	1287	188	26.81	2	2	50/19
†E. Bird	42	4	1016	116	26.73	—	1	17
†J. Bailey	50	3	1254	89	26.68	—	6	6
P. Davis	17	1	427	104	26.68	1	1	7/1
E. D. R. Eagar	49	4	1200	118	26.66	1	5	26
J. H. G. Deighton	17	1	426	79	26.62	—	2	3
C. Walker	50	9	1087	112	26.51	2	3	7
R. W. V. Robins	23	2	552	68	26.28	—	1	25
C. Gladwin	45	10	914	124*	26.11	1	1	13
R. Horsfall	10	1	235	95	26.11	—	1	11
P. Clift	50	3	1226	125*	26.08	3	3	11
†L. H. Compton	41	7	884	88	26.00	—	2	35
†W. Watson	35	2	853	119	25.84	2	2	18
†E. Davies	54	1	1366	158	25.77	2	8	12
†H. Winrow	32	3	746	105*	25.72	1	2	9
A. E. G. Rhodes	46	1	1156	127	25.68	2	6	12
†H. T. Bartlett	19	0	483	82	25.42	1	2	5
†M. H. Stevenson	23	1	556	96	25.27	—	4	6
M. L. Y. Ainsworth	10	1	226	45	25.11	—	—	8
Rev. W. E. G. Payton	23	3	502	72	25.10	—	—	2
†A. Riddington	20	1	475	77	25.00	—	3	8
L. Johnson	14	3	273	54	24.81	—	1	4
A. C. Shirreff	55	2	1311	122	24.73	1	7	17
F. G. Mann	54	5	1200	143*	24.48	3	5	72/23
A. J. McIntyre	48	4	1077	94	24.47	—	5	21
F. R. Brown	43	1	1012	104	24.09	1	4	26
M. F. Tremlett	48	4	1056	76	24.00	—	7	33
A. Townsend	11	2	213	70	23.66	—	—	1
W. G. Keighley	33	2	729	74	23.51	—	4	16
†P. D. Hearn	48	9	914	87*	23.43	—	3	11
†R. T. Spooner	34	9	587	73	23.48	—	1	46/14
D. Shackleton	48	3	1053	101*	23.40	1	3	27
M. R. Barton	20	1	443	68	23.31	—	—	11
W. B. Morris	22	2	466	61	23.30	—	2	4
†F. W. Stocks	23	0	531	113	23.08	1	2	4
J. E. Timms	40	1	899	190	23.05	1	2	8
M. Robinson	46	5	943	100	23.00	1	5	27
W. Wooller	46	3	980	80	23.00	—	5	11
†V. H. Broderick	45	3	965	100	22.97	1	2	5
A. F. T. White	30	2	643	193*	22.96	1	—	23
†B. Edrich	42	3	893	92*	22.89	—	1	28
C. A. Milton	45	3	960	102	22.85	1	1	—
F. H. L. Mooney (N.Z.)	39	5	774	102	22.76	—	1	46/20

Batting (Cont.)	I.	N.O.	R.	H.S.	Avge.	100	50	Ct/St
†R. Sale	12	0	273	146	22.75	1	—	2
H. T. F. Buse	48	3	1020	117	22.66	2	4	17
†A. H. Kardar	35	1	700	60	22.58	—	2	22
†R. W. Clarke	40	12	627	51*	22.39	—	2	24
A. H. Parnaby	12	0	267	87	22.25	—	3	3
O. B. Popplewell	16	4	267	37	22.25	—	—	21/2
S. S. Rogers	20	2	400	61	22.22	—	1	3
A. Jepson	29	7	487	45*	22.13	—	—	12
P. Greenwood	32	6	572	52	22.00	—	2	5
R. H. Maudsley	13	0	286	107	22.00	1	—	8
R. Smith (Essex)	45	4	883	112	21.53	1	4	8
S. G. Symington	36	5	659	65*	21.25	—	3	13
A. Coxon	32	9	487	65*	21.17	—	3	28
P. J. Hall	11	3	165	49	20.62	—	—	4
S. C. Griffith	42	4	783	111	20.60	1	3	58/22
M. Coope	42	1	826	102*	20.14	1	3	4
L. B. Muncer	48	6	837	81	19.92	—	3	18
A. H. Phebey	28	0	554	68	19.78	—	4	10
G. E. S. Woodhouse	51	8	849	59	19.74	—	1	6/1
A. Smithson	15	2	256	46	19.69	—	—	5
G. Dews	15	2	255	45	19.61	—	—	8
L. Harrison	11	4	137	24*	19.57	—	—	10/3
D. M. Young	20	2	349	63*	19.38	—	1	3
†R. Howorth	49	4	860	72	19.11	—	4	15
W. Stephenson	45	4	782	88	19.07	—	3	42/43
C. J. Scott	11	3	151	40*	18.87	—	—	5
J. H. H. Anton	15	1	264	45	18.85	—	1	—
D. R. Guard	17	0	319	85	18.76	—	2	1
G. Dawkes	45	9	665	88	18.47	—	1	69/11
E. Hill	40	1	718	60	18.41	—	2	6
A. James	29	11	331	37*	18.38	—	—	5
†J. E. Walsh	46	3	785	97	18.25	—	4	27
R. W. H. Sutcliffe	12	0	218	38	18.16	—	1	5
W. V. Divecha	14	6	145	68*	18.12	—	—	8
G. Hill	36	5	561	53	18.09	—	1	11
J. A. Young	35	9	469	62	18.03	—	—	14
A. V. Bedser	34	8	468	53*	18.00	—	1	29
N. D. Howard	57	4	936	95	17.66	—	5	20
E. A. Marsh	26	1	437	71	17.48	—	2	9
†T. B. Burtt (N.Z.)	31	6	436	68*	17.44	—	1	12
†D. E. Blake	18	0	311	81	17.27	—	1	15
†J. H. Wardle	28	0	412	70	17.16	—	2	15

Batting (Cont.)	I.	N.O.	R.	H.S.	Avge.	100	50	Ct/St
J. C. Laker	39	7	548	100	17.12	1	1	26
G. L. Watson	22	2	337	85	16.85	—	1	3
L. P. Campbell	12	0	202	43	16.83	—	1	8/6
W. A. Sime	29	3	432	68	16.61	—	3	12
T. P. B. Smith	37	4	548	115	16.60	1	1	16
C. Monks	17	2	248	51	16.53	—	1	3
K. A. Taylor	15	0	247	89	16.46	—	1	5
†V. Munden	31	5	426	67	16.38	—	1	11
J. Sims	38	6	523	61	16.34	—	2	10
†J. K. Graveney	35	4	505	62	16.29	—	1	5
H. B. Cave (N.Z.)	23	9	228	36	16.28	—	—	12
R. G. Garlick	31	9	358	51	16.27	—	1	5
C. R. D. Rudd	20	4	260	54	16.25	—	1	7
T. A. Chapman	27	1	414	38	15.92	—	—	9/1
G. Lambert	43	7	568	61	15.77	—	1	11
L. M. Cranfield	12	2	157	41	15.70	—	—	—
D. V. P. Wright	30	18	184	50*	15.33	—	—	11
†G. R. Langdale	10	1	138	63*	15.33	—	1	1
J. Warr	24	12	182	47	15.16	—	—	6
G. Evans	15	2	192	65*	14.76	—	1	3
E. Crush	36	3	486	51	14.72	—	1	11
A. E. Nutter	37	4	440	76*	14.66	—	1	21
P. F. Harvey	20	4	233	50*	14.56	—	1	13
J. H. Cowie (N.Z.)	17	8	131	47	14.55	—	—	4
G. H. Chesterton	11	3	160	43	14.54	—	—	9
J. N. Bartlett	11	3	116	28	14.50	—	—	7
J. Pleass	25	2	330	49	14.34	—	—	5
C. C. Burke (N.Z.)	17	5	171	44*	14.25	—	—	8
D. G. Clark	44	6	537	58*	14.13	—	2	15
W. B. Roberts	27	5	311	41*	14.13	—	—	6
H. Yarnold	46	11	494	61	14.11	—	1	63/47
D. A. Skinner	35	1	474	63	13.94	—	3	28
†J. Lawrence	49	7	583	45	13.88	—	—	8
†E. H. Wade	36	7	384	44	13.24	—	—	38
E. A. Watts	10	1	119	44	13.22	—	—	47/18
F. Cooper	12	2	131	52	13.10	—	1	2
†J. Ransom	13	2	144	58	13.09	—	1	2
A. Carty	15	3	154	53	12.83	—	1	6
W. H. Rayment	14	2	154	35	12.83	—	—	8
C. W. Grove	43	3	511	81	12.77	—	3	4
H. G. Davies	42	6	457	45	12.69	—	—	41/9
†R. R. Dovey	46	8	482	52*	12.68	—	1	8

Batting (Cont.)

	I.	N.O.	R.	H.S.	Avge.	100	50	Ct/St
†G. F. Cresswell (N.Z.)	15	11	50	12*	12.50	—	—	6
†J. Eaglestone	35	3	395	62	12.34	—	1	10
A. F. Townsend	20	1	233	41	12.26	—	—	2
R. Pollard	34	4	365	53	12.16	—	1	14
N. G. Hever	35	22	156	23*	12.00	—	—	10
F. Ridgway	40	5	420	89	12.00	—	1	7
B. Boobbyer	12	0	143	28	11.91	—	1	7
†R. T. D. Perks	51	4	544	51	11.57	—	1	17
P. Corrall	42	10	370	38	11.56	—	—	38/18
†H. L. Hazell	39	23	185	29	11.56	—	—	15
W. S. Surridge	28	2	300	41*	11.53	—	—	27
N. S. Mitchell-Innes	14	0	157	42	11.21	—	—	10
G. A. R. Lock	33	14	212	29	11.15	—	—	27
†E. P. Robinson	22	8	151	40	10.78	—	—	12
†L. T. Pritchard	35	4	332	44	10.70	—	—	8
A. Barlow	18	3	160	44	10.66	—	—	23/7
J. Cornford	36	12	252	34	10.50	—	—	5
L. Angell	18	2	160	45	10.00	—	—	6
K. Fiddling	25	12	116	23	8.92	—	—	3
Sir D. Bailey	10	2	70	29	8.75	—	—	3
C. J. Knott	35	13	188	21	8.54	—	—	9
T. W. Goddard	40	15	227	20	8.40	—	—	14
†J. Sperry	39	15	201	30	7.90	—	—	5
H. J. Butler	15	4	87	26*	7.66	—	—	4
P. F. Jackson	27	12	115	29	7.66	—	—	5
E. A. Meads	25	7	133	25	7.38	—	—	39/18
F. E. Woodhead	24	4	145	40*	6.90	—	—	3
M. H. Wrigley	14	4	69	17	6.90	—	—	4
J. Redman	10	3	45	12	6.42	—	—	1
W. H. Copson	41	8	211	28	6.23	—	—	4
†R. Berry	18	1	106	22	6.23	—	—	7
L. H. Gray	26	16	62	17*	6.20	—	—	14
D. V. Brennan	33	11	125	14*	5.68	—	—	47/19
G. R. Pullinger	19	10	51	18	5.66	—	—	14
C. Cook	38	14	133	18	5.54	—	—	6
†E. Price	32	9	118	19*	5.13	—	—	14
J. Jackson	43	24	134	24	4.96	—	—	6
†D. J. Wood	30	7	94	12*	4.08	—	—	9
W. E. Hollies	29	15	55	8*	3.92	—	—	7
B. J. K. Pryer	15	3	38	12	2.62	—	—	6
†J. W. McMahon	15	7	21	6*	2.62	—	—	4
A. Wilson	19	8	25	8*	2.27	—	—	22/10

BOWLING

(Qualification: 10 wickets, 5w and 10w = 5 wkts. in innings and 10 in a match. † a left-arm bowler.)

	Overs	Mdns.	Runs	Wkts.	Avge.	5w	10w
R. Aspinall	133.1	32	289	30	9.63	4	1
G. O. Allen	81.3	15	216	14	15.42	1	—
†A. W. Goddard	1187.2	326	3069	160	19.18	13	5
†A. H. Kardar	922.5	366	1777	92	19.31	6	1
†R. Howorth	1113.4	386	2278	117	19.47	8	2
†H. L. Hazell	923.1	303	2065	106	19.48	6	2
†J. A. Young	1453.3	526	2948	150	19.65	8	2
J. C. Laker	1191.1	419	2422	122	19.85	7	1
L. Jackson	1030.1	256	2450	120	20.41	6	—
W. E. Hollies	1626.4	584	3413	166	20.56	16	6
A. Coxon	920.2	238	2100	101	20.79	5	1
M. H. Wrigley	314.4	75	792	38	20.84	3	—
W. K. Laidlaw	54	6	209	10	20.90	1	—
R. O. Jenkins	1146.1	187	3879	183	21.19	16	5
A. V. Bedser	1005.2	244	2344	110	21.30	5	1
C. Gladwin	1045.4	297	2513	117	21.47	8	—
M. F. Tremlett	492	116	1324	61	21.70	2	—
†W. B. Roberts	892.4	354	1556	71	21.91	2	—
G. V. P. Wright	755.1	125	2829	129	21.93	5	1
D. H. Chesterton	423.2	129	1010	46	21.95	1	—
†J. H. Wardle	1093.1	407	2333	103	22.65	12	4
J. Lawrence	771.3	123	2433	107	22.73	9	1
†T. B. Burtt (N.Z.)	1245	405	2929	128	22.88	11	2
F. Berry	429.3	151	919	40	22.97	3	1
F. Trueman	243.3	49	719	31	23.19	1	—
B. L. Muncer	1124.3	328	2656	114	23.21	7	2
J. P. Whitehead	137	31	325	14	23.29	2	1
P. F. Ridgway	922.3	201	2449	105	23.32	2	—
C. W. Grove	949.1	244	2243	95	23.61	5	—
†C. Cook	1052.2	343	2397	101	23.73	5	—
E. A. Townsend	435	100	1052	44	23.90	2	—
E. A. Bedser	847.3	251	2116	88	24.04	4	—
†T. E. Bailey	1020	186	3146	130	24.20	11	2
†J. N. Bartlett	165.3	33	514	21	24.47	1	—
W. Wooller	1127.2	290	2947	120	24.55	7	1
T. L. Pritchard	1043	189	2794	113	24.72	7	1
J. J. Warr	604	128	1585	64	24.76	3	—

Bowling (Cont.)

	Overs	Mdns	Runs	Wkts	Avge.	5w	10w
†G. A. R. Lock	754.5	287	1672	67	24.95	—	—
R. G. Garlick	787	193	2052	81	25.33	2	—
R. T. D. Perks	1134.2	298	3083	121	25.47	7	1
O. J. Watt	284.5	58	842	33	25.51	1	1
J. Cornford	880.5	200	2476	97	25.52	6	2
H. T. F. Buse	729.2	163	2017	79	25.53	5	—
P. Greenwood	858.4	259	1927	75	25.69	4	—
R. Carty	276.4	42	878	34	25.82	3	—
A. E. Nutter	685	169	1716	66	26.00	3	—
†J. Webster	98.4	17	286	11	26.00	1	—
J. Sims	1159	188	3284	126	26.06	9	2
G. F. Cresswell (N.Z.)	995.1	184	1618	62	26.09	4	—
D. Shackleton	941.2	206	2616	100	26.16	7	1
R. G. Wilson	142	18	421	16	26.31	1	—
†A. J. Watkins	709.2	176	1799	68	26.45	1	—
†M. Hilton	156.3	44	372	14	26.57	—	—
W. S. Surridge	548.5	98	1813	68	26.66	2	—
L. H. Gray	792.5	185	1895	71	26.69	3	—
W. H. Copson	673.2	150	1902	71	26.78	3	—
P. A. Whitcombe	212.1	53	536	20	26.80	—	—
N. G. Hever	819	220	1904	71	26.81	3	—
C. J. Knott	897.4	175	2717	101	26.90	6	1
†W. E. Jones	308	72	836	31	26.96	1	—
J. H. G. Deighton	355.1	66	971	36	26.97	2	—
F. R. Brown	1054.4	249	2997	111	27.00	6	—
K. Grieves	699.4	189	1705	63	27.06	4	—
R. Tattersall	430.3	137	976	36	27.11	3	—
J. A. Cowie (N.Z.)	616.5	129	1601	59	27.13	5	—
J. F. Parker	537.5	123	1331	49	27.16	—	—
R. V. Divecha	194.1	52	471	17	27.70	—	—
D. B. Close	1245	324	3150	113	27.87	6	1
H. J. Butler	487.4	112	1227	44	27.88	1	—
W. V. Robins	109	15	391	14	27.92	—	—
†R. W. Clarke	842.5	156	2467	88	28.03	4	—
†A. Mason	464.3	164	1038	37	28.05	1	—
J. K. Graveney	533.4	106	1661	59	28.15	1	—
R. Pollard	884.4	241	2062	73	28.24	4	1
†J. T. Ikin	536.2	130	1452	51	28.47	1	—
†J. E. Walsh	1061.1	135	3800	132	28.78	10	3
†S. Trick	129.2	42	291	10	29.10	—	—
P. F. Harvey	567.1	120	1698	58	29.27	4	1
J. G. Lomax	143	33	322	11	29.27		

Bowling (Cont.)

	Overs	Mdns	Runs	Wkts	Avge.	5w	10w
A. G. J. Rimell	201.2	75	473	16	29.56	—	—
C. C. Burke (N.Z.)	598.3	144	1611	54	29.83	1	—
J. W. Martin	159.1	31	449	15	29.93	1	—
†James Langridge	127.4	20	390	13	30.00	—	—
†D. B. Carr	765.1	183	2076	69	30.08	3	—
E. A. Watts	90.2	19	331	11	30.09	1	—
T. P. B. Smith	899.4	153	2472	82	30.14	5	—
V. E. Jackson	959.1	302	2275	75	30.33	2	—
R. R. Dovey	934.1	289	2234	73	30.60	—	—
†J. Bailey	1026.4	267	2662	86	30.95	4	—
C. Oakes	626.1	131	1920	62	30.96	2	—
H. Sharp	136.5	27	373	12	31.08	1	—
A. W. Wellard	1019.1	221	2725	87	31.32	4	—
T. A. Dean	100.1	25	316	10	31.60	1	—
R. Smith (Essex)	1175.5	252	3290	104	31.63	7	—
E. P. Robinson	737.3	239	1458	46	31.69	1	—
†V. H. Broderick	839.4	250	2130	67	31.79	2	—
R. T. Simpson	208.4	73	511	16	31.93	—	—
G. E. M. Heath	153.3	22	512	16	32.00	1	—
C. B. Harris	430.4	135	834	26	32.07	—	—
F. H. Vigar	234.2	31	909	28	32.46	1	—
C. W. Foord	185.5	31	520	16	32.50	1	—
†A. C. Shirreff	285.2	67	816	25	32.64	2	—
†D. Compton	740.4	125	2386	73	32.68	4	—
†E. Price	613.5	133	1765	54	32.68	3	—
G. Lambert	771.5	146	2401	73	32.89	3	—
B. Edrich	432.2	112	1228	37	33.18	2	—
†J. Sperry	920	190	2397	72	33.29	2	—
†Derief Taylor	205	79	402	12	33.50	—	—
J. A. Hayes (N.Z.)	301.4	60	873	26	33.57	1	—
N. W. D. Yardley	372.4	110	745	22	33.86	—	—
P. J. Hall	289.4	52	826	24	34.41	2	—
†D. J. Wood	973.2	199	2905	84	34.58	2	—
A. E. James	611.2	166	1523	44	34.61	2	—
J. G. W. Davies	199.4	52	522	15	34.80	—	—
G. Lester	449	92	1323	38	34.81	1	—
G. R. Pullinger	459.3	101	1333	38	35.07	1	—
†W. J. Edrich	563.1	95	1688	48	35.16	1	—
P. F. Jackson	617.1	129	1704	48	35.50	3	—
G. O. Rabone (N.Z.)	558.4	118	1785	50	35.70	1	—
F. G. Woodhead	829.4	249	1916	53	36.15	2	—

Bowling (Cont.)

	Overs	Mdns.	Runs	Wkts.	Avge.	5w	10w
A. Jepson	799.3	155	2213	61	36.27	3	—
G. H. G. Doggart	243.5	69	626	17	36.82	—	—
C. B. Van Ryneveld	383.3	62	1196	32	37.37	2	—
A. E. G. Rhodes	802	133	2549	66	38.62	—	—
C. H. Palmer	205	77	698	18	38.77	—	—
B. J. K. Pryer	354	63	1049	27	38.85	—	—
†W. A. Sime	379.5	95	990	25	39.60	—	—
†F. W. Stocks	124	29	402	10	40.20	—	—
A. W. H. Mallett	192	44	489	12	40.75	1	—
†B. Sutcliffe (N.Z.)	185.4	37	654	16	40.87	—	—
H. S. Squires	168.1	33	452	11	41.09	—	—
G. Evans	197.5	42	664	16	41.50	—	—
J. Oakes	377.2	80	1168	28	41.71	—	—
C. J. Cox	314.2	73	843	20	42.15	—	—
C. J. Scott (N.Z.)	203.5	41	552	13	42.46	—	—
H. B. Cave (N.Z.)	657	133	1809	42	43.07	—	—
E. Crush	536	106	1563	36	43.41	—	—
S. J. Symington	411.5	83	1312	30	43.73	1	—
J. Redman	153.1	19	498	11	45.27	—	—
G. Hill	432.4	110	1227	27	45.81	—	—
†J. W. McMahon	267	48	909	19	47.84	2	—
†C. Walker	366.4	94	1063	22	48.31	2	—
†M. H. Stevenson	276	88	728	14	52.00	—	—
V. J. Ransom	300.2	61	872	16	54.50	—	—
C. A. Milton	265	71	640	11	58.18	—	—
†H. Winrow	265.2	75	769	10	76.90	—	—
Total			928,949	34,590	26.85		

ABOUT THE AVERAGES

During the 1949 season no fewer than ninety-four batsmen reached a 1,000 run aggregate—a new record exceeding the previous figure of ninety-one, established in 1928 and equalled in 1933, 1934 and 1947. Twenty-nine bowlers achieved a 100 wicket aggregate, equalling the record set up in 1935.

It can be seen from the table below which were the wet summers and which the dry. The cost per wicket in 1949 is a record.

	Runs	Wickets	Average
1946	202,611	24,511	8.266
1947	248,243	27,752	8.945
1948	221,852	26,458	8.385
1949	256,243	28,490	8.994

PLAYFAIR WHO'S WHO 1950

By ROY WEBBER and PETER WEST

To the best of our belief this Who's Who of English cricketers is the most accurate and the most complete record of its kind ever published. It embraces almost everyone who appeared in first-class cricket in England in 1949 and also some that did not play last year; and therefore includes nearly all who are likely to play in 1950. The exceptions are a few players new to county cricket this season.

Respective lists have been checked by the counties but it is easy for errors to creep in and we should be very pleased to hear of any inaccuracies. Details are complete to the end of February.

To economise in space several abbreviations have been used and readers might like to familiarise themselves with the " key " before studying the records in detail. This Who's Who should be read in conjunction with CAREER RECORDS 1950 on following pages and with the achievements of 1949 as set out in other parts of this Annual.

ABBREVIATIONS

†	*Amateur*
B	*Born*
RHB	*Right-hand bat*
LHB	*Left-hand bat*
MF ..	*Medium-fast*
FM ..	*Fast-medium (rather quicker than MF)*
RFM	*Right-arm fast-medium*
LFM	*Left-arm fast-medium*
RMF	*Right-arm medium-fast*
LMF	*Left-arm medium-fast*
M ..	*Medium right*
ML ..	*Medium left*
OB ..	*Off-break*
LB ..	*Leg-break*
LBG	*Leg-break & googly*
LA ..	*Left arm*
C.Cap	*County cap*
*	*Not out or unbroken stand*
HS ..	*Highest score*
BB ..	*Best bowling performance*

†ABLACK, R. K. ("Ken") (Northants) B.Port of Spain (Trinidad) 5/1/1919. Slow LA bowler. Played 2 matches for county in 1946 and 1 in 1949.

†AINSWORTH, M. L. Y. (" Mike ") (Worcs.) B.Hooton (Cheshire) 13/5/1922. Attractive RHB. Educated at Shrewsbury. R.N. officer, plays for Combined Services. Debut 1946. C.Cap 1949. HS—100 v Warwick (Dudley) 1948.

AITCHISON, John (Kent) B.Gillingham 27/12/1928. Useful OB bowler. Played 1 match in 1949—3-33 v Glamorgan (Gravesend). On staff of Q P R. football club.

ALDERSON, Ralph (Lancs.) B.Newton-le-Willows 7/6/1920. Sound RHB. Debut in 1948. Scored 55 v Kent (Manchester)—only innings in 1949.

†ALLEN, Basil O. (Glos.) B.Bristol 13/10/1911. Reliable and realistic LHB. Used to open, now bats lower down. Fearless field close to wicket. Educated at Clifton. Debut 1932.

Cambridge Blue 1933. Has scored 1000 runs in season 7 times. Glos. capt. 1937-38 and 1947-50. Played for Gents. at Lord's 1938. HS—220 v Hants. (Bournemouth) 1947.

†ALLEN, G. O. ("Gubby") (Middx.) B.Sydney (Australia) 31/7/1902. One of the best fast bowlers of his time, now near final retirement. Forceful, stylish RHB. Educated at Eton. Debut 1921. Cambridge Blue 1922 and 1923. Toured S. America 1926-27, Australia and N.Z. 1932-33 and 1936-37. W. Indies 1947-48, captain on last two tours. Played in 22 Tests since debut v Australia (Lord's) 1930, 11 times as captain. Took all ten Lancs. wickets (8 clean bowled) for 40 runs at Lord's in 1929. HS—180 Free Foresters v Cambridge U. (Cambridge) 1948.

†ALTHAM, R. J. L. (Hants.) B.Winchester 21/1/1924. Educated at Marlborough. Played one match for Oxford U. 1947. Qualified for Hants. Son of H. S. Altham.

AMES, Leslie E. G. (Kent) B.Elham 3/12/1905. Probably the best batsman-wicketkeeper the game has ever seen. Debut 1926. Toured Australia 1928-29, 1932-33, 1936-37. S. Africa 1938-39, W.Indies 1929-30, 1934-35 and N.Z. 1932-33. Played for England in 47 Tests between 1929-30 and 1938-39. Dismissed 100 batsmen in a season three times (1928, 1929 and 1932), his "bag" of 127 in 1929 being a record. In each season he also completed the wicketkeeper's double. Benefits in 1937 (£1,265) and 1948 (£4 336). Played soccer for Folkestone, Gillingham and Orient. Has scored 1000 runs in a season 16 times (1927-1949 except 1936 when he was injured). In 1936 and 1939 hit fastest century of the season. Scored 3058 runs (av. 58.80) in 1933. Has scored two 100s in a match twice. Represented Players at Lord's 1931-2-4-7-47. Has stumped more batsmen (415) than any other wicketkeeper, but has not kept wicket since 1939. 95 centuries. HS—295 v Glos. (Folkestone) 1933.

ANGELL, Leslie (Somerset) B.Norton St. Phillip 29/12/1922. Steady RHB. Debut 1947. Turned pro. 1949. HS—45 v N. Zealanders (Taunton) 1949.

†**ANSON, G. F.** (Kent) B.Sevenoaks 8/10/1922. Stylish RHB. Educated at Harrow. At Cambridge U. in 1947 but left to take business appointment before gaining almost certain Blue. Did not play in 1949. HS—106 Cambridge U. v Middlesex (Cambridge) 1947.

†**ANTON, J. H. H.** (Cambridge U.) B.Kidderminster 19/9/1926. RHB. Educated at Rugby. Debut 1949, when he just failed to gain a Blue.

ARMSTRONG, T. R. (Derby) B.Clay Cross 13/10/1909. Useful LA change bowler. RHB. Debut 1929. Plays occasionally for county. BB—7-57 v Somerset (Frome) 1933.

ARNOLD, Johnny (Hants.) B.Cowley (Oxford) 26/11/1907. Attractive RHB; Opened regularly until 1949. Still a fine cover point. Debut 1929. Test v N.Z. (Lord's) 1931. Represented Players at Lord's 1931 and 1936. Soccer (OL) with Southampton and Fulham. Only present-day cricketer to gain full England "caps" at cricket and football, playing for England v Scotland, April, 1933. 1000 runs every season since 1930. Joint benefit 1948-50. HS—227 v Glamorgan (Cardiff) 1932.

ASHMORE, William (Middx.) B.St. John's Wood (Mddx.) 1929. LMF bowler. Debut 1946. Combined Services 1948. Did not play for county in 1949.

ASPINALL, Ronald (Yorks.) B.Almondbury 26/10/1918. RFM bowler and RHB. Debut 1946. C.Cap 1948. Was bowling exceptionally well in May 1949 when injury kept him out for rest of season. HS—75* v. Notts. (Nottingham) 1948. BB—7-46 (13-100 match) v Somerset (Leeds) 1949.

AVERY, A. V. ("Sonny") (Essex). B. East Ham 12/12/1914. Very sound and correct opening RHB. Debut 1935. Leyton CF in 1937 A.F.A. Cup Final. Toured world with Islington Corinthians in 1937-38. Has been unlucky with several injuries to his right hand, one of which kept him out for two months in 1949. Best year 1948—1890 runs (av. 46.09). 1000 runs in season three times. Benefit 1950. HS—214* v Worcs. (Clacton) 1948.

†**BAILEY, Sir Derrick** (Glos.) B.South Africa 15/8/1918. Useful RHB and M bowler. Son of Sir Abe Bailey. Debut 1949. C.Cap 1949.

BAILEY, Jim (Hants.) B.Shawford (Winchester) 6/4/1908. Fine LA spinner. Sound LHB, especially against slow bowling. Built on ample lines, usually fields in gully. Debut 1929. Left county in 1933 for League cricket, returning in 1939. Performed "double" in 1948—1399 runs and 121 wickets. Joint benefit 1948-50. HS—133 v Worcs. (Southampton) 1946. BB—7-7 v Notts. (Southampton) 1932.

†**BAILEY, Trevor E.** (Essex) B.Westcliff 3/12/1923. Sound RHB, splendid FM bowler (moves either way) and fine field. Educated at Dulwich. Played in Lord's Victory Test v Australia in 1945. Debut for Essex 1946. C.Cap 1947. Cambridge Blue 1947 and 1948. Joined Essex administrative staff 1948. Played in all 4 Tests v N.Z., 1949, and for Gents. at Lord's 1947 and 1949. Took all 10 Lancs. wickets for 90 at Clacton 1949. "Double" in 1949. HS—205 v Sussex (Eastbourne) 1947.

BARLOW, Alfred (Lancs.) B.Little Lever 31/8/1915. Regular wicketkeeper at end of 1949 season. RHB. Debut 1947. HS—44 v Derby (Manchester) 1949.

BARRACLOUGH, Eric S. (Yorks.) B. Bradford 30/3/1923. FM bowler and RHB. Debut 1949, playing 1 match

BARRICK, Desmond (Northants) B.Fitzwilliam (Pontefract) 28/4/1926. Promising RHB and LBG bowler. Debut 1949. HS—147* v New Zealanders (Northampton) 1949.

BARRON, W. ("Bill") (Northants.) B.Herrington (County Durham) 26/10/1917. Attacking LHB. Fine slip field, can keep wicket in emergency. Played for Durham pre-war. Played one match for Lancs. 1945. Debut for Northants. 1946. C.Cap 1946. Soccer for Northampton Town. HS—161* v Cambridge U. (Cambridge) 1948 and shared in 2nd wkt. county record with Brookes (265).

†**BARTLETT, Hugh T.** (Sussex) B.Balaghat (India) 7/10/1914. Attractive LHB—a real murderer of bowling pre-war. Educated at Dulwich. Cambridge Blue 1934-5-6, captain 1936. Played for Surrey 1933 to 1935. Debut for Sussex in 1937. C.Cap 1938. Represented Gentlemen at Lord's 1938 and 1939, scoring 175* in 1938. Scored fastest 100 of 1938—in 57 minutes v Australians (Hove). In same season hit Verity for seven sixes in one innings. Toured S. Africa in 1938-39 and was selected for the 1939-40 Indian tour which was cancelled. Won D.F.C. during war while with Airborne Forces. Sussex captain 1947 to 1949.

1000 runs in season four times (1938-9-47-8). HS—183 Cambridge U. v Notts. (Cambridge) 1935.

†**BARTLETT, John N.** (Sussex) B.Mickleover (Derby) 16/6/1928. Steady LA spinner and RHB. Educated at Chichester. Oxford Blue 1946. Debut in 1946. Represented Gentlemen at Lord's in 1946. BB—5-102 Oxford U. v. Lancs. (Oxford) 1946.

†**BARTON, Michael R.** (Surrey) B.Dereham (Norfolk) 14/10/1914. Solid RHB of forward type. Good slip field. Educated at Winchester. Oxford Blue 1936-7. Played for Norfolk before war. Joined Surrey 1948 (vice-capt.) and gained cap. Surrey capt. 1949-50 HS—192 Oxford U. v. Glos. (Oxford) 1937.

†**BEDFORD, P. Ian** (Middx.) B.Friern Barnet 11/2/1930. LBG bowler, RHB. Debut 1947 while still at Woodhouse G.S. (Finchley). While in R.A.F. played for Combined Services in 1949. BB—6-52 Middx. v Yorks. (Bradford) 1948.

BEDSER, Alec V. (Surrey) B.Reading 4/7/1918. Excellent FM bowler and a very useful RHB who has rescued England more than once. Good field. England's most consistent bowler since the war. Debut 1939. C.Cap 1946. Played in 23 Tests since the war, taking 89 wickets, including 11 in each of his first two Tests (v India). Toured Australia and New Zealand 1946-47 and S. Africa 1948-49, but declined trip to W. Indies 1947-48. In 1948 shared in two century partnerships in Tests v. Australia. Has taken 100 wkts each season since war. HS—126 v. Somerset (Taunton) 1947. BB—8-42 v Middlesex (Lord's) 1949.

BEDSER, Eric A. (Surrey) B.Reading 4/7/1918, the identical twin of A. V. Sound and improving opening RHB. Very promising OB bowler. Now one of the best all-rounders in England. Good field. Travelled with Alec on both his overseas tours. Enjoyed best season in 1949—1740 runs and 88 wkts. Has shared in several large opening partnerships with Fishlock. HS—163 v Notts. (Oval) 1949. BB—7-99 v Middlesex (Lord's) 1949.

†**BENNETT, A. C. L. ("Leo")** (Northants.) B.West Norwood (London) 31/12/1914. Useful RHB. Educated at Dulwich. Debut 1947. Plays rarely owing to duties with B.B.C. Prolific scorer in London club cricket. HS—68 v Notts. (Northampton) 1947.

BERRY, Leslie G. (Leics.) B.Dorking (Surrey) 28/4/1906. Sound and very consistent opening RHB, back to his best form in 1949. Debut 1924. Has scored most runs (27616) and centuries (39) for Leics. Appointed Leics. captain 1946 to 1948, the first professional to skipper regularly in county cricket for many years. Has scored 1000 runs in a season 17 times. HS—232 v Sussex (Leicester) 1930.

BERRY, Robert (Lancs.) B.Manchester 29/1/1926. Most promising slow LA bowler. Debut 1948. Played for Minor Counties 1949, then gained frequent place in county team. BB—7-40 (10-96 match) Minor Counties v. Yorks. (Lord's) 1949.

†**BIRD, R. E. ("Ronny")** (Worcs.) B. Quarry Bank (Staffs.) 4/4/1915. Forcing RHB. Debut 1946. C.Cap 1946. Batted well early in 1949 but had poor August. HS—116 v Yorks. (Sheffield) 1949.

†**BLAKE, P. D. S.** (Sussex) B.Calcutta 23/5/1927. Stylish RHB and fine field. Educated at Eton. Debut in 1946. C.Cap 1948—the first awarded by Sussex after war. Now at Oxford. HS—77 v Northants. (Hove) 1948.

†**BLAKE, David E.** (Hants.) B.Havant (Portsmouth) 27/4/1925. Useful LHB and promising wicketkeeper. Educated at Aldenham. Debut 1949. HS—60 v Worcs. (Portsmouth) 1949.

†**BOOBBYER, B.** (Oxford U.) Educated at Uppingham. Sound RHB, fine field. Blue 1949. Rugger Blue 1949, England centre 1950. HS—27 v. Hants. (Bournemouth) 1949.

BRAZIER, Alan F. (Surrey) B.Paddington (Mddx.) 7/12/1924. Sound RHB who has had few chances in first team. Debut 1948. Scored 1212 runs for Surrey 2nd XI in 1949—a record in Minor County cricket.

BREARLEY, H. (Middx.) B.Yorks. 26/6/1913. Useful RHB. Yorkshire colt before making Middx. debut 1949.

†**BRENNAN, Don. V.** (Yorks.) B.Eccleshill (Bradford) 10/2/1920. Talented wicketkeeper, capable of brilliance. RHB. Debut 1947. C.Cap 1947. Test Trial 1949. HS—34 v Glos. (Bradford) 1947. Injured eye 1949.

BRICE, Gordon H. J. (Northants.) B. Bedford 4/5/1924. Promising RHB. FM or OB bowler. Reading footballer. Debut 1949, playing 3 matches.

†**BRIDGER, Rev. John R.** (Hants.) B. Dulwich (Surrey) 8/4/1920. Stylish RHB who lacks first-class practice. Educated at Rugby. Played for Cambridge U. in war-time. Debut 1945 for Under 33 at Lord's. Schoolmaster, available in August only. HS—142 v Middlesex (Bournemouth) 1946.

BRODERICK, V. H. ("Vince") (Northants.) B.Bacup (Lancs.) 17/8/1920. Most useful all-rounder—stylish LHB and slow spinner. Debut 1939. C. Cap 1947. Achieved "double" in 1948 and was not far short in 1947. Test Trials in 1948 and 1949. HS—

135 v Warwick (Northampton) 1948.
BB—9-35 v Sussex (Horsham) 1948
and 8-16 v Derby (Rushden) 1947.

BROMLEY, Philip H. (Warwick) B.
Stratford-on-Avon 30/7/1930. RHB
and OB bowler. Debut 1947. Has
played only 3 matches to date.
Played for R.A.F. in 1949; available
for county 1950.

†**BROOKE-TAYLOR, David C.** (Derby)
B.Bakewell 15/6/1920. RHB. Educated at Cheltenham. Debut 1947.
Plays in August. HS—61* v Northants. (Rushden) 1947.

BROOKES, Dennis (Northants.) B.Kip-
pax (Leeds) 29/10/1915. Skilful
and consistent opening RHB. Excellent field. Debut 1934. England
12th man v India at Lord's and
Manchester 1946. Played in both
Test Trials 1946. Toured W. Indies
1947-48, but chipped finger bone
compelled early return. Scored two
100s in match v Sussex (Eastbourne)
1946. Shares record 2nd wkt. county
partnership with Barron. Scored
1000 runs in season seven times.
HS—257 v Glos. (Bristol) 1949—
sharing record of Northants. highest
innings with A. H. Bakewell.

†**BROWN, F. R.** ("Freddie") (Northants)
B.Lima (Peru) 16/12/1910. Forcing RHB, dangerous LBG bowler,
fine field. Can also bowl OB's and
seamers. Educated at The Leys.
Cambridge Blue 1930 and 1931.
Played for Surrey 1930 to 1948
before joining Northants. on registration in 1949. Captain in 1949.
Toured Australia and N.Z. 1932-33.
Six England "caps" between 1931
and 1937. Captained England v
N.Z. at Manchester and the Oval
1949. "Doubles" in 1932 and 1949.
HS—212 (in 145 minutes) v Middlesex (Oval) 1932.

BROWN, Sidney M. (Middx.) B.Eltham
(Kent) 8/12/1917. Quick-scoring
attractive RHB. Brilliant outfield.
Debut 1937. With J. D. Robertson
added 310 for 1st wkt. v Notts.
(Lord's) 1947. 1000 runs each
season since war. Can keep wicket
in emergency. HS—200 v Kent
(Canterbury) 1949.

†**BURNETT, A. Compton** (Cambridge U.)
B.Chipstead (Surrey) 26/10/1923.
Forceful RHB. Good slip field. 18
catches in 1949 University season.
Emergency wicketkeeper. Educated
at Lancing. Blue 1949. HS—79*
v Middx. (Cambridge) 1949.

BUSE, H. T. F. (Somerset) B.Ashley
(Wilts.) 5/8/1910. Very useful all-
rounder. Steady RHB and MF
bowler who swings ball considerably
either way. Debut 1929 as amateur.
Has played rugger for Bath and
Somerset. 1000 runs in a season 4
times. HS—132 v Northants (Kettering) 1938. BB—7-26 v
Northants. (Taunton) 1949.

BUTLER, Harold J. (Notts.) B.Clifton
(Nottingham) 12/3/1913. Talented
RFM bowler, not blessed with the best
of health or luck. Moves either way,
gains pace and lift off pitch. RHB.
Debut 1933. Has achieved " hat-
trick" three times—v Surrey and
Leics. in 1937 and Hants. in 1939,
all at Nottingham. Played v S. Africa
(Leeds) 1947 and toured W. Indies
1947-48, only playing in one Test
because of illness. Represented
Players at Lord's 1947. HS—62 (in
30 minutes) v Glamorgan (Swansea)
1939. BB—6-36 (11-115 match)
v Derby (Ilkeston) 1947.

†**CAMPBELL, Ian P.** (Kent) B.Purley
(Surrey) 5/2/1928. Hard-hitting
RHB. Wicketkeeper. Educated at
Canford where he had a remarkable
batting record. Oxford Blue 1949.
Played 1 match for Kent in 1946.
Also Kent Rugby player. HS—43
Oxford U. v Leics. (Oxford) 1949.

CANNINGS, Victor H. D. (Hants.) B.
Bighton (Hants.) 3/3/1920. Useful
RHB and M bowler. Debut for
Warwick 1947. Joined Hants. for
1950. Served in Palestine Police
for seven years. HS—61 v. Notts.
(Birmingham) 1947. BB—5-49 v
Sussex (Hove) 1947.

†**CARR, Donald B.** (Derby) B.Weisbaden
(Germany) 28/12/1926. Attractive
RHB. Useful SL bowler and brilliant
field. Educated at Repton. Oxford
Blue 1949 and capt. for 1950. Also
soccer Blue (OL). Played in Lord's
"Victory" Test in 1945. Debut for
Derby 1946. HS—170 Oxford U. v
Leics. (Oxford) 1949. BB—6-111
v Glos. (Chesterfield) 1949.

CARTER, R. (Sussex) B.West Hoathly
1/6/1933. Promising LB bowler,
who can really spin. Useful RHB.

CARTY, R. (Hants.) B.Southampton
28/7/1922. Promising RFM bowler.
RHB. Debut 1949. HS—53 v
Oxford U. BB—6-110 v. Middlesex
(both at Bournemouth, 1949).

CASTLE, Fred (Somerset) B. in Kent
9/4/1909. RHB. Schoolmaster, only
available in August. Debut 1946.
HS—60* v Surrey (Weston-super-
Mare) 1946.

CHAPMAN, Tommy A. (Leics.) B.Bar-
well 14/5/1919. Much improved
RHB. Brilliant field. Debut 1946.
HS—74 v. Warwick (Leics.) 1947.

†**CHESTERTON, G. H.** (Oxford U.) B.
Chisbury (Salop) 15/7/1922. M in-
swing bowler and RHB. Educated at
Malvern. Blue 1949. Played for
Cornwall. HS—43 v. Free Foresters
(Oxford) 1949. BB—6-11 v. F.F.
(Oxford) 1949. Now master at Mal-
vern, available for Worcs.

CHRISTENSEN, Dan (Warwick.) London all-rounder of Swedish extrac-
tion; joined staff for 1950. B.
Edgware 27/6/32.

†**CLARK, David G.** (Kent) B.Maidstone

27/1/1919. RHB. Keen field close to wicket. Debut 1946. Kent capt. 1949-50. HS—58* v. Notts. (Nottingham) 1949.

CLARK, Tom H. (Surrey) B.Luton (Beds.) 5/10/1924. Sound RHB. Played for Bedfordshire before joining Surrey. Debut 1947. HS—59 v Cambridge U. (Guildford) 1949.

†**CLARKE, C. B. ("Bertie")** (Northants.) B.Bridgetown (Barbados) 7/4/1918. LBG bowler and RHB. Excellent fielder. Toured England in 1939 with W. Indies, playing in all three Tests and taking 87 wickets in all matches. During war qualified as Physician at Guy's Hospital, playing for British Empire XI. Joined Northants. 1946. C.Cap 1947. Plays for B.B.C. in club cricket. HS—86 v. Worcs. (Worcester) 1947. BB— 7-75 (13-107 match) W. Indies v Hants. (Portsmouth) 1939.

CLARKE, R. W. ("Bob") (Northants.) B.Finedon 22/4/1924. Promising LFM bowler—swings in with arm and sometimes comes back off pitch. Hard-hitting LHB. Debut 1947. C.Cap 1949. HS—56 v Notts. (Nottingham) 1948. BB—7-83 (13-190 match) v Surrey (Northmptn) 1949.

†**CLAY, John C.** (Glamorgan) B.Bonvilston (Mon.) 18/3/1898. Outstanding slow OB bowler, over 6ft. tall. Aggressive RHB. Educated at Winchester. Debut 1921. Test v S. Africa (Oval) 1935. Glamorgan capt. 1924-1927. and 1946. Test Selector 1947 and 1948. Best season 1937 when he took 176 wkts. (av. 17.34) inc. 17-212 v Worcs. (Swansea). Took 100 wkts. in season three times. HS— 115* v. N.Zealanders (Cardiff) 1927. BB—9 wkts. in an innings three times and 17-212 in match (above).

CLAY, J. D. (Notts.) B.West Bridgeford 15/10/1924. Useful RHB. Debut 1948. HS—57* v Leics. (Nottingham) 1949.

CLIFT, Phil. B. (Glamorgan) B.Usk (Mon.) 3/9/1920. Stylish opening RHB. Brilliant field close to wicket. Debut in 1937 aged 16. C.Cap 1947. HS—125* v Derby (Cardiff) 1949.

CLOSE, D. Brian (Yorks.) B.Rawdon 24/2/1931. Forcing LHB. Right OB bowler who also bowls in and out swingers. Good field. Debut 1949. C.Cap 1949. Had outstanding debut season—performing "double" (youngest player ever to do so) and playing for England v. N.Z. at Manchester (youngest player to appear for England in Test cricket). Represented Players at Lord's, scoring 65— highest in the match. Soccer for Leeds U. (Central League). Joined Army in October 1949. HS—88* v Essex (Leeds) 1949. BB—6-47 v Worcs. (Worcester) 1949. In hospital during past winter with thigh injury (soccer).

†**COLES, W. N.** (Cambridge U.) B.Northwood (Middx.) 11/2/1928. Educated at Eton. Played two matches for Cambridge U. in 1949.

COMPTON, Denis C. S. (Middx.) B.Hendon (Middx.) 23/5/1918. RHB—a genius. Versatile, sometimes brilliant, slow left bowler of "chinaman" and other varieties. Excellent field anywhere. Debut 1936. Played first Test v N.Z. (Oval) 1937, and has not missed a Test in England since. Owing to football commitments with Arsenal he could not tour S. Africa 1938-39, but since the war has toured Australia and N.Z. 1946-47 and S. Africa 1948-49. Has played in 36 Test matches, scoring 3132 runs, including 13 centuries. While in India during war he played for Holkar in Ranji Trophy, scoring 249* v Bombay in 1944-45. Record season in 1947 when he scored 3816 runs and 18 centuries—both records. With Edrich had shared in many huge partnerships including 424* for 3rd wkt. v Somerset (Lord's) 1948, and 370 for 3rd England wkt. v S. Africa (Lord's) 1947. Has never failed to score 1000 runs in a season either home or abroad. Best bowling season 1947—73 wkts. (av. 28.12) Benefit in 1949 (£12,200). HS— 300 M.C.C. v N.E. Transvaal (Benoni) 1948-49 runs scored in 181 minutes, the fastest triple century on record. BB—6-80 (12-174 match) v Surrey (Oval) 1947—when he scored 137* in his only innings in the match.

COMPTON, Leslie H. (Middx.) B.Woodford (Essex) 12/9/1912. Sound wicketkeeper. Capable RHB who hits hard on the off. Would be a better bat if necessary but goes in at No. 8. Can also bowl M seamers. Debut 1938. C.Cap 1947 Replaced Price as wicket-keeper in 1947. Excellent CH with Arsenal. HS—107 v. Derby (Derby) 1947.

CONSTABLE, Bernard (Surrey) B.East Molesey 19/2/1921. Correct RHB. Useful LB bowler and fine field. Debut 1939. Gained regular place in 1949. HS—107 Combined Services v Surrey (Oval) 1946.

CONSTABLE, Dennis (Northants.) B.East Molesey 14/8/1925. Younger brother of Surrey Constable. Reserve wicketkeeper. Debut 1949 when he played 1 match.

COOK, Cecil ("Sam") (Glos.) B.Tetbury 23/8/1921. Very accurate LA spin bowler. RHB. Debut 1946, taking a wicket with his first ball in first-class cricket. Test Trial 1946. C.Cap 1946. Test v S. Africa (Nottingham) 1947. Has taken 100 wkts. in each season, 1946-49. BB— 9-42 v Yorks. (Bristol) 1947.

F

†COOMB, A. G. (Comb. Services) B. Bedford 3/4/1929. M bowler (moves either way), RHB. Educated at Bedford Modern School. Played for Comb. Services in 1948 and 1949 while in the R.N.

COOPER, Edwin (Worcs.) B.Bacup (Lancs.) 30/11/1915. Neat and consistent opening RHB. Debut 1938. Scored 191 & 106* v Northants. (Kidderminster) 1946. Had outstanding opening season in 1949—1916 runs with av. 43.54. 1000 runs each season since 1937 HS—216* v Warwick (Dudley) 1938.

COOPER, Fred (Worcs.) B.Bacup (Lancs.) 18/4/1921. RHB, reserve opener. Brother of Edwin. Debut 1946. HS—113* v Notts. (Nottingham) 1948.

†COOPER, Rusi S. (Middx.) B.Bombay (India) 14/12/1922. Useful RHB. Played 2 matches in 1949.

CORNFORD, Jim (Sussex) B.Crowborough 9/11/1911. Whole-hearted FM bowler; moves either way with pace off pitch. Has rarely hit the headlines but his bowling has served his county well. RHB. Best season 1949 when he took 97 wickets (av. 25.52) Benefit in 1950. HS—34 v Leics (Ashby de la Zouch) 1949. BB—9-53 v Northants. (Rushden) 1949.

CORRALL, P. ("Paddy") (Leics.) B. Leicester 16/7/1906. Sound wicket-keeper, brilliant on his day. Debut 1930, scoring 4 and adding 112 for 9th wkt. with G. Geary v Cambridge U. (Cambridge). Dismissed 10 batsmen (7 ct. 3 st.) v Sussex (Hove) 1936. Benefit 1949 (£2,333—county record). HS—64 v Sussex (Hove) 1934.

COX, Dennis R. (Surrey) B.Bermondsey 21/12/1925. Useful FM bowler. Debut in 1949 when he played in first two county matches. England 12th man at the Oval 1949.

COX, George (Sussex) B.Horsham 23/8/1911. A most attractive RHB but rather inconsistent; best on hard wickets. Useful change bowler and splendid cover. Famous son of equally famous father. Debut in 1931. Played soccer for Arsenal, Fulham and Luton Town. Best season in 1947—2032 runs (av. 37.62). 1000 runs each season since 1937. HS—234 v Indians (Hove) 1946. BB—6-125 v M.C.C. (Hastings) 1946.

COXON, Alec (Yorks.) B.Huddersfield 18/1/1917. Aggressive whole-hearted MF bowler, moves either way. Useful well-equipped RHB. Debut 1945. C.Cap 1947. Test v Australia (Lord's) 1948. Has played soccer for Bradford. HS—83 v Notts. (Leeds) 1948. BB—8-31 v Worcs. (Leeds) 1946 — including "hat-trick."

CRANFIELD, L. M. ("Monty") (Glos.) B.Bristol 29/8/1910. Good OB bowler who lacks chances, having been understudy to Goddard. Can also bowl LB's. Useful RHB. Debut 1934. HS—90 v Essex (Bristol) 1947. BB—8-45 (13-54) v Cambridge U. (Gloucester) 1946. Testimonial 1950.

†CRANMER, Peter (Warwick) B.Olton (Birmingham) 10/9/1914. Patently aggressive RHB and occasional bowler. Fine field. Failed to gain cricket Blue at Oxford, but won rugger Blue 1933 and 1934. England rugger captain and centre—16 caps. Debut 1934. Captain Warwick 1938 to 1947. HS—113 v Northants. (Birmingham) 1934.

†CRANSTON, Kenneth (Lancs.) B.Liverpool 20/10/1917. Stylish RHB and very useful MF swing bowler. Debut 1947. Lancs. captain 1947 and 1948. Played in 3 Tests v. S. Africa in his first season, in all four Tests on 1947-48 W. Indian tour and v Australia at Leeds, 1948. At Leeds in 1947 took last four S.A. second innings wickets in one over (w.ww.w). His profession of surgeon-dentist at Liverpool prevents regular appearance. HS—156* M.C.C. v. Yorks. (Scarborough) 1949. BB—7-43 (10-82 match) v. Surrey (Oval) 1948.

CRAPP, John F. (Glos.) B.St.Columb (Cornwall) 14/10/1912. Extremely sound LHB with fine scoring shots. Brilliant field at first slip. Debut 1936. Scored 1000 runs each season since 1936, and 2014 in 1949—only left-hand bat to score 2000 runs in a season purely for Glos. Test Trial at Canterbury 1946. Played in 3 Tests v. Australia in 1948 (Manchester, Leeds and Oval). Toured S. Africa in 1948-49, playing in last four Tests. HS—175 v. Cambridge U. (Cambridge) 1947.

CRAY, S. J. ("Chick") (Essex) B.Stratford 29/5/1921. Stylish RHB. Very fast in outfield with accurate return. Debut 1938. C.Cap 1947. Coached in S. Africa in 1948-49 and 1949-50 winters. HS—139 v. Northants (Clacton) 1948.

†CRICK, F/Lt. Harry (Combined Services). Wicketkeeper and RHB. Played for Yorkshire 1947.

†CRUSH, E d d i e (Kent) B.Dover 25/4/1917. Very useful RHB and M bowler who moves either way. Debut 1946. C.Cap 1948. HS—78 v. Hants. (Canterbury) 1948. BB—6-50 v. Hants. (Canterbury) 1948.

DARE, R. (Hants.) B.Blandford (Dorset) 26/11/1921. Slow LA spinner. Debut 1949, playing in 3 matches.

DARKS, Geoffrey (Worcs.) B.Bewdley 28/6/1926. RHB and M bowler. Debut 1946, but has played few matches. HS—20 v. Combined Services (Worcester) 1949.

†DAVIDSON, W. W. (" Bill ") (Sussex) B.Poplar (London) 20/3/1920. Wicketkeeper. Educated at Brighton. Oxford Blue 1947-8. Debut 1947.

DAVIES, Emrys (Glamorgan) B.Llanelly 27/6/1904. Very sound opening LHB. Originally clever LA spinner but now rarely bowls. " Double " in 1935 and 1937. Has scored 1000 runs in a season 12 times. Selected for cancelled 1939-40 tour to India. Benefit in 1938 (£688). Added 313 for 3rd wkt. with W. E. Jones v. Essex (Brentwood) 1948—the record Glamorgan partnership for any wkt. Shared 1st wkt. stand of 274 with A. H. Dyson v. Leics. (Leicester) 1937 and achieved " hat-trick " in same match. HS—287* v. Glos. (Newport) 1939. BB—5-19 (10-74 match) v. Worcs. (Llanelly) 1938.

DAVIES, Haydn G. (Glamorgan) B. Llanelly 23/4/1912. Wicketkeeper capable of brilliance. Adventurous RHB who can also defend stubbornly. Debut 1935. Test Trial at Lord's 1946. Has dismissed nearly 300 batsmen behind the wicket. HS— 68 v. Northants. (Cardiff) 1939.

†DAVIES, J. G. W. (" Jack ") (Kent) B.Blackheath 10/9/1911. Attractive RHB. Accurate OB bowler. Excellent cover. Educated at Tonbridge. Cambridge Blue 1933 and 1934. Clean bowled Bradman for a " duck " in 1934. Fine rugger centre (Blackheath and Kent). HS—168 v. Worcs. (Worcester) 1946. BB—6-28 (10-91 match) v. Worcs. (Dover) 1947.

DAVIS, Eddie (Northants.) B.Brackley 8/3/1922. Sound RHB. Debut 1947. Added 259 for 2nd wkt. with Brookes when making his HS—171 v. Leics. (Northampton) 1949

DAVIS, Percy (Northants.) B.Brackley 24/5/1915. Sound RHB. Debut 1935. Can keep wicket in emergency. Coached in S. Africa 1949-50. Testimonial 1950. HS—237 v. Somerset (Taunton) 1947.

DAWKES, George (Derby) B.Leicester 19/7/1920. Excellent wicketkeeper and sound RHB. Debut for Leics. in 1937 and C.Cap 1938. Joined Derby in 1947 and C.Cap 1947. Has kept goal for Leicester City. Toured India with Commonwealth team 1949-50. HS—95 v. Notts. (Ilkeston) 1948.

DEBNAM, A. F. H. (Hants.) See page 173.

†DEIGHTON, John H. G. (Lancs.) Good RFM bowler, swinging either way with nip off the pitch. Robust RHB. Educated at Denstone. Debut for Lancs. 1948. Serving in Army. HS—79 v. Leics. (Blackpool) 1949. BB—6-64 Comb. Services v. Worcs. (Worcester) 1949.

DEVEREUX, L. (Worcs.) B.Paignton (Devon) 1932. Useful RHB. Debut in 1949—2 matches for Middx. Represented England at table tennis at Prague in 1949. At present in Forces. Playing in "friendlies" for Worcs. 1950.

†DEW, John A. (Sussex) B.Horsham 12/5/1920. RHB. Good wicketkeeper. Educated at Tonbridge. Cambridge war-time " Blue " (1941). Debut 1947. Did not play 1948-49.

†DEWES, John G. (Middx.) B.Latchford (Cheshire) 11/10/1926. Very sound opening LHB and fine field. Educated at Aldenham. Played for England in Lord's " Victory " Test in 1945, after scoring 1000 runs for Cambridge U. in May (minor matches only). While in R.N. played for Combined Services. Cambridge Blue 1948 and 1949. Played in Test v. Australia (Oval) 1948, opening innings with Hutton. Debut for Middx. 1948. C.Cap 1948. Played for Gentlemen at Lord's 1948 and 1949. With G. H. G. Doggart shares English 2nd wkt. record (429 unseparated v. Essex at Cambridge 1949). HS—204* Cambridge U. v. Essex (Cambridge) 1949.

DEWS, George (Worcs.) B.Ossett (Yorks.) 5/6/1921. Forceful RHB. Fine outfield. Debut 1946. Plays soccer for Plymouth Argyle. HS— 78 v. R.A.F. (Worcester) 1946.

†DIVECHA, R. V. ("Buck") (Oxford U) B.Bombay 18/10/1927. Useful RHB and RFM bowler. Educated at Podar H.S. and Bombay Univ. Played for Oxford in 1948 and 1949, just failing to gain Blue, for Northants. 1948 and for Oxfordshire 1949. HS—68* v. Leics. (Oxford) 1949.

DODDS, T. C. (" Dicky ") (Essex) B.Bedford 29/5/1919. Attractive, enterprising and consistent opening RHB. Debut 1946 as amateur. C.Cap 1946. Turned pro. 1947. Took a wicket with his first ball in first-class cricket, but now rarely bowls. Scored 1000 runs in a season four times, 1946-1949. HS—157 v. Leics. (Leicester) 1947.

†DOGGART, A. Peter (Sussex) B.London 3/11/1927. RHB. Debut 1947—5 matches. Did not play in 1948 or 1949, but made runs for Sussex 2nd XI. Now on staff of " Cricketer ".

†DOGGART, G. Hubert G. (Sussex) B.Earl's Court 18/7/1925. Most promising stylish and forceful RHB and accurate OB bowler. Fine field and catch. Educated at Winchester. Cambridge Blue 1948-9, captain in 1950. Soccer, squash, rackets and fives Blue—Cambridge captain at four games. Debut 1948—1169 runs (av. 34.38); 2063 runs (av. 45.84) in 1949. Played for Gentlemen at Lord's in 1949. Scored 215*

v. Lancs. (Cambridge) on debut in 1948. C.Cap 1949. Added 429* for second wicket with J. G. Dewes v. Essex (Cambridge) 1949—English record. HS—219* Cambridge U. v. Essex (Cambridge) 1949. BB—3-57 (5-67 match) in 1949 University match. Joint Sussex captain 1950.

DOLLERY, H. E. (" Tom ") (Warwick) B.Reading (Berks.) 14/10/1914. Very consistent RHB, plenty of shots, good in crisis. Can keep wicket in emergency. Played for Berks. before joining Warwick. Debut for Warwick. 1934. Has scored 1000 runs every season since 1935. 2084 runs (av. 47.36) in 1949. Played in 4 Test Trials before making Test debut v. S. Africa (Nottingham) 1947. Played v. Australia at Lord's and Manchester 1948. Played soccer for Reading. Shared captaincy with R. H. Maudsley in 1948 and was appointed pro. captain of Warwick. in 1949—a great success. Benefit 1949 (£6,362 —county record). HS—200 v. Glos. (Gloucester) 1949

†**DONNELLY, Martin P.** (Warwick) B.Ngaruawahia (New Zealand) 17/10/1917. One of the three best LHB's in the world today. A superb on-side player. Can bowl LA slows. Made debut in 1936-37 in N.Z. and toured England in 1937, playing in all 3 Tests. Came to England during war and stayed in 1946 to go up to Oxford. Blue 1946 and 1947, captain second year. Played 1 match for Middlesex in 1946. Debut for Warwick. 1948. Played for N.Z. touring team in 1949, showing wonderful consistency — 64 (Leeds), 206 (Lord's), 75 and 80 (Manchester). Oxford rugger Blue 1946 and England centre v Ireland 1947. Holds unique record by scoring centuries for Oxford U. in 1946 'Varsity match (142), Gentlemen at Lord's (162* in 1947), and New Zealand in 1949 Lord's Test (206)—all glorious innings. Played for Gentlemen at Lord's 1946-7-8. HS—208* M.C.C. v. Yorks. (Scarborough) 1948.

DOVEY, Raymond R. (Kent) B.Chislehurst 7/7/1920. Very accurate and thoughtful RA bowler of OB's and " cutters." Sound LHB. Plays in glasses. Debut 1938. C.Cap 1946. Best season 1947—94 wkts. (av. 25.23). HS—54 v. Worcs. (Dover) 1947. BB—5-51 (10-113 match) v. Somerset (Bath) 1946.

DOWNTON, G. (Kent) B.Sidcup 1/11/1928. Reserve wicketkeeper. Debut 1948. Did not play in 1949.

DUNHAM, Norman (Leics.) B.Quorn 9/12/1925. RM bowler. Played 1 match in 1949.

†**EAGAR, E. D. R. (Desmond)** (Hants.) B.Cheltenham (Glos.) 8/12/1917. Attractive and enterprising RHB. Excellent field anywhere, but especially at backward short leg. Zealous, inspiring skipper. Debut for Glos. 1935 while still at Cheltenham. Oxford Blue 1939. 1000 runs in season 1939-47-48-49. Appointed Captain-Secretary to Hants. in 1945, making debut in 1946. HS—147 Oxford U. v. Minor Counties (Oxford) 1938.

EDRICH, Brian (Kent) B.Cantley (Norfolk) 18/8/1922. Forceful LHB. ROB bowler; spins well but needs better length and direction. Youngest of the four county cricketing brothers. Joined Kent staff 1939. Debut 1947. C.Cap 1946. HS—193* v. Sussex (Tunbridge Wells) 1949—adding 191 for 9th wkt. with F. Ridgway. BB—7-64 v. Glos. (Tunbridge Wells) 1949.

EDRICH, Geoffrey A. (Lancs.) B.Lingwood (Norfolk) 13/7/1918. Attractive RHB. Brilliant outfield, rarely seen close to wicket now. Debut 1946. C.Cap 1946. Held 6 catches in match v. Eessex (Colchester) 1946. HS—136* v. Somerset (Taunton) 1949.

†**EDRICH, William J.** (Middx.) B.Lingwood (Norfolk) 26/3/1916. Outstanding RHB and brilliant field at first slip. Fields splendidly in most positions. As a bowler (FM) he was at his best in 1946 and 1947, but a strain in August 1947 has reduced his ability since. First played for Norfolk but joined M.C.C. staff in 1934, when he was transferred from Norwich City to Tottenham Hotspur (OL). Debut for Middx. 1937. Scored 1000 runs before end of May 1938 —all at Lord's. Played in Tests v. Australia 1938 and South Africa 1938-39 without success until he scored 219* at Durban in the " timeless " Test. Turned amateur in 1947. Has appeared for the Players at Lord's in 1938 and Gents. 1947-8-9. Toured India with Lord Tennyson's team 1937-38, South Africa 1938-39, Australia and N.Z. 1946-47. Has played in 29 Tests. Scored 3539 runs in 1947—second highest aggregate. Has scored 1000 runs in season seven times. Served in R.A.F. during war as Sqdn.-Ldr. and won D.F.C. HS—267* v. Northants. (Northampton) 1947. BB—7-48 v. Worcs. (Worcester) 1946.

†**EGGAR, John D.** (Derby) B.Nowshera (N.W.F.P.) 1/12/1916. Very sound RHB. Good field. Educated at Winchester. Oxford Blue 1938. Now master at Repton. HS—219 v. Yorks. (Bradford) 1949.

ELLIOTT, Charles S. (Derby) B.Bolsover 17/7/1912. Consistent opening RHB. Good slip field. Debut 1932. Played soccer for Coventry City. Has played in Birmingham League. Testimonial 1950. HS—215 v. Notts. (Nottingham) 1947.

EMMETT, George M. (Glos.) B.India 2/12/1912. Elegant and consistent opening RHB; a delightful stroke player. Very keen fielder. Played for Devon before joining Glos. 1937. Test v. Australia (Manchester) 1948. 1000 runs in a season 5 times (1938-39, 1947-49)—2005 runs in 1949. Scored 115 and 103* v. Leics. (Leicester) 1947. HS—165* v Surrey (Bristol) 1938.

†**EVANS, Gwyn** (Leics.) B.Bala 13/8/1915. Useful RHB and M bowler. Educated at St. Asaph. Oxford Blue 1939. Played for Glamorgan 1939. Debut for Leics. 1949. C.Cap 1949. HS—65* v. Glos. (Leicester) 1949. BB—6-80 Oxford U. v. Leics. (Oxford) 1939.

EVANS, T. Godfrey (Kent) B.Finchley (Middx.) 18/8/1920. Brilliant wicketkeeper, at his best on big occasions. Dashing but unsound RHB. Debut 1939. C.Cap 1946. Has played cricket regularly since 1946 and not missed a tour. Toured Australia and N.Z. 1946-47, W. Indies 1947-48, S. Africa 1948-49. Debut for England v. India (Oval) 1946. Has now played in 27 Tests. Nearly reached wicketkeeper's "double" in 1947—1110 runs and 93 dismissals. Dismissed 9 batsmen (8 ct. 1 st.) for Kent v New Zealanders (Canterbury) 1949. HS—101 M.C.C. v. Otago (Dunedin) 1946-47—his only first-class hundred.

†**EVE, Stanley C.** (Essex) B.Stepney 8/12/1925. Attractive RHB and very good field. Debut 1949, scoring maiden century in 2nd match. HS—120 v. Warwick. (Brentwood) 1949.

FAGG, Arthur E. (Kent) B.Chartham 18/6/1915. Very sound, accomplished, opening RHB, at his best against quick bowling. Splendid onside player. Still a good slip field. Debut 1932. Played 5 Tests—2 v. India 1936, 2 v. Australia 1936-37, 1 v. W. Indies 1939. Returned home early from Australian tour owing to rheumatic trouble. Scored 244 and 202* v Kent (Colchester) 1938—only instance of two 200's in a match. Scored 1000 runs each season since 1934 except when he missed 1937 season owing to ill health. Coach at Cheltenham 1946. Returned to Kent in 1947. HS—257 v. Hants. (Southampton) 1936.

†**FAIRBAIRN, Alan** (Middx.) B.Winchmore Hill 25/1/1923. Opening LHB. Educated at Haileybury. Scored 108 v. Somerset (Taunton) 1947 when making debut for Middx. C.Cap 1947. Did not play in 1949. HS —110* v. Notts. (Nottingham) 1947.

FARAGHER, Harold A. (Essex) B.Reddish (Lancs.) 20/7/1917. Sound RHB and good field. Scored 501

runs in 9 innings for Essex 2nd XI in 1949 and made debut in last match of season.

†**FARR, B. H.** (Notts.) B.Worksop. Educated at Harrow. RFM bowler. War-time (1943) "Blue" for Cambridge. Debut 1949, playing in 2 matches.

†**FENNER, O/Cadet M. D.** (Combined Services) LHB. Kent 2nd XI.

FIDDLING, Ken (Northants.) B.Hebden Bridge (Yorks.) 13/10/1917. Dependable wicketkeeper. Played for Yorks. 1938 to 1946 before joining Northants. in 1947. C.Cap 1947. HS—68 v. Surrey (Oval) 1947.

FIRTH, Jack (Yorks.) B.Cottingley 27/6/1919. Reserve wicketkeeper. Debut 1949, playing in 4 matches.

FISHLOCK, L. B. ("Laurie") (Surrey) B.Battersea (London) 2/1/1907. Attractive, forceful and very consistent opening LHB. Still a fine outfield. Debut 1931. Toured Australia 1936-37 and 1946-47, a broken finger on each tour causing him to miss matches. Played in 4 Tests— 2 v. India 1936, 1 v. India 1946, 1 v. Australia 1946-47. Gained an England amateur soccer cap with Dulwich Hamlet and played pro. soccer for Crystal Palace, Millwall, Aldershot, Southampton, and Gillingham. When he scored his first century for Surrey he became the first left-handed Surrey century scorer for over 60 years. Has scored two 100's in a match 3 times and 1000 runs in a season 9 times. Benefit 1950. HS—253 v. Leics. (Leicester) 1948.

FLAVELL, John (Worcs.) B.Brierley Hill (Staffs.) 14/5/1929. RMF bowler and RHB. Debut in 1949 when he played one match.

FLETCHER, David G. W. (Surrey) B. Sutton 7/7/1924. Stylish opening RHB of whom much is expected. Debut 1946. C.Cap 1947, when he scored 1857 runs and appeared for Players at Lord's. Missed end of 1948 season through ill-health. Test Trial 1949. HS—194 v. Notts. (Nottingham) 1947.

FOORD, C. W. ("Bill") (Yorks.) B. Scarborough 11/6/1924. RFM bowler of possibilities. RHB. A schoolmaster who plays as a pro. Wears glasses. Debut 1947. BB—5-35 v. Glos. (Huddersfield) 1949.

†**FORD, W/Cmdr. W. R.** (Combined Services) Wicketkeeper and LHB.

†**FREDERICK, M.** (Derby) B.Barbados (B.W.I.) 6/5/1927. Useful RHB. Very good field. Debut 1949. HS— 84 v. Essex (Burton-on-Trent) 1949.

†**GARDINER-HILL Peter** (Oxford U.) B. London 22/10/1926. Educated at Eton. Played 2 matches for Oxford, 1949. Opening RHB.

GARDNER, Freddie C. (Warwick.) B. Coventry 4/6/1922. Consistent and much improved opening RHB. Debut

1947 as amateur. C.Cap 1949. Plays soccer for Newport County. Enjoyed good season in 1949—1657 runs (av. 34.52). HS—140* v. Worcs. (Birmingham) 1949—carrying bat through innings.

GARLICK, R. Gordon (Northants.) B. Kirkby Lonsdale (Westmoreland) 11/4/1917. Much improved ROB bowler. RHB. Good humoured and whole-hearted. Played for Lancs. 1938 to 1947. Debut for Northants. 1948. C.Cap 1949. HS—51 v. Essex (Westcliff) 1949. BB—6-27 (10-46 match) Lancs. v. Derby (Buxton) 1946.

†**GAY, Capt. David W. M.** (Sussex) B. London 2/4/1920. RHB and M bowler. Debut in 1949, playing 2 matches for Combined Services and Sussex. Plays for Army; regular soldier who won M.C. during war.

†**GENDERS, W. Roy** (Somerset) B.Sheffield 21/1/1915. RHB and change bowler. Man of many counties— Derby (1946), Worcs. (1947 and 1948) and Somerset (1949). HS— 55* Worcs. v Derby (Chesterfield) 1947.

GILES, Ronald J. (Notts.) B.Chilwell 17/10/1919. Useful RHB and change bowler (LA seamers). Debut 1937. Has had limited opportunities. HS— 59 v Glamorgan (Cardiff) 1949.

GIMBLETT, Harold (Somerset) B.Bicknoller (Somerset) 19/10/1914. Attractive forcing opening RHB who who should have played for England more often. A really fine straight driver, he can be tremendously severe on anything short. Good fielder with very powerful throw from deep. Debut 1935, scoring 123 v. Essex (Frome) in his first match (he reached his century in 63 minutes and won the Lawrence Trophy for the season). Played in 3 Tests—2 v. India 1936 and 1 v. W. Indies 1939. Has scored most centuries (34) for Somerset. 1000 runs each season since 1936. Holds every Somerset batting record except one—most runs for the county (15198) still held by F. S. Lee. HS—310 v. Sussex (Eastbourne) 1948—at that time the highest in England since 1939.

GLADWIN, Clifford (Derby) B.Doe Lea 3/4/1917. Very accurate RFM bowler of in-swing and leg cutters. Hard-hitting RHB. Debut 1939. C.Cap 1946. Toured S. Africa 1948-49. Played in 8 Tests—2 v. S. Africa 1947, 5 v. S. Africa 1948-49, 1 v. N.Z. 1949. It was a leg-bye off Gladwin that won the Durban Test for England in 1948-49, off the last ball of the match. Only 86 runs short of the "double" in 1949. 100 wkts. each season since war. HS—124* v. Notts. (Nottingham) 1949. BB—9-119 v. Lancs. (Buxton) 1947.

GODDARD, Tom W. (Glos.) B.Gloucester 1/10/1900. Outstanding and everlasting OB bowler. Originally a fast bowler. Debut 1922, gained regular place in 1929. Played in 8 Tests—1 v Australia 1930, 2 v N.Z. 1937, 3 v. S. Africa 1938-39, 2 v. W. Indies 1939. Toured S. Africa in 1930-31 and 1938-39. Best season 1937 (248 wkts.) Has taken 100 wkts. in a season 15 times. Took 17-106 in a day v. Kent (Bristol) 1939. Took all ten wkts. v. Worcs. (Cheltenham) 1937. Has performed "hat-trick" six times, including one v. S. Africa (Johannesburg Test) 1938-39. Benefits 1936 (£2,097) and 1948 (£3,355). HS—71 v. Essex (Southend) 1932.

GRAVENEY, J. Kenneth (Glos.) B. Hexham 16/12/1924. Promising RFM bowler, moves either way. LHB. Debut 1947, gaining regular place in 1949. Took all ten wkts. for 66 v. Derby (Chesterfield) 1949. HS— 62 v. Leics. (Leicester) 1949.

GRAVENEY, Thomas W. (Glos.) B. Riding Mill 16/6/1927. Most promising forceful and stylish RHB of forward type—at his best on firm wicket. Fine outfield. Debut 1948. C.Cap 1948. Represented Players at Lord's 1949, a season which brought him 1784 runs. HS—159 v. Somerset (Bristol) 1949.

GRAY, J. R. (Hants.) B.Southampton 19/5/1926. Useful RHB and good field. Debut 1948. Made 2 appearances 1949. On Arsenal staff. HS —46 v. Combined Services (Aldershot) 1948.

GRAY, Laurie H. (Middx.) B.Tottenham 16/12/1915. Good RFM bowler who moves either way, mostly out. Good field near wicket. RHB. Debut 1934. C.Cap 1937. Took 5 wkts. in 11 balls (inc. 4 in 6) v. Sussex (Hove) 1938. Has only taken 100 wkts. in a season once (1946), but returns good "bag" each season. Test Trial at Canterbury 1946. Benefit (£6,000) 1948. BB—7-17 (11-34 match) v. Hants. (Lord's) 1946.

GREENSMITH, W. T. ("Bill") (Essex) B.Middlesbrough (Yorks.) 16/8/1930. Promising all-rounder. RHB and LB bowler. Debut 1947. Played for county in 1947 and 1948 and Combined Services in 1949. May be available for Essex in 1950.

GREENWOOD, Peter (Lancs.) B.Todmorden 11/9/1924. Very useful promising all-rounder. Bowls OB's and out-swingers. Improving RHB and very keen field. Debut 1948. C.Cap 1949. HS—52 v. Northants. (Peterborough) 1949. BB—6-35 v. Northants. (Manchester) 1949.

GRIEVES, KEN. (Lancs.) B.Sydney (N.S.W.) 27/8/1925. Realistic aggressive RHB bat and slow bowler of parts (LB's and all sorts). Played for N.S.W. in 1945-46. Played for Rawtenstall in League cricket. Keeps goal for Bury. Debut for Lancs. 1949. C.Cap 1949. HS—128 v New Zealanders (Manchester) 1949. BB— 6-60 v. Kent (Manchester) 1949.

†**GRIFFITH, Stewart C.** ("Billy") (Sussex) B.Surrey 16/6/1914. Has been outstanding amateur wicket-keeper for many years—neat and quiet. Better RHB than figures suggest. Educated at Dulwich. Debut 1934. Cambridge Blue 1935. Toured Australia and N.Z. 1935-36. Selected for cancelled 1939-40 Indian tour. Played in all five Victory Tests in 1945. Toured W. Indies in 1947-48 and S. Africa 1948-49. Has played in 3 Tests, opening the innings and scoring 140—his maiden century —in his first Test at Trinidad 1947-48. Played for Gentlemen at Lord's five times 1939-46-7-8-9. Won D.F.C. with Airborne Forces. HS— 140 England v. West Indies (Trinidad) 1947-48. County secretary 1946-50; resigned February. Now on staff of "Sunday Times," will play mid-week games only.

GROVE, C. W. ("Charlie") B.Birmingham 16/12/1912. Accurate inswing RFM bowler. Hard-hitting RHB. Debut 1938. C.Cap 1947. HS—104* v Leics. (Leicester) 1948. BB-7-48 v Somerset (Taunton) 1947

†**GUARD, David R.** (Hants.) B.Romsey 19/5/1928. Stylish RHB. Educated at Winchester. Debut 1946, but played only occasionally until 1949. HS—89 v Glamorgan (Cardiff) 1949.

†**HALL, P. J.** (Cambridge U.) B.Hong Kong 4/12/27. M bowler (outswing), useful RHB, good field. Educated at Geelong G.S., Victoria, but he is not an Australian. Blue 1949. HS—49 v Sussex (Horsham) 1949. BB—5-51 v Somerset (Bath) 1949.

†**HALL, T. A.** (Derby). B.Durham 19/8/1930. Promising RFM bowler. Educated at Uppingham (1948 capt.) One match in 1949.

HALLIDAY, Harold (Yorks.). B.Pudsey 9/2/1920. Sound opening RHB; hits hard off back foot. Thoughtful and useful slow change bowler. Debut 1938. C.Cap 1948. Rheumatism kept him out for part of 1949. HS— 130 v Glos. (Bristol) 1948.

HAMER, Arnold (Derby). Aged 33. RHB. Played for Yorks. 1938. Last season scored 1106 runs for Pudsey St. Lawrence—an aggregate record in Bradford League. Has played soccer with York City.

HARBIN, L. (Glos.). B.Trinidad (B.W.I) 26/4/1915. RHB, slow-medium spinner. Scored 89 for Trinidad v. Jamaica in Trial 1938-39. Debut in 1949, taking 9-133 in his only match v Combined Services (Bristol).

HARDSTAFF, Joe. (Notts.). B.Nuncargate 3/7/1911. Handsome RHB; splendid driver and cutter. Fine outfield. Son of equally famous father. Joined Notts. staff 1927 making debut 1931. Has played in 23 Tests. Toured Australia and N.Z. 1935-36. 1946-47, Australia 1936-37, India 1937-38, N.Z. 1938-39 (Sir J. Cahn's team), W. Indies 1947-48. Has coached in N.Z. Scored 205* for England v India (Lord's) in first postwar Test. Represented Players at Lord's six times, 1935-1939 and 1946. Scored over 2,500 runs in 1937, when he hit fastest century of season in 51 minutes. 1000 runs in season ten times. Benefit (£3,063) in 1948. More centuries (64) than any Notts. player. HS—266 v Leics. (Leicester) 1937.

HARRIS, Charles B. (Notts.) B.Underwood 6/12/1908. Determined RHB of unpredictable mood. Regular opener till 1948 when he went in lower down. Useful change bowler. Debut 1928. C.Cap 1931. Has shared in over 40 opening century partnerships with W. W. Keeton. 1000 runs in season ten times. Benefit 1949 (£3,500 approx.—record for Club). HS—234 v Middlesex (Nottingham) 1933.

HARRISON, Leo. (Hants.). B.Mudeford 8/6/1922. Reserve wicketkeeper; can field splendidly anywhere. Useful RHB who would improve with more confidence and experience. Debut 1939. Now plays in glasses. HS— 61* v Yorks (Bournemouth) 1947.

HARVEY, Peter F. (Notts.). B.Linby 15/1/1923. Promising RHB and LBG bowler. Fine slip field. Debut 1947. Scored 125* v Derby (Nottingham) in his second match in first-class cricket (did not bat in first). C.Cap 1949. HS—125* v Derby (Nottingham) 1947. BB—8-122 v Somerset (Nottingham) 1949.

HARVEY, Peter V. (Oxford U.) B.Wallington (Surrey) 6/1/1926. Educated at Epsom College. Played one match for Oxford U. in 1949. LHB.

†**HAWKEY, R. B.** (Cambridge U.). B.Teddington (Middx.) 7/8/1923. Educated at Merchant Taylors' School. Played for Cambridge 1948 and 1949, but failed to gain Blue.

†**HAYLES, Major B. R. M.** (Combined Services). B.Andover (Hants.) 29/10/1916. Wicketkeeper, RHB. Educated at Haileybury. Has played occasional matches for Army and Combined Services since 1938.

HAZELL, Horace L. (Somerset). B.Brislington 30/9/1909. One of the best slow LA spinners and No. 11 bats in England. Good slip or gully. Debut 1929. Bowled 105 successive balls without conceding a run v Glos. (Taunton) 1949—a world

record. Benefit 1949 (£2,324). HS
—43 v Glos. (Bristol) 1946. BB—
6-18 (11-52 match) v Kent (Canterbury) 1946 and 8-27 (12-63
match) v Glos. (Taunton) 1949.

HEARN, Peter. (Kent). B.Tunbridge
Wells 18/11/1925. Promising LHB.
Change bowler (LA slow). Keen outfield. Debut 1947, scoring 124 v
Warwick (Gillingham) in first
match. C.Cap 1947. HS—138
Combined Services v Northants.
(Northampton) 1947.

HEATH, David M. W. (Warwick).
B.Birmingham 4/12/1931. Opening
RHB. Debut 1949—2 matches.

†**HEBDEN, G. G. C.** (Hants.) B.London
14/7/1918. MF bowler. Debut
1937, has rarely played for county.

HEDGES, B. (Glamorgan) see page
173.

†**HENDERSON, Derek** (Oxford U.) Played
one match in 1949. M bowler, RHB.

HEVER, Norman G. (Glamorgan).
B.Marylebone (London) 17/12/1924.
Accurate RFM in-swing bowler.
Rather slightly built; always attacks
stumps. Debut for Middlesex 1947,
but joined Glamorgan 1948. C.Cap
1948. Played in Test Trial 1949.
HS—29 v Combined Services (Pontypridd) 1948. BB—6-34 v Somerset (Taunton) 1949.

HILL, Eric. (Somerset). B.Taunton
9/7/1923. Stylish and correct
opening RHB. Debut 1947. C.Cap
1949, when he was out of luck and
out of form. Splendid outfield and
safe catch. HS—85 v Northants.
(Kettering) 1948.

HILL, Gerry (Hants.). B.Totton
15/4/1913. RHB and off-spin bowler.
A thoroughly sound and dependable
all-rounder, and safe catch. At his
best as a batsman when attacking
the bowling. Debut 1932. In 1935
was hit for 32 off one over by C.
Smart (Glamorgan at Cardiff)—a
world record. 1000 runs in 1946
and 1947. Joint Benefit 1948-50.
HS—161 v Sussex (Portsmouth)
1937. BB—8-62 (14-146 match)
v Kent (Tonbridge) 1935.

HILTON, Malcolm J. (Lancs.). B.Chadderton 2/8/1928. Promising slow
LA bowler who spins and flights well
Fields keenly. Dismissed Bradman
twice in a match at Manchester
1948. Debut 1946. Did not play
regularly in 1949. 103 wkts. for
Lancs. 2nd, 1949. BB—5-19 v.
Notts. (Manchester) 1948.

HITCHCOCK, R. E. ("Ray"). (Warwick). B.Christchurch (N.Z.)
28/11/1929. Forcing LHB and LB
bowler. Debut 1949—1 match.

†**HOFMEYR, M. B.** (Oxford U.). B.Pretoria (South Africa) 9/12/1925.
Solid, watchful opening RHB. Educated at Pretoria H.S. and Rhodes
Univ. Coll, Grahamstown. Blue 1949.
Rugby Blue 1948 and 1949. Carried his bat through a completed
innings twice in 1949—his performance in the 'Varsity match being only
the second time in the series. HS—
154 v Hants. (Bournemouth) 1949.
English Rugby international 1950
(full-back). Oxford cricket secretary 1950.

HOLLIES, W. Eric (Warwick.) B.Old
Hill (Staffs.) 5/6/1912. Outstandingly accurate LBG bowler. RHB, but
not a very serious one. Has scored
less runs than he has taken wickets,
but can offer a stubborn defence.
Debut 1932. Toured W. Indies
1934-35. Declined invitation to
tour S. Africa 1948-49 owing to leg
injury. Played in 11 Tests—3 v
W. Indies 1934-35 (headed Test
bowling averages), 3 v S. Africa
1947, 1 v Australia 1948, and 4 v
N.Z. 1949. Took 184 wkts. in 1946,
including all ten Notts. wkts. for 49
in an innings at Birmingham, all
without assistance from the field—7
bowled and 3 l.b.w. Benefit (£4,896)
1948. Took 100 wkts. in 1935 and
in each season since 1937. Has
taken most wickets for Warwick.
HS—24 v Leics. (Oakham) 1937.
BB—10-49 (see above).

†**HOLMES, Errol R. T.** (Surrey) B.Calcutta (India) 12/8/1905. Forcing
RHB and useful M change bowler.
Debut 1924. Educated at Malvern.
Oxford Blue 1925-6-7, also soccer
Blue. Captain of Surrey 1934 to
1938 and 1947-1948. Toured W.
Indies 1934-35, playing in all 4
Tests. Test v S. Africa 1935. Captained M.C.C. team to Australia
and N.Z. 1935-36. HS—236
Oxford U. v Free Foresters (Oxford)
1927.

†**HOLMES, J. R. R.** Played one match
for Free Foresters in 1949.

HORSFALL, Richard (Essex) B.Todmorden (Lancs.) 26/6/1920. Most
promising forceful RHB. Debut
1947. C.Cap 1948. Unable to
play for most of 1949 owing
to back injury received during practice in April. HS—170 v Hants
(Bournemouth) 1947.

†**HOSKYNS, Sir John, Bart.** (Cambridge
U.) B.Cambridge 28/5/1926. Opening LHB. Played 2 matches for
Cambridge U. in 1949.

†**HOSSELL, Jack J.** (Warwick). B.Birmingham 25/5/1914. LHB. Change
bowler. Debut 1939. C.Cap 1946.
Played for 2nd XI in 1948 and
1949 HS—83 v Leics. (Birmingham) 1946.

HOUGH, Philip (Lancs.) RHB from
Macclesfield. Ex-Cheshire player
specially registered for 1950.

†**HOWARD, Barry J.** (Lancs.) B.Preston
21/5/1926. Sound RHB. Debut
1947. C.Cap 1947. Captain of
Lancs. 2nd XI. HS—114 M.C.C. v
Essex (Lord's) 1949.

HOWARD, Jack H. (Leics.) B.Leicester 24/11/1917. Useful LHB and reserve wicketkeeper. Debut 1946. Did not play in 1949 owing to illness which is likely to prevent his return as a pro. HS—38* v Middlesex (Lord's) 1946.

†**HOWARD, Nigel D.** (Lancs.) B.Preston 18/5/1925. Stylish RHB of forward type. Very keen field. Debut 1946. C.Cap 1948. Lancs. captain 1949-50. HS—145 v. Derby (Manchester) 1948.

HOWORTH, Richard (Worcs.) B.Bacup (Lancs.) 26/4/1909. Sound LHB and very good slow LA bowler. Debut 1933. C.Cap 1934. "Doubles" in 1939, 1946 and 1947—missing by 3 runs in 1938. Reached 100 wkt. aggregate 8 times. Played in 5 Tests—1 v S. Africa 1947 and all 4 on 1947-48 W. Indian tour. Took wkt. with first ball in Test cricket. Benefit (£3,000 approx.) 1949. Best season 1947—1510 runs and 164 wkts. HS—114 v Kent (Dover) 1936 and for H. D. G. L-Gower's XI v Indians (Scarborough) 1946. BB—7-18 (10-57 match) v Northants. (Kettering) 1949.

†**HUNT, R. G.** (Sussex)—see page 173.

HURST, Gordon T. (Sussex) B.Kenley (Surrey) 26/8/1920. Useful OB bowler. Debut 1947. BB—6-80 v Warwick (Hove) 1947.

HUTTON, Len (Yorks.) B.Fulneck (Pudsey) 23/6/1916. Technically the finest RHB in the world today and the soundest opener. Safe catch anywhere. Debut 1934, when he was hailed as the successor to Herbert Sutcliffe. Debut in Test cricket v N.Z. at Lord's in 1937—scoring a "duck"—and has since played in 41 out of 47 Tests for England. With C. Washbrook added 359 for England 1st wkt. v S. Africa (Johannesburg) 1948-49—a record for all Tests. In scoring 364 v Australia (Oval) 1938 he stayed at the wicket for 13 hours 20 minutes—the longest innings in cricket history and the highest in Tests. Represented Players at Lord's 1937-8-9-48-9. Scored 3429 runs in 1949—4th highest season's aggregate. Passed 1000 runs aggregate every season since 1936. Toured S. Africa 1938-39 and 1948-49, Australia 1946-47 and W. Indies 1935-36 (Yorks. tour) and 1947-48 (flew out to join team for second half of tour). Benefit in 1950. HS—364 (above).

IKIN, John T. (Lancs.) B.Bignall End (Staffs.) 7/3/1918. Very sound LHB; opened for county with increased success for most of 1949. Useful RLB bowler and brilliant field close to wicket. Played for Staffs. before making Lancs. debut 1939. C.Cap 1946—awarded after he had gained first England cap. Played in 12 Tests—2 v India 1946, 5 v Australia 1946-47, 1 v N.Z. 1946-47, 4 v W. Indies 1947-48. Two tours as above. Held 55 catches in 1946. Reached 1000 run aggregate 4 times. HS—167 v New Zealanders (Manchester) 1949. BB—6-21 (11-119 match) v Notts. (Manchester) 1947 and 4-14 (inc. "hat-trick") v Somerset (Taunton) 1949.

†**INGRAM, Eddie A.** (Mddx.) B.Dublin 4/8/1910. Useful RHB and M bowler. Plays mainly for Ireland, but has made several appearances for Middx., gaining his cap in 1948. Debut 1928. HS—64 Ireland v Scotland (Belfast) 1937.

†**INSOLE, Douglas J.** (Essex) B.Clapton 18/4/1926. Unorthodox but highly effective RHB with a fine eye. Brilliant fielder; can keep wicket if necessary. Occasional change bowler. Educated at Monoux, Walthamstow. Cambridge Blue 1947-8-9, capt. in 1949. Also soccer Blue. Debut 1947. C.Cap 1949. Joint Essex Capt., 1950. HS—219* v. Yorks. (Colchester) 1949

†**IVEY, Michael** (Oxford U.) B.Leeds 11/7/1928. Educated at Leeds G.S. Opening RHB, M bowler.

JACKSON, Leslie (Derby) B.Whitwell 5/4/1921. Promising RFM bowler of rugged build who hits the ground hard, moves either way with low trajectory. RHB. Debut 1947. C.Cap 1949. Played v N. Zealand (Manchester) 1949. BB—7-51 v Leics (Derby) 1949.

JACKSON, Peter F. (Worcs.) B.Aberfeldy (Perthshire) 11/5/1911. Talented ROB bowler and RHB. Debut 1929. Achieved "hat-trick" v Glamorgan (Neath) 1936. 100 wkts. in season four times. Benefit (£2,150) 1948. HS—40 v Glos. (Worcester) 1933. BB—8-64 (12-119 match) v Middlesex (Lord's) 1935.

JACKSON, Victor E. (Leics.) B.Sydney (Australia) 25/10/1916. Forcing RHB. Good MOB bowler. Fine slip field. Played for N.S.W. in 1935-36. Came to England and played for Sir J. Cahn's XI. Debut for Leics. 1939. C.Cap 1946. Performed "hat-trick" v Derby (Derby) 1946. HS—170 v Northants. (Leicester) 1948. BB— 7-74 v Lancs. (Barwell) 1946.

JAKEMAN, Freddie (Northants.) B. Holmsfirth (Yorks.) 10/1/1921. Attacking LHB, still rather lacking in concentration. Played for Yorks. 1946-47. Registered for Northants. 1949. HS—169 v Derby (Derby) 1949.

JAMES, A. E. ("Ted") B.Bletchley (Bucks.) 7/8/1924. RHB and accurate M bowler, mostly cutters. Played for Bucks. before making Sussex debut in 1948. HS—37* v

Somerset (Eastbourne) 1949. BB—5-40 v Kent (Tunbridge Wells) 1949.

JAQUES, Peter (Leics.) B.Leicester 20/11/1919. Useful RHB. Played 1 match in 1949, scoring 55 and 14 v Northants. (Northampton).

JENKINS, Roland O. (Worcs.) B.Worcester 24/11/1918. Sound RHB. Fine LBG bowler. Brilliant field at cover point. Debut 1938. C.Cap 1939. Made great advance in 1948, scoring first century, achieving first "hat-trick" and totalling 1356 runs and 88 wickets. Toured S. Africa 1948-49, replacing Hollies, and played in all 5 Tests. Another good summer in 1949, achieving "double" for first time and representing Players at Lord's. Chosen for Test Trial but passed over for the Tests against N.Z. Did the "hat-trick" in each innings v Surrey (Worcester) 1949—the fourth bowler to perform the feat. HS—109 v Notts. (Nottingham) 1948. BB—8-92 v. Lancs. (Manchester) 1946.

JEPSON, Arthur (Notts.) B.Selsdon 12/7/1915. Whole-hearted RFM bowler who moves either way. Useful RHB. Good catch near wicket. Debut 1938. C.Cap 1939. Has played soccer (goal) for Port Vale, Stoke City and Lincoln City. HS—93 v Lancs. (Nottingham) 1938. BB—7-50 (12-139 match) v Kent (Nottingham) 1947.

†**JOHNSON, L.** (Derby) B.Barbados (B.W.I.) 8/11/1927. Attractive RHB. Useful change OB bowler and brilliant field. Debut 1949. HS—77 v Sussex (Worthing) 1949.

†**JONES, A. Trevor M.** (Somerset) B.Wells 9/4/1920. RHB. Debut 1938. Did not play in 1949. HS—106 v Leics. (Leicester) 1938.

JONES, William E. (Glamorgan) B.Carmarthen 31/10/1916. A most attractive LHB with delightful off-side strokes. Useful slow LA spinner. Excellent deep-field. Debut 1937. C.Cap 1946. Test Trial 1949. Wartime Welsh rugger international and prodigious kicker of goals for Gloucester and Gloucestershire. Best season was 1948 (1656 runs and 47 wkts.). HS—212* v Essex (Brentwood) 1948. BB—5-50 v Kent (Gravesend) 1948. Knee injury 1949.

†**KARDAR, Abdul Hafeez** (Warwick.) B. Lahore (Pakistan) 17/1/1925. Aggressive LHB and dangerous LA spinner (has length, flight and spin). Good slip or gully. Played in Ranji Trophy matches before coming to England with 1946 touring team, playing in all 3 Tests under the name of Abdul Hafeez, but on going up to Oxford played under his correct name. Oxford Blue 1947-8-9. Debut for Warwick 1948. C.Cap 1949. Played

for Gents at Lord's 1949. HS—138* Oxford U. v Middlesex (Oxford) 1948. BB—7-58 (12-136 match) Oxford U. v Hants. (Bournemouth) 1949.

†**KEELING, Michael E. A.** (Oxford U.) B. London 6/11/1925. Played for Oxford 1948-49. Opening RHB.

KEETON, Walter W. (Notts.) B.Shirebrook 30/4/1905. Attractive and remarkably consistent opening RHB. Fine on-driver and cutter. Debut 1926. C.Cap 1931. With Harris has shared in over 40 century opening partnerships. Test Trials in 1932. Played in 2 Tests—v Australia (Leeds) 1934 and v W. Indies (Oval) 1939. Scored 1000 runs each season since 1931 except 1935. Benefit 1947. HS—312* v Middlesex (Oval) 1939—the Notts. record.

†**KEIGHLEY, W. Geoffrey** (Yorks.) B. Nice (France) 10/1/1925. Sound opening RHB. First non-Yorkshire-born player to appear for county for over 40 years. Educated at Eton. Oxford Blue 1947-8. Deputy Yorks. captain 1949. Debut 1947. HS—105 Oxford U. v S. Africans (Oxford) 1947.

†**KELLAND, P. A.** (Cambridge U.) B.Pinner (Middx.) 20/9/1926. Educated at Repton. Played 2 matches for Cambridge in 1949.

KELLY, John (Derby) B.Bacup (Lancs.) 19/3/1922. Correct, promising RHB. Debut for Lancs. 1947. Signed for Derby for 1950. HS—58 Lancs. v Glos. (Bristol) 1949.

KENYON, Donald (Worcs.) B.Wordsley 15/5/1924. Sound opening RHB who played many fine innings in 1949 but is inclined to be impetuous. Debut 1946. C.Cap 1947. 1000 runs in 1947 and 1949. HS—182 v Somerset (Kidderminster) 1949.

KIRBY, Geoffrey N. G. (Surrey) B. Reading 6/11/1923. Reserve wicketkeeper. RHB. Debut 1947. Held six catches in innings v Cambridge U. (Guildford) 1949.

†**KNOTT, Charles J.** (Hants.) B. Southampton 28/11/1914. Dangerous slow ROB bowler who spins as much as any of his type; particularly dangerous when wicket helps. Debut 1938. Test Trial at Canterbury 1946. Played for Gents. at Lord's 1946. BB—8-85 v Surrey (Portsmouth) 1939.

†**LAKER, J. C. (Jim)** (Surrey) B.Bradford 9/2/1922. Excellent ROB bowler. Useful RHB and good field. Debut 1946. C.Cap 1947. 100 wkts. 1947-8-9. Toured W. Indies in 1947-48, playing in all 4 Tests. Tests v Australia at Nottingham, Lord's and Manchester 1948 and v N.Z. at Oval 1949. Scored splendid 63 v Australia at Nottingham when eight England wickets had fallen for 74. Coached in S. Africa 1949-50.

HS—100 v Cambridge U. (Guildford) 1949. BB—8-42 v Warwick (Oval) 1949.

LAKER, Peter G. (Sussex) B.Hurstpierpoint 5/12/1926. RHB and LB bowler. Debut in 1948—2 matches. One match in 1949.

LAMBERT, George (Glos.) B.London 5/5/1919. Opening RFM bowler. In 1949 was one of the quickest English bowlers. His best deliveries can be devastating. Aggressive RHB. Originally on Lord's ground staff. Debut 1938. HS—68 v Sussex (Eastbourne) 1948. BB—7-93 v Oxford U. (Oxford) 1949.

†**LANGDALE, George R.** (Somerset) B. Thornaby-on-Tees (Yorks.) 11/3/1916. Forcing LHB and ROB bowler. Played for Derby 1936 to 1939. Debut for Somerset 1946. C.Cap 1946. Instructor at R.M.A. Sandhurst. HS—146 v Yorks. (Taunton) 1946. BB—5-30 v Warwick (Birmingham) 1946.

LANGRIDGE, James (Sussex) B.Newick 10/7/1906. Very sound LHB and slow LA bowler of remarkable consistency; flight and accuracy. Toured India in 1933-34 and 1937-38 and Australia and N.Z. in 1935-36 and 1946-47. Represented Players at Lord's 1933-5-7. Performed "double" six times, scoring 1000 runs in a season 17 times. Played in 8 Tests—v W. Indies 1933 (2), v India 1933-4 (3), 1936 (1), 1946 (1), v S. Africa 1935 (1). Benefit (over £4,000) 1947. HS—167 v Notts. (Nottingham) 1936. BB—9-34 v Yorks. (Sheffield) 1934.

LANGRIDGE, John (Sussex) B.Chailey 10/2/1910. Very sound and consistent opening RHB, extremely strong on on-side. Excellent first slip. Debut 1928. With E. H. Bowley added 490 for first wkt. v Middlesex (Hove) 1933—Sussex record. Has passed the 2000 run aggregate 8 times and 1000 runs 12 times. Best season 1949—2914 runs (av. 60.70) including 12 centuries. Represented Players at Lord's 1949. HS—250* v Glamorgan (Hove) 1933.

†**LAVERS, Alan B.** (Essex) B.Melbourne (Australia) 6/9/1912. Sound RHB. Change bowler (ROB). Debut 1937. Can play only occasionally because of business. BB—4-68 v Kent (Gravesend) 1949.

LAVIS, George (Glamorgan) B.Sebastopol (Mon.) 17/8/1908. Useful RHB and M bowler. Debut 1928. Now official county coach, so appearances restricted. Testimonial 1950. HS—154 v. Worcs. (Cardiff) 1934.

†**LAW, J. A. G. G.** (Oxford U.) B.Bangalore (India) 25/3/1923. Educated Edinburgh Acad. 2 matches for Oxford U. 1949. WK and RHB.

LAWRENCE, John (Somerset) B.Carlton (Yorks.) 29/3/1914. Diminutive RHB and LBG bowler, who displayed fine bowling form in 1949. Plenty of flight and spin. Brilliant field near wicket. Played in Bradford League during war. Debut 1946. C.Cap 1946. HS—88 v Hants. (Portsmouth) 1946. BB—8-63 v Hants. (Portsmouth) 1949.

†**LAWS, M. L.** (Middx.) B.Finchley (Middx.) 12/8/1926. Reserve wicketkeeper. Educated at Highgate. Debut 1948.

LEADBEATER, Eddie (Yorks.) B.Huddersfield 15/8/1927. RHB and LBG bowler. Good field. Debut 1949, when he played 4 matches.

LESTER, E. (Yorks.) B.Scarborough 18/2/1923. Forceful and entertaining RHB, not always orthodox, but hits ball very hard. Debut in 1945. Turned pro. 1948. Scored two 100's in a match twice. HS—186 v Warwick (Scarborough) 1949.

LESTER, Gerry (Leics.) B.Long Whatton 27/12/1915. Sound opening RHB and useful LBG bowler. Debut 1937. C.Cap 1946. Has scored 1000 runs in last three seasons. HS—131 v Oxford U. (Oxford) 1949. BB—6-42 v S. Africans (Leicester) 1947.

LEWIS, Claude (Kent) B.Sittingbourne 27/7/1910. LA spinner. Debut 1933, but now county coach and rarely plays. C.Cap 1935. HS—27 v Surrey (Oval) 1939. BB—6-46 v Worcs. (Gillingham) 1939.

†**LEWIS, David** (Oxford U.) B.Bulawayo (S. Rhodesia) 27/7/27. Played 1 match for Oxford U. in 1949. RHB.

LEWIS, Esmond B. (Warwick) B.Shirley 5/1/1918. Wicketkeeper. RHB. Debut 1949, dismissing nine batsmen in his first match v Oxford U. (Birmingham).

LEWIS, K. H. (Glamorgan) B.Newtown (Montgomeryshire) 10/11/1928. RFM bowler. Joined staff for 1950.

†**LEWIS, Reg. C. V.** (Oxford U.) B.Cape Town (S.A.) 4/10/1927. Educated at Diocesan College, S.A. Played 1 match for Oxford U. in 1949; later for Oxfordshire. LBG bowler, RHB.

LIVINGSTONE, L. (Northants.) B. N.S.W. (Australia) 3/5/1920. Opening LHB and wicketkeeper. County has applied for registration for 1950. Played for New South Wales in one match in 1941-42 before war compelled stoppage of first-class cricket in Australia. He reappeared in 1946-47, scoring 100* v Queensland (Sydney), before transferring to League cricket with Royton (Lancs.). Capt. Commonwealth team to India 1949-50.

LOCK, G. A. R. ("Tony") (Surrey) B. Limpsfield 5/7/1929. Promising LA spinner. Good field. RHB. Debut 1946. Gained regular place 1949. HS—29 v Oxford U. (Oval) 1949

BB—6-43 Combined Services v Glamorgan (Pontypridd) 1948.

LOMAX, James G. (Lancs.) B.Rochdale 5/5/1925. RMF bowler. Debut 1948. Played 6 matches in 1949.

LOWE, G. (Derby) B.Mastin Moor 25/5/1915. RHB. Played 1 match for county in 1949.

LOWSON, Frank A. (Yorks.) B.Bradford 1/7/1925. Most promising opening RHB; neat and well equipped. Fair field. Debut 1949. C.Cap 1949. Scored 1799 runs in first season. Test Trial 1949. HS—104 v Middlesex (Sheffield) 1949.

†**LUMSDEN, Ian J. M.** B.Edinburgh 6/4/1923. Forceful RHB, brilliant field. Debut 1946. Has played for Scotland and Combined Services. Educated at George Watson's, Edinburgh.

†**MALLETT, A. W. H. ("Tony")** B.Dulwich 28/8/1924. Adventurous RHB. RMF in-swing bowler. Educated at Dulwich. Played for Under 33 at Lord's 1945. Debut for Kent 1946. Oxford Blue 1947-8. Played for Gents. at Lord's 1946-7. Only available in August. HS—97 v Sussex (Tunbridge Wells) 1946. BB—6-76 v Leics. (Oxford) 1947.

†**MANN, F. George** (Middx.) B.Byfleet (Surrey) 6/9/1917. Attractive forcing RHB of forward type. Good field at mid-off Educated at Eton. Cambridge Blue 1938 and 1939. Debut 1937. C.Cap 1939. Played for Gents. at Lord's 1948-9. Middx. capt. 1948 and 1949. Captained M.C.C. S. African team 1948-49, playing in all five Tests. Captained England v N.Z. at Leeds and Lord's 1949. HS—136* England v S. Africa (Port Elizabeth) 1948-49.

†**MANNERS, Lt.-Cmdr. John E.** (Hants.) B.Exeter 25/9/1913. Aggressive, unorthodox RHB. Debut 1936, but rarely available owing to service in R.N. HS—147 Combined S. v Glos. (Gloucester) 1948.

†**MARSHALL, Jack M. A.** (Warwick) B.Kenilworth 26/10/1916. RHB and LB bowler. Debut 1946. C.Cap 1946. Master at Warwick School, available in August only. HS—47 v Derby (Derby) 1946. BB—5-65 v Worcs. (Dudley) 1946.

MARTIN, E. (Notts.) B.Lambley (Notts.) 17/8/1925. RHB. Fourth in Minor County batting averages (61.62) in 1949. Debut 1949, playing 5 matches for county.

†**MARTIN, John W.** (Kent) B.Catford 16/2/1917. FM in-swing bowler. Hard-hitting RHB. Debut 1939. C.Cap 1946. Test Trial 1946. Test v. S. Africa (Nottingham) 1947. HS—34 v. Northants. (Northampton) 1946. BB—6-37 v Hants. (Southampton) 1948.

MASON, Alan (Yorks.) B.Addingham 2/5/1921. Promising LA spin

bowler. LHB. Debut 1947. HS—22 v Sussex (Hove) 1949. BB—5-56 v Northants. (Bradford) 1949.

†**MAUDSLEY, Ronald H.** (Warwick.) B. Lostock-Graham (Cheshire) 8/4/1918. Sound RHB and M bowler. Educated at Malvern. Oxford Blue 1946 and 1947. Debut 1946. C.Cap 1946. Warwick capt. 1948. Oxford Don, available only in vacations. HS—130 Oxford U. v Sussex (Chichester) 1946. BB—6-54 v Surrey (Oval) 1946.

†**MAXWELL, Charles R.** (Worcs.) B. Middlesex 21/5/1913. RHB. Wicketkeeper who deputises for Yarnold. Debut for Notts. 1932. Played for Middlesex in 1946. Joined Worcs. 1948. HS—268 Sir J. Cahn's XI v Leics. (Nottingham) 1935.

†**MAY, Peter B. H.** (Cambridge U.) B. Reading 31/12/1929. Very promising stylish RHB. Educated at Charterhouse. Scored many runs in Navy and Combined Services cricket. Up at Cambridge U. in 1950. Qualified to play for Surrey, but has not yet appeared for them owing to claims of Services cricket. Soccer Blue (IR) 1949. HS—175. Combined S. v Worcs. (Worcester) 1949 — after scoring 97 in first innings.

MAYES, R. ("Dickie") (Kent) B.Littlebourne 7/11/1921. Useful RHB. Joined Kent staff 1939. Debut 1947. HS—37 v Glamorgan (Swansea) 1949.

McCORKELL, Neil (Hants.) B.Portsmouth 23/3/1912. Very sound opening RHB and wicketkeeper. Debut 1932. Represented Players at Lord's 1936. Toured India 1937-38 with Lord Tennyson's team. Scored 1000 runs in a season seven times (1935-6-7-8-9-47-9). Joint Benefit 1948-50. Has son on county staff. HS—154* v Lancs. (Liverpool) 1935.

McHUGH, F. P. ("Mac") (Yorks.) B. Leeds 15/11/1925. 6ft. 3ins. RFM bowler. Debut 1949 when he played 3 matches for county.

McINTYRE, A. J. ("Mac") (Surrey) B. Kennington 14/5/1918. Attacking, attractive RHB, very quick on his feet. Good wicketkeeper. Debut 1938. C.Cap 1946. Took over 'keeping from Mobey in 1947. Dismissed 95 batsmen (71 ct. 24 st.) and scored no less than nine "ducks" in 1949. Coached in W. Indies 1949-50. HS—143* v Kent (Blackheath) 1949.

McMAHON, J. W. (Surrey) B.Balaclava (S. Australia) 28/12/1919. Unorthodox slow LA bowler with no pretensions to batsmanship. Wears glasses. Has played in Australian Grade cricket. Debut 1947. C.Cap 1948. BB—8-46 v. Northants. (Oval) 1948.

MEADS, Eric A. (Notts.) B.Nottingham 17/8/1916. Diminutive wicketkeeper and RHB. Debut 1939.

C.Cap 1939. Has missed only one match for county since the war. HS—56* v. Worcs. (Nottingham) 1948.

MERCER, W. Norman (Sussex) B. Prescott 30/5/1922. RHB and change bowler. Debut 1948—1 match. Did not play in 1949.

†**MEYER, R. J. O.** ("Jack") (Somerset) B.15/3/1905. Aggressive, stylish RHB. Versatile slow medium RA bowler. Educated at Haileybury. Cambridge Blue 1924-5-6. Also Golf Blue. Debut 1924. Somerset captain 1947—had serious back trouble. HS—202* v. Lancs. (Taunton) 1936.

†**MILLS, J. Michael** (Warwick.) B. Birmingham 27/7/1921. RHB and OB bowler. Educated at Oundle. Cambridge Blue 1946-7-8, captain 1948. Debut 1946. HS—44 Cambridge U. v Essex (Cambridge) 1947. BB—7-69 Cambridge U. v Yorks. (Cambridge) 1946.

MILTON, C. Arthur (Glos.) B.Bristol 10/3/1928. Very promising all-rounder. Attractive RHB, strong off back foot. Medium pace out-swing bowler. Superb field. Debut 1948. C.Cap 1949. With Arsenal F.C. HS —92* v. Derby (Chesterfield) 1949.

†**MISCHLER, N. M.** Wicketkeeper and RHB. Educated at St. Paul's. Cambridge Blue 1946 and 1947. HS— 76 v Somerset (Bath) 1947.

†**MITCHELL, I. N.** (Cambridge U.) B. Bristol 17/4/1925. Educated at Harrow. Played 2 matches for Cambridge U. in 1949.

†**MITCHELL-INNES, Norman S.** (Somerset) B.Calcutta (India) 7/9/1914. Stylish RHB. Change bowler. Safe field in slips. Debut in 1931 while still at Sedbergh. Oxford Blue 1934-5-6-7, captain in 1936. Test v. S. Africa (Nottingham) 1935. Toured Australia and N.Z. 1935-36. Also Oxford Golf Blue. Played for Gents. at Lord's 1935-6-7. Has played for county one month each year while on leave from Sudan Civil Service, so lacks match practice. County Captain, May, 1948. HS—207 Oxford U. v. H. D. G. L-Gower's XI (Reigate) 1936.

MONTGOMERY, Stan W. (Glamorgan) B.West Ham (Essex) 7/7/1920. Sound RHB. Originally on Essex staff. Debut 1949. Cardiff City A.F.C. centre half. Turned pro. 1950. HS—and maiden century— 117 v Hants. (Bournemouth) 1949— sharing in county 5th wkt. record of 264 with M. Robinson.

†**MORRIS, R. J.** (Cambridge U.) Sound opening RHB and useful OB bowler. Educated at Blundell's. Blue 1949. HS—96 v Sussex (Cambridge) 1949.

MORRIS, William B. (Essex) B.Kingston (Jamaica) 28/5/1917. Promising RHB who should do well in

1950. Injury in 1949 retarded his advance. Useful OB bowler. Debut 1946. HS—68 v. Cambridge U. (Cambridge) 1949.

MUNCER, B. Leonard (Glamorgan) B. Hampstead (London) 23/10/1913. Excellent ROB bowler. Hard-hitting RHB. Good slip field. Debut for Middlesex in 1933 but received few opportunities and joined Glamorgan in 1947. C.Cap 1947. Since then has been one of the best all-rounders —689 runs and 107 wkts. in 1947, 906 and 159 in 1948, 837 and 114 in 1949. Represented Players at Lord's 1948. HS—87 v. South of England (Swansea) 1948. BB—9-62 (15-151 match) v. Essex (Brentwood) 1948.

MUNDEN, Victor (Leics.) B.Leicester 7/4/1924. Useful, rather impetuous LHB. Slow LA bowler. Debut in 1946. HS—67 v. Northants. (Northampton) 1949. BB—5-48 v. Derby (Chesterfield) 1948.

†**NEWMAN, D. L.** (Middx.) B.Harringay (Middx.) 25/6/1920. Useful RHB. Son of L. W. Newman, the well-known North London club cricketer. Debut 1948. D d not play in 1949.

NOTLEY, B. (Notts.) B.Nottingham 31/8/1918. Debut 1949, when he played one match v. Surrey (Oval).

NUTTER, A. E. ("Bert") (Northants.) B.Burnley (Lancs.) 28/6/1913. Forcing RHB and MF bowler; moves either way, quick off pitch. Fine slip field. Played for Lancs. 1935 to 1939, falling only 9 runs short of "double" in 1938. Played in Lancashire League 1946-7. Joined Northants. 1948. C.Cap 1948. HS —109* Lancs. v. Notts. (Manchester) 1939. BB—7-52 (12-86 match) Northants. v. Kent (Northampton) 1948.

OAKES, Charles (Sussex) B.Horsham 10/8/1912. Forceful RHB (fine driver) and LBG bowler—a very useful all-rounder. Debut 1935. C.Cap 1937. 1000 runs in a season 4 times—best 1607 (av. 29.21) in 1949. Took 63 wickets (av. 27.12) in 1948. HS—148* v. Worcs. (Worthing) 1938. BB—5-10 v. Yorks. (Hove) 1946.

OAKES, John (Sussex) B.Horsham 3/3/1916. Younger brother of Charles. Useful RHB (a fine hitter) and OB bowler. Brilliant field near wicket. Debut 1938. C.Cap 1949. HS—99 v. Kent (Tunbridge Wells) 1949. BB—6-78 v. Glos. (Bristol) 1948.

OAKMAN, Alan (Sussex) B.Hastings 20/4/1930. Useful RHB and OB bowler. Debut 1947. Played for Combined Services in 1949 while in Army. HS—79* Combined Services v. Hants. (Portsmouth) 1949. BB— 4-31 Sussex v. Worcs. (Stourbridge) 1948.

OLDFIELD, Norman (Northants.) B. Dukinfield (Manchester) 5/5/1911. Neat, attractive and remarkably consistent opening RHB. Played for Lancs. 1935-1939, scoring 1000 runs each season. Played Test v. W. Indies (Oval) 1939. League cricket 1946-7. Joined Northants. 1948. C.Cap 1948. Scored 1000 runs in season seven times. In 1949 recorded highest run aggregate in season for Northants. batsman (2192). Toured India in 1949-50 with Commonwealth team. HS—168 Northants. v. Worcs. (Worcester) 1949.

ORD, Jimmie S. (Warwick.) B.Backworth (Newcastle) 12/7/1912. Diminutive stylish RHB; possessed of one of the best square cuts in the game. Debut 1933. C.Cap 1938. Scored 107* and 101 v. Notts. (Nottingham) 1948. Benefit 1950. HS—156* v. Hants. (Bournemouth) 1949.

OUTSCHOORN, Laddie (Worcs.) B.Ceylon 26/9/1918. Wristy, rather unpredictable RHB. Useful seam bowler. Brilliant slip or gully, holding 54 catches in 1949. Played cricket in Singapore before capture by the Japs. Debut 1946. C.Cap 1948. HS—215* v. Northants. (Worcester) 1949.

†**PALMER, Charles H.** (Leics.) B.Old Hill (Staffs.) 15/5/1919. Attractive RHB and useful swing and OB bowler. Debut for Worcs. 1938. Gents. at Lord's 1948. Toured S. Africa 1948-49 while a master at Bromsgrove but did not play in the Tests. Appointed Leics. secretary, Feb., 1950; Captain when registered by M.C.C. HS—177 v. Notts. (Dudley) 1947.

†**PARKER, Graham W.** (Glos.) B.Bristol 11/2/1912. Sound RHB. Educated at Crypt School (Gloucester), now runs cricket at Blundell's. Cambridge Blue 1934 and 1935. Also rugger Blue 1932-3-4-5. Two England rugger caps. HS—210 v. Kent (Dover) 1937.

PARKER, John F. ("Jack") B.Battersea (London) 23/4/1913. Stylish forcing RHB of forward type. Very useful M swing bowler. Slip field. Might well have played for England as all-rounder but for war and attack of fibrositis in 1946. Now fit again. Selected for 1939-40 cancelled tour to India. Debut 1932. 1000 runs in season six times. HS—255 v. New Zealanders (Oval) 1949 (highest against N.Z. in England). BB—5-46 v. Kent (Blackheath) 1946.

PARKHOUSE, W. Gilbert A. (Glamorgan) B.Swansea 12/10/1925. Most promising stylish RHB. Good outfield. Made considerable reputation in wartime cricket, but could not play for county until 1948, owing to service duties. Scored 1204 runs in first season and gained C.Cap. HS—145 v. Notts. (Nottingham) 1949.

PARKS, J. M. ("Jim") B.Haywards Heath 21/10/1931. RHB and M bowler. Son of J. H. Parks. Debut 1949—2 matches.

†**PARNABY, Major A. H.** (Combined Services). Solid opening RHB. Debut 1949. HS—87 v. Kent (Gillingham) 1949.

†**PAWSON, H. Anthony** (Kent) B.Chertsey (Surrey) 22/8/1921. Stylish RHB and excellent outfield. A fine cutter and superb runner between wickets. Educated at Winchester. Oxford Blue 1947-8 (capt. 1948), scoring 135 in 1947 'Varsity match. Debut for Kent 1946, scoring 90 v. Hants. (Canterbury). Played for Gents. at Lord's 1947. Oxford soccer Blue. Now master at Winchester. HS—150 Oxford U. v. Worcs. (Worcester) 1947.

†**PAYTON, Sqdn.-Ldr. The Rev. W. E. G.** (Derby) B.Nottingham 27/12/1913. Son of W. Payton (Notts. pro.) Sound RHB, good opener. Debut for Notts. 1935. Cambridge Blue 1937. Chaplain in R.A.F. Joined Derby 1949. HS—98 Combined S. v. Glamorgan (Pontypridd) 1948.

†**PEARCE, Thomas N.** (Essex) B.London 3/11/1905. Very sound and realistic RHB. Educated at Christ's Hospital. Debut 1929. From 1933 to 1939 he was one of several joint Essex captains. Essex capt. 1946-49. Played for Gents. at Lord's 1936 and 1948. 1000 runs in season six times (1935-6-46-7-8-9). International rugger referee. Test Selector 1949-50. HS—211* v. Leics. (Westcliff) 1948. Joint County Captain with Insole, 1950.

PERKS, Reginald T. D. (Worcs.) B. Hereford 4/10/1911. Splendid wholehearted RFM bowler; moves either way. Adventurous, often effective LHB. Debut 1930. Played in 2 Tests—v. S. Africa (Durban) 1938-39 and v. W. Indies (Oval) 1939. Tour as above. Represented Players at Lord's 1931 and 1949. Has taken 100 wkts. each season since 1934. Benefit (£3,000) 1947. HS—75 v. Notts. (Nottingham) 1938. BB—9-42 (14-96 match) v. Glos. (Cheltenham) 1946, and 8-63 (15-106 match) v. Essex (Worcester) 1937.

PHEBEY, Arthur H. (Kent) B.Catford 1/10/1924. Promising RHB. Good field. Debut 1946. Played football for English Schools and now for Dulwich Hamlet. HS—68 v Derby (Chesterfield) 1949.

PLACE, Winston (Lancs.) B.Rawtenstall 7/12/1914. Attractive RHB, usually opening, but went in lower down after injury in 1949. Rather uncertain starter but fine player at his best. Useful slip field. Debut 1937. Toured W. Indies in 1947-48, playing in 3 Tests and scoring 107 at

Kingston. With Washbrook formed a most successful opening partnership, their highest stand being 350 unseparated v. Sussex (Manchester) 1947—a season when they did great things together. 1000 runs each season since war. Toured India with Commonwealth team in 1949-50. HS—266* v. Oxford U. (Oxford) 1947.

PLEASS, J. E. (" **Jim** ") (Glamorgan) B.Cardiff 21/5/1923. Useful RHB. Fine field. Debut 1947, turning pro. in 1948. HS—77* v. Hants. (Cardiff) 1948.

†**POCOCK, H. John** (Kent) B.Maidstone 8/4/1921. RHB. Debut 1947. HS—34 v. Yorks. (Hull) 1947.

POLLARD, Richard (Lancs.) B.Westhoughton 19/6/1912. Splendid whole-hearted RFM bowler (moves either way), now reaching end of his career. Hard-hitting RHB. Debut 1933. Played in 4 Tests—1946 v. India (Manchester), 1946-47 v N.Z. (Christchurch), 1948 v. Australia (Manchester and Leeds). Toured Australia and N.Z. 1946-47. 100 wkts. in season seven times. Benefit (£8,500 approx.) 1949. HS—63 v. Derby (Manchester) 1947. BB—8-33 v. Northants. (Manchester) 1947.

POOLE, Cyril J. (Notts.) B.Forest Town 13/3/1921. Fast-scoring LHB of forward type. Good field. Debut 1946. C.Cap 1949. Plays soccer for Mansfield Town. HS—154* v. Leics. (Nottingham) 1949—reaching his 100 in an hour.

†**POPPLEWELL, O. B.** (Cambridge U.) Sound unobtrusive wicketkeeper. Solid RHB. Educated at Charterhouse. Debut 1949. Blue 1949. HS—37 v Surrey (Guildford) 1949.

†**PORTER, Arthur** (Glamorgan) B.Clayton-le-Moors (Lancs.) 25/3/1914. Useful RHB. Debut 1937. Plays infrequently owing to duties as a welfare supervisor. HS—105 v. Surrey (Oval) 1946.

†**POSTINS, M. H.** (Warwick.) All-rounder —RHB and bowler.

POTTER, Gordon (Sussex) B.Dorman's Land 26/10/1931. Debut 1949 when he played one match.

†**POTTS, H. Jimmy** (Oxford U.). B. 23/1/1925. Educated at Stand G.S. (Manchester). Debut in 1949 when he played 3 matches for Oxford U. and appeared in Lancs. 2nd XI. Oxford soccer Blue (capt. 1949) (OR).

PRENTICE, Frank T. (Leics.) B.Knaresborough (Yorks.) 22/4/1912. Consistent and enterprising RHB and useful OB change bowler. Debut 1934. Has scored 1000 runs each season since war—in all 5 times (inc. 1937). Testimonial 1950. HS—191 v. Notts. (Loughborough) 1949.

PRESSDEE, J. (Glamorgan) B.Mumbles (Swansea) 19/6/1933. Slow LA bowler. Debut v. Notts. (Cardiff) 1949—only match to date.

PRESTON, Kenneth C. (Essex) B.Goodmayes 22/8/1925. Very promising RFM bowler. Debut 1948. Missed 1949 season owing to broken leg received at football, but gradually regained confidence in 2nd XI with 26 wkts. in 7 matches towards end of season. BB—6-85 v. Worcs. (Clacton) 1948.

PRITCHARD, Tom L. (Warwick.) B. Manaia, Taranaki (N.Z.) 10/3/1917. Attacking RFM bowler—probably the fastest in England in 1949. Hard-hitting RHB when under way. Twice took ten wkts. in an innings in minor matches in N.Z.—when his pace was faster than it is now. Debut 1946. C.Cap 1947. Represented Players at Lord's 1948. Took 172 wkts. (av. 18.75) in 1948 and 113 wkts. (av. 24.72) in 1949. HS—81 v. Notts. (Birmingham). 1947. BB —8-43 (13-153 match) v. Northants. (Northampton) 1948.

†**PRYER, Barry J. K.** (Kent) B.Plumstead 1/2/1925. Useful LB bowler and RHB. Good field. Educated at City of London School. Cambridge Blue 1948. Debut for Kent 1947. HS—75* v. Middlesex (Cambridge) 1948. BB—4-65 v. Worcs. (Worcester) 1949.

†**PULLINGER, George R.** (Essex) B. Islington 14/3/1920. RMF bowler, mostly out-swing. Safe catch. Debut 1949. C.Cap 1949. BB— 5-54 v. Somerset (Bath) 1949.

†**RANSOM, Victor J.** (Hants.) B.New Malden (Surrey) 17/3/1918. Very useful MF bowler; moves ball either way. Agricultural RHB. Plays for Malden Wanderers in London club cricket. Debut 1947. C.Cap 1949. HS—58 v Glos. (Portsmouth) 1949. BB—5-50 v. Northants. (Northampton) 1947.

RAYMENT, Allan W. H. (Hants.) B. Finchley (Middlesex) 29/5/1928. Keen, promising RHB and good fielder. Can bowl seamers. Played for Combined Services in 1947 and Middlesex 2nd XI in 1948. Joined Hants. 1949. HS—35 v. Northants. (Northampton) 1949.

REDMAN, James (Somerset) B.Bath 1/3/1926. RHB and MF bowler. Debut 1948. Turned pro. 1949.

REVILL, Alan (Derby) B.Bolsover 27/3/1923. Fast improving and stylish RHB. Useful change bowler. Brilliant field near wicket on leg side. Debut 1946. C.Cap 1947. HS—156* v. Leics. (Ashby-de-la-Zouch) 1949.

RHODES, A. E. G. (" **Dusty** ") (Derby) B.Tintwhistle (Cheshire) 10/10/1916. Attractive forcing RHB. Originally fast bowler, now LBG. Debut 1937. Performed " hat-trick " three times —twice in 1948. Scored century before lunch on 3rd day v. Notts. (Ilkeston) 1949. HS—127 v. Somerset (Taunton) 1949. BB—7-109 v. Glamorgan (Cardiff) 1946.

RICHARDSON, Alan (Notts.) B.Woodbeck 28/10/1926. RFM bowler. Debut 1949, when he played 5 matches for county.

†**RICHARDSON, Peter E.** (Worcs.) B. Hereford 4/7/1931. Promising RHB Educated at Cathedral School, Hereford. Debut 1949, playing 4 matches for county.

RIDDINGTON, A. (" Tony ") (Leics.) B.Countesthorpe 22/12/1911. Useful LHB and slow LA bowler. Debut 1931, but has not played regularly. HS—104* v. Northants. (Northampton) 1946. BB—5-34 v. Yorks. (Leicester) 1946.

RIDGWAY, Frederick B.Stockport (Lancs.) 10/8/1923. Good FM bowler who moves either way. On short side but well built. RHB—a hitter. Fine field. Debut 1946. C.Cap 1947. Test Trial 1949. Soccer for Ramsgate in Kent League. HS—89 v. Sussex (Tunbridge Wells) 1949. BB—7-27 (12-66 match) v. Yorks. (Hull) 1947.

†**RIMELL, A. G. J.** (Cambridge U.) B. India 29/8/1928. Stylish LHB and accurate ROB bowler. Educated at Charterhouse. Blue 1949. Qualified for Hants., has yet to play for them. HS—160 v. Worcs. (Worcester) 1949. Cambridge secretary 1950.

RIMMER, J. (Derby) B.Longwith 26/1/1925. RFM bowler. Debut 1949, when he played in 3 matches.

RIPPON, T. J. (" Jack ") (Glamorgan) B.Swansea 6/7/1919. Reserve wicketkeeper. P.O.W. in Poland for 5 years during war. Played 2 matches in 1947 and 1 in 1948.

RIST, Frank (Essex) B.Wandsworth 30/3/1914. Steady RHB and reserve wicketkeeper. Debut 1934. C.Cap 1949. Played soccer for Charlton Athletic. Appointed county coach 1949. HS—53 v. Glos. (Westcliff) 1939.

ROBERTS, Harry E. (Warwick.) B. Coventry June 1924. Opening LHB. Debut 1949, playing 2 matches.

†**ROBERTS, W/Cmdr. J. F.** (Combined Services) Opening LHB, very good slip field.

ROBERTS, William B. (Lancs.) B. Kirkham 27/9/1914. Very accurate, thoughtful slow LA spinner. Splendid field. Debut 1939. C.Cap 1939. Played in 3 " Victory " Tests in 1945 and might have played in Tests since if his attack had a little more sting. Style reminiscent of J. C. White. HS—51 v. Glamorgan (Manchester) 1948. BB—8-50 v. Oxford U. (Oxford) 1949.

ROBERTSON, John D. (Middx.) B. Chiswick 22/2/1917. Most accomplished and consistent opening RHB. Beautiful extra-cover drive. Can bowl OB's. Good field. Debut 1937. C.Cap 1937. Tests v. S. Africa (Oval) 1947, N.Z. (Lord's) 1949 and all 4 on 1947-48 W. Indies tour. With S. M. Brown added 310 for 1st wkt. v. Notts. (Lord's) 1947. HS—331* v. Worcs. (Worcester) 1949—all scored in a day's play.

†**ROBINS, R. Walter V.** (Middx.) B. Stafford 3/6/1906. In his prime a very aggressive RHB; can still hit very hard. LBG bowler, brilliant on his day. Excellent field. Educated at Highgate. Debut 1925. Cambridge Blue 1926-7-9. Also soccer Blue. Test debut in 1929; has played in 19 Tests. Captain in 3 Tests v. N.Z. 1937. Toured Australia 1936-37. Inspiring Middlesex capt. 1935 to 1938 and 1946-47—winning championship in 1947. Test Selector 1947 and 1948. Achieved " double " 1929. Played soccer for Corinthians and Notts. Forest. Performed " hat-trick " v. Leics. (Lord's) 1929 and v. Somerset (Lord's) 1937. Played for Gents. at Lord's 4 times, 1928-1931. HS 140 v. Cambridge U. (Cambridge) 1930. BB—8-69 v. Glos. (Lord's) 1929. County Captain again 1950.

†**ROBINSON, Maurice** (Glamorgan) B. Lisburn (Ulster) 16/7/1921. Sound RHB, useful quick bowler—and humourist too. Joined Glamorgan 1946 after R.A.F. service at St. Athans. C.Cap 1946. Did not play in 1948 but appeared regularly in 1949. HS—190 v. Hants. (Bournemouth) 1949

ROGERS, Neville H. (Hants.) B.Oxford 9/3/1918. Sound opening RHB; fine stroke player when under way. Splendid field anywhere. Scored 696 runs in 1946, 1722 in 1947, 1311 in 1948 and 1747 in 1949. Debut 1946.. C.Cap 1947. HS—178 v. Surrey (Portsmouth) 1949.

†**ROGERS, Stuart S.** (Somerset) B.Muswell Hill 18/3/23. Attacking RHB and splendid field. Educated at Highgate. War-time Cambridge " Blue " 1942. Debut 1946. C.Cap 1949. HS—61 v. Hants. (Portsmouth) 1949. County Captain 1950.

ROUTLEDGE, R. (Middx.) B.Middlesex 7/7/1920. Useful RM bowler. Debut 1946.

ROWE, E. J. (Notts.) B.Netherfield (Notts.) 21/7/1920. Reserve wicketkeeper. Debut 1949 when he played 1 match.

†**RUDD, C. R. D.** (Oxford U.) B.Kenilworth (Cape, S.A.) Stylish RHB. Educated at Eton. Blue 1949. HS —54 v. Leics. (Oxford) 1949.

†**SALE, Richard** (Derby) B.Shrewsbury 4/10/1919. One of the most

attractive LHB's in county cricket. Educated at Repton, where he is now a master. Oxford Blue 1939 and 1946. Debut for Warwick. 1939. Joined Derby 1949. HS—157 v. Indians (Birmingham) 1946.

SCOTT, Colin J. (Glos.) B.Bristol 1/5/1919. Originally RFM bowler but has now turned to OB's. Brilliant field. Took 121 wkts. in 1939, but has been unable to recapture this form since the war. HS 90 v. Surrey (Oval) 1947. BB—7-86 v. Surrey (Gloucester) 1939.

†**SEAMER, John W.** (Somerset) B.Shapwick 23/6/1913. RHB. Wears glasses. Educated at Marlborough. Oxford Blue 1934-5-6. Debut 1932. One of three Somerset captains in 1948. HS—194 Oxford U. v. Minor Counties (Oxford) 1934.

SHACKLETON, Derek (Hants.) B.Todmorden (Lancs.) 12/8/1924. Very promising all-rounder—FM bowler (moves either way) and very useful RHB. Good field. Debut 1948. Fell 86 runs short of " double " in 1949—a fine achievement in his first full season. HS—87* v. Essex (Bournemouth) 1949. BB—7-83 (12-214 match) v. Glos. (Portsmouth) 1949.

SHARP, Harry (Middx.) B.Kentish Town (Middx.) 6/10/1917. Sound RHB—a good opener. Useful OB bowler. Debut 1946. C.Cap 1948. HS—102 v. Glos. (Bristol) 1949. BB—5-52 v. Oxford U. (Oxford) 1949.

SHAW, Dennis G. (Warwick.) B.Manchester 16/2/1931. RHB and LB bowler. Splendid field. Debut 1949 when he played 1 match.

†**SHEARWOOD, K. A.** (Derby) B.Derby 5/9/1921. Wicketkeeper. RHB. Played 2 matches for Oxford U. and 1 for Derby in 1949.

†**SHEPPARD, D. S.** (Sussex) B.Reigate (Surrey) 6/3/1929. Promising and stylish RHB. Educated at Sherborne. Debut 1947. C.Cap 1949. Service in Army has delayed his appearance at Cambridge U. HS—204 v. Glamorgan (Eastbourne) 1949.

†**SHIRREFF, Sqdn.-Ldr. Alan C.** (Kent) B.Ealing (Middx.) 12/2/1919. Sound RHB and useful M bowler. Educated at Dulwich. Cambridge Blue 1939. Debut for Hants. 1946. Specially registered for Kent 1950. Captains Combined Services. HS—91 v. Surrey (Oval) 1946. BB—7-81 v. Glos. (Bristol) 1947.

SHORTLAND, Norman A. (Warwick.) B.Coventry 16/7/1916. RHB and change bowler. Debut 1938 but rarely plays. HS—70 v. Sussex (Birmingham) 1946.

†**SIME, W. A.** (Notts.) B.Wepener (O.F.S., S.A.) 8/2/1909. Hardhitting RHB. Useful LA spin bowler and safe field. Educated at Bedford and Oxford. Played for Beds. in Minor county cricket (also county rugger player). Debut for Notts. 1945. Notts. captain 1947-8-9. Barrister by profession. HS—176* v. Sussex (Hove) 1948.

†**SIMPSON, Reggie T.** (Notts.) B.Sherwood (Notts.) 27/2/1920. Handsome RHB, brilliant field, occasional OB bowler. Debut in 1946 after playing in Ranji Trophy matches in India during war. C.Cap 1946. England 12th man v. Australia in 1948. Toured S. Africa 1948-49, playing in first Test. Played for England v. N.Z. in 1949, scoring a memorable 103 at Manchester and 68 at the Oval. Played for Gents. at Lord's 1947 and 1949. HS—238 v. Lancs. (Manchester) 1949.

SIMS, J i m (Middx.) B.Leyton 13/5/1904. Everlasting LBG bowler, who has given Middx. great service. Hard-hitting RHB, difficult to dislodge in a crisis. Debut 1929. Played in 4 Tests—v. S. Africa (Leeds) 1935, India (Oval) 1936 and twice on 1936-37 Australian tour. Also toured Australia and N.Z. 1935-36 and S. America 1937-38. Decided to retire at end of 1948 season, but signed a new contract after taking ten West wkts. for 90 runs in Kingston festival. Benefit 1946. HS—123 M.C.C. v. Kent (Lord's) 1931. BB—10-90 East v. West (Kingston) 1948. Benefit 1950.

†**SKINNER, David A.** (Derby) B.Duffield 22/3/1920. RHB. Debut 1947. Derby captain 1949—resigned for business reasons at end of season. HS—63 v. Sussex (Worthing) 1949.

SMALES, Ken (Yorks.) B.Horsforth 15/9/1927. RHB and OB bowler. Debut 1948. Did not play in 1949. BB—5-65 v Surrey (Oval) 1948.

SMITH, Denis (Derby) B.Somercotes 24/1/1907. Stylish opening RHB, at his best a most attractive strokemaker. Sound slip field. Debut 1927. Played 2 Tests v. S. Africa 1935. Toured Australia and N.Z. 1935-36. Testimonial (£1,950) 1947. Originally decided to retire at end of 1949, but has been engaged for 1950. HS—225 v. Hants. (Chesterfield) 1935.

SMITH, Don V. (Sussex) B.Broadwater (Sussex) 14/6/1923. Promising opening LHB and good field. Debut 1946. Originally a slow bowler. HS—85 v. Middlesex (Lord's) 1949.

SMITH, G. S. (Leics.) B.Leicester 18/1/1923. Useful RHB. Debut 1949 when he played 1 match.

SMITH, Ray (Essex) B.Boreham 10/8/1914. Whole-hearted all-rounder—very useful aggressive RHB, swings either way and also bowls OB's. Splendid field, usually cover. Debut 1934. C.Cap 1938. " Double " 1948. Has taken 100 wkts. each season since the war. Scored fastest 100 of 1948—104 in 63 mins. v. Yorks. (Westcliff). Toured India with Commonwealth team in 1949 -50. HS—112 v. Derby (Colchester) 1948 and for South v. North (Scarborough) 1949. BB—7-51 v. Worcs. (Chelmsford) 1946.

SMITH, Roy (Somerset) B.Taunton 14/4/1930. LA spinner and RHB. Debut 1949, scoring 40 v. Cambridge U. (Bath) in his only match.

SMITH, T. Peter B. (Essex) B.Ipswich (Suffolk) 30/10/1908. Skilful LBG bowler. Forceful RHB. Debut 1929. Toured India 1937-38 with Lord Tennyson's team and Australia and N.Z. 1946-47 with M.C.C. Played in 4 Tests, v. India (Oval) 1946, v. Australia (twice at Sydney) 1946-47 and v. N.Z. (Christchurch) 1946-47. " Double " 1948. Has taken 100 wkts. in season 5 times. Benefit (£3,000) 1947. Shared in last wkt. partnership of 218 v. Derby (Chesterfield) 1947. HS—163 v. Derby (Chesterfield) 1947. BB—9-108 v. Kent (Maidstone) 1948 and 9-121 v. N.S.W. (Sydney) 1946-47—most wickets by an Englishman in a single innings in Australia.

SMITHSON, Gerald A. (Yorks.) B. Spofforth 1/11/1926. Forcing LHB. Fine outfield. Debut 1947. C.Cap 1947. Toured W. Indies in 1947-48, playing in 2 Tests, after being granted leave from the mines. Injury received on tour prevented appearance in 1948 and ill-luck and loss of form still followed him in 1949 when he played only a few matches. HS—169 v. Leics. (Leicester) 1947.

SNAPE, M. D. (Derby) B.Creswell 7/7/1923. RHB. Played 2 matches in 1949.

SPERRY, J. (Leics.) B.Thornton 10/3/1910. LFM bowler who gets good wickets. Swings in to right-hander and moves away off seam. Debut 1937. Best season 1948 (81 wkts.) HS—33 v. Worcs. (Barwell) 1947. BB—7-19 v. Hants. (Leicester) 1939.

SPOONER, Richard T. (Warwick.) B. Stockton-on-Tees 30/12/1919. Most promising wicketkeeper, neat and quiet. Useful LHB. Played for Durham before joining Warwick. Debut 1948. C.Cap 1948. Not in best of health in 1949. HS—70 v. Derby (Derby) 1949.

†**STAINTON, R. G.** ("Bob") B.Kent 23/5/1911. Sound RHB. Educated at Malvern. Oxford Blue 1933. Also soccer Blue. Debut 1932. A schoolmaster, he is only available in August. Did not play in 1948 or 1949. HS—89 Oxford U. v. W. Indians (Oxford) 1933.

STEPHENSON, Harold W. (Somerset) B.Haverton Hill Durham 18/7/1920. Wicketkeeper of great promise; very quick in his stumping; very useful RHB. Headed Durham batting averages 1947. Debut 1948. C.Cap 1949 when he took over stumping from Luckes. In Somerset matches dismissed 83 batsmen—a county record—and totalled 85 dismissals in the season. HS—88 v. Surrey (Oval) 1949.

†**STEVENSON, M. H.** (Cambridge U.) B.Chinley 3/6/1927. Sound RHB and useful change bowler (slow LA). Educated at Rydal. Blue 1949. HS—62 v. Free Foresters (Cambridge) 1949. Qualified for Derby but has not yet played for them.

STOCKS, Frederick W. (Notts.) B. Hucknall 6/11/1918. Sound LHB and RA change bowler. Debut 1946. C.Cap 1946. Performed unique feat of century in his first match (114 v. Kent at Nottingham) and a wicket with his first ball in first-class cricket (v. Lancs. at Manchester). Test Trial at Lord's 1946. HS—166 v. Northants. (Nottingham) 1948.

STONE, Donald H. (Lancs.) Well-built RFM bowler. Debut 1949 when he played 2 matches.

†**SURRIDGE, W. Stuart** (Surrey) B. Herne Hill 3/9/1917. Hard-hitting RHB. Whole-hearted, much improved, RFM bowler; moves either way, mostly out. Very good slip field, holding 28 catches in 1949. Debut 1939. Member of cricket equipment firm, but is a farmer. HS —41* v. Middlesex (Oval) 1949. BB—6-49 v. Middlesex (Oval) 1949.

†**SUTCLIFFE, W. H. H.** (" Billy ") B. Pudsey 10/10/1926. Forcing RHB and change bowler (LB's). Son of Herbert Sutcliffe. Educated at Rydal. Debut 1948. HS—56 v. Glamorgan (Hull) 1948.

†**SUTHERLAND, I.** (Cambridge U.) B. Leicester 7/7/1926. Educated at Wyggeston G. S. One match for Cambridge U. in 1949.

SUTTLE, Ken (Sussex) B.Kensington (London) 25/8/1928. Promising LHB. Quick outfield. Debut 1949. Soccer for Chelsea and Brighton & Hove Albion. HS—43* v. Yorks. (Hove) 1949.

†**SWANN, J. L.** (Middx.) B.Ealing (Middx.) 3/10/1926. Debut 1949, when he played one match for county.

†**SYMINGTON, S. J.** (Leics.) B.Bexhill-on-Sea 16/9/1926. Hard-hitting RHB and useful FM bowler. Educated at Canford. Debut 1948. Captain 1949—Regular Army duties prevent continuance in 1950. C.Cap 1949. HS—65 v. Essex (Leicester) 1949. BB—5-45 v. Derby (Ashby-de-la-Zouch) 1949.

†**TANNER, John D. P.** (Oxforw U.) B. Harrogate 2/7/1921. Wicketkeeper. Educated at Charterhouse. Played for Oxford U. 1947-8-9 but failed to win Blue. On debut in first-class cricket, v. Lancs. (Oxford) 1947, did not concede a bye in an innings of 512. LHB.

TATTERSALL, Roy (Lancs.) B.Bolton 17/8/1922. Promising ROB bowler, his height giving him lift off pitch; quickish through air; can also use seam. LHB. Debut 1948. HS—39 v. New Zealanders (Manchester) 1949. BB—6-39 v. Derby (Buxton) 1949.

TAYLOR, Brian (Essex) B.West Ham 19/6/32. Wicketkeeper. RHB. Played in 1 match in 1949, keeping wicket 5 times for 2nd XI.

TAYLOR, Derief (Warwick.) B.Kingston (Jamaica) 17/9/1918. LHB and slow LA spinner. Debut 1948. HS—121 v. Leics. (Birmingham) 1949—maiden century.

TAYLOR, Donald D. (Warwick.) B. Auckland (N.Z.) 2/3/1923. Diminutive and attractive RHB. Useful change bowler (OB's). Played for Auckland from 1946-47 to 1948-49. Test v. England 1946-47. Shared in opening partnerships of 220 and 286 with B. Sutcliffe v. Canterbury in 1948-49—a world record. Missed selection for 1949 N.Z. team so came to England for trial with Surrey. Debut for Warwick. 1949. Will be qualified for county 1951—meanwhile is playing for Old Hill in Birmingham League. HS—143 Auckland v. Canterbury (Auckland) 1948-49.

†**THACKARA, Lt./Cmdr. A. L.** (Combined Services). Correct opening RHB.

THOMPSON, Alec (Middx.) B.Liverpool 17/4/1916. Forceful RHB. Debut 1939. C.Cap 1946. Opportunities have usually been limited. HS—100* v. Surrey (Oval) 1946.

†**THOMPSON, John R.** (Warwick.) B. Berkhamsted (Herts.) 29/9/1918. Attractive opening RHB. Good field. Educated at Tonbridge. Cambridge Blue 1938-9. Debut 1938. C.Cap 1947. Now a master at Marlborough and available only in August. Batted extremely well in 1947 and 1949, finishing 5th in English batting averages 1949. HS—191 Cambridge U. v. Free Foresters (Cambridge) 1938.

†**THOMPSON, L. B.** (Middx.) B.Ealing (Middx.) 12/11/1908. Useful OB bowler. Captain Middx. 2nd XI. Debut 1946.

†**THOMPSON, Roland G.** (Warwick.) B.Coventry 26/9/1932. RHB and FM bowler. Debut 1949, when he played 1 match. See page 173.

†**TILLARD, Robert J.** (Sussex) B.London 26/5/1924. Educated at Winchester Debut 1949—one match. Regular soldier on a course at Oxford.

TITMUS, Frederick (Middx.) B.Kentish Town (Middx.) 24/11/1932. Most promising young RHB. Bowls quick or slow. Inside left on Watford F.C. staff. Debut v. Somerset (Bath) 1949. Had outstanding record in Cross Arrow matches at Lord's in September, 1949. (12 inns. 656 runs, 82 avge.)

TODD, Leslie J. (Kent) B.Catford 19/6/1907. Sound, well-equipped opening LHB who can vary his game. Useful LM bowler pre-war, now rarely bowls. Debut 1927. " Double " 1936. Benefit 1947. Scored 1000 runs each season since 1933 except 1938. In 1948 shared with Fagg in nine century opening partnerships for Kent—county record. Out of luck and form for most of 1949. Played for England at table tennis. HS—174 v. Leics. (Maidstone) 1949. BB—6-26 (11-64 match) v. Notts. (Tonbridge) 1936.

TOMPKIN, Maurice (Leics.) B.Countesthorpe 17/2/1919. Attractive RHB; an uncertain starter but fine strokes when set. Debut 1938. C.Cap 1946. Fine season in 1947 (1781 runs) and has scored 1000 runs each season since war. Played soccer for Leicester City and Huddersfield. HS—163 v. Sussex (Hastings) 1947.

TOWNSEND, Alan (Warwick.) B. Stockton-on-Tees 26/8/1921. Improving RHB, M in-swing bowler and brilliant slip field. Played for Durham before joining Warwick. Debut 1948. C.Cap 1948. Held 33 catches in 1949—county record for fieldsman. HS—80* v. Lancs. (Birmingham) 1948. BB—7-84 v. Essex (Brentwood) 1949.

TOWNSEND, Arnold F. (Derby) B.Long Eaton 29/3/1912. Sound opening RHB, but uncertain starter. Debut 1934. Played very occasionally pre-war, but scored 1188 runs in 1946—his first full season. 1348 runs in 1947, but not so successful since. HS—142* v. Somerset (Taunton) 1939.

TREMLETT, Maurice F. (Somerset) B. Stockport (Lancs.) 5/7/1923. Capable RHB, fine driver, and MF bowler. Splendid field in front of wicket on off-side. Joined Somerset staff in 1938. Debut 1947, taking 8-86 in his first match (v. Middx. at Lord's). Toured W. Indies 1947-48 and S. Africa 1948-49. 3 Tests, all v. W. Indies 1947-48. Scored over 1000 runs 1948 and 1949. HS—105 M.C.C. v. Natal XI (Pietermaritzburg) 1948-49. BB—8-31 v. Glamorgan (Weston-super-Mare) 1948.

†**TRICK, W. M.** Stanley (Glamorgan) B.Briton Ferry 31/10/1916. ML bowler. Debut 1946, but missed 1947 season. Showed good form in 1948 at Swansea (29 wkts. for 480 runs) where wicket suits his bowling. BB—6-29 (12-106 match) v. Somerset (Swansea) 1948.

TRUEMAN, Freddie (Yorks.) B.Stainton 6/2/1931. Promising RFM bowler of possibilities; RHB. Solidly built. Debut 1949. BB—8-70 v. Minor Counties (Lord's) 1949.

UFTON, Derrick G. (Kent) B.Crayford 31/5/1928. LHB and reserve wicketkeeper. On Charlton Athletic staff. Debut 1949 when he played in 2 matches.

UNDERWOOD, A. J. (Notts.) B.Wiseton (Notts.). Medium LA bowler. Debut in 1949 when he played 2 matches. Now in Army.

†**UNWIN, F. St. George** (Essex) B. Halstead 23/4/1911. Forcing RHB. Debut 1932. One of three Essex captains 1939. Now captain Essex 2nd XI. HS—60 v. Kent (Colchester) 1946.

†**VALENTINE, Brian H.** (Kent) B. Blackheath 17/1/1908. Attractive forcing RHB. Educated at Repton. Cambridge Blue 1929. Debut 1929. Toured India 1933-34 and S. Africa 1938-39. Played in 7 Tests, scoring 136 v. India (Bombay) on debut in 1933-34. Kent captain 1932 to 1934, 1937 (joint with R. T. Bryan) and 1946 to 1948. Wounded in Normandy 1944. 1000 runs nine times. Brilliant lawn tennis player, winning Public Schools doubles with H. W. (Bunny) Austin. HS—242 v. Leics. (Oakham) 1938.

†**VAN RYNEVELD, Clive B.** (Oxford U.) B.Cape Town (S.A.) 19/3/1928. Fine all-rounder—forceful RHB and excellent LBG bowler. Educated at Diocesan College, S.A. Played for Western Province (S.A.) before coming to England. Oxford Blue 1947-8-9, captain 1949. Oxford Rugby Blue 1947-8-9; 4 English caps at centre. Played for Gents. at Lord's 1949. HS—102 v. Worcs. (Oxford) 1949. BB—7-57 University match 1948.

†**VAULKHARD, Patrick** (Derby) B. Nottingham 15/9/1911. Attacking RHB and useful wicketkeeper. Debut for Notts. 1934. Joined Derby 1946. HS—264 v. Notts. (Nottingham) 1946.

†**VERNON, Lt. J. Michael** (Combined Services) RHB and M bowler.

VIGAR, Frank H. (Essex) B.Bruton (Somerset) 14/7/1917. Very sound all-rounder; RHB, LBG bowler and fine field and catch near wicket. Debut 1938. C.Cap 1946. Shared in last wkt. partnership of 218 with T. P. B. Smith v. Derby (Chester-

field) 1947. HS—145 Middlesex & Essex v. Surrey & Kent (Kingston) 1947. BB—8-128 v. Leics. (Clacton) 1946.

WADE, Thomas H. (Essex) B.Maldon 24/11/1910. Sound, unspectacular wicketkeeper and useful LHB. Debut 1929 as bowler, but changed to wicketkeeping 1934. Assisted M.C.C. in Australia 1936-37 and was awarded touring colours. Benefit (£3,900 — Essex record) 1948. Played soccer for Southend. HS—96 v. Oxford U. (Leyton) 1932.

†**WAIT, O. J.** (Cambridge U.) B.Dulwich 2/8/1926. Tall MF in-swing bowler. Educated at Dulwich. Blue 1949. Debut 1949. Qualified for Surrey. BB—6-94 (10-144 match) Cambridge U. v. Somerset (Bath) 1949.

†**WALFORD, Michael M.** (Somerset) B. Durham 27/11/1915. Stylish opening RHB and brilliant field. Educated at Rugby. Oxford Blue 1936 and 1938. Also rugger and hockey Blues. Played hockey for Great Britain in 1948 Olympic Games. Is now a master at Sherborne and available only in August. Scored 141* v. Indians (Taunton) on debut for Somerset 1946. HS—264 v. Hants. (Weston-super-Mare) 1947.

WALKER, Clifford. B.Huddersfield 27/6/1920. Sound RHB and useful M bowler; dips ball away. Debut for Yorks. 1947. Joined Hants. in 1949 and was regular member of team. C.Cap 1949. HS—112 v. Lancs. (Bournemouth) 1949. BB—5-40 v. Oxford U. (Bournemouth) 1949.

WALKER, Jack (Kent) B.Cobham (Kent) 2/3/1914. Reserve wicketkeeper and RHB. Debut 1949 when he played 2 matches.

WALSH, Jack E. (Leics.) B.Sydney (Australia) 4/12/1912. Most dangerous slow LA spinner, who bowls " chinaman " and sundry other varieties. Hard-hitting LHB. Good slip field. Debut 1937. C.Cap 1946. Represented Players at Lord's 1947. Hit seven sixes in scoring 106 v. Essex (Loughborough) 1948 —his HS. Took 174 wkts. in 1948 —county record. Has taken 100 wkts. each season since war. BB— 8-103 (15-164 match, including " hat-trick ") v. Notts. (Loughborough) 1949.

WARD, Geoffrey H. (Kent) B.Rainham 22/11/1926. Reserve wicketkeeper. Debut 1949, when he played 2 matches.

WARDLE, John H. (Yorks.) B.Ardsley 8/1/1923. Skilful LA spinner; aggressive LHB. Debut 1946. C.Cap 1947. Toured W. Indies 1947-48, playing in one Test. Represented Players at Lord's 1948. Lost form early in 1949 but came back at a vital time and bowled as well as ever. HS—70 v. Worcs. (Sheffield) 1949. BB—8-87 v. Derby (Chesterfield) 1948.

†**WARR, John J.** (Middx.) B.Ealing (Middx.) 16/2/1927. Very promising, industrious FM bowler; moves either way. RHB. Educated at Ealing G.S. Debut 1949. C.Cap 1949. Cambridge Blue 1949. HS —47 v. Yorks. (Sheffield) 1949. BB—6-35 Cambridge U. v. Lancs. (Cambridge) 1949.

WASHBROOK, Cyril. (Lancs.) B. Barrow 6/12/1914. Most attractive opening RHB, especially strong on leg-side. Plays all bowling with assurance; favours the hook and cut; brilliant field, usually cover. With Len Hutton forms England's best opening pair since Hobbs and Sutcliffe. Debut 1933. Played in 26 Tests —v. Australia (5 in 1946-7, 4 in 1948), v. S. Africa (5 in 1947, 5 in 1948-9), v. India (3 in 1946), and v. N.Z. (1 in 1937, 2 in 1949). Two tours as above. Benefit (£14,000—the highest on record) 1948. Scored 195 v. S. Africa (Johannesburg) 1948-49, adding 359 for first wkt. with Hutton—a record for all Tests. Has scored 1000 runs in season 9 times in England — best 1947 2662 runs (avge. 68.25). HS—251* v. Surrey (Manchester) 1947.

WATKINS, A. J. (" Allan ") (Glamorgan) B.Usk ((Mon.) 21/4/1922. Very sound LHB and LMF swing bowler. Magnificent field close to wicket. Debut 1939. C.Cap 1947. On Cardiff City F.C. staff. Made Test debut v. Australia (Oval) 1948, but did not do himself justice owing to injury. Toured S. Africa 1948-49, playing in all 5 Tests and scoring first Test century—111 at Johannesburg. Test v. N.Z. (Lord's) 1949. 1000 runs in 1947, 1948 and 1949. HS—146 v. Northants. (Kettering) 1947. BB—5-19 v. Warwick (Neath) 1949. Cartilage operation in 1950.

†**WATKINS, David** (Essex) B.St. Albans 18/8/1928. RHB and M bowler. Debut 1949, playing in one match for county. Regular member of 2nd XI 1949.

WATSON, G. S. (Leics.) B.Sittingbourne (Kent) 10/4/1909. Enterprising RHB who likes fast bowling. Debut for Kent 1928. Joined Leics. 1934. Testimonial 1950. Played soccer for Charlton Athletic and Crystal Palace and in amateur internationals v. Ireland and Scotland 1930. HS —145 v. Glamorgan (Leicester) 1939.

WATSON, W. (Yorks.) B.Bolton-on-Dearne 7/3/1920. Sound LHB.

Debut 1939. Test Trial 1946. C.Cap 1947. Played soccer for Huddersfield Town and Sunderland, gaining England cap v. Italy 1949-50. HS—172 v Derby (Scarborough) 1948.

†**WATTS, Hugh E.** (Somerset) B.Bath 4/11/1922. Attacking LHB. Educated at Downside—now runs cricket there. Cambridge Blue 1947. Debut 1947. C.Cap 1947. Available only in August. Wears glasses. HS—110 v. Glamorgan (Weston-super-Mare) 1949.

†**WEBB, H. E.** (Hants.) B. In India 10/5/1927. Wristy, stylish RHB. Educated at Winchester. Oxford Blue 1948, scoring 115 in University match at Lord's. Also soccer Blue. Qualified for Hants.

WEBB, Rupert T. (Sussex) B.Harrow (Middx.) 11/7/1922. Reserve wicket-keeper. On Lord's staff before joining Sussex. Debut 1948.

†**WEBSTER, Jack** (Northants.) B.Bradford 28/10/1917. MF bowler and RHB. Educated at Bradford G.S. Debut 1938. Cambridge Blue 1939. Debut for Northants. 1946. Available only in August. HS—65 v Surrey (Oval) 1948. BB—7-78 Cambridge U. v Essex (Brentwood) 1939.

WEEKS, Raymond (Warwick.) Slow LA bowler. Has played for Cornwall. B.Camborne 30/4/30. Not yet registered.

WELLARD, Arthur W. (Somerset) B. Southfleet (Kent) 8/4/1903. Wonderfully consistent RFM bowler who also bowls OB's. Famous as a hitting RHB—the best since World War I. Safe slip field. Debut 1927. "Doubles" in 1933, 1935 and 1937. Has twice scored five sixes off successive balls bowled to him—off T. R. Armstrong in 1936 and Frank Woolley in 1938. Played in two Tests— v Australia (Lord's) 1938 and v N.Z. (Manchester) 1937. Playing Birmingham League cricket with Kidderminster in 1950 but is re-engaged on a match basis with Somerset. Testimonial 1951. HS—112 v Surrey (Oval) 1934. BB—8-52 (15-101 match) v Worcs. (Bath) 1947.

WEST, Gordon H. (Essex) B.Upton Park 7/8/1923. Sound RHB and good field. Played v Cambridge U. (Cambridge) 1949, scoring 55 in his first county match.

WESTERMAN, Peter (Surrey) B.Barnes 8/12/1920. Useful RMF bowler and RHB. Educated at Hampton G.S. Debut 1949, playing in 4 matches. BB—5-51 v Glos. (Oval) 1949— his first match.

WHARTON, Alan (Lancs.) B.Heywood 30/4/1923. Attacking LHB, useful seam bowler and very fine outfield. Debut 1946. C.Cap 1946. Test v N.Z. (Leeds) 1949. Rugby League for Salford. HS—139 v Oxford U. (Oxford) 1949.

†**WHEATLEY, G. A.** (Surrey) B.Twickenham 28/5/1923. Useful RHB. Sound wicketkeeper. Educated at Uppingham Oxford Blue 1946. Played 5 matches for Surrey 1947. Injured in 1949. HS—66 Oxford U. v Sussex (Chichester) 1946.

†**WHITCOMBE, Philip A.** (Middx.) B. Kensington 23/4/1923. Tall RFM bowler, highly thought of in 1948. Hard-hitting RHB. Educated at Winchester. Oxford Blue 1947-8-9 Played for Gents. at Lord's 1948. County debut 1948. Did not play for Middx. in 1949. HS—68 Oxford U. v Glos. (Oxford) 1949. BB—7-51 University match 1948.

†**WHITCOMBE, Peter J.** (Worcs.) B.Worcester 11/11/1926. Reserve wicketkeeper. RHB. Educated Worcester R.G.S. Debut 1949—one match.

WHITEHEAD, John P. (Yorks.) B. Uppermill 3/9/1925. RHB and FM bowler of considerable pace. Very keen field. Debut 1946. At London University—now professional for Littleborough in Central Lancs. League. HS—71 Combined Services v Northants. (Northampton) 1947. BB—5-10 Combined Services v. Worcs. (Hereford) 1947.

†**WHITE, Alan F. T.** (Worcs.) B.Coventry 5/9/1915. Forceful RHB. Educated at Uppingham. Cambridge Blue 1936. Played for Warwick 1936 to 1939. Debut for Worcs. 1946. C.Cap 1946. Captain 1947-8, joint with R. E. S. Wyatt 1949. HS—95 v Combined S. (Worcester) 1946.

†**WHITE, Major W. Michael E.** (Northants.) B.Barnes (Surrey) 22/5/1913. RHB and FM bowler. Educated at Dover. Played for Cambridge U. 1937 but did not win Blue. Appearances limited owing to Army duties.

WHITING, Norman H. (Worcs.) B. Stourbridge 2/10/1920. RHB. Debut 1947. HS—56 v Combined Services (Worcester) 1949.

WHITTAKER, Geoffrey J. (Surrey) B. Peckham 29/5/1916. Aggressive RHB. Fine field. Has been dogged by injuries. Debut 1937. C.Cap 1949. Hit nine sixes in 148 v Northants. (Northampton) 1949 (short on-boundary). Was P.O.W. in Italian hands during war, when he had top of right thumb amputated. Kingstonian footballer. HS—148 v Northants. (Northampton) 1949—scoring 89* in second innings.

†**WILCOX, Dennis R.** (Essex) B.Westcliff 4/6/1910. Very correct RHB. Educated at Dulwich. Cambridge Blue 1931-2-3, captain in 1933. Debut for Essex 1929. Headmaster of Prep. school at Westcliff. Joint Essex captain 1933 to 1939. HS—157 in 1932 University match.

†**WILEY, John W. E.** (Oxford U.) Educated at Cape Town University. 4 matches for Oxford U. in 1949. RHB.

†**WILLATT, G. L.** (Notts.) B.Nottingham 7/5/1920. Sound opening LHB. Educated at Repton. Cambridge Blue 1946-7, captain 1947. Also soccer Blue. Debut for Cambridge 1938; for Notts. 1946; possibly for Derbyshire 1950. Plays for Scotland—has tutorial post at Edin. Univ Played for Gents. at Lord's 1947. HS—131 v Surrey (Oval) 1947.

WILLIAMS, E. L. (Leics.) B.Shaftesbury (Dorset) 15/9/1925. Useful all-rounder, M pace bowler. Played 1 match in 1949.

WILLSON, R. (Sussex) B.Burgess Hill 14/7/1933. Slow LA bowler, LHB. Very promising; remarkably steady for his age.

WILSON, Alan (Lancs.) B.Newton-le-Willows 24/4/1921. Wicketkeeper with no pretentions to batting (RHB). Debut 1948.

WILSON, Andrew E. (Glos.) B.London 18/5/1912. Most useful and compact LHB, who can open or bat in the middle of the order. Cuts and hooks strongly. Sound wicketkeeper. Debut for Mddx. 1932. Joined Glos. 1936 but could not play in Championship until 1938, when he scored over 1000 runs. 1000 every season since war. HS—188 v Sussex (Chichester) 1949. Appointed county coach 1950.

WILSON, J. Victor (Yorks.) B.Scampston 17/1/1921. Solid and forceful LHB; drives and cuts well. Useful field. Debut 1946. C.Cap 1948. With Watson added 302 for 2nd wkt. in 165 mins. v Derby (Scarborough) 1948. Plays soccer for Leeds United. HS—157* v Sussex (Leeds) 1949.

†**WILSON, Sqd.-Ldr. R. G.** (Combined Services). Aggressive RHB. FMR bowler—mainly in-swing. Debut 1948. HS—100 v Hants. (Portsmouth) 1949. BB—5-51 (8-109 match) v Worcs. (Worcester) 1949 B.Arnside (Westm'land) 20/12/1922.

†**WINN, Chris E.** (Sussex) B.Beckenham (Kent) 13/11/1926. Forceful LHB of forward type. Educated at K.C.S., Wimbledon. Oxford Blue 1948-9. Debut 1948. HS—95 Oxford U. v Worcs. (Oxford) 1949.

WINROW, Harold B.Manton 17/1/1916. Useful all-rounder; LHB and LA spinner. Cuts and drives well. HS—204* v Derby (Nottingham) 1947. BB—5-18 v Derby (Nottingham) 1948.

WOOD, D. Jim (Sussex) B.Horsted Keynes 19/5/1914. Much improved LFM opening bowler; moves either way and straightens off seam. LHB. Debut 1936. C.Cap 1938. HS—31 v Oxford U. (Eastbourne) 1939. BB—7-24 v Middlesex (Hove) 1949.

WOODHEAD, Frank G. (Notts.) B. Edwinstone (Notts.) 30/10/1912. Steady FM bowler, mostly in-swing. RHB. Debut 1934. Played League cricket in 1947. HS—52* v Hants. (Nottingham) 1937. BB—7-24 v Worcs. (Nottingham) 1938.

†**WOODHOUSE, George E. S.** (Somerset) B.Blanford (Dorset) 15/2/1924. Resolute, stylish RHB, but average probably affected by cares of captaincy. Educated at Marlborough. War-time Cambridge "Blue" 1943. Debut 1946. C.Cap 1947. One of three Somerset capts. in 1948; appointed sole captain in 1949. HS—109 v Leics (Leicester) 1947.

WOLTON, Albert V. (Warwick) B. Maidenhead (Berks.) 12/6/1919. Promising RHB. Fine field in deep. Debut 1947. C.Cap 1949. HS—111* v Somerset (Birmingham) 1949.

WOOLER, Charles (Leics.) B.Rhodesia 30/6/1930. RFM bowler, at present qualifying for county. Played one match in 1949.

†**WOOLLER, Wilfred** (Glamorgan) B.Rhos-on-Sea (N. Wales) 20/11/1912. Forceful RHB who gets runs when most wanted. Accurate and lively MF bowler. Brilliant field close to wicket. Educated at Rydal. Cambridge Blue for cricket (1935-6) and rugger (1933-4-5) Famous Welsh centre three-quarter (18 caps). Glamorgan captain 1947 to 1950. Played for Gents at Lord's 1948. P.O.W. in Japanese hands during war. HS—111 v W. Indies (Cardiff) 1939. BB—7-20 v Warwick (Cambridge) 1936.

WRIGHT, Douglas V. P. (Kent) B.Sidcup 21/8/1914. Skilful LBG bowler, devastating on his day, but inconsistent form makes him an enigma. Quick through air for his type. Useful RHB. Debut 1932. Toured S. Africa 1938-39, Australia (23 Test wkts.) and N.Z. 1946-47, S. Africa 1948-49. Played in 26 Tests since his debut in 1938 against Australia. Holds world record with seven "hat-tricks," the seventh being v Hants. (Canterbury) 1949. Taken 100 wkts each season since 1937 (except 1948). Benefit 1950. HS—84* v Hants. (Southampton) 1939. BB—9-51 (15-163 match) v Leics. (Maidstone) 1949.

†**WRIGLEY, Michael H.** (Oxford U.) B. Knutsford (Cheshire) 30/7/1924. Good RFM bowler. RHB. Educated at Harrow. Debut 1948. Blue 1949. Qualified for Lancs. in 1950. BB—6-57 v Surrey (Oval) 1949.

†**WYATT, R. E. S.** ("Bob") (Worcs.) B.Milford (Surrey) 2/5/1901. Extremely sound and consistent RHB. Formerly good MF bowler. Played for Warwick 1923-1939, captain 1930 to 1937. Debut for Worcs.

1946. C.Cap 1946. Joint-captain with A. F. T. White 1949. Most travelled of all cricketers, touring Australia and N.Z. 1932-33, 1936-37, S. Africa 1927-28, 1930-31, W. Indies 1929-30, 1934-35, India 1926-27 and S. America 1937-38—only other cricketer to tour in six countries was Sir Pelham Warner. Played 40 Tests for England, acting as captain v Australia (Oval) 1930 and in the 1934, 1934-35 and 1935 series of Tests. Has scored more runs than any other batsman now playing. Played for Gents. at Lord's 13 times between 1926 and 1939. Test Selector 1949. HS—232 Warwick v Derby (Birmingham) 1937.

†**YARDLEY, Norman W. D.** (Yorks.) B. Barnsley 19/3/1915. Very sound attractive RHB, fine driver. More than useful M swing bowler. Fine field anywhere. Educated at St. Peter's, York. Cambridge Blue 1935-6-7-8, captain 1938. Debut for Yorks. 1936. Played for Gents. at Lord's 1937-8, 1946 to 1949. Toured India 1937-38, S. Africa 1938-39, Australia and N.Z. 1946-47. Played in 17 Tests—1 v S. Africa 1938-39, 5 v Australia 1946-47 (in 5th as capt.), 1 v N.Z. 1946-47, 5 v S. Africa 1947 (capt.), 5 v Australia 1948 (capt.) In 1946-47 dismissed Bradman in three successive Test innings. Gained hockey Blue and is good squash player. Yorks captain 1948-1949. HS—182* M.C.C. v Orange Free State (Bloemfontein) 1938-39. BB—6-29 M.C.C. v Camb. U. (Lord's) 1946.

YARNOLD, H. (Worcs.) B.Worcester 6/7/1917. Good wicketkeeper. Useful RHB. Debut 1938. C.Cap 1947. Dismissed 110 batsmen (63 ct. 47 st.) in 1949—only Ames has dismissed more. HS—68 North v South (Kingston) 1947.

YOUNG, D. Martin (Glos.) B.Coalville (Leics.) 15/4/1924. Sound RHB. who may be the opener Glos. need. Drives and cuts well. Debut for Worcs. 1946. Joined Glos. 1949. HS—90 Worcs. v Cambridge U. (Cambridge) 1947.

YOUNG, J. A. ("Jack") (Middx.) B. Paddington (Middx.) 14/10/1912. Excellent LA spinner; very accurate. Useful and improving RHB. Fine field in gully. Debut 1933, but not a regular until 1946 when he gained his cap. Played in 8 Tests—v S. Africa (Leeds) 1947, v Australia (Nottingham, Manchester, Oval) 1948, v S. Africa (Johannesburg, Port Elizabeth) 1948-49, v N.Z. (Leeds, Lord's) 1949. Bowled 11 successive maiden overs v Australia (Nottingham) 1948—a Test record. HS—62 v Yorks. (Sheffield) 1949. BB—8-31 (12-72 match) v Yorks. (Lord's) 1946.

CAREER RECORDS 1950

Compiled by ROY WEBBER

The following table gives the full career record in first-class cricket of every player likely to appear in the 1950 season. All figures are complete to 30th September, 1949, and with the exception of Dawkes, Place, Oldfield and R. Smith—who toured India in 1949-50—and Hardstaff, who played in New Zealand last winter, will be correct at the start of the season.

	Batting				Bowling		
	Runs	H.S.	Avge.	100s	Runs	Wkts.	Avge.
Ablack, R. K.	24	16	12.00	—	220	0	—
Ainsworth, M. L. Y.	1188	100	28.62	1	21	0	—
Aitchison, J.	2	2	1.00	—	33	3	11.00
Alderson, R.	55	55	27.50	—	—	—	—
Allen, B. O.	13023	220	29.13	12	406	3	135.33
Allen, G. O. J. L.	8535	180	27.71	9	17298	778	22.23
Altham, R. G. J. L.	14	14	4.66	—	—	—	—
Ames, L. E. G.	35190	295	43.93	95	718	22	32.63
Angell, F. L.	207	45	9.85	—	—	—	—
Anson, G. F.	450	106	25.55	1	—	—	—
Anton, J. H. H.	264	45	18.85	—	—	—	—
Armstrong, T. R.	311	28*	6.34	—	3183	133	23.93
Arnold, J.	20712	227	32.46	35	1161	17	68.29
Ashmore, W.	24	15*	12.00	—	129	3	43.00
Aspinall, R.	709	75*	18.65	—	2516	126	19.96
Avery, A. V.	7948	214*	34.11	17	503	8	62.87
Bailey, Sir D.	70	29	8.75	—	49	2	24.50
Bailey, J.	9500	133	24.73	5	12822	470	27.28
Bailey, R. A.	0	0*	0.00	—	250	2	125.00
Bailey, T. E.	3789	205	33.53	3	8314	314	26.47
Barlow, A.	346	44	10.17	—	—	—	—
Barraclough, E. S.	27	24*	27.00	—	34	1	34.00
Barrick, D.	595	147*	42.50	1	285	5	57.50
Barron, W.	3799	161*	26.02	6	167	5	33.40
Bartlett, H. T.	9907	183	32.16	16	269	10	26.90
Bartlett, J. N.	214	28	8.91	—	2016	69	29.21
Barton, M. R.	3914	192	26.53	6	—	—	—
Bedford, P. I.	94	20	6.82	—	1585	52	30.49

	Batting				Bowling		
	Runs	H.S.	Avge.	100s	Runs	Wkts.	Avge.
Bedser, A. V.	2729	126	18.43	1	13729	575	23.87
Bedser, E. A.	4355	163	25.76	4	5770	197	29.28
Bennett, A. C. L.	536	68	20.20	—	—	—	—
Berry, L. G.	27629	232	31.14	39	—	—	—
Berry, R. E.	105	22	6.23	—	596	10	59.60
Bird, R. E.	2349	116	22.80	2	968	42	23.04
Blake, D. E.	311	60	17.27	—	435	13	33.46
Blake, P. D. S.	491	77	18.88	—	—	—	—
Boobbyer, B.	143	28	11.91	—	6	0	—
Brazier, A. F.	57	20	8.14	—	—	—	—
Brearley, H.	55	24	13.75	—	—	—	—
Brennan, D. V.	542	34	7.22	—	—	—	—
Brice, G. H. J.	27	20	13.50	—	200	5	40.00
Bridger, J. R.	771	142	32.12	1	34	0	—
Broderick, V. H.	2918	135	22.27	4	6843	256	26.73
Bromley, P. H.	20	12	6.66	—	46	1	46.00
Brooke-Taylor, D. C.	375	61*	15.00	—	—	—	—
Brookes, D.	13599	257	35.04	33	90	2	45.00
Brown, F. R.	8338	212	26.03	14	22308	829	26.90
Brown, S. M.	8156	200	29.98	13	20	0	—
Burnett, A. C.	565	79*	37.66	—	—	—	—
Buse, H. T. F.	6733	132	22.74	5	11780	437	26.95
Butler, H. J.	1832	62	11.33	—	17222	712	24.18
Campbell, I. P.	224	43	14.00	—	—	—	—
Cannings, V. H. D.	745	61	16.00	—	—	—	—
Carr, D. B.	1523	170	25.81	3	2914	88	33.11
Carty, H.	154	53	12.83	—	841	25	33.64
Castle, F.	686	60*	20.78	—	878	34	25.82
Chapman, T. A.	948	74	13.94	—	43	1	43.00
Chesterton, G. H.	160	43	14.54	—	6	0	—
Clark, D. G.	643	58*	11.69	—	1010	46	21.95
Clark, T. H.	130	59	14.44	—	—	—	—
Clarke, C. B.	1036	86	12.18	—	89	2	44.50
Clarke, R. W.	1038	56	18.21	—	6536	243	26.89
Clay, J. C.	7158	115*	15.42	2	25953	1315	19.73
Clay, J. D.	190	57*	23.75	—	5093	161	31.63
Clift, P. B.	2594	125*	22.36	4	49	0	—
Close, D. B.	1098	88*	27.45	—	436	5	87.20
Coles, W. N.	26	14	8.66	—	3150	113	27.87
Compton, D.	23287	300	59.35	83	9377	334	28.07
Compton, L. H.	2799	107	21.53	2	565	13	43.46
Constable, B.	1719	107	24.21	1	1209	27	44.77

Name	Runs	HS	Avge	100s	Runs	Wkts	Avge
Eagar, E. D. R.	6243	147	24.87	5	988	24	41.16
Edrich, B.	1372	193*	18.29	1	2302	70	32.88
Edrich, W. J.	20881	267*	36.67	57	10874	341	31.88
Eggar, J. D.	1659	219	33.18	4	70	—	—
Elliott, C. S.	6724	215	25.18	3	143	4	—
Emmett, G. M.	8382	165*	30.92	12	481	10	48.10
Evans, A. E.	824	65*	16.48	—	2039	52	39.21
Evans, T. G.	4767	101	22.06	1	2458	72	34.13
Eve, S. C.	717	120	27.57	1	20	0	—
Fagg, A. E.	16797	257	39.89	40	—	—	—
Fairbairn, A.	463	110*	27.23	2	52	0	—
Faragher, H. A.	26	26	26.00	—	—	—	—
Farr, B. H.	5	3	1.66	—	—	—	—
Fenner, M.		2	2.00	—	130	1	130.00
Fiddling, K.	983	68	11.58	—	—	—	—
Firth, J.	42	22*	21.00	—	429	9	47.66
Fishlock, L. B.	19221	253	40.46	43	39	0	—
Flavell, J.	6	6	6.00	—	—	—	—
Fletcher, D. G. W.	3356	194	33.22	5	956	34	28.11
Foord, C. W.	23	11	5.75	—	6623	246	26.92
Ford, W. R.	65	36	10.83	—	—	—	—
Frederick, M.	98	50	32.66	—	—	—	—
Gardiner-Hill, P.	78	50	39.00	—	—	—	—
Gardner, F. C.	2395	140*	31.93	3	—	—	—
Garlick, R. G.	1335	51	13.76	—	—	—	—
Gay, W. M.	16	11	3.20	—	288	9	32.00
Genders, W. M.	245	55*	16.53	—	98	3	32.66
Giles, R. J.	1282	59	18.57	—	1129	19	59.42
Gimblett, H.	14351	310	35.78	34	2026	41	49.41
Gladwin, C.	2904	124*	20.59	1	10009	513	19.51
Goddard, T. W.	4883	71	9.48	—	54281	2760	19.65
Graveney, J. K.	557	62	15.47	—	1695	64	26.48
Graveney, T. W.	2757	159	19.06	5	53	0	—
Gray, J. H.	305	46	19.06	—	—	—	—
Gray, L. H.	807	35*	7.01	—	14591	600	24.31
Greensmith, W. T.	33	10	4.12	—	187	2	93.50
Greenwood, P.	792	52	20.30	—	3085	119	25.92
Grieves, K.	1741	128	38.68	3	1845	65	28.38
Griffith, S. C.	4487	140	17.06	3	23	0	—
Grove, C. W.	1805	104*	13.47	3	7825	294	26.61
Guard, D. R.	430	89	15.35	1	—	—	—

Name	Runs	HS	Avge	100s	Runs	Wkts	Avge
Constable, D.	20	12	10.00	—	—	—	—
Cook, C.	455	18	7.00	—	10815	497	21.76
Coomb, A. G.	30	16	10.00	—	202	5	40.40
Cooper, E.	10436	216*	31.72	15	23	0	—
Cooper, F. S.	1225	113*	19.14	1	23	0	—
Cooper, R. S.	48	36	16.00	—	—	—	—
Cornford, J.	1094	34	5.58	—	22285	852	26.15
Corrall, P.	2562	64	9.70	—	—	—	—
Cox, D. R.	18	9	9.00	—	238	5	49.50
Cox, G.	13690	234*	32.28	32	4145	128	32.38
Coxon, A.	2222	83	18.51	—	7456	342	21.80
Cranfield, L. M.	2457	90	14.28	—	7580	233	22.53
Cranmer, P.	5430	113	21.98	4	1110	22	50.45
Cranston, K.	3008	156*	34.57	3	4881	177	27.57
Crapp, J. F.	13653	175	37.50	23	270	5	54.00
Gray, S. J.	3379	139	24.48	7	38	1	38.10
Crick, H.	124	22	9.53	—	—	—	—
Crush, J.	1078	78	16.08	—	3163	83	47.66
Dare, R.	13	7	6.50	—	143	3	51.83
Darks, R.	43	20	10.75	—	311	6	30.02
Davidson, W. W.	76	18*	5.42	—	—	—	—
Davies, E.	20711	287*	27.61	28	24768	825	29.51
Davies, H. G.	3096	68	14.07	—	—	—	—
Davies, J. G. W.	5435	168	24.26	4	7408	251	67.00
Davis, J.	1976	171	29.49	2	0	0	—
Davis, P.	6047	237	23.08	10	402	6	41.81
Dawkes, G.	2851	95	16.86	—	—	—	25.46
Debnam, A. F. H.	88	18	7.33	—	669	16	—
Deighton, J. H. G.	577	79	20.60	—	1655	65	30.72
Devereux, L. N.	43	32	21.50	—	—	—	—
Dew, J. A.	51	29	17.00	—	—	—	—
Dews, G.	3764	204*	39.20	3	22	0	—
Dews, J. G.	1019	78	17.87	—	8	0	—
Divecha, R. V.	193	68*	19.30	—	553	18	41.25
Dodds, T. C.	6769	157	34.53	8	330	8	20.50
Doggart, A. P.	93	20	13.28	—	41	2	37.09
Doggart, G. H. G.	3232	219*	40.91	8	816	22	41.07
Dollery, H. E.	13961	200	36.64	28	32	0	26.07
Donnelly, M. P.	8994	208*	47.58	22	1068	26	—
Dovey, R. R.	1527	54	12.02	—	8838	339	—
Downton, G.	37	16	6.16	—	—	—	—
Dunham, N.	15	12*	15.00	—	60	0	—

First group (H – J):

	Batting				Bowling		
	Runs	HS	Avge.	100s	Runs	Wkts.	Avge.
Hall, P. J.	172	49	19.11	—	1002	27	37.11
Hall, T. A.	0	0	0.00	—	55	0	—
Halliday, H.	3404	130	27.67	5	948	31	30.58
Hamer, A.	3	3	1.50	—	64	1	64.00
Harbin, L.	15	15	7.50	—	133	9	14.77
Hardstaff, J.	24951	266	45.78	64	1370	23	59.56
Harris, C. B.	17091	234	34.66	28	7231	167	43.29
Harrison, L.	1172	125*	13.95	1	18	0	—
Harvey, P. F.	740	125*	15.10	1	4058	128	31.70
Harvey, P. V.	9	9	9.00	—			
Hawkey, R. B.	42	13	7.00	—	139	1	139.00
Hayles, B. R. B. M.	69	40	7.66	—			
Hazell, H. L.	1909	43	8.71	—	17538	735	23.86
Hearn, P.	2077	138	24.15	2	577	14	41.21
Heath, D. M. W.	24	13*	6.00	—	124	3	41.33
Hebden, G. G. C.	44	29	8.80	—	55	0	—
Henderson, D.	10	10	5.00	—			
Hever, N. G.	321	29	9.17	—	3845	169	22.75
Hill, E.	1577	85	17.52	—	1288	56	23.00
Hill, G.	6431	161	18.42	4			
Hilton, M.	123	18	9.46	—	29571	1354	21.83
Hitchcock, R. E.	15	15	7.50	—	9488	283	33.52
Hofmeyr, M. B.	879	154	43.95	3	10	0	—
Hollies, W. E.	1036	24	5.34	—	25385	1135	22.36
Holmes, E. R. T.	13061	236	32.49	23	370	7	52.85
Holmes, E. R. R.	28	24	14.00	—	895	30	29.83
Hoskyns, Sir J. C.	63	42*	21.00	—			
Horsfall, R.	2224	170	21.32	4	760	28	27.14
Hossell, J. J.	1217	114	21.35	3			
Howard, B. J.	1099	114	28.17	1			
Howard, J. H.	589	38*	11.32	—	4728	164	28.82
Howard, N. D.	2011	145	22.85	1			
Howorth, R.	9774	114	20.36	4	6639	204	32.54
Hunt, R. G.	802	117	20.56	—			
Hurst, G. T.	27	9	3.00	—	1530	65	23.53
Hutton, L.	25982	364	55.99	85	462	12	38.50
Ikin, J. T.	6957	167	36.42	9	4139	186	22.25
Ingram, E. A.	631	64	15.39	—			
Insole, D. J.	3493	219*	37.55	6			
Ivey, M. L.	175	24	3.97	—			
Jackson, P. F.	1943	40	5.97	—	28330	1088	26.03

Second group (J – L):

	Batting				Bowling		
	Runs	HS	Avge.	100s	Runs	Wkts.	Avge.
Jackson, V. E.	5793	170	27.98	9	9532	361	26.40
Jakeman, F.	1225	169	27.22	2			
James, A. E.	430	37*	14.33	—	2352	77	30.54
Jaques, P.	69	55	34.50	—			
Jenkins, R. O.	2248	109	24.62	1	12777	540	23.66
Jepson, A.	4998	93	16.65	—	13304	440	30.23
Johnson, L.	475	77	25.00	—	297	4	74.25
Jones, A. T. M.	299	106	11.40	1	132	3	44.00
Jones, W. E.	4628	212*	28.56	4	2473	85	29.09
Kardar, A. H.	2132	138*	25.38	2	3527	177	19.91
Keeling, M. E. A.	67	40	13.40	—			
Keeton, W. W.	22592	312*	40.34	52	103	2	51.50
Keighley, W. G.	1516	105	28.07	1	79	0	—
Kelland, P. A.	1	1*	1.00	—	172	6	28.66
Kelly, P.	150	58	18.75	—	14	0	—
Kenyon, D.	3753	182	25.70	4	0	0	—
Kirby, G. N. G.	54	27	13.50	—			
Knott, C. J.	671	22	7.06	—	9986	412	24.23
Laker, J. C.	1999	100	19.99	1	7885	349	22.59
Laker, P. G.	14	8*	14.00	—	70		
Lambert, G. R.	2153	68	14.07	1	9287	321	28.93
Langdale, G. R.	695	146	18.78	—	902	22	41.00
Langridge, James	27233	167	35.04	38	32230	1417	22.74
Langridge, John	23949	250*	39.26	56	1784	43	41.48
Lavers, A. B.	652	39	15.52	—	469	13	36.07
Lavis, G.	4957	154	18.42	3	7768	156	49.79
Lawrence, J.	3178	88	18.47	—	7253	300	24.17
Law, J. A. G. G.	22	12	5.50	—			
Laws, M. N. L.	5	3	1.33	—			
Leadbeater, E.	68	29*	13.60	—	427	8	53.37
Lester, E.	3669	186	35.62	11	67	1	67.00
Lester, G.	4897	131	24.24	4	6691	182	36.76
Lewis, C.	728	27	6.50	—	8047	300	26.82
Lewis, D.	7	7	7.00	—			
Lewis, R. C. V.	64	51	21.33	—	44	1	44.00
Livingstone, L.	34	34	34.00	—			
Lock, G. A. R.	253	100*	10.95	1	1905	79	24.11
Lomax, J. G.	241	29	32.00	—	322	11	29.27
Lowe, G.	51	14	8.50	—	15	0	—
Lowson, F. A.	1799	104	35.98	1			
Lumsden, I. J. M.	379	66	27.07	—			

Name	Batting Runs	HS	Avge.	100s	Bowling Runs	Wkts	Avge.
Mallett, A. W. H.	1360	97	18.63	—	4510	167	27.00
Mann, F. G.	5512	136*	25.40	7	389	3	129.66
Manners, J. E.	827	147	33.08	3	—	—	—
Marshall, J. M. A.	717	47	17.07	—	1499	44	34.06
Martin, E.	41	18*	8.20	—	—	—	—
Martin, J. W.	249	34	8.58	—	2149	86	24.98
Mason, A.	77	22	6.41	—	1286	42	30.61
Maudsley, R. H.	2340	130	24.12	3	1391	51	27.27
Maxwell, C. R.	1439	268	26.64	1	—	—	—
May, P. H. B.	700	175	53.84	1	—	—	—
Mayes, R.	202	37	10.10	—	18	0	—
McCorkell, N.	13693	154*	25.45	14	15	0	—
McHugh, F. P.	0	0	0.00	—	147	4	36.75
McIntyre, A. J.	4187	143*	25.22	6	180	4	45.00
McMahon, J. W.	139	17*	3.86	—	4017	128	31.38
Meads, E. A.	780	56*	14.46	—	—	—	—
Mercer, W. N.	34	24	17.00	—	45	0	—
Meyer, R. J. O.	4014	202*	23.89	2	8941	348	25.69
Milton, C. A.	1031	92*	23.97	1	655	14	46.78
Mills, J. M.	520	44	15.75	—	1943	73	26.61
Mischler, N. M.	434	46	14.46	—	—	—	—
Mitchell, I. N.	63	27	15.75	—	—	—	—
Mitchell-Innes, N. S.	6944	207	31.42	13	2846	82	34.70
Montgomery, S. W.	183	117	30.50	1	—	—	—
Morris, R. J.	550	96	28.94	—	192	2	96.00
Morris, W. B.	1058	68	17.93	—	1840	40	46.00
Muncer, B. L.	4451	87	19.10	—	8080	403	20.04
Munden, V.	596	67	13.85	—	1289	23	56.04
Newman, D. L.	33	19	16.50	—	—	—	—
Notley, B.	0	0	0.00	—	90	1	90.00
Nutter, A. E.	3258	109*	21.86	1	8822	332	26.59
Oakes, C.	7684	148*	26.04	10	10794	329	32.80
Oakes, J.	2692	99	21.88	—	3820	88	43.40
Oakman, A.	181	79*	13.92	—	828	20	41.40
Oldfield, N.	10996	168	38.71	20	85	2	42.50
Ord, J. S.	7993	156*	27.18	11	205	2	102.50
Outschoorn, L.	3334	215*	27.33	3	696	14	49.71
Palmer, C. H.	3898	177	29.98	7	2099	56	37.48
Parker, J. F.	10389	210	23.12	5	2223	54	41.16
Parkhouse, W. G. A.	2695	145	32.06	16	13987	476	29.38
Parks, J. M.	26	12	8.66	—	9	1	9.00

Name	Batting Runs	HS	Avge.	100s	Bowling Runs	Wkts	Avge.
Parnaby, A. H. C.	267	87	22.25	—	187	4	46.75
Pawson, H. A.	3084	150	40.05	5	—	—	—
Payton, W. E. G.	930	98	22.14	—	915	15	61.00
Pearce, T. N.	11737	211*	35.24	22	36666	1556	23.56
Perks, R. T. D.	6406	75	12.71	—	—	—	—
Phebey, A. H.	632	68	19.75	—	—	—	—
Place, W.	8606	266*	39.65	25	42	1	42.00
Pleass, J.	769	77*	15.38	—	—	—	—
Pocock, H. J.	118	34	11.80	—	70	1	70.00
Pollard, R.	3438	63	13.32	—	24841	1105	22.48
Poole, C. J.	1704	154*	38.72	5	23	0	—
Popplewell, O. B.	267	37	22.25	—	—	—	—
Porter, A.	1292	105	23.07	2	480	16	30.00
Potter, G.	5	5	5.00	—	63	0	—
Potts, H. J.	142	49	23.66	—	—	—	—
Pressdee, F. T.	0	0	0.00	—	35	0	—
Prentice, F. T.	10454	191	28.48	17	5847	117	49.97
Preston, K. C.	65	23*	5.00	—	1211	42	28.83
Pritchard, T. L.	1276	81	12.63	—	8583	383	22.40
Pryer, B. J. K.	239	75*	9.19	—	1810	46	39.34
Pullinger, G. R.	51	14*	5.66	—	1333	38	35.07
Ransom, V. J.	405	58	9.64	—	3167	89	35.58
Rayment, A. W. H.	159	35	12.33	—	58	0	—
Redman, J.	63	12	6.30	—	639	16	39.93
Revill, A.	3497	156*	23.46	3	791	21	37.66
Rhodes, A. E. G.	5022	127	20.08	4	10758	369	29.15
Richardson, A	9	5	3.00	—	280	5	56.00
Richardson, P. E.	108	39	15.42	—	—	—	—
Riddington, A.	3576	104*	18.92	1	3019	76	39.72
Ridgway, F.	780	89	9.39	—	6653	255	26.09
Rimell, A. G. J.	467	160	31.13	1	473	16	29.56
Rimmer, J. J.	9	1*	1.00	—	264	5	52.80
Rippon, T. J.	45	30	22.50	—	—	—	—
Rist, F.	1344	56*	14.93	—	—	—	—
Roberts, S. N.	158	48*	15.80	—	21	0	—
Roberts, H. E.	33	30	10.67	—	—	—	—
Roberts, W. B.	865	51	11.72	—	8296	392	21.16
Robertson, J. D.	13017	331*	41.72	36	1134	27	42.00
Robins, R. W. V.	13299	140	26.97	11	21620	912	23.76
Robinson, M.	2035	190	23.12	2	405	13	31.15
Rogers, N. H.	5476	178	26.58	7	8	0	—
Rogers, S. S.	517	61	16.67	—	—	—	—

Name	Batting Runs	HS	100s	Avge.	Bowling Runs	Wkts.	Avge.
Routledge, R.	57	12		5.18	502	11	45.63
Rowe, E. J.	1	1		0.50			
Rudd, C. R. D.	260	54		16.25			
Sale, R.	2361	157	3	28.44			
Scott, C. J. W.	1955	90		11.92	9406	288	32.64
Seamer, J. W.	2483	194	4	20.35	171	4	42.75
Shackleton, D.	1142	87*		19.35	3237	121	26.75
Sharp, H.	1720	102	1	24.95	856	27	31.70
Shaw, D. G.	17	17		17.00	106	2	53.00
Shearwood, K. A.	40	28		10.00			
Sheppard, D. S.	996	204	3	34.34			
Shirreff, A. C.	1382	91		19.46	4000	135	29.62
Shortland, N. A.	471	70		15.19	50	0	-
Sime, W. A.	1909	176*	1	21.21	1982	42	47.19
Simpson, R. T.	7104	238	19	41.78	709	20	35.45
Sims, J. M.	7798	123	4	17.72	33281	1379	24.13
Skinner, D. A.	475	63		13.57	182	2	91.00
Smales, K.	149	45		14.90	546	12	45.50
Smith, D.	20363	225	31	31.81	718	21	34.19
Smith, D. V.	1381	85		24.66	243	2	121.50
Smith, G. S.	29	22		14.50			
Smith, Ray	5380	112	2	19.11	20254	669	30.27
Smith, Roy	40	40		20.00	29	0	-
Smith, T. P. B.	8807	163	8	18.04	39148	1481	26.43
Smithson, G. A.	1345	169	2	26.37	84	1	84.00
Snape, M. G.	0	0*		0.00			
Sperry, J.	861	33		6.94	10894	380	28.66
Spooner, R. T.	1410	70		23.89			
Stainton, R. G.	2330	89		24.27	25	1	25.00
Stephenson, H. H. W.	948	88		17.88	728	14	52.00
Stevenson, M. H. H.	483	82	3	25.42	2034	36	56.50
Stocks, F. W.	2747	166		27.47	253	3	84.33
Stone, D. R.	47	46		23.50			
Surridge, W. S. S.	877	41*		11.69	4188	150	27.92
Sutcliffe, W. H. H.	419	56		19.95	115	4	28.75
Sutherland, I.	9	9		9.00	23	0	-
Sutle, K.	127	43*		21.16	6	0	-
Swann, J. L.	32	19		16.00	53	2	26.50
Symington, S. J.	744	65		21.88	1448	36	40.22
Tanner, J. D. P.	109	25*		13.62			
Tattersall, R.	252	39		31.50	1333	50	26.66
Taylor, B.	2	2		2.00			

Name	Batting Runs	HS	100s	Avge.	Bowling Runs	Wkts.	Avge.
Taylor, Derief	473	121	1	36.38	587	15	39.13
Taylor, D. D.	806	143	1	32.24	325	14	23.21
Thackara, A. L.	49	42		24.50			
Thompson, A.	3235	100*	1	29.40	483	6	80.50
Thompson, J. R.	2655	191	6	37.39	7	0	-
Thompson, L. B.	16	13		4.00	248	5	49.60
Thompson, R. G.	17	17		17.00	66	1	66.00
Tillard, R. J.	3	3		1.50			
Titmus, F. J.	17	13		17.00	9	0	-
Todd, L. J.	19866	174	37	32.09	15773	570	27.67
Tompkin, M.	7508	163	10	29.21	39	0	-
Townsend, A.	1605	80*		21.98	1592	59	26.88
Townsend, A. F.	4285	142*	5	23.54	39	0	-
Tremlett, M. F.	3090	105	2	21.02	6625	233	28.43
Trick, W. M. S.	45	15		5.62	1023	47	21.74
Trueman, F. S.	12	10		3.00	719	31	23.19
Ufton, D. G.	52	27*		17.33			
Underwood, A. J.	1099	60		14.65	175	1	175.00
Unwin, F. St. G.					41	0	-
Valentine, B. H.	18223	242	35	30.12	1115	27	41.29
Van Ryneveld, C.	1602	102	1	21.60	1834	57	32.17
Vaulkhard, P.	1383	264	1	16.75	88	2	88.00
Vernon, J. M.	67	25		28.44	44	2	22.00
Vigar, F. H.	5234	145	11	15.04	6658	182	36.41
Wade, T. H.	4770	96		3.16	1418	48	29.54
Wait, O. J.	19	7		37.21	842	33	25.51
Walford, M. M.	4131	264	7	28.23	215	7	30.71
Walker, C.	1355	112	1	19.00	1134	24	47.33
Walker, J.	19	106		16.56			
Walsh, J. E.	2948	106		9.50	15116	664	22.76
Ward, G. H.	19	6*		17.02			
Wardle, J. H.	1549	47		15.16	7897	345	22.88
Warr, J. J.	182	251*		46.97	1585	64	24.76
Washbrook, C.	19729	251*	55	46.97	247	3	82.33
Watkins, A. J.	4698	146	12	29.00	3577	116	30.83
Watkins, D. S.	2	7		2.00			
Watson, G. S.	7989	145	6	22.76	86	3	28.66
Watson, W.	4048	172	4	29.76	51	1	51.00
Watts, H. E.	2225	110	1	25.57	51	0	-
Webb, R. T.	401	145*	1	28.64	107	1	107.00
Webster, J.	182	22		9.10	10	1	10.00
	497	65		9.20	2990	107	27.94

	Batting				Bowling		
	Runs	HS	100s	Avge.	Runs	Wkts.	Avge.
Wellard, A. W.	12468	112	2	19.82	38991	1604	24.30
West, G. H.	63	55	—	31.50			
Westerman, P.	24	10*	—	6.00	258	7	36.85
Wharton, A.	3545	139	7	34.08	743	17	43.70
Wheatley, G. A.	465	66	—	17.88			
Whitcombe, P. A.	779	68	—	19.97	1805	90	20.05
Whitcombe, P. J.	12	8*	—	12.00			
Whitehead, J. P.	265	71	—	16.56	1320	52	25.38
White, W. M. E.	398	35	—	13.72	1524	42	36.28
White, A. F. T.	5026	95	—	21.85	26	0	—
Whiting, N. H.	255	56	—	13.42	3	0	—
Whittaker, G. J.	2107	148	4	30.98	47	1	47.00
Wilcox, D. R.	8361	157	15	31.59	136	3	45.33
Wiley, J. W. E.	103	30	—	12.87			
Willatt, G. L.	2689	131	7	32.79	59	2	29.50
Williams, E. L.	17	14	—	8.50	33	2	16.50
Wilson, A.	48	8*	—	3.20			
Wilson, A. E.	6599	188	6	25.98	1	0	—
Wilson, J. V.	3033	157*	4	31.59	26	0	—

	Batting				Bowling		
	Runs	HS	100s	Avge.	Runs	Wkts.	Avge.
Wilson, R. G.	388	100	1	29.84	516	21	24.57
Winrow, F. H.	3214	204*	3	27.23	3778	89	42.44
Winn, C. E.	1128	95	—	28.20	9	0	—
Wood, D. J.	504	31	—	5.66	8635	272	31.74
Woodhead, F. G.	1095	52*	—	8.62	10257	318	32.25
Woodhouse, G. E. S.	1959	109	1	20.84	8	1	8.00
Wolton, A. V.	1377	111*	1	25.03	21	0	—
Wooler, C. A.	6	6*	—	—	132	3	44.00
Wooller, W.	5021	111	2	23.13	11689	407	28.71
Wright, D. V. P.	3743	84*	—	14.39	29202	1206	24.21
Wrigley, M. H.	70	17	—	7.00	880	42	20.95
Wyatt, R. E. S.	37785	232	85	40.41	28942	885	32.70
Yardley, N. W. D.	12388	182*	21	32.85	4897	155	31.59
Yarnold, H.	1607	68	—	11.31	0	0	—
Young, D. M.	1115	90	—	19.22			
Young, J. A.	1226	62	—	10.56	11618	610	19.04

WICKETKEEPERS

The career figures of the leading wicketkeepers are as follows:—

	Total	Ct.	St.
Barlow, A.	86	64	22
Brennan, D. V.	164	118	46
Compton, L. H.	218	168	50
Corrall, P.	486	319	167
Dawkes, G. O.	295	203	92
Davies, H. G.	269	232	37
Evans, T. G.	376	259	117
Fidding, K.	175	135	40
Griffith, S. C.	368	292	76
McCorkell, N.	630	459	171
McIntyre, A. J.	220	179	41
Meads, E. A.	235	192	43
Spooner, R. T.	119	90	29
Stephenson, H. W.	89	44	45
Wade, T. H.	530	367	163
Wilson, A.	58	42	16
Wilson, A. E.	314	211	103
Yarnold, H.	297	174	123

ADDITIONS TO WHO'S WHO

HUNT, R. G. (Sussex) B. 13/4/1915. Sound RHB and useful change bowler. Educated at Aldenham. Debut 1935. Cambridge Blue 1937. Played for Sussex 1936, 1946 and 1947. Joint Sussex Captain with G. H. G. Doggart in 1950. 117 Camb. U. v. Army (Cambridge) 1937, BB—5-91 Camb. U. v. Sussex (Worthing) 1937.

CARTER, Ray (Warwick) B.Birmingham 14/4/'33. RMF bowler—2 games for 2nd XI, 1949.

KING, I. (Warwick) B.Leeds 10/11/'31. Left-arm bowler, useful bat. Educated Worcester R.G.S. Due for call-up in May.

HEDGES, Bernard (Glamorgan) B.1927. RHB from Pontypridd.

HARRON, Don G. (Leics.). B.Durham 12/9/1921. Opening RHB registered from Durham.

GOODWIN, Jeff (Leics.) B.Bignall End 22/1/1929. LFM bowler from Bignall End in N. Staffordshire League.

DERHAM, A. F. H. (Hants.) B.Belvedere (Kent) 12/10/'22. LB bowler. RHB. Specially registered from Kent for whom he made debut in 1948.

THOMPSON, J. (Warwick) B. 26/2/'32. Educated at Worcester R.G.S. Wicketkeeper and RHB. Due for call-up in May.

THOMPSON, G. (Warwick). Twin brother of "J." LB bowler and RHB. Same school. Played in England Schoolboys XI v. Wales at Bournemouth 1949. Both are fine Rugby players.

Leading Fixtures 1950

SAT., 29th APRIL

Lord's	M.C.C. v. Yorkshire
Cambridge	Cambridge U. v. Sussex
Oxford	Oxford U. v. Gloucestershire
Oval	Surrey v. Glamorgan

WED., 3rd MAY

Lord's	M.C.C. v. Surrey
Southampton	Hampshire v. Warwicks.
Hove	Sussex v. Lancashire
Cambridge	Cambridge U. v. Essex
Oxford	Oxford U. v. Yorkshire
Cardiff	Glam. v. Som. (friendly)

SAT., 6th MAY

Lord's	Middlesex v. Hampshire
Worcester	Worcs. v. West Indies
Swansea	Glamorgan v. Notts.
Gloucester	Gloucestershire v. Warwicks.
Manchester	Lancashire v. Leicestershire
Peterborough	Northamptonshire v. Surrey
Taunton	Somerset v. Sussex
Cambridge	Cambridge U. v. Yorkshire

WED., 10th MAY

Lord's	Middlesex v. Warwickshire
Oval	Surrey v. Derbyshire
Bradford	Yorkshire v. West Indies
Brentwood	Essex v. Northamptonshire
Pontypridd	Glamorgan v. Leicestershire
Cambridge	Cambridge U. v. Lancs.
Oxford	Oxford U. v. Hampshire
Worcester	Worcs. v. Combined Services

SAT., 13th MAY

Lord's	Middlesex v. Somerset
Oval	Surrey v. West Indies
Derby	Derbyshire v. Northants.
Brentwood	Essex v. Glamorgan
Bristol	Gloucestershire v. Kent
Manchester	Lancashire v. Hampshire
Nottingham	Nottinghamshire v. Sussex
Worcester	Worcestershire v. Leics.
Oxford	Oxford U. v. Warwicks.

WED., 17th MAY

Lord's	Middlesex v. Glamorgan
Cambridge	Cambridge U. v. West Indies
Bristol	Gloucestershire v. Yorkshire
Northampton	Northamptonshire v. Kent
Nottingham	Nottinghamshire v. Leics.
Wells	Somerset v. Surrey
Hove	Sussex v. Worcestershire
Birmingham	Warwickshire v. Essex
Oxford	Oxford U. v. Lancashire

SAT., 20th MAY

Lord's	M.C.C. v. West Indies
Oval	Surrey v. Essex
Chesterfield	Derbyshire v. Somerset
Portsmouth	Hampshire v. Leicestershire
Gillingham	Kent v. Glamorgan
Nottingham	Notts. v. Northants.
Birmingham	Warwickshire v. Lancashire
Worcester	Worcestershire v. Glos.
Leeds	Yorkshire v. Sussex
Cambridge	Cambridge U. v. The Army

WED., 24th MAY

Lord's	Middlesex v. Derbyshire
Romford	Essex v. Hampshire

Leicester	Leicestershire v. Surrey
Hove	Sussex v. Warwickshire
Huddersfield	Yorkshire v. Somerset
Oxford	Oxford U. v. West Indies

SAT., 27th MAY

Lord's	Middlesex v. Sussex
Cardiff	Glamorgan v. West Indies
Derby	Derbyshire v. Warwickshire
Romford	Essex v. Worcestershire
Southampton	Hampshire v. Kent
Leicester	Leicestershire v. Northants.
Nottingham	Nottinghamshire v. Surrey
Taunton	Somerset v. Gloucestershire
Sheffield	Yorkshire v. Lancashire
Oxford	Oxford U. v. Free Foresters

WED., 31st MAY

Bradford	Test Trial
Lord's	Middlesex v. Worcestershire
Taunton	Somerset v. West Indies
Birmingham	Warwickshire v. Glamorgan
Gillingham	Kent v. Sussex
Leicester	Leicestershire v. Derbyshire
Northampton	Northants v. Yorkshire
Manchester	Lancashire v. Surrey

SAT., 3rd JUNE

Lord's	Middlesex v. Kent
Manchester	Lancashire v. West Indies
Ilford	Essex v. Warwickshire
Cardiff	Glamorgan v. Somerset
Bristol	Gloucestershire v. Notts.
Portsmouth	Hampshire v. Sussex
Worcester	Worcestershire v. Northants.
Bradford	Yorkshire v. Derbyshire
Cambridge	Cambridge U. v. Leics.

WED., 7th JUNE

Lord's	Middlesex v. Leicestershire
Oval	Surrey v. Somerset
Ilkeston	Derbyshire v. Worcestershire
Ilford	Essex v. Nottinghamshire
Gloucester	Gloucestershire v. Lancs.
Gravesend	Kent v. Northamptonshire
Birmingham	Warwickshire v. Yorkshire
Oxford	Oxford U. v. Sussex
Cambridge	Cambridge U. v. Hampshire
Cardiff	Glamorgan v. Combined S.

THURS., 8th JUNE

Manchester	ENGLAND v. WEST INDIES (1st Test Match—5 days)

SAT., 10th JUNE

Lord's	Middlesex v. Lancashire
Oval	Surrey v. Northamptonshire
Gloucester	Glos. v. Glamorgan
Gravesend	Kent v. Somerset
Coalville	Leicestershire v. Warwicks.
Nottingham	Nottinghamshire v. Hants.
Horsham	Sussex v. Essex
Stourbridge	Worcestershire v. Yorkshire
Cambridge	Camb. U. v. F. Foresters
Oxford	Oxford U. v. Derbyshire

WED., 14th JUNE

Lord's	M.C.C. v. Oxford U.
Newcastle (Jesmond)	Northumberland v. West Indies (2 days)
Manchester	Lancashire v. Glos.
Northampton	Northants. v. Middlesex

Neath	Glamorgan v. Derbyshire
Horsham	Sussex v. Nottinghamshire
Sheffield	Yorkshire v. Essex
Southampton	Hampshire v. Worcestershire

SAT., 17th JUNE

Lord's	Middlesex v. Yorkshire
Swansea	Glamorgan v. Surrey
Nottingham	Notts. v. West Indies
Bristol	Glos. v. Derbyshire
Manchester	Lancashire v. Kent
Northampton	Northamptonshire v. Essex
Taunton	Somerset v. Hampshire
Dudley	Worcestershire v. Warwicks.
Hove	Sussex v. Cambridge U.

WED., 21st JUNE

Lord's	Beaumont v. Oratory (1day)
Hove	Sussex v. West Indies
Derby	Derbyshire v. Glamorgan
Colchester	Essex v. Yorkshire
Bristol	Gloucestershire v. Hants.
Rushden	Northants v. Somerset
Nottingham	Nottinghamshire v. Middx.
Guildford	Surrey v. Oxford U.
Birmingham	Warwicks. v. Cambridge U.
Dudley	Worcestershire v. Kent

SAT., 24th JUNE

Lord's	ENGLAND v. WEST INDIES
	(2nd Test Match—5 days)
Buxton	Derbyshire v. Lancashire
Colchester	Essex v. Gloucestershire
Ebbw Vale	Glamorgan v. Northants.
Bath	Somerset v. Leicestershire
Guildford	Surrey v. Hampshire
Birmingham	Warwickshire v. Kent
Leeds	Yorkshire v. Notts.
Chichester	Sussex v. Oxford U.
Worcester	Worcs. v. Cambridge U.

WED., 28th JUNE

Oval	Surrey v. Cambridge U.
Chesterfield	Derbyshire v. Yorkshire
Portsmouth	Hampshire v. Middlesex
Tun. Wells	Kent v. Lancashire
Nottingham	Nottinghamshire v. Worcs.
Bath	Somerset v. Essex
Chichester	Sussex v. Glamorgan
Ashby-de-la-Z.	Leicestershire v. Oxford U.
Portsmouth	R.N. v. Warwicks (2 days)

SAT., 1st JULY

Lord's	Middlesex v. Essex
Southampton	Hampshire v. West Indies
Ilkeston	Derbyshire v. Notts.
Bristol	Glos. v. Cambridge U.
Tun. Wells	Kent v. Worcestershire
Kettering	Northants v. Glamorgan
Bath	Somerset v. Lancashire
Coventry	Warwickshire v. Leics.
Sheffield	Yorkshire v. Surrey
Hove	Sussex v. Scotland

WED., 5th JULY

Lord's	M.C.C. v. Camb. U. (2 days)
Liverpool	Lancashire v. West Indies
Westcliff	Essex v. Somerset
Cardiff	Glamorgan v. Middlesex
Loughborough	Leicestershire v. Kent
Northampton	Northants. v. Notts.
Worthing	Sussex v. Gloucestershire
Birmingham	Warwickshire v. Surrey
Worcester	Worcestershire v. Derbyshire
Bradford	Yorkshire v. Hampshire

SAT., 8th JULY

Lord's	OXFORD v. CAMBRIDGE
Oval	Surrey v. Kent
Northampton	Northants. v. West Indies
Westcliff	Essex v. Leicestershire
Llanelly	Glamorgan v. Glos.
Manchester	Lancashire v. Derbyshire
Nottingham	Nottinghamshire v. Yorks.
Worthing	Sussex v. Somerset
Birmingham	Warwickshire v. Middlesex

WED., 12th JULY

Oval	Surrey v. Gloucestershire
Leicester	Leicestershire v. West Indies
Derby	Derbyshire v. Hampshire
Manchester	Lancashire v. Sussex
Nottingham	Nottinghamshire v. Kent
Taunton	Somerset v. Warwickshire
Worcester	Worcestershire v. Middx.
Edinburgh	Scotland v. Yorkshire
Barry	Glam. v. R.A.F. (2 days)

FRI., 14th JULY

Lord's	Eton v. Harrow (2 days)

SAT., 15th JULY

Chesterfield	Derbyshire v. West Indies
Bristol	Gloucestershire v. Sussex
Blackheath	Kent v. Surrey
Manchester	Lancashire v. Essex
Leicester	Leicestershire v. Notts.
Northampton	Northants. v. Warwicks.
Kidderminster	Worcs. v. Glamorgan
Leeds	Yorkshire v. Middlesex

MON., 17th JULY

Lord's	R.A. v. R.E. (2 days)

WED., 19th JULY

Lord's	R.N. v. The Army (2 days)
Swansea	Glamorgan v. Lancashire
Bristol	Gloucestershire v. Surrey
Birmingham	Warwickshire v. Somerset
Dudley	Worcs. v. Hampshire
Harrogate	Yorkshire v. Leicestershire

THURS., 20th JULY

Nottingham	ENGLAND v. WEST INDIES
	(3rd Test Match—5 days)

SAT., 22nd JULY

Lord's	M.C.C. v. Minor Counties
Oval	Surrey v. Yorkshire
Chesterfield	Derbyshire v. Essex
Cardiff	Glamorgan v. Sussex
Bournemouth	Hampshire v. Somerset
Folkestone	Kent v. Leicestershire
Liverpool	Lancashire v. Notts.
Northampton	Northants. v. Worcs.
Birmingham	Warwickshire v. Glos.

WED., 26th JULY

Lord's	GENTLEMEN v. PLAYERS
Burton	Derbyshire v. Sussex
Bournemouth	Hampshire v. Northants.
Maidstone	Kent v. Essex
Manchester	Lancashire v. Middlesex
Worcester	Worcestershire v. Surrey
Hull	Yorks. v. Gloucestershire
Sunderland	Durham v. West Indies
	(2 days)

SAT., 29th JULY

Lord's	M.C.C. Young Pros. v.
	Young Amateurs of
	Middx. (1 day)

Oval	Surrey v. Middlesex
Sheffield	Yorkshire v. West Indies
Clacton	Essex v. Sussex
Southampton	Hampshire v. Derbyshire
Maidstone	Kent v. Gloucestershire
Leicester	Leicestershire v. Glamorgan
Nottingham	Nottinghamshire v. Lancs.
Frome	Somerset v. Northants.
Birmingham	Warwickshire v. Worcs.

MON., 31st JULY

Lord's	Clifton v. Tonbridge (2days)

WED., 2nd AUGUST

Lord's	Rugby v. Marlboro (2 days)
Oval	Surrey v. West Indies
Clacton	Essex v. Kent
Bristol	Gloucestershire v. Northants.
Blackpool	Lancashire v. Glamorgan
Leicester	Leicestershire v. Middlesex
Nottingham	Notts. v. Warwicks.
Taunton	Somerset v. Yorkshire
Worcester	Worcestershire v. Sussex

FRI., 4th AUGUST

Lord's	Cheltenham v. Haileybury and I.S.C. (2 days)

SAT., 5th AUGUST

Oval	Surrey v. Nottinghamshire
Swansea	Glamorgan v. West Indies
Bristol	Gloucestershire v. Somerset
Canterbury	Kent v. Hampshire
Manchester	Lancashire v. Yorkshire
Northampton	Northants. v. Leicestershire
Hove	Sussex v. Middlesex
Birmingham	Warwickshire v. Derbyshire
Worcester	Worcestershire v. Essex

MON., 7th AUGUST

Lord's	R.N. v. R.A.F. (2 days)

WED., 9th AUGUST

Lord's	M.C.C. Young Pros. v. English Schools C.A. (1 day)
Birmingham	Warwicks. v. West Indies
Derby	Derbyshire v. Glos.
Swansea	Glamorgan v. Hampshire
Canterbury	Kent v. Middlesex
Manchester	Lancashire v. Worcestershire
Leicester	Leicestershire v. Essex
Weston-s-M	Somerset v. Notts.
Hastings	Sussex v. Surrey
Leeds	Yorkshire v. Northants.

THURS., 10th AUGUST

Lord's	M.C.C. Young Pros. v. London Fedtn. of Boys' Clubs (1 day)

FRI., 11th AUGUST

Lord's	Southern Schools v. The Rest (2 days)

SAT., 12th AUGUST

Oval	ENGLAND v. WEST INDIES (4th Test Match—5 days)
Chelmsford	Essex v. Surrey
Cheltenham	Gloucestershire v. Middx.
Leicester	Leicestershire v. Hants.
Wellingboro	Northants. v. Lancashire
Nottingham	Notts. v. Derbyshire
Weston-s-M	Somerset v. Glamorgan
Hastings	Sussex v. Kent
Bradford	Yorkshire v. Warwickshire

Belfast	N. Ireland v. Worcs. (2days)

MON., 14th AUGUST

Lord's	Combined Services v. Public Schools (2 days)

WED., 16th AUGUST

Chesterfield	Derbyshire v. Leicestershire
Cheltenham	Gloucestershire v. Worcs.
Bournemouth	Hampshire v. Lancashire
Northampton	Northamptonshire v. Sussex
Weston-s-M	Somerset v. Middlesex
Coventry	Warwickshire v. Notts.
Scarborough	Yorkshire v. Kent
Chelmsford	Essex v. Combined Services

THURS., 17th AUGUST

Lord's	M.C.C. v. C.C.C. (1 day)

SAT., 19th AUGUST

Lord's	Middlesex v. Surrey
Cheltenham	Glos. v. West Indies
Derby	Derbyshire v. Kent
Newport	Glamorgan v. Essex
Bournemouth	Hampshire v. Notts.
Leicester	Leicestershire v. Lancs.
Worcester	Worcestershire v. Somerset
Eastbourne	Sussex v. Yorkshire
Birmingham	Warwickshire v. Northants.

WED., 23rd AUGUST

Lord's	Middlesex v. Northants.
Oval	Surrey v. Worcestershire
Southend	Essex v. West Indies
Cardiff	Glamorgan v. Yorkshire
Dover	Kent v. Derbyshire
Manchester	Lancashire v. Warwickshire
Leicester	Leicestershire v. Glos.
Nottingham	Notts. v. Somerset
Eastbourne	Sussex v. Hampshire

SAT., 26th AUGUST

Lord's	Middlesex v. West Indies
Oval	Surrey v. Lancashire
Southend	Essex v. Derbyshire
Portsmouth	Hampshire v. Yorkshire
Dover	Kent v. Nottinghamshire
Leicester	Leicestershire v. Sussex
Northampton	Northamptonshire v. Glos.
Swansea	Glamorgan v. Warwickshire
Taunton	Somerset v. Worcestershire

WED., 30th AUGUST

Lord's	The Army v. R.A.F. (2days)
Oval	Surrey v. Leicestershire
Canterbury	Kent v. West Indies
Portsmouth	Hampshire v. Glamorgan
Nottingham	Nottinghamshire v. Essex
Hove	Sussex v. Derbyshire

SAT., 2nd SEPTEMBER

Bournemouth	Hampshire v. Glos.
Leicester	Leicestershire v. Worcs.
Scarborough	Yorkshire v. M.C.C.
Hastings	S. of England v. West Indies
Kingston	Surrey XI v. The Rest

WED., 6th SEPTEMBER

Norwich	Minor Counties v. W. Indies
Hastings	Under Thirty v. Over Thirty
Scarborough	North v. South
Kingston	Festival match

SAT., 9th SEPTEMBER

Scarborough	H. D. G. Leveson Gower's XI. v. West Indies

Printed in England by Welbecson Press Ltd., 39/43, Battersea High Street, S.W.11.